Stephen Coote

Stephen Coote was educated at Magdalene College, Cambridge and at Birkbeck College, University of London. He now lives in Oxfordshire.

Also by Stephen Coote

Byron – The Making of a Myth
William Norris
A Short History of English Literature
A Play of Passion – The Life of Sir Walter Ralegh
Keats – A Life
W. B. Yeats

Royal Survivor
A Life of Charles II

Stephen Coote

SCEPTRE

Copyright © 1999 by Stephen Coote

First published in 1999 by Hodder and Stoughton
A division of Hodder Headline
A Sceptre Paperback

The right of Stephen Coote to be identified as the Author of
the Work has been asserted by him in accordance with the
Copyright, Designs and Patents Act 1988.

10 9 8 7 6 5 4 3 2 1

A CIP catalogue record for this title is available from
the British Library

ISBN 0 340 69619 2

Printed and bound in Great Britain by
Clays Ltd, St Ives PLC

Hodder and Stoughton
A division of Hodder Headline
338 Euston Road
London NW1 3BH

For Mack and Iris

Contents

List of Illustrations

Section One

Charles I and Henrietta Maria, by Daniel Mytens
Five children of Charles I, artist unknown

Oliver Cromwell, by Robert Walker

Edward Hyde. 1st Earl of Clarendon, by Thomas Simon

Archibald Campbell, 1st Marquis of Argyll, by David Scougall

Charles II and Wiliam Carlos in the Boscobel Oak, by Isaac Fuller
Charles II escaping with Mrs Lane, by Vandergucht

Charles II in exile, by Adrian Hanneman

Charles II and Mary of Orange dancing at The Hague, by Hieronymus
   Janssens

Charles II, by Samuel Cooper

Section Two

Andrew Marvell, artist unknown
John Evelyn, by Robert Nanteuil
Samuel Pepys, by John Hayls
John Wilmot, Earl of Rochester, artist unknown

Catherine of Braganza, by Dirk Stoop
Barbara Palmer, Countess of Castlemaine, artist unknown
Frances Stuart, Duchess of Richmond and Lennox, by William Wissing
Louise de Kéroualle, Duchess of Portsmouth, by Pierre Mignard

Nell Gwynn, by Sir Peter Lely (?)
Hortense Mancini, Duchess of Mazarin, artist unknown
Henriette Anne, Duchess of Orleans, artist unknown

George Villiers, 2nd Duke of Buckingham, by Sir Peter Lely

Thomas Clifford, 1st Baron Clifford of Cudleigh, artist unknown
Henry Bennet, 1st Earl of Arlington, artist unknown
Anthony Ashley Cooper, 1st Earl of Shaftsbury, artist unknown
John Maitland, 1st Duke of Lauderdale, Jacob Huysmans

Titus Oates, by Robert White
George Saville, 1st Marquis of Halifax, by Mary Beale
James II and Anne Hyde, by Sir Peter Lely

Charles II in 1685, by John Riley

William III, artist unknown

Acknowledgements

Illustrations 1 and 9 The Royal Collection © Her Majesty The Queen.
The remainder are reproduced by courtesy of the National Portrait
Gallery.

Preface

This is a biography of a popular king. Charles II is one of those historical figures – Elizabeth I and Queen Victoria are others – who live most vividly in the myths that have been wished on them. Charles II is 'the merry monarch', a tall, saturnine man walking briskly with his little dogs or beguiling long hours of leisure with his many mistresses. He is allowed to be sexy, glamorous and just a little sinister – a sort of seventeenth-century Dutch uncle. To complete the picture and add the necessary grit, a thousand pub signs remind everyone of his most famous adventure: Charles's hiding himself in the royal oak at Boscobel while narrow-eyed Cromwellian soldiers tried to hunt him down.

Like all such simplifications, there is a grain of truth in these images, but I have found the larger reality to be more interesting. The Charles I have tried to present here was not a carefree playboy but a hard-bitten politician: wily, manipulative and cynical, a survivor in a dangerous world. The extraordinary course of his life ensured that this was so, and one of the great pleasures of writing this book has been focusing on adventures and unexpected turns, on narrative and plot. After all, a historian's first duty is to tell the story, and Charles's life was a remarkable tale of sumptuous security stripped to bare necessity, of peace, war and intrigue, of poverty and power.

These were the forces that shaped the man, but what of the man who tried to shape events? By the time Charles was returned to his throne in 1660 he had schooled himself to become an enigma, a man at once affable and impenetrable. Such characteristics were not universally popular. 'One great objection made to him', wrote a contemporary, 'was the concealing of himself, and disguising his thoughts.'[1] It is the biographer's task to try and strip away something of that disguise and reveal the workings of the inner man. As I started to do this, so one special factor began to become clear to me. Beneath the quick wit, deeper than the love of pleasure, more certain than religious belief and overmastering them all was Charles's conviction that the ancient rights of the English monarchy should be preserved unimpaired and, where possible, fully displayed. If he was often an idler, Charles was always a king.

It is this particular quality that throws light on the rest and gives Charles's very human inconsistencies a sort of coherence. He was, first of all, a fearless man. The little boy who waved his pistol at the enemy during the Battle of Edgehill is recognisably the youth who raised a Scots army in the vain hope of regaining his throne. Charles's courage at the close of that campaign is undeniable, but fearlessness itself is not a moral quality. It belongs equally to the greatly honest and the deeply devious, and Charles's conduct towards his Scots allies shows that he would stoop to virtually anything to try and establish his power.

The Machiavellian amateur of the months in Scotland is again recognisable in the King who was returned to his throne in 1660. The period immediately following Charles's restoration suggests the aims and conflicts he would have to face throughout his reign. He would not, if he could possibly avoid it, be the servant of those who had given him back his power, the puppet of the Anglican gentry, the King of just the parson and the squire. He was determined to exalt the monarchy, and with the Restoration came the return of his ancient prerogative powers, the King of England's right to summon, prorogue and dismiss his parliaments, to appoint the peers, bishops and judges who made his laws and governed his church, his right to declare war and make peace.

It is in this area of Charles's personal authority that the clue to his conduct as a king can be found, and I have tried to show him as a monarch consistently determined to assert his power and taking enormous risks in the process. There is a breath-taking audacity in

Charles's political guile which helps to account for his abiding fascination, just as the forces raised in opposition to him provide a link between his age and our own. Finally, it was this struggle that provided me with my title, for throughout his extraordinary career Charles showed himself to be above all a man of almost limitless resource – a royal survivor.

The Black Boy

The King was at prayers when they brought him the news. He showed no emotion, and only when the service was over did he collapse in grief at being told that his favourite, the great Duke of Buckingham, had been savagely murdered. The assassin was one John Felton, a half-crazed army officer with a grudge and, as he believed, a divine mission to rid the England of Charles I of the man who was hastening it to ruin.

In his preparations for this task Felton had, a few days earlier, made his way to Tower Hill, where he bought a tenpenny knife. The London through which he stole his way was seething with anger. From open-air pulpits preachers thundered against the Duke's policies, their words mingling in Felton's mind with his own fury at being passed over for a promotion. In the House of Commons, exasperated Members framed a resolution declaring the Duke to be 'the cause of all the evils the kingdom suffered, and an enemy to the public'.[1] These words, along with a couple of brief prayers, Felton copied out on a piece of paper which he then sewed into his hat. If he were to be killed by the Duke's attendants in the confusion that was bound to follow the murder, there should at least be no doubt as to his motive. His was the anger of the people of England with a grandee who had led them into a series of disastrous foreign wars, who had persuaded the King to marry a brazenly Catholic French princess and who was even now marshalling in Portsmouth another great army to help those Frenchmen trapped in La Rochelle by the forces of Richelieu. The compulsory billeting of these raucous soldiers infuriated those obliged to provide for them, and Felton's anger caught the mood of the time.

Felton himself left London on foot and made his way to the coast. He arrived in Portsmouth on Saturday, 22 August 1628, a little before nine in the morning. He went straight to the house where the Duke lodged. Buckingham's servants were putting the last touches to his finery, adjusting his lace ruff, arranging the rope of pearls he wore over his doublet and scenting his hair. His chamber was crowded with his fellow peers and officers of the fleet and the army, as well as a group of voluble Frenchmen loudly insisting that the expedition be launched with all speed. Felton would have to bide his time.

When Buckingham's toilette was at last complete, the noisy company was informed that breakfast was ready. The Duke rose and made his way to the door, the rich hangings were drawn up, and, as he walked along the passage, he turned to speak to one of his aides. This was Felton's moment. The tenpenny dagger flashed from his side. Rising over the Duke's shoulder, it fell with such vehemence into its victim's chest that those around could hear the dull thud it made as Felton called out for mercy on the Duke's soul. The fatally wounded man then staggered forward, pulling at the blade in his heart and crying out that the villain had killed him. He died almost instantly, his body ignominiously spreadeagled across the dining table.

The murder affected everybody, and, while the people of London lit bonfires in the streets and the grief-stricken King retired to his bed, Queen Henrietta Maria seized her opportunity. Her marriage to Charles had been rancorous from its earliest days, and after six weeks the couple had parted only to meet and row again. Henrietta Maria had found her husband cold, formal and inhibited by a serious stutter. Above all, she resented his being so wholly subdued by the Duke. For his part, Charles quickly discovered that his bride was an immature and spoiled girl of fifteen, and he proceeded to treat her with contempt. But the daughter of Marie de Medici and Henri IV was not easily cowed and she had, besides, a naturally manipulative mind. Sensing that the depth of her husband's grief might yet put him in her power, she went to the King's side and offered him comfort.

What started as a ruse laid bare an emotional truth. To their mutual delight, the couple soon found that the murder of the favourite had removed an impediment to their intimacy, and over the following months courtiers noticed that the reserved, humourless Charles and his vivacious little Queen were gradually falling in love. The King, wrote one observer, 'wholly made over all his affection to his wife'.[2] Peace was settling on the royal household. When Henrietta Maria was ill, Charles was constantly at her side. When she recovered, he jousted before her in kingly magnificence. Soon it was noticed that the Queen was pregnant. In an age of terrible child mortality, the premature baby was 'cut down the same instant that it saw the light', but the Queen, entering her halcyon days, wrote thanking God that 'the danger is past, and as to my loss, I wish to forget it'.[3]

She went to Tunbridge Wells to complete her recuperation and to take the waters which were well known for their effects on women wishing to bear children. Fretting at being parted from her husband, the restless Queen soon decided to move on to Oatlands Palace near Weybridge, where Charles paid her a surprise visit, and there, in the rapture of their meeting, another child was conceived. By the last months of 1629, Henrietta Maria was certain she was pregnant again, and news of her condition rapidly spread. A soothsayer predicted that she would give birth to 'a son and a strong child'.[4] The King confessed that his happiness entirely depended 'on this new hope that God has given us'.[5] The weeks passed, the rounding out of the Queen's body was keenly observed, and in October one of her servants was seen scurrying about London in search of mussels that were urgently needed to satisfy a royal craving.

Expectation mounted, and the Queen's mother sent her daughter voluminous advice, a beautiful sedan chair and a little jewelled heart to wear around her neck. This charm became so important to the Queen, so absolute an assurance of her future happiness, that she would tremble if she found she had forgotten to put it on. As her pregnancy advanced

3

and her time approached, her dwarf and her dancing master were sent to France to fetch a famous midwife. This was considered by many to be a slight. Surely the heir to the English throne should be brought into the world by good, Protestant, English hands? Such murmurs of disapproval were rapidly followed by public pleasure when it was learned that the unlikely emissaries had been captured by pirates, but the arrival from France of a band of Capuchin friars was an altogether more ominous sign. Here, once again, was a flagrant display of that Roman Catholicism whose presence at the centre of power caused such concern.

It was decided that the palace at Whitehall was not a suitable place for the lying-in, and the quieter St James's was chosen instead. There, in a room off the Colour Court, a bed sumptuously hung with green satin was prepared, and in this, around four in the morning of 29 May 1630, as Venus hovered brilliantly in the skies, the Queen's labours began. They were to continue through nearly eight hours, and a while after midday she was delivered of a large and swarthy boy – the second Charles Stuart of that name. He was handed over almost at once to a wet nurse and, as the King rode away to give thanks in St Paul's, six women of impeccably Protestant credentials came forward to rock the royal cradle.

While church bells pealed and bonfires once again flamed along the streets, men and women listened to every scrap of gossip they could glean about the heir to the throne. Distinguished foreigners wrote home with the tiniest details. The Venetian ambassador, having carefully approached the royal nurses, gravely informed the Senators of the Serene Republic that the future King of England 'never clenched his fists but always kept his hands open'. This, he was told, was a good sign. Charles would be 'a prince of great liberality'.[6] Such old wives' tales certainly had more to recommend them than the laborious predictions of the astrologers. The sturdy baby curled in his cradle and sucking his thumb would, they said, grow into a man with a thin beard, a shrill voice and a 'mincing gait'. It was not quite clear if he would live to be 108 or a mere 66 years old, but it was certain that he would be 'very fortunate' and 'attain wealth by marriage and war'. In only one respect were these pious hopes correct. Charles, the fortune-tellers declared, would be a nimble-witted, practical king, 'particularly fond of mathematicians, sailors, merchants, learned men, painters and sculptors'.[7]

While the gossips and astrologers looked to the Prince's worldly fortunes, the clergy prepared for his christening. This was the first step in inducting him into his future role as the head of the Church of England, and thus the defender of the true, Protestant, Anglican faith. This was a matter of the gravest importance, and the King insisted on what he considered a suitable measure of Protestant ceremonial. He wrote to the Capuchin friars telling them 'not to trouble themselves about the baptism of his son, as he would attend to that himself'.[8] He then arranged for his friend Bishop Laud to conduct the ceremony, which was held on 27 June in the private chapel of St James's Palace.

The rooms through which the little Prince was carried were hung with fresh tapestries, and the baptismal gifts were lavish. The Duchess of Richmond presented the child with a diamond ring worth £8000. The City fathers offered a gold cup 'a yard in length'. The Lord Mayor of London donated a silver font which was placed on a rostrum in the middle of the aisle so that the use of the Anglican rite would be clear to all. The choice of godparents nonetheless caused some concern. The Queen's family had to be involved, but Marie de Medici and Louis XIII embodied for most English people that horror of continental Roman Catholicism which ran so deeply through the nation's mind. The appointment of the Catholic Countess of Roxburgh as governess of the Prince's household also raised alarm (although she was soon replaced), and ardent Protestants, some of whom had secretly hoped that the Queen would prove barren, again muttered in discontent. For all the King's efforts, a suspiciously papist atmosphere clung round his son's baptism, and, as it ended and cannons thundered from the Tower, so a Puritan minister complained that he could see little cause for joy since he was 'uncertain what religion the King's children will follow, when brought up under so devoted a mother to the Church of Rome'.[9]

The mother herself was alternately bemused and enthralled by her child. He was, first of all, a very large baby who at four months could have passed for an infant a year old. This was a characteristic he may have inherited from his large-boned Danish grandmother on his

5

father's side, but, if this was so, his other prominent feature was a marked contradiction to this Scandinavian background. 'He is so dark I am ashamed of him,' the Queen wrote.[10] This swarthiness was something Charles almost certainly acquired from his Italian, Medici ancestors, and it was so obvious a characteristic that he would later be referred to as 'the black boy'.[11] What was also clear was that the Prince was both strong and intelligent. At four months he was teething, and his proud mother wrote that 'his size and fatness supply the want of beauty. I wish you could see the gentleman, for he has no ordinary mien; he is so serious in all he does', she added prophetically, 'that I cannot help fancying him far wiser than myself.'[12]

A household was provided for the Prince in St James's Palace. There, at an annual cost of £5000, some two to three hundred servants – chamberlains, doctors, lawyers, needlewomen, pages and scullions – presented a suitable air of opulence as they went about their business in the richly carved and painted rooms. The Queen was not expected to nurse her baby herself, but she had her own ideas on how infants should be reared, and, at her insistence, Prince Charles was not wrapped in the swaddling bands of conventional babyhood but was dressed in loose white linen cloths and soon afterwards in tiny shirts. At seven months he was reported as 'continuing in a blessed prosperity of health' which lasted through 1631, when the Countess of Dorset became his official governess.[13] Among other matters, the Countess replaced the Prince's first wet nurse with Mrs Christabella Wyndham, who stayed with Charles for four years. The baby became strongly attached to this woman, and Mrs Wyndham was later to play a significant role in Charles's youth. Meanwhile, as the little Prince toyed with his sweet-tasting gum and sugar dolls, and began to take 'a strange and unaccountable fondness for a wooden billet, without which in his arms he would never go abroad or lie down in his bed', so siblings were regularly added to the royal nursery.[14] Princess Mary was born when Charles was eighteen months old and was followed, two years later, by his mother's favourite, the blue-eyed James, Duke of York. Of the other royal children to survive into adulthood, Henry, Duke of Gloucester, was born in 1639, and Princess Henriette Anne in 1644.

There came the inevitable childhood illnesses to prove the toughness of the Prince's constitution. In 1633, just before his father was due to travel to Scotland, he caught a fever. He had been with the King in the royal park at Greenwich until after sunset, and later insisted on watching his father from a window at which he was allowed to stand 'with no hat upon his head or neck-cloth upon his neck'. The following day he was 'very heavy and drowsy', and was found to have a cold. As the fever rose, his doctor became alarmed. He consulted with colleagues who diagnosed the cause of the illness as a boil on the Prince's neck. Various remedies were prescribed. An ointment was ineffectually applied, a cooling drink was vomited up, and the eight experts gathered in the stuffy room eventually decided on the extreme measure of administering milk clysters 'to refresh his intestines and assuage his pain'. The agonising result was that Charles began to vomit blood, and a panacea of chicken broth laced with senna and rhubarb was ordered. By this time the child's natural resilience was beginning to assert itself. Although he was still nauseous and suffering from diarrhoea, his fever started to abate. He was made to swallow more broth 'with every good success' and, a week later, was eating 'heartily' despite being in poor spirits. He continued to recover, and by the time his father returned to Greenwich in July he was able to greet the King 'with the prettiest innocent mirth'.[15]

Such nursery delights were a world away from the political forces gathering outside. After Buckingham's death the King resolved to continue with his favourite's policies, but the widely unpopular attack on La Rochelle which had stirred the ire of Buckingham's murderer proved a humiliating disaster and, with this defeat still rankling, King Charles had been obliged to face a session of Parliament during the summer of 1629. The small love he already had for that institution was darkening to deep mistrust. His mind preyed on the fact that words from Parliament's remonstrance against Buckingham had been sewn into his murderer's hat and were recognised as a principal reason for the favourite's death. This document (known as the Petition of Right) had also pressed on royal powers, prohibiting imprisonment without trial and the levying of taxes 'without common consent by act of parliament'.

Charles had been obliged to accept the Petition, but he was resolved that the Commons should not tamper with his ancient prerogative powers, and by the time Members met in July 1629 the prejudice was hardening in his mind that certain of them at least were evil men resolved on destroying the fabric of society.

The session rapidly became acrimonious, King Charles insisting on his right to collect such long-established taxes as tonnage and poundage, while Puritan Members of the House insisted on their right to discuss financial and religious matters. The clash, noted the Venetian ambassador, 'generates very great rancour, and there is great fear of a rupture'.[16] This soon came about. Charles, realising that he was losing control of the House, ordered it to adjourn for a week. Cries of 'No! No!' greeted the announcement, and the Speaker was forcibly held down in his chair so that proceedings could continue. Angry motions against Catholicism and arbitrary taxes were then passed as royal officers hammered on the locked doors. Eventually the session ended, but at the urgent meetings of the Privy Council that followed, the King resolved on a course of action that would determine not only the next eleven years of his reign but the entire course of his son's youth.

He made his announcement with all the dramatic resources at his disposal. He rode to the House of Lords dressed in his most sumptuous regalia and there, having pointedly refused to grant the Commons the ancient courtesy of being invited to hear his speech, he addressed the peers on the matters nearest his heart. There was, he now firmly believed, a conspiracy by a handful of ill-affected persons who were determined to wreck the ancient practices of the realm. Although, as he assured the House, 'princes are not bound to give account of their actions but to God alone', Charles felt it became him to tell 'his loving and faithful nobility' about the plot he believed was launched against him. The loyal need not fear. Rather than tolerate dangerous novelty and insubordination, the King would 'maintain the ancient and just rights and liberties' of his subjects and rule without a parliament.[17] He rode home, an observer wrote that evening, as if he had freed himself from a great yoke. The House at Westminster was now silent, and Prince Charles would pass the years of his boyhood with only the

8

vaguest knowledge of Parliament as an institution bitterly opposed to his father's wishes.

The King himself, entering on the period of his personal rule, retreated to his various palaces. Of these, Whitehall was the most important, and it was in this vast, rambling conglomeration of buildings, spread out over twenty acres, that the boy Prince began to learn the ways of English royal life. The palace itself was situated on the north bank of the Thames, between the law courts at Westminster and the great commercial hub of the City of London. The seething life of the capital stretched up to its walls and even beyond since a public thoroughfare ran through the site. For all that a knight marshal was supposed to keep the area clear of undesirables and make sure that no squatters' shacks were built near by, the little silk-clad Prince would have seen the stalls selling fish and other perishables that were clustered all around. This press of people, the noises and the smells, were all unavoidable. Even the royal family, when in residence at Whitehall, could never wholly escape them. Porters were supposed to control those who entered the court itself, to turn away those not wearing 'gowns or fit habits', and deny access especially to those carrying offensive weapons. Nonetheless, for all the care that was taken, robbers occasionally broke in and, if condemned by the Court of the Royal Palaces, were hanged outside the Holbein Gate. Their dangling corpses were a ghastly warning to others, and an indication to the boy Prince of his father's powers.

Beyond this pullulating and often brutal world lay the decorous life of the court. Here, amid the ceremoniousness, the Prince came to know his father as a remote, sad-eyed and fastidious man, 'imperious and lofty' as contemporaries described him.[18] Order and hierarchy obsessed the King, for these were his way of convincing himself that his authority could create the dignity he craved. At the start of his reign he had cleared the gilded gothic and renaissance rooms of the crowd of 'fools and bawds, mimics and catamites' that had revelled through them in the days of his father, James I.[19] Now the palace rules were pinned up for all to read. Fifty-eight gentlemen pensioners were in constant attendance on the King, while 210 yeoman warders guarded him night and day. Here too, immortalised in the portraits of Van Dyck, gathered that generation of refined, silken courtiers, the women with their perfect complexions enhanced by glorious pearls, the superciliously beautiful young men idly displaying their long legs and graceful hands. It was for such a world that Van Dyck also painted that perfect invocation of royal childhood, the canvas in which the sallow and plump-faced Prince Charles, just seven years old and surrounded by his brothers and sisters, stares out at the spectator with dark, observant eyes as he rests his hand on the head of a subdued but watchful dog.

Mealtimes especially saw this little boy learning the ways of one of the most refined royal houses in Europe. Both for dinner (which was served between midday and two o'clock) and for evening supper, the Prince was required to enter the elaborate dining hall with his hat on. This was removed while the chaplain said grace and then replaced as the boy sat down at the right-hand end of the table. Kneeling pages then held out a silver-gilt ewer of scented water and a napkin. When Prince Charles had rinsed his hands, he made his choice from the dishes that were shown him, and a gentleman carved and tasted his portion before serving it. Other kneeling pages surrounded him while he ate. One offered bread, another wine, while a third held a bowl beneath the Prince's chin to catch any drops that might fall. No one spoke on these occasions unless the King led the conversation, but as the Prince looked round the elaborate, pillared dining room, so he could see, in the soft light that filtered down from the high windows, the luxurious formality of his father's court. On a service table richly draped in crisp linen stood an array of gold and silver plates, crystal flagons and drinking vessels. A silver wine-cooler held a collection of bottles. Liveried servants made their silent way across the black and white marble-paved floor. At the far end of the great room, from the respectful distance of a gracefully proportioned gallery, privileged observers gazed down on the scene and were watched in their turn by the royal dogs lying on the cool of the floor.

While such ceremony appeared to surround the King with dignity, the ways of his wife's circle were altogether more contentious and, from the time of his earliest boyhood, they made Prince Charles a subject of the public's often irate concern. The Queen's chapel was the particular focus of attention. This exquisite building had been designed for her by the architect Inigo Jones, and the Queen herself had laid the silver foundation stone at a lavish ceremony conducted in front of some 2,000 people. In the remarkably short space of three months the completed chapel – now 'a paradise of glory' fitted out with huge sculpted angels, 'hidden lights', gold plate and a Rubens altarpiece – was ready for consecration.[20] At the service a priest preached on the text 'This is the Lord's doing and it is marvellous in our eyes'.

To the serious Puritan merchant passing by, his mind running on profits and predestination, this was the last thing the chapel was. To such people it was a building to inspire shuddering distaste and call up a host of deep and bitter fears. Were not Roman Catholics the national enemy? There were still grandfathers alive who might just remember the sailing of the Spanish Armada. Many more could recall the hysteria that had gripped the country when the Gunpowder Plot was uncovered. And for all good Protestants there was the work popularly known as Foxe's *Book of Martyrs*. There, in lurid and bludgeoning detail, they were offered accounts of those of the godly who had been executed in the great battle between true religion and the papal Antichrist. To such minds, the Roman church's belief in the transubstantiation of the communion bread and wine into the body and blood of Christ was obscene. Its veneration for the Virgin and the saints had no warrant in the sacred authority of Scripture. Such things, it was believed, were superstitions urged by a cunning priesthood who exercised an excessive power over their followers and were attempting to extend the tyranny of Catholicism to the shores of England itself.

For some there was evidence that they were getting their way. The Queen's priests, it was said, had made her house a safe haven for the loathed Jesuits, and she herself willingly accepted the undignified penances that were inflicted on her. The news letters made it clear to those willing to believe such things that Henrietta Maria was sometimes made to go barefoot and to eat out of wooden dishes like a servant. Worst of all, she had gone to Tyburn to say prayers for the souls of those Roman Catholics who had been executed there. She had been so carried away with her enthusiasm, it was alleged, that she had fallen to her knees by the gallows and clutched her rosary in her fingers. Now she had persuaded the King to relax restrictions on entry to her chapel. There were those who had seen that the heir to the throne himself was regularly brought there to worship in the Catholic rite. So great was the outcry that the King declared that the boy's visits should cease. For a while he was persuaded to change his mind, but when the irresolute father finally put his foot down resentment against the Queen had deepened and she took to organising private parlour games for the Prince. The prizes in these were sacred medals and crucifixes. Coming upon one such occasion, the dismayed King ordered his son to hand back all he had won.

This little incident took place in the Queen's apartments where the growing Prince came to know a world more intimate but no less sumptuous than that of his father. Here, in the wainscoted rooms, hung with tapestries and the Italian masterpieces sent to her by the Pope's envoys, Henrietta Maria housed her Negro servants whose colour set off the pallor of her own skin. Here she was entertained by her dwarves, among them Jeffrey Hudson who, at a bare eighteen inches tall, had once been brought to the dinner table hidden in a pie. It was in these rooms, among the silver-plated tables and cabinets of lignum vitae, that Henrietta Maria, careless of expense, ordered lace, embroidery, rare flowers and precious stones. Here, too, the Queen sat countless times to Sir Anthony Van Dyck as he perfected her image, ignoring, as a courtier must, her protuberant teeth and concentrating instead on her ripening beauty, on the dark ringlets that fell so alluringly round her brow, and on her exquisite taste in dresses, whether of formal black, amber, oyster or stormy blue.

When she was bored or feeling a mother's love, Henrietta Maria summoned her eldest son to her apartments. There his quick eyes watched those courtiers who were drawn to her by the lure of influence – men happy to chatter in that thin, heady mixture of Catholic piety and Platonic love which characterised the Queen's circle. Mr Waller might be reading a poem. The soft-handed clerics – Monsignor Panzani or George Conn – might deftly turn the conversation to matters of the faith, while beside his mother would be Harry Jermyn, 'the Queen's prize servant', a handsome man in an ox-like way, a gambler and a swordsman who was obviously her best friend. All of these people were careful to flatter the Prince when he appeared, leaning forward with their worldly, attentive faces to take what seemed a genuine interest in his enthusiasms. Then, when his presence was no longer required, attendants took Charles back to the nursery and his mother returned to her other interests – a fitting for a new gown perhaps, or a last look at the lines of the masque in which she and her husband were to dance that night.

The court masques were the most splendid of the occasions on which Prince Charles observed his mother and father. These entertainments were made up from a lavish combination of drama, opera and ballet. Immense amounts of money were spent on them, and extraordinary ingenuity was lavished on their effects. On the nights of their performance, in the blaze of a thousand candles, the delighted Prince saw his richly costumed parents dancing their way round painted pastoral plains and horrid dens, ideal cities and remote wildernesses. Scene followed scene with extraordinary profusion. Suddenly there would appear before the boy's wondering eyes 'magnificent buildings composed of several select pieces of architecture'. People, coaches and horses crossed marvellous bridges. Great cities were dimly descried in the distance, while 'from the highest part of the heavens came forth a cloud . . . in which were eight persons richly attired representing the spheres'. Other clouds would then appear bearing musicians, 'and at that instant, beyond all these, a heaven opened full of deities; which celestial prospect, with the chorus below, filled all the whole scene with apparitions and harmony'.[21]

The purpose of such spectacles was to exalt the love of the King and Queen and illustrate the benefits this supposedly brought to the country at large. In such a world of make-believe it seemed there was nothing that the love of Charles's parents could not achieve. If the gods reordered the heavens after their human example, how much more could the devotion of the royal couple banish from Britain the vices of drinking, smoking and licentiousness. Even the Prince himself, barely out of his infancy, occasionally found a role in such celebrations, appearing for example in *The King and Queen's Entertainment* of 1636. He was as yet too young for a speaking part but, along with Buckingham's glamorous sons George and Francis Villiers (with whom he shared his nursery), he appeared in a country dance and then sat while a comically pompous usher tried to shoo away some country people who had come to present the King and Queen with baked pumpkins.

To the audience of aristocrats gathered to watch the performance, the message was as clear as it was comforting: for all the difficulties presented by officious busybodies throughout the land, Charles and Henrietta Maria retained the love of the common people. The drama proved it and, when such moments of fantasy failed to hide the truth, more brutal methods could be resorted to. When the Puritan William Prynne published a diatribe against the court and its entertainments, writing that 'women actors are notorious whores', he was tried and sentenced to life imprisonment, to a fine of £5000 and to having his ears cropped. By such means as these was arbitrary rule enforced in the little Prince's world.

The masques were insubstantial pageants and have long since faded, but a more lasting record of the world in which Prince Charles grew up was provided by his father's interest in the visual arts. During the years of his personal rule the King put together one of the most remarkable collections of renaissance and baroque paintings ever made. He was lavish in his spending, paying £18,280, for example, to purchase the masterpieces gathered by the Dukes of Mantua. The King thereby acquired works by Mantegna, Raphael, Titian and Correggio, and these were frequently supplemented by gifts from foreign rulers. The money spent on this activity – and the frankly papist subject-matter of many of the canvases themselves – once again roused suspicions about the court's religious sympathies. It is clear, however, that for the King (who kept a Raphael Madonna and Child in his bedroom) these works appealed through their aesthetic genius to what his friend Bishop Laud termed 'the beauty of holiness', to that tradition within the Anglican church which saw the church itself as a powerful estate of the realm that exalted reason, ritual and cultivated feeling over narrow dogmatism.

Laud himself, described by one observer as 'a little low, red faced man, of mean parentage', rose rapidly under the King's patronage by uniting agreeable religious beliefs with exceptional personal energy.[22] At a time of intense doctrinal controversy, both men were drawn by temperament and conviction to the teachings of the Dutch theologian Arminius, who held that there was an innate spark of salvation in all people. This spark had to be protected, tended and fed by the sacraments of the church over which the King was head. As a consequence, he and Laud encouraged the restoration and beautifying of church buildings and the imposition of order and ceremony on the services conducted in them. In churches across the land statues were replaced and stained glass was repaired, while the clergy were required to wear surplices, rail off their altars and cover them with a cloth to ensure that the sacrament of the host was made something special and set apart.

Prince Charles was encouraged to develop similar tastes. The King ordered a richly bound Bible to be prepared for him by the Ferrars at their 'Protestant monastery' at Little Gidding, and John Ferrar brought the completed volume to the Prince at Richmond. Here he was ushered into the presence chamber to find Charles accompanied by Bishop Duppa, the Villiers boys and the Duke of York. As was proper, Ferrar knelt to kiss the Prince's hand and then presented his Bible. He was delighted by the way the boy received it.

'Here's a gallant outside!' Charles exclaimed as he examined the binding. Then, as he began turning over the pages, so he said: 'Better and better!'

A courtier asked somewhat needlessly: 'How liketh Your Highness that rare piece?'

'Well, well *very*,' came the enthusiastic reply. 'It pleaseth me exceedingly'. Then, with the quick-witted tact that was already natural to him, Charles added: 'I wish daily to read in it.'[23] Only the Duke of York, an obstinate little boy, marred the charm of the occasion by insisting that he be presented with a Bible as lovely as his brother's, and that as soon as possible.

While the Prince treasured his Bible, his father's subjects were less gently encouraged to appreciate the beauty of holiness. Laud pursued his High Church policies with a vigour that often amounted to vindictiveness. This was an approach that was to have the gravest political consequences. While many felt that his imposition of ritual revealed a dangerously papist tendency, they also realised that the methods by which Laud and the King enforced these ideas touched on their privileges. Laud especially promoted the beauty of holiness through the most arbitrary means: by exacting money, by disregarding property rights and by sneering at the existence of parliaments. His religious doctrines were increasingly felt to be part of a political programme which exalted royal absolutism and, as a reward for his labours, the King appointed him Archbishop of Canterbury.

The result was increasing disquiet among all sorts and conditions of sober and serious people, both those Protestants who felt they could remain within the severer confines of the Church of England, and those Puritans who increasingly fretted at what they saw as unreformed and accumulating abuse. The latter were always a minority, although an articulate and influential one. Coming from all classes of society, they set a special value on the spiritual intensity generated by periods of strict self-examination and the often agonised probing of the soul which preceded their becoming convinced of their election to a state of grace.

One of the best-known and certainly one of the most influential instances of such an experience occurred in the Fens towards the end of the 1620s, at the time when Oliver Cromwell was setting up as a gentleman farmer at the village of St Ives. Although Cromwell had served as MP for Huntingdon in the Parliament of 1629, he had not distinguished himself by the vehemence of his anti-monarchical views. Indeed, he seems to have been more troubled by personal problems, for he took time off from the business of the House to visit a well-known London physician who diagnosed him as suffering from depression. When Cromwell returned home, his doctor was frequently called out to help ease the morbid thoughts which Cromwell himself, then in his early thirties, clothed in the religious vocabulary of dry springs and barren wildernesses.

In Puritan terms, Cromwell was entering that period of the helpless conviction of personal sinfulness from which the grace of God alone could redeem the soul. 'You know what my manner of life hath been,' he wrote to a relation. 'O I have lived in and loved darkness, and hated the light. I was a chief, the chief of sinners.' Eventually, with all human resources drained, there broke across such desolation the absolute certainty of a calling. 'O the riches of his mercy!'[24] Such experiences had an all-transforming power, and now, as one of the godly, Cromwell became whole-heartedly committed to urging forward true reformation and taking Christian life in England beyond what were seen as the compromises of the church of Laud with its bishops, its royal head, its clergy in vestments and its celebration of such papist festivals as Christmas.

The Prince's own religious instruction was put in the hands of Dr Brian Duppa, the devout and learned Bishop of Chichester. Duppa was a sufficiently shrewd teacher to wear his scholarship lightly, and Charles became fond of him. The greatest influence on his life at this period however was the Duke of Newcastle, the grandee who had been appointed as his governor to breed in him the bearing of an aristocrat. Many of Newcastle's precepts were permanently to influence Charles's behaviour, encouraging that affability and courtesy which he had already displayed to Ferrar and which were so to mark him as a man, becoming the often deceptive mask for an altogether darker political astuteness.

Newcastle was an ambitious man and his position as the Prince's governor gave him prestige and influence, but once he had accepted the task he became so devoted to his charge that he would brook no criticism of him. He was himself a fervent monarchist, so fervent indeed that his wife complained that he loved the boy Charles better than their own children, better indeed than her. Charles in his turn found a forty-five-year-old man with a nimble if not profound mind, an immense range of interests, an unfailing courtesy and, above all, an open and pragmatic view of the world. Here was an adult very different to the Prince's reserved and chilly father, and a figure the boy could easily see as a hero. How could he resist a man who disdained to treat him merely as a child, who was rarely narrow and who pulsated with energy? Here was a governor who adored animals and was one of the most skilled horsemen in Europe. When he visited his stables he was invariably greeted by the neighing of his 'rejoicing' stud, each member of which he seemed to know intuitively. Soon he had taught Charles to be a competent rider, while also making him a skilled fencer and an able dancer. Newcastle could, besides, talk of chemistry and literature, but the wide range of his interests never became a burdensome pedantry, and he was determined that his charge should be similarly alert and able to deal with the world in a natural, broad-minded way.

It is clear that Newcastle was trying in part to counter the influence over the boy of those elements in his father's personality which were to some degree responsible for his growing unpopularity. For instance, if the Prince was always to be conscious of his exalted station, he should not cultivate the fastidious reserve of his father which distressed many as haughtiness. 'Though you cannot put on too much King,' ran one of Newcastle's maxims, 'yet even there sometimes a hat or a smile in the right place will advantage you.' How very different this was to the King's catchphrases: 'Sir, I am not of your opinion,' or the chilling, 'I mean to be obeyed.' By such light, human touches as Newcastle urged, Prince Charles might win a wide regard. 'How easy a way is this to have the people.'

It went along with such an approach that Charles was not to be too bookish. Developing ideas that were soon to be at the forefront of intellectual enquiry, Newcastle urged that he would sooner have the boy 'study things than words, matter than language'. Although a knowledge of foreign tongues was useful, Charles was not to become a walking dictionary. Similarly, while remaining loyal to the Anglican church, he was to avoid an excessive religiosity. Newcastle could see that the little boy who had so relished the gift of a lovely Bible was 'in your own disposition religious', but he was to 'be beware of too much devotion', for a virtuous man might be a bad king since 'divinity teaches us what we should be, not what we are'. Finally, Charles was to cultivate an easy respect for the opposite sex. 'To women you cannot be too civil,' Newcastle declared, 'especially to great ones.'[25] Little of this advice was to fall on stony ground, and it is clear that Newcastle was trying to fashion Charles into a man at once well bred and worldly-wise, a future ruler who was both pragmatic and shrewd. It is evident too that he early on achieved some measure of success. By the time he was a mere eight years old, Charles was already beginning to practise the delicate arts of manipulation.

At the close of 1638 he again fell ill. The previous drastic remedies were recommended but the boy refused them. He also refused to listen to persuasion and knew that he was safe from punishment. The doctors decided that all they could do was ask Henrietta Maria to intervene. She wrote urging her son to swallow his medicine, 'for if you will not I must come to you, and make you take it, for it is for your health.'[26] The Duke would tell her, she added, whether he had been a good boy or not. Unwilling to risk a confrontation with either his mother or his governor, Charles resorted to shrewd boyish diplomacy. Asking someone to rule lines on a sheet of paper for him, he wrote to Newcastle saying: 'My Lord, I would not have you take too much physic; for it doth always make me worse, and I think it will do the like to you.' Then, suggesting that he was really quite fit, obedient and affectionate, the boy added: 'I ride every day, and am ready to follow any other directions from you. Make haste to return to him that loves you. Charles P.'[27] Newcastle took the hint, and nothing more was heard of the Prince swallowing bitter medicines.

Charles had won his first victory, but while schoolroom politics were one thing the adult world was another, and the most important lesson the Prince had to learn was the nature of the Stuart monarchy as his father envisaged this. Few occasions revealed the King's power with more ceremony than the reception of ambassadors from foreign states, and no room in all his palaces more splendidly displayed the mysteries of kingship than the Banqueting Room in Whitehall where these occasions took place. Here Prince Charles could observe his father as both connoisseur and autocrat.

The King himself sat on a throne at the far end of the chaste but sumptuous hall which Inigo Jones had designed for him in his most refined Palladian style. Down the immense length of this room were then ranged the King's courtiers, the great of the realm dressed in a dazzling display of many-coloured silks, jewels and feathers. The ambassador to be received advanced between these impressive ranks, bowing deeply to the King as the source of all authority in his three realms of England, Scotland and Ireland. The King was the head of the church and appointed all the bishops. He was the ultimate power of the law and appointed all the judges. He was the crown of society and even the peers addressed him as 'dread sovereign'. Over such people as these, and over all those below them, the King held absolute power. His word was literally the law. This he could express either through proclamations (issued with or without consultation with his Council) or as statutes promulgated with the advice of Parliament, a body it was universally recognised he could call or dismiss at will. The levying of taxes, the declaration of war, the settling of peace, the pardoning of criminals, the regulation of trade were all his final responsibility. In such a world as this, kings 'make and unmake their subjects; they have power of raising, and casting down; of life, and of death.'[28]

The great painted panels the King had commissioned from Rubens for the ceiling of the Banqueting Room elaborated this idea, and whenever Prince Charles cast his eyes up to them he was given a glorious lesson in the divine right of kings. In a panel over the throne his grandfather James I pointed to the embracing figures of Peace and Plenty. Royal Bounty trod down on the shrunken breasts of Avarice, Wise Government triumphed over Discord, Heroic Virtue kicked at the face of writhing Envy, while, in the great central panel of the ceiling, Rubens had portrayed James I being drawn to heaven as a reward for his earthly labours. Here indeed was the apotheosis of the King who had once declared that 'the state of monarchy is the supremest thing upon earth: for kings are not only God's lieutenants, and sit upon God's throne, but even by God himself are called Gods.'[29]

Nonetheless, as Prince Charles stared up at these images of Stuart power, so murmurings outside the palace were beginning to threaten the foundations of his father's rule. Men and women across the country, unable to find comfort in the High Church rituals forced on them by Laud, were separating into dangerously independent or 'gathered' congregations. They were also putting their faith in the coming of the

Millennium. Revelation was at hand, and many were ardent for a New Jerusalem where the Stuarts would have no power at all. Soon Baptists, Presbyterians and Independents, Muggletonians, Ranters and fearsome, vision-crazed Fifth Monarchy men would all be asserting their claims to exclusive religious insight and political power. Whole nations even began to challenge the King. Angry voices in Scotland objected to his attempt to force a prayer book on their land, and the Scots eventually united in agreeing to a Covenant by which they bound themselves to a rigid and repressive form of Presbyterianism that was wholly at odds with the teachings of the Anglican church.

The King would brook no compromise and readied his militia, saying he would rather die 'than yield to their impertinent and damnable demands.'[30] Nonetheless, when, in July 1640, a Scots army invaded England, marching unopposed as far as Newcastle, Charles was obliged to agree to a truce. The Scots were allowed to remain in Northumberland and Durham on a subsidy of £860 a day. But the King's obstinacy had worked against him. The paying of so large a sum necessitated the recall of MPs to Westminster, and when the so-called Long Parliament opened in November 1640 such leading figures as John Pym were determined to address the nation's grievances. They spoke out against what they saw as the growing influence of popery at the court, objected to the arbitrary way in which King Charles had imposed taxes to fund his personal rule, and attacked his ministers and eventually even the monarch himself. Amid this rising cacophony, Prince Charles's years of childhood security were coming to a close, and soon his very survival would be at stake.

2

The End of Peace

The voices of protest across his father's realms rose to a storm whose force would soon expose Prince Charles to the brutalities of civil war, sunder him from his parents and eventually drive him into years of penniless and hopeless exile. Even now, in 1640, the turmoil impinged on the royal schoolroom, and whisperings among the boy's household began to disturb him. No one offered comfort, and eventually the Prince's worried state became evident even to the preoccupied King. He asked his son what the matter was.

'Your Majesty should have asked me that sooner,' came the resentful reply.

'Tell me,' said the King.

The little boy summoned up his courage and the words of the gossips spilled out. 'My grandfather', he began, 'left you four kingdoms – I am afraid Your Majesty will leave me never a one.'

Prince Charles was already fearful that he might lose his right to the crowns of England, Scotland and Ireland (along with traditional English claims to the crown of France), and it was a measure of his father's lack of spontaneity that he did not try to calm his son's fears but merely asked: 'Who hath been your tutors in this?'

He was met with the silence of a little boy who perhaps feared he had already gone too far and, instead of offering comfort, the King turned impatiently away.[1]

The world nonetheless demanded that the ten-year-old Prince be more than just a bewildered child. He had public duties to perform, and the public's eyes were on him. In their pursuit of the King's 'evil counsellors', the House of Commons had resolved on the destruction of the Earl of Strafford, whom they saw as the military arm of royal absolutism. The trial of 'Black Tom Tyrant' took place in Westminster Hall, where a throne had been set on a dais. A shamefaced King Charles preferred to listen to the mauling of his great servant from a private box, and it was his eldest son who was required to represent the monarchy, sitting by himself on the throne from the start of the day's proceedings until noon as the furious, bewildering process raged about him.

While the Prince spent his mornings in this way, his nights were passed in celebration. In an urgent attempt to prove his Protestant credentials and raise much-needed money, the King had resolved on marrying nine-year-old Mary, the little fair-haired Princess Royal, to the young Dutch Prince, William of Orange. To the Queen, this was an insult to her religion, and on William's landing in the country she had petulantly refused to kiss him. It was left to Prince Charles to greet the good-looking fifteen-year-old on the great staircase in Whitehall. William was then told that his future bride had caught a cold and that he could not see her until she had recovered. The eager boy insisted, and eventually Prince Charles accompanied him to meet his sister. A week later, in a distinctly subdued ceremony, the children were married in the chapel at Whitehall, and a delightful double portrait by Van Dyck portrays them holding each other's fingers in a gesture of affection.

On the evening of the wedding itself, after a stroll in Hyde Park, a supper and a dance, the time came for the bedding of the young people. The King accompanied Prince William to the state chamber where the Princess lay, surrounded by her ladies. Assisted by Prince Charles, the bridegroom removed his dressing gown, got into the bed and very gently gave his bride three kisses. He than lay beside her for about three quarters of an hour 'in the presence of the great lords and ladies of

England' and the Dutch representatives.[2] For the marriage to be officially 'consummated' the couple's bare legs had to touch, but Mary's nightgown reached to her ankles, and it was only when the Queen's ever-useful dwarf produced a pair of scissors to cut the garment that matters could be concluded to the delight of all.

But Whitehall was no longer safe. A furious London mob, avid for Strafford's head, was howling about the palace, and the pressure on the King to collude in his servant's death became irresistible. He wrote one last, wretched appeal to both Houses of Parliament. If they would commute the sentence on Strafford to imprisonment, he declared, it would be 'an unspeakable contentment to me'.[3] According to the Venetian ambassador, the Queen then suggested a twist of pathos which she clearly thought would carry the day. She proposed that Prince Charles deliver the letter in person. Surely the sight of such innocence involved in a matter of such gravity would soften the hearts of those terrible men? A coach was called and the driver was ordered to take the Prince to the House of Lords. The coach duly set off through the back-streets of a dangerous London, but the Prince's appeal was in vain. For the first time in his life he was brusquely dismissed, the King's letter was returned and the people had Strafford's head.

The mounting state of tension in the country began to bring advisers of the highest calibre to the King's side. Among these men was Edward Hyde, a lawyer and the Member of Parliament for Saltash in Cornwall. Hyde's sense of decorum had already been annoyed by the 'indecency and rudeness' shown by Oliver Cromwell at a meeting of a Commons committee, and he had told him in characteristically orotund tones that if he continued in the same manner, 'he would presently adjourn the committee and complain of you to the House'.[4] Some of Hyde's colleagues were suspicious and feared for his career.

'You will undo yourself by adhering to the Court,' warned Henry Marten.

Hyde returned somewhat disingenuously that he had 'no relation to the Court'. He was 'only concerned to maintain the Government and to preserve the law'. He then proceeded to expatiate on his favourite theme at length.

Marten made his own position clear in a sentence. 'I do not think one man wise enough to govern us all.'

Hyde was dumbstruck at such attack on the monarchy. 'It was the first word', he wrote, 'he had ever heard any man speak to that purpose.'[5]

Armed with well-bridled indignation, Hyde had a private meeting with King Charles the following day, and it is a significant measure of his stature that he managed to win the confidence of his fastidious and often chilly monarch. The depth of Hyde's loyalty was his outstanding recommendation for he had, in his own words, 'a very particular devotion and passion for the person of the King'.[6] The fact that Charles was inspired to some feeble jokes in his presence also suggests that he warmed to Hyde's cultivated affability, but just as important to the naturally shy and often lazy King was this ally's unflagging administrative energy and aura of massive assurance. Hyde could be pompous – sometimes magisterially so, as Prince Charles would soon learn – but the authority he exuded even in his thirties was deeply attractive to the beleaguered monarch.

With the mounting political tension, the whole of London was now in uproar and the King himself was increasingly confused and uncertain what to do. Then, quite suddenly, he left his capital with his family, fleeing so abruptly that nothing was prepared for them when the royal household arrived at Hampton Court. There, Prince Charles was obliged to sleep in the same bed as his parents. The securities of an ordered boyhood were collapsing around him. He was being hurried out of ceremonious palaces where power was a Rubens gesture, and soon he would be made to confront a world where he would need all his cunning to survive. Meanwhile, in an empty Whitehall, the curious wandered about with no guards to prevent them staring at the trappings of royalty: the state rooms, the pictures, the tapestries and the throne, on which some even sat to feel what it was like to be a king.

During this uncertain time, the Prince could see that his father was preparing for war against his own subjects. Even here the difficulties and reverses the King faced suggested how perilous the state of monarchy was, how uncertain the divine right of kings. Newcastle, the

Prince's old tutor, was despatched to Hull to secure the huge arsenal there, but failed to do so. In a desperate attempt to gather arms and ammunition, the King then sent his wife to Holland. The couple left Windsor Castle for Dover on 7 February, but had to skirt a hostile London, skulking on the byways like debtors or thieves. The days of the gorgeous masques with which the Prince's mother and father had convinced themselves that their love could order the world had come to an abrupt end. Henrietta Maria was now obliged to pawn her jewels for guns.

There was an emotional parting between the royal parents at Dover, and then the Prince's peregrinations started again. Father and son's eventual destination was York, but inevitably there were stops on the way, and attempts were made to secure those who, it was hoped, were loyal to the King's cause. The Prince had an important role to play in this, and he performed it with a patience and sophistication remarkable in a little boy not yet twelve. His visit to Cambridge particularly showed how training and instinct had already made him a royal actor, an important child who, as the focus of attention, had considerable responsibilities.

Prince Charles arrived in the city several days before his father, was welcomed with a Latin speech by the Vice Chancellor, and then, along with the Villiers boys, was given his honorary degree. Pairs of gloves and a Bible were presented to him and if, in King's College Chapel, he failed to follow custom and cover his face with his hat during prayers, he was excused for what was seen as a minor and even a delightful lapse. The Regent House offered a sterner challenge. A three-hour play of a dullness so intense that even the actors were concerned awaited the boy. He sat through it quietly and, at the end, applauded with 'all signs of acceptance which he could' before being obliged to watch a second play, which was received with an equal appearance of pleasure.[7] When the long day was over, the Prince was escorted by enthusiastic members of the university to a coach in which he set off to meet his father at Newmarket.

When father and son returned to Cambridge they were to find that royal visits could show the state of the divisions in the country at large.

While the royal pair were greeted outside Trinity College with cries of 'Vivat Rex!' and were generously entertained at St John's, the townspeople were determined to express their feelings. Some surrounded the King's departing coach and began 'humbly and earnestly' begging him to 'return to your Parliament, or we shall be undone'. Others were blunter in their response. As the King's coach proceeded along the road to Huntingdon, it soon became apparent to the already irritated monarch that, in an act of pointed defiance, none of the county's gentry had mustered to escort him. Worse was to follow. After refusing a Parliamentary request that he transfer the vast armoury at Hull to the Tower of London, the King made a second attempt to seize it for himself but was refused entry. As the country headed ever more surely towards civil war, the first act of military defiance had occurred. The Royal Navy then deserted to the Parliamentarian cause, yet another attempt to seize Hull proved a failure and, by August, war was inevitable. Senior officers in the rebel army were commanded by the King to surrender their commissions or be accused of treason. Then, on 12 August, he issued a proclamation urging his subjects to meet with him at Nottingham. 'The time is now come', he wrote, 'for my faithful friends to show themselves.'[8] For the moment, few did.

Prince Charles was increasingly involved in the preparations for war. Arms, men and money were all desperately needed for the royal cause, and in the middle of September his father moved westwards to Shrewsbury, from where he could gain access to the royalist heartlands of Wales and the Marches. The Prince, attended by Lord Hertford who had been appointed his governor in Newcastle's absence, was sent to Raglan. There he was entertained to metheglin or spiced mead and other local delights in a tapestry-hung room where the local people presented him with what gifts they could: engraved antique plate or the fruits of their farms. In return, they were treated to a graceful speech. 'Gentlemen,' the prince began, 'I have formally heard of the great minds, the true affections and meanings of the ancient Britannies* – but

* That is, the ancient Britons, supposed ancestors of the contemporary Welsh.

my kind entertainment hath made me confide in your love, which I shall always remember. I give you commendation, praise and thanks for your love, your bounty and liberal entertainment.'[9] With such words, the boy then continued his progress through Radnorshire, being 'very gracious and loving' to all, and exercising that affability he was later to use with such political adroitness. Soon his success was apparent. Quantities of men and money began to reach the King from North Wales, Cheshire and Denbighshire. A mint was set up, and pay was promised to those who enlisted. The close of September saw the King commanding over 6000 footsoldiers and 2000 horse.

On 12 October, the King ordered this gallimaufry of mostly inex-perienced men to march south-east towards London so that he might regain his capital. He and his son were riding to battle. As their forces proceeded, so others joined them, and the Royalists' manpower swelled beyond all expectation. The Prince was now to become familiar with the ways of an army that consisted of thirteen regiments of foot, ten of horse and three of dragoons, with an artillery train of twenty guns. It is hardly surprising that this large, unwieldy force progressed at a rate of a mere ten miles a day, but the reason why they were doing so at all had to be made clear to them. On 19 September, Prince Charles listened as his father addressed his assembled troops on the perils of the 'dark, equal chaos of confusion' he believed would sweep across the country if ever he surrendered to the twin evils of religious radicalism and Parliamentary insubordination.[10] Later, he gave orders to proceed to Edgehill, where, from the advantage of a slight ridge, he intended to engage with his enemies. There, too, Prince Charles would have his first experience of battle.

Early on the morning of 23 October, with drums beating, Royalist soldiers emerged from the barns and cottages where they had been billeted, buckled on their armour and prepared to march off in the frosty cold. The King, dressed in a black, ermine-lined cloak, mounted his charger attended by the Lords Richmond and d'Aubigny, along with Sir Edmund Verney, who was carrying a larger than ordinary scarlet banner. Prince Charles and the Duke of York rode just behind. It is probable that the Prince himself was mounted on the 'very goodly white horse' he had been presented with when the royal progress reached York, its richly studded velvet trappings reaching nearly to the ground and embroidered all over 'with burning waves of gold'.[11] He doubtless also wore his sumptuous battledress, which consisted of a burnished and oiled black breastplate beautifully decorated with engraved and gilded bands. A marvellously contrived helmet matched this, while beneath his breastplate the Prince wore a shirt of oyster-coloured silk decorated with gold bands and lace at the cuffs. There was an abundant red sash around his waist, and a sword at the side of his buff leather jerkin. He also carried a pistol which he was determined to use should the opportunity arise.

The army was given its orders to march, and the Prince and his brother, put in the care of the eminent physician Dr William Harvey, watched the opposing troops draw up their battle formations. The battle itself commenced towards one o'clock in the afternoon. Ineffective artillery fire was exchanged for about an hour until the Royalist army resolved to move down the hill. When, after another hour, they had completed their descent, they again opened fire. Then, at about three o'clock, Prince Rupert of the Rhine, the King's fierce and glamorous nephew who was in England to widen his military experience, ordered his cavalry on the right to charge. Prince Charles looked on as, amid the terrible, unfamiliar noise and the drifting of white gunpowder smoke, the Royalists trotted forward for 200 yards. Trumpeters then sounded the gallop and they swept through the enemy cavalry, wreaking revenge until they had chased the enemy two miles to Kineton. There, joined by the cavalry of the Royalist left, they wasted valuable time looting the Parliamentary baggage train.

Wrongly believing that they would be supported by the swift return of these men, the King's foot now advanced 'with a slow steady pace, and a daring resolution'.[12] Heavy carnage was inflicted by each side, yet neither broke or ran. But by now the initiative had passed to the remaining Parliamentarian cavalry. They charged so successfully that the King was obliged to watch his own centre fleeing back towards the hill. He resolved to march up to them and encourage them by his presence, but as nothing would induce him to put his sons in danger he turned to the Duke of Richmond and ordered him to conduct the boys to safety. The Duke refused, as did the Earl of Dorset, and probably for the same reason. 'He would not be thought a coward', the Duke huffily declared, 'for the sake of any king's sons in Christendom.'[13] Charles and James were then entrusted to Sir William Howard, who, with others, began to lead them away.

They had not gone a musket shot towards the hill when they saw a body of horse galloping in their direction through the failing light. Thinking the men must be Royalists, they rode towards them. The dangerous truth emerged only when the royal party sent out an equerry and saw the man beaten from his horse and stripped. While the equerry feigned death, the princes and their escort made rapidly for a barn which was being used as a field hospital for the Royalist wounded. But by now a full body of Roundheads was within easy shooting distance. 'I fear them not!' Prince Charles called out and drew a pistol from one of his holsters.[14] A horrified Sir John Hinton earnestly and 'at last somewhat rudely' begged the Prince not to attack, persuading him instead to ride quickly away as a well-mounted Roundhead broke from his ranks and careered towards Charles himself. Hinton received his charge, shots were exchanged, and, although Hinton unseated his enemy, the man was so heavily armed that Hinton's sword was useless against him. A Royalist soldier then came up and poleaxed the fallen man while the Princes themselves rode safely away.

The Battle of Edgehill was a bitterly fought draw after which, having failed to capture London, the King retreated to Oxford. Prince Charles followed him there. For a boy on the verge of adolescence, wartime Oxford had all the appeal of a raffish, exciting garrison city. His father set up his lodgings in imperious Christ Church, but was obliged to use the vast main quadrangle there as a cattle pen. The royal party tried to maintain the appearance of a court, dining in state, attending chapel, playing games, watching entertainments, reading the elegantly syco-phanic verse of William Waller and having their portraits painted by William Dobson, who portrayed the prince himself in his battledress. But danger and a sense of improvisation were never far away. Every morning the King rose punctually to inspect the city's defences, while the colleges and lecture halls were turned into barracks and workshops. Tailors stitched uniforms in the Music School, there was a granary in the Schools of Logic and Law, and portable bridges were sawn in the School of Rhetoric. Here was a chaotic world that would rapidly harden the Prince. Passing a captured Parliamentarian officer in the streets, he asked the man's guards where they were escorting their prisoner. They said he was being taken to be questioned before the King. Charles replied that the man should be hanged before his father had a chance of pardoning him, a remark which suggests the unblinking ease with which he would much later condemn his own enemies.

In the streets and public places of Oxford, there was the glitter of uniforms, the tread of parading troops and the harsh bark of orders shouted to men at drill. There was also what for many was an unacceptable level of drunkenness and lewd behaviour. The Cavaliers might be 'neat enough and gay in their appearance, and yet they were very nasty and beastly . . . vain, empty and careless, rude whoremongers'.[15] Royal proclamations were regularly issued in an attempt to curb excesses of behaviour, while chaplains were commanded to hold services twice a day in front of their troops and to preach to them every Sunday morning. Nonetheless, even the royal family could not always be relied upon to set a shining example. Portraits of Prince Charles from this time show a boy's face starting to become shadowed with a new, adult sensuality. His sexual interests were beginning to stir, and on one occasion in church, beguiled by the presence of a row of women 'half-dressed, like angels' in the Royalist fashion, he started to snigger during the sermon. His new governor, the ineffectual Lord Berkshire, felt obliged to tap him sharply on the head with his staff.

Henrietta Maria now returned to England with a supply of arms and men, and on 13 July 1643, the King, attended by Prince Charles and the Duke of York, rode out to meet her. A medal was struck to commemorate the occasion and bore on one side an image of Charles and Henrietta Maria seated on thrones, the planets benign above them, while below the Python of rebellion lay dead at their feet. But all was not such harmony when the couple returned to Oxford. From her rooms at Merton, the Queen meddled persistently in political manoeuvres altogether too subtle for her domineering but shallow mind. Wholly committed to the war, contemptuous of the heretics about her and rejoicing in her easy dominance over her husband, Henrietta Maria tried constantly to subvert the well-considered plans of such bourgeois Anglicans as the newly knighted Sir Edward Hyde, the King's Chancellor of the Exchequer. In the meantime, she also pursued her own brand of international diplomacy. She realised that in her eldest son she had a valuable commodity to trade on the European marriage market, and she now began to make overtures to those surrounding Louis XIV's first cousin, Anne-Marie de Montpensier. In addition to her acknowledged charms, La Grande Mademoiselle, as this lady was known, had three more solid attractions: she was incalculably rich, she was devoutly Catholic and she was French. She was, in Henrietta Maria's eyes, a perfect match for Prince Charles.

While the Queen pursued her fantasies, the summer saw a number of Royalist military successes. Bristol, the second largest port in the land, was captured, and as the Cavaliers' northern army besieged Hull, so their western army left Oxford to concentrate on securing Plymouth. In the long term, none of these campaigns was to prove a lasting victory, and, even while reports of success came in, the Parliamentarians were consolidating their position. At Marston Moor they decided on an heroic evening attack. Cromwell and Sir David Leslie broke the Royalist horse and then, returned from the pursuit, destroyed the Royalist foot. It gradually became apparent that the battle was a turning point and that the Royalist cause was collapsing. The strain told on the Prince's family. The Queen, heavily pregnant with the daughter she would christen Henriette Anne, resolved that Oxford was too dangerous a place to give birth and decided to move to the West Country. From there she set sail for France where, amid humiliations she could never have imagined, she would continue her increasingly desperate efforts at diplomacy and marrying off her son.

As she did so, Parliament set about the raising of a national force to be called the New Model Army. Such initiatives ensured the further steady defeat of the Royalist cause, and the loss of Shrewsbury partic-ularly was a disaster both in practical terms and for morale. Even the

King recognised the increasing hopelessness of his situation and, for the first time, feared that he might fall into enemy hands. He saw it as one of his prime duties to ensure the safety of the Prince. 'While his son was at liberty they would not dare to do him harm,' or so he thought. The question of where Prince Charles might be sent was rapidly solved. Division and weakness in the west were draining the Royalists of support there. Newly appointed as the General of the Western Association, the heir might yet work the healing magic of royalty. Besides, it was time for the fourteen-year-old Prince to face his responsibilities, and it was partly to 'unboy' him that the King now sent him to Bristol.

There was not enough money for a glorious send-off. Lord Capel had to raise what he could on his credit and, in return, was put in charge of the single regiments of horse and foot which were all the King could spare. He had however provided his son with a council. This included the indispensable Hyde, who, while worrying that the King would fall victim to the influence of ultra-Royalist fanatics, was also preparing to educate the heir to the throne with all the well-intentioned pomposity that came so naturally to him. But now, as the Royalist cause entered its darkest days, even the weather seemed to conspire in the atmosphere of gloom. When Prince Charles and his Council rode out from Oxford on 4 March 1645, the great clouds lumbering across the sky burst in torrential rain as if to acknowledge that the Prince would never see his father again.

Accompanied by Hyde, the Earl of Berkshire and the Lords Capel, Hopton and Culpepper, Charles rode through the torrential rain to Faringdon. From there he moved on to Devizes, to Bath and finally to Bristol. There he discovered that none of the promises made at Oxford had been kept. Not an extra man or horse had been provided, while of the £100 a week supposedly allowed for his support there was 'not one penny ready or likely to be'. Eventually, matters became so serious that Charles 'was forced to borrow from the Lord Hopton's store to buy bread'.[16]

Quite as damaging as these shortages were the divisions soon found to be rife among the local Royalist officers. Charles had been sent to the

West Country so that 'by his presence, direction, and authority, the many factions and animosities which were between particular persons of quality and interest in those parts . . . might be composed and reconciled'.[17] There was little hope of achieving this. The King had appointed Lord Goring as his regional Commander-in-Chief but, although an undoubtedly brave and vigorous man, Goring was both shifty and an alcoholic. At the start of the war he had been a distinguished cavalry leader, but the notorious plundering he permitted his troops made him widely hated by ordinary people, just as his slide into drink and vindictive apathy made him increasingly unpopular with the Royalists. Worst of all, Goring was incapable of working with such fellow officers as Sir Richard Grenville. Giving and taking orders in such an atmosphere would be extremely difficult, and, as the Royalist cause in the west began to collapse, Prince Charles was to learn at first hand the frustrations of being surrounded by able but vainglorious men who were as much concerned for their own reputations as his father's cause.

Hyde now felt it incumbent on him to begin training the Prince for his future responsibilities. In order to familiarise the boy with the twists and compromises of policy making, he insisted that Charles be present at all sessions of the Council, 'to mark and consider the state of affairs and to accustom himself to speaking and judging upon what was said'. With the censoriousness that was second nature to him, Hyde believed that such lessons were badly needed. Hitherto, he declared, Charles had been 'very little conversant with business'. Nor, he added, had the boy 'spent his time so well towards the improvement of his mind and understanding as might have been expected from his years and fortune'.[18] Hyde was constantly to berate Charles for inattention and laziness, but he was oblivious to the fact that the dark-eyed, observant Prince was taking in everything about him with the fascination of a clever adolescent.

At fifteen, Charles was a tall, vigorous and highly sexed boy with the coarse, saturnine looks which were far from being what was then considered conventionally handsome. His large and sensuous mouth was particularly disparaged, but it is clear that he had intense animal magnetism and the equally potent allure of monarchy. For some, these were irresistible qualities to be exploited for a variety of ends. During the week he spent helping to raise troops at Bridgwater, for instance, the Prince renewed his acquaintance with Christabella Wyndham, his old wet nurse. She was, Hyde declared, a woman who had nothing feminine about her but her fleshy exterior, and this she now used to attract the boy in the hope of gaining advancement for herself and her family. Mrs Wyndham played on Charles's natural rebelliousness, trying to keep him away from meetings of his Council and speaking 'negligently and scornfully' of his advisers. She also behaved towards him in public with a degree of intimacy that Hyde found distressing.

Over-familiar with the easily distracted Charles, Mrs Wyndham started wheedling him into granting land. Hyde cautioned the boy, and Mrs Wyndham herself retaliated with a campaign of backbiting. This eventually got so out of hand that she told the Prince it was his father who was really responsible for the disasters that had been inflicted on the country. An appalled Council wrote to the King, who at once ordered his son's return to Bristol, but it is significant that Hyde himself could never find out if the Prince really believed all he had been told by Mrs Wyndham. Charles was a quick-witted boy growing up in wartime, and he was learning that, in a world where propriety had all but collapsed, it was best to cultivate an affable exterior but keep his opinions to himself. The lesson would in time engender an inveterate habit of mind.

Charles nonetheless had a public role to play. The West Country had suffered terribly from the ravages of troopers, and in some places the people were paying double taxes which Goring's army collected with a greed and savagery that made them widely detested. Like many others across the country, the local people started to band into associations of Clubmen who, in the last resort, were prepared to defend their well-being by fighting any forces who disrupted their livelihoods.[19] They came to present their case to the Prince. Charles, realising the threat these people posed, received them with every appearance of understanding and courtesy. He was grieved, he said, at the sufferings undergone by such good subjects and he promised redress. He also told them how concerned he was that they organised large, unauthorised meetings, saying that he feared 'others of different affections might mingle with them and pervert them to actions they did not at first intend'. What was really needed, he suggested, was a large army that could secure peace for all. Surely there were those among the Clubmen who would join such a force? If only they would give him their names, he would see to it that they were 'supplied with arms and ammunition'. Behind the scenes meanwhile – and showing that hard, manipulative nature which was later to mark him as a mature politician – Charles ordered Goring to suppress the Clubmen's meetings. Goring tried to do so, but the Clubmen, sensing where their advantage lay, switched their support to the Parliamentarian side and its ruthlessly impressive New Model Army.

It was the New Model Army which, on 14 June 1645, inflicted ruinous defeat on the Royalist cause at Naseby. In public, the King tried to put a brave face on matters and claimed that he was 'no wise disheartened by our late misfortune', but in the letters he wrote to his son it is clear that his true thoughts were running in a different direction. The safety of the heir and his own defeat preoccupied him. 'Charles,' the King declared, 'it is very fit for me now to prepare for the worst . . . Wherefore know that my pleasure is, whensoever you find yourself in apparent danger of falling into the rebels' hands, that you convey yourself into France, and there to be under your mother's care; who is to have the absolute full power of your education in all things, except religion.'[20] This was an order the Prince was to obey 'without grumbling', but the Council were horrified. Flight from British soil would be a glaring admission of defeat, and France especially posed the dangers of Roman Catholicism. The King, with characteristic indecisiveness, later changed his mind and urged Denmark as an altogether better place for his son, while Hyde urged Scotland and Ireland as the safest havens. At least they were part of the King's domains. Hyde was determined nonetheless that flight would be the last resort, and, as Fairfax and the New Model Army pressed ever closer to the Prince, retreat into the far reaches of the West Country seemed the most advisable course.

The exhausted state of the Royalist troops meant that they could only fight an increasingly hopeless defensive operation. Although Goring attacked with considerable cunning, he was no match for the New Model Army, and in a conflict outside Langport he was overwhelmed by the Parliamentary forces. As he retreated west, his army began to disintegrate, and Fairfax set about building a chain of fortresses from coast to coast which would effectively bottle up the Prince and the remaining Royalist forces in Devon and Cornwall. From there they were obliged to watch the withering of their hopes. The disillusioned Goring retired abroad, and the Royalists' was now an army which, in Hyde's words, 'only their friends feared, and their enemies laughed at'.[21] Hopton made what stand he could at Torrington, but a night attack by Fairfax put his men to flight, and when the Council, sheltering in Pendennis Castle, learned of a madcap scheme to kidnap the Prince himself, they resolved on the only course of action they thought they could take: flight to the remotest peripheries of the kingdom. A frigate was 'ready upon an hour's warning' to convey the Prince to safety and, at ten o'clock on the evening of Monday, 2 March, the Prince of Wales, accompanied by Hyde, Culpepper and Berkshire, set sail for the Scilly Isles.

They arrived at St Mary's, the principal island of the Scilly group, after a rough passage of thirty-six hours, during which the crew of their boat broke open trunks and plundered the passengers. Conditions once the royal party had landed were scarcely more comfortable. Food was in short supply, lodgings were damp, and there was little fuel with which they could dry themselves out and hope to keep warm. Culpepper was despatched to France 'to acquaint the Queen with His Highness's being at Scilly', but then, on 12 April, the Parliamentary fleet suddenly arrived off the Scillies.[22] There was another hurried session of the Council, and this showed the Prince to be an altogether more subtle and even devious youth than Hyde had suspected. At the end of the meeting he drew from his pocket the letter sent him months earlier by his father in which the King had ordered his son to keep out of Parliament's grasp at all costs. Charles now used his father's words to urge that they all make at once for Jersey. Chance, as it was so often to do, supported his resolve. A storm blew up and raged for three days, scattering the enemy gathered off St Mary's. When it was over, the Prince and his Council hurried aboard the *Black Proud Eagle*, and, with an excited Charles himself at the helm, made for the relative safety of Jersey.

There was no roaring of cannon to greet the ship as it dropped anchor beneath Elizabeth Castle. The Royalist cause was in retreat, and the people of Jersey recognised the fact with a suitable chastened sympathy. Prince Charles disembarked with the members of his Council, a number of attendant lords and six clergymen. Later that evening, another ship brought over his chief household servants, while a third vessel conveyed such necessary members of his entourage as laundresses, tailors and shoemakers. In all, there were some three hundred people to make up his court. When they had finally disembarked, Lord Wentworth was despatched to Paris to tell Henrietta Maria of her son's safe arrival. Hopton then busied himself making the necessary arrangements for the Prince's accommodation in Elizabeth Castle. Charles was still on sovereign territory and had, it appeared, no interest in leaving it. Indeed, as Hyde wrote, 'the Prince himself seemed to have the greatest averseness and resolution against going into France, except in the case of danger of surprisal by the rebels, that could be imagined'.[23]

Living arrangements had to be sorted out in detail. The sudden arrival of so many strangers placed the island's resources under considerable strain. Although the royal party had brought supplies of beef, cheese, flour and dried peas with them, thought had to be given to how they might be fed in the long term, and it was eventually ordered that the local butchers and farmers should bring their produce to the marketplace at nine o'clock every Wednesday morning and reserve it for the Prince's servants until midday, after which the islanders could buy what they themselves needed. Similar demands were made of Jersey's fishermen, while, for the rest of the week, the country people were required to supply Elizabeth Castle daily with two sheep, a lamb, a calf, two pigs, two chicken, two goslings, two pots of butter and two dozen eggs.

So heavy an imposition required tactful handling, and the affable nature of the Prince was a considerable advantage, winning him the immediate regard of the greater part of the islanders. Even those of a Parliamentary persuasion were quickly won round by an adroit act of royal generosity. The women in particular were concerned that Royalist agents would confiscate their jewellery and other precious possessions and had sent them for safekeeping to relatives living in the island's more distant villages. Prince Charles promptly issued an order that what had already been seized should be returned, and then declared that any of the local people who had complaints against members of his party should refer these to the island's Governor, Sir George Carteret, in the expectation of 'justice exemplaire'.[24]

The days of public receptions that followed again proved the Prince to be 'grandement benin'. To satisfy the loyalty and curiosity of the people, he dined in public, treating them to a glimpse of that high cere-moniousness which had characterised mealtimes at Whitehall. For all that Charles's fortunes were in the steepest decline, here was the same profusion of gold and silver plate, the same decorous kneeling of page-boys, and a precision and deftness to the whole occasion that won instant admiration. As one observer wrote in his native French: 'as to the main-tenance of the Prince's table, it was such that everyone knew his place and matters were handled with such good order that all was done with pleasure and was a delight to behold, since everyone was prompt to his office'. The rituals of royal living were being preserved, much to the islanders' satisfaction, and their loyalty was confirmed when Charles made Sir George Carteret a baronet. A few days later there was a royal progress round the island. A state lunch was held at the old castle of Mount Orgeuil, and there was a grand military field-day at which all the male islanders between fifteen and seventy were commanded to appear and shout 'Dieu sauve le Roi et le Prince.'[25] Charles eagerly reviewed them, raising his beaver hat and bowing in a friendly, courteous manner as they passed. When the various exercises had been performed – the dragoons putting on an especially spectacular display as they charged across the sands in pursuit of an imaginary enemy – the Prince summoned the officers before him and declared that, through his treasurer, he would distribute a thousand livres to the soldiers in appreciation of their efforts and discipline.

Charles returned from the military parade to discover that Lord Culpepper had arrived in Jersey with news from Henrietta Maria. The Queen was now insisting that her son be brought to her in France with all speed. She was prepared to use every means at her disposal to ensure this, and she had already succeeded in persuading Culpepper himself that the Prince's proper place was at her side. Culpepper began to work on the boy, doing so with such conviction that the suggestible Charles 'became as averse to remaining in Jersey as he had previously been disinclined to leaving it'.[26] Letters from the Queen then arrived in which she made her intentions plain. It was the King's express desire that Charles go to France and, that being his wish, 'I have no doubt but that you will obey it suddenly' – that is, immediately. There were, in Henrietta Maria's view, compelling reasons of state behind the order. 'Your coming hither is the security of the King your father,' she declared. 'Therefore make all haste you can to show yourself a dutiful son.'[27] The vexed Hyde could not have disagreed more strongly but he was in the difficult position of having to persuade the Prince's parents to act against their natural inclinations. Determined that Charles should not leave the country until it was absolutely necessary, he sent Culpepper back to France not only to inform the Queen of his view that Jersey was a safe place for her son to be but to argue that to remove him from there would be sheer folly.

Then, to his utter exasperation, Hyde discovered that he had not only a worried mother and her foolish friends to deal with. Lord Digby now arrived from Ireland, his head running over with absurd and dangerous plans. In Ireland, he said, Prince Charles 'would find the whole kingdom devoted to his service'.[28] Carried away with his zeal, Digby turned to the Prince 'and thereupon positively advised him, without further deliberation,' to hurry himself aboard one of Digby's waiting ships 'which were excellent sailers, and fit for his secure transportation'. Charles turned his fifteen-year-old's eyes towards the over-excited peer. He had learned a great deal about such men in the last few months and was becoming skilled in handling them. He quietly replied that it would be strange indeed to take so decisive a step before he had consulted with his father.

Such reasonableness only made Digby the more enthusiastic for his madcap scheme. Having failed to persuade the Prince of its merits, he set about tackling Hyde. To Hyde's utter amazement, Digby proposed kidnapping the boy. It was well known that Charles adored ships. Had he not been at the helm of the *Black Proud Eagle* during part of the way to Jersey? What could be easier than to invite him aboard one of Digby's vessels and, while he was sitting down to a meal, 'cause the sails to be hoisted up, and make no stay till he came to Ireland'? Hyde at once quashed this idea, but the indignant peer was not to be gainsaid. If Hyde would not help him save the Royalist cause then he would go to France and use his influence with Henrietta Maria.

29 May saw the Prince's sixteenth birthday, and there were extensive celebrations. In the early morning a royal salute was fired from the ramparts of Elizabeth Castle. Batteries all along the coast responded, and the numerous frigates out at sea fired answering salvoes. The great cannons at Mount Orgeuil were discharged, while, in villages across the island, artillery and musket men fired their weapons in celebration. The militia then assembled on the beach in front of Elizabeth Castle before marching off to parade on the highest part of the island. Feasting and merrymaking filled the rest of the day, but it was the coming of night that saw the most spectacular scenes. Bonfires were lit on the peaks around St Aubin's Bay. Every vessel in the harbour hung lights from its masts and yardarms, while a vast crowd assembled on the beach as guns fired yet again and loyal toasts were drunk.

Charles himself had spent the afternoon reviewing the island's fortifications and revealing the practical intelligence that was to become so marked a characteristic. As he made his inspection, it came to his notice that there was a point on the south-east coast of Jersey where the enemy could land. He at once ordered that a fortress capable of mounting four cannons should be built there at his own expense. But military matters were not his only interest. Charles's love of the sea was also deepening, and it was at this time that he was presented with his first boat. Taking the helm of the *Black Proud Eagle* had thrilled the boy, and on his arrival in Jersey he had commanded that a yacht should be built for him in the yards at St Marlo. By 8 June the vessel was ready. Long in the keel, it was beautifully painted, decorated with the Prince's achievement of arms, and also comfortably cushioned. In addition, the boat had two masts and twelve oars so that it could either be sailed for sport or rowed for more formal and stately occasions. The vessel was at once in constant use. The Prince would no longer ride the causeway leading from Elizabeth Castle to the town. He insisted on sailing. He always steered for himself and he let no one else touch the tiller. Now, as the high summer wore on, he passed hours tacking across the secure and beautiful St Aubin's Bay.

He could not be left to such pleasures. Lord Digby had arrived in Paris, where the Queen listened to him and then despatched the ever useful Harry Jermyn to Fontainebleau, where he was to inform the French court of events. Cardinal Mazarin, who fully realised the political advantages of having Prince Charles in France, attended with particular care and suggested that Digby himself be summoned to explain his plans. Smiling his soft, perpetual smile, Mazarin inclined his ear as Digby spilled out his ideas. When he had finished he gently pointed out their shortcomings. It was surely unnecessary, Mazarin said, for Prince Charles to go to Ireland in person. Besides, it was natural that his mother should want him at her side, and natural, too, that the boy should want to be there. It would be altogether more satisfactory if Digby himself went to Ireland to raise troops for the Royalist cause. Money would be provided for him if only he would urge the Prince to come and live with the Queen.

Digby was easily convinced. It was now clear to him that the Prince should go to France rather than to Ireland. The French had shown themselves to be the most willing and generous allies, and clearly they had the Prince's best interests at heart. Henrietta Maria agreed, and letters from her husband deepened her resolve. 'I do not think Prince Charles safe in Jersey,' the King had written. There was no telling what might happen, and so 'in God's name let him stay with thee, till it is seen what ply my business will take'.[29] The King's will was plain, and Henrietta Maria would have her son in France. She would brook no delay, and Harry Jermyn was despatched to Jersey with strict orders to return with the boy. He duly set off, accompanied by Digby, Capel, Culpepper and an entourage of some sixty to eighty gentlemen.

The party had no sooner landed in Jersey than Digby went straight to speak with Hyde and tried to convince him of the necessity of the

43

Prince's going to France, while Jermyn worked on the teenage boy himself. He showed him copies of the letters exchanged between his parents and extolled to him the delights of Paris. Charles listened intently and, when a meeting of his Council was eventually called in his bedroom, he insisted that Jermyn and Digby, along with Lord Wentworth, stay by his side while sections of the royal correspondence were read out to the assembled company. All eyes were now focused on the Prince. The moment of decision had come. A worried Hyde pointed out that five of Charles's six official counsellors had advised him not to leave the country, but the boy had listened to softer persuasions. He was making his first important political decision and was determined to go to Paris, saying in a few words that 'he conceived it a command from the King and Queen, and resolved to obey it as soon as might be'.[30] Tuesday was chosen for the day of departure.

Tuesday morning saw Charles up early and ready to depart. He had forbidden his attendants to leave Elizabeth Castle even for a minute 'lest they might be absent in that article of time when the wind should serve', but he was to learn that the royal will was not automatically complied with. There was as yet no sign of the ship in which he was due to sail since 'the seamen would not stir, declaring themselves that they would not carry the Prince into France'.[31] Charles at once required Sir George Carteret to go and sort matters out, but by the time the vessel appeared the wind had changed and the sailing had to be postponed. Charles then gave orders that all those who were to travel with him should be ready by four o'clock the following morning, and that nobody was to go to bed.

Again, as dawn rose, the weather turned against him. 'The wind was so high, that no man durst put to sea.' By the time evening came the storm had blown itself out and Charles was bursting with impatience. He would set sail come what may. He would head for St Malo or any other port on the French coast. Once more he had to abandon his plans, 'there being a very slender wind, and that against him, and the Channel reported to be full of Parliament ships'.[32] Thursday morning was decided on for his departure.

On Thursday morning the Prince once again hurried aboard his frigate, but the wind turned against him for yet a third time and he was

driven back to the shore, where he was obliged to loiter all the afternoon. By five o'clock he could tolerate the delay no longer. Suddenly
he gave orders that all who were to sail with him should board the frigate
at once. He himself was resolved to row across to France if needs be –
anything rather than remain in Jersey! He wanted to be in Paris, wanted
to be away from Hyde and his censorious superiority. As Charles
resolved to make his break for freedom, the Lords Digby and Jermyn
frogmarched him down to his yacht. Then the wind changed for a last
time. Thoughts of the yacht were abandoned and Charles boarded the
waiting frigate. By eleven o'clock that night he had reached the French
coast and there he lay impatiently at anchor until the sun rose.

3

The Prince in France and Holland

O
n landing in France it was discovered that Mazarin's plans for Charles did not extend to organising a suitable royal welcome for him. No grand seigneur had been despatched from the French court. There was no band of elegant chevaliers reining in their horses as the Prince stepped on to French soil. Indeed, the Cardinal's eyes were not on him at all but were levelled at the victorious Parliamentarians across the Channel. To them it must be made to seem that Prince Charles had not come to France at Mazarin's insistence but had abandoned his country of his own will. He was not a guest but a refugee.

Attended by four chaplains and a party of his nobles, Charles rode first to Coutainville, and from there to Paris. Finally he arrived at St Germain, where he greeted the mother he had not seen for more than two years. Charles found her sadly changed. The birth of her youngest daughter had gravely impaired Henrietta Maria's health, and now, by 1646, she was a little, emaciated woman ever more frantically given to solving problems beyond her capacity and influence. She was constantly worried about money, about the progress of the Royalist cause in England, about the fate of her husband and about the future of her eldest son. Her commitment to her cause was beyond question. So too was her courage. 'There is nothing that lies so near my heart as your safety,' she had written to her husband, and Henrietta Maria was prepared to suffer anything to help him.[1] To this end she had willingly sent the King all she could spare from the pension of 1200 francs a day provided by her family. Carriages, guards, maids-of-honour, all were sacrificed to the greater cause, and, as Charles entered his mother's apartments, it was obvious to him that 'nothing could have been further from her dignity than were her train and her surroundings'.[2]

Such poverty was embittering and its effects were dangerous. Far from being the world of hope and easy luxury Charles had been expecting, France was to offer the teenage boy a lesson in hardship and frustration. In a matter of days he learned that the ever useful Lord Jermyn kept such a tight hold on the royal purse-strings (except when his own needs were concerned) that many of the loyal but impoverished Cavaliers in exile felt aggrieved. The effect on morale was disastrous. Endymion Porter, who had once helped the King assemble his art collection, complained that he could not attend the court since he had nothing to wear 'but that poor riding suit I came out of England in'. Henrietta Maria's tactlessness only made matters worse, and Porter was particularly upset that 'the Queen thinks I lost my estate for want of wit rather than from loyalty to my master'.[3]

Such bitterness among the exiled Royalists was to prove a liability, and when these people applied to the Prince for funds they discovered that he was unable to help them. The Queen was determined to keep Charles in her power by keeping him poor. She was also determined that he should have no say in policy making. She would herself be the saviour of the Royalist cause. Hyde was appalled. 'The Prince of Wales remained all that time in Paris under the government of his mother,' he wrote indignantly. For years Hyde had secretly despised the Queen for what he considered the baleful mastery she had achieved over her husband, and now he feared for her effect on her son. It infuriated him that his erstwhile pupil was not allowed to take part 'in any business or be sensible of the unhappy condition the royal family was in'. Hyde's love of propriety was also offended by the fact that the Prince was never 'master of ten pistoles to dispose of as he desired'. The result was obvious. Charles, Hyde wrote, was not 'so much respected as he would have been if he had lived more like himself and appeared more concerned in his own business'.⁴ The Prince of Wales had been reduced to a cipher.

Henrietta Maria was determined nonetheless that her teenage son should make an impression on the French. She and her bickering little court had put a great part of their trust in the French royal family, but the fact that it took five weeks of delicate negotiation before the Bourbons agreed to meet the penniless Prince might have given the Queen pause for thought. The manner of his reception should also have indicated that they were altogether less enthusiastic about supporting her cause than she was in urging it. Mazarin, the Queen Regent and the eight-year-old Louis XIV (already being trained to the most exacting standards of royal absolutism) were determined that Prince Charles should not be accorded the full honours of a state visit. How much better, then, to make the meeting between them all an informal, family occasion! Apparently spontaneous gatherings were planned with the utmost care. It was agreed that the parties should meet 'as if by chance' in the forest of Fontainebleau. The French, arriving first, sat in their coaches until, by happy coincidence, Charles and Henrietta Maria were seen nearing. The royal persons then descended from their respective vehicles, and Charles had his first view of his hosts.

Henrietta Maria, taking her son by the arm, presented him to the King. Louis XIV was then an attractive little boy of eight with wide hazel eyes, pink cheeks and a mass of curly chestnut hair. He already seemed rather serious, rarely laughing or playing. He was also insistent on the honours due to him. 'He knows that he is King and wants to be treated as such,' one observer wrote, adding that 'if he lives and receives a good education, he gives promise of being a great King'. Charles was then presented to the Queen Regent, Anne of Austria, a handsome, auburn-haired woman with beautiful eyes, and a throat and hands that were the admiration of Europe. Charles kissed one of these extended hands, and the Queen Regent, in her turn, kissed his cheek. Charles was then presented to the other great members of the French court: to the Duc d'Anjou, to Gaston d'Orléans, the younger brother of the previous King, and lastly to his daughter, La Grande Mademoiselle.

Here was the woman Charles's mother had promised should be his bride. Mademoiselle, it transpired, was a tall, imperious, but empty-headed blonde of nineteen with an aquiline nose and a conspicuous lack of feminine charm. For all her haughty concern with rank and protocol she was also betrayed into vulgarity from time to time. As her friend Madame de Motteville wrote (and Mademoiselle's feminine friendships were passionate), she had 'wit, riches, virtue and royal birth, but her vivacity rendered her actions lacking in that gravity which becomes persons of her rank, and she was too easily carried away by her feelings. This temperament', the lady added, 'sometimes spoilt the beauty of her complexion by causing her to flush, but as she was fair, had fine eyes, a lovely mouth, and a good figure, she had on the whole an air of great beauty.'[5] Naturally, Mademoiselle was dressed in the height of fashion. Her vast dress trailed behind her, a hand-mirror dangled on a ribbon from her waist, her décolletage was cut seductively low, while, on her large cheek, she had placed a *mouche* or 'beauty spot' which Charles would soon learn was called by admirers the 'kiss' or even the 'assassin'.

Wondering if the throne of England might one day be appropriate to her massive fortunes and considerable bulk, La Grande Mademoiselle looked on intrigued but unimpressed at the scene being played out before her. Prince Charles was, she recalled, 'only sixteen or seventeen, but very tall for his age. His head was noble, his hair black, his complexion brown, his person passably agreeable.'[6] The more obser-vant Madame de Motteville added that 'his mouth was large and ugly'.[7] Mademoiselle was determined this time not to allow herself to be carried away by her tepid feelings, for if the Prince was far from being as repulsive as the King of Spain (to whom she had once been agreeably promised) he suffered from one very serious defect: 'he neither spoke nor understood French, a most inconvenient thing'. Mademoiselle did not realise that Charles was playing a shrewd game before the crowned heads of Europe. Whatever his personal feelings for the lady, reports from England and his own growing political sense made it perfectly obvious that he could not mortgage his destiny to a Catholic heiress who might, in the last resort, fail to provide him with the men and money he needed to regain his father's throne. Feigning ignorance of French, but refusing wholly to disobey his mother's wishes, the lanky and dissembling Prince played the role of the dumbstruck, hopeless lover.

La Grande Mademoiselle was not so foolish as to be wholly taken in either by this charade or by Henrietta Maria's plans for her son. 'It was clear to me', Mademoiselle wrote, 'that the Queen of England wished me to believe that he was in love with me.'[8] It was evident that he was not, but, if Charles was unwilling to court his fortune, Henrietta Maria would do so for him. Characteristically, she overplayed her hand, and the imperious blonde was pleased to recall that she saw through Henrietta Maria's designs 'from the moment that she told me that he talked of me incessantly'. Mademoiselle was led to believe that she was just the Prince's physical type and that if it had not been for Henrietta Maria's maternal concern with decorum 'he would be in your apartments at all hours'. There was also, the Queen implied, a political aspect to the Prince's *tristesse*. He was in despair at the death of the wife of the Holy Roman Emperor since he feared terribly that that potentate might win Mademoiselle's hand. 'I listened to all she said,' the great lady wrote in her memoirs, 'but I did not put all the faith in it that perhaps she desired. I do not know whether the Prince might have fared better had he spoken for himself.'[9] But Charles, shrewdly, did not speak at all.

He was nonetheless obliged to continue with the enforced dumb-show. Balls, ballets and fêtes beguiled the aristocracy's evenings, and Charles duly attended. On one occasion the aristrocratic Choisys were to give a party to which Henrietta Maria and her son had been invited, along with La Grande Mademoiselle. The English Queen, thrilled by the prospect, announced that she herself would dress Mademoiselle's often unkempt blonde hair. The Prince meanwhile, to show the depths of his emotion, would hold a candelabra aloft like any pageboy as Henrietta Maria decked La Grande Mademoiselle with a generous selection of the crown jewels of France, along with some remaining trinkets of her own. The Prince, wearing his Garter, a diamond-hilted sword and a shoulder-knot or *petite oie* made up from Mademoiselle's heraldic colours of black, white and rose, played his part with the complaisance that was becoming second nature to him. His *belle amie* meanwhile looked adoringly at herself in the mirror. 'Nothing could have been seen better or more magnificently arrayed than I was that day,' she recalled, 'and I did not fail to find many people who assured me that my fine figure, my good looks, my pale complexion, and the splendour of my fair hair became me better than all the riches that shone upon my person.'[10]

Thus bedecked, Mademoiselle arrived at the Choisys' to find a melancholy Charles lingering in the portico and waiting to hand her from her coach. When she paused to rearrange her hair in front of a mirror, the Prince yet again held up lights for her and then followed her to the ballroom, where he did not leave her side. It was all rather agreeable, but the sudden appearance of Prince Rupert of the Rhine ensured that the course of true love did not run quite as smoothly as it might have done. Rupert proposed that he act as Charles's translator, declaring, to the utter mystification of Mademoiselle, that Charles understood all she said despite the fact that he could not speak French to her. When the ball came to an end and the intrigued lady returned in her coach to the Tuileries, she once again found her besotted lover waiting bareheaded by the lodge gates. 'His gallantry', she recalled, 'was carried to such lengths that it caused great comment.'[11]

This caused her to think about her future, and at the close of an operatic extravaganza Mademoiselle seated herself on a throne placed on the stage. There, in unescorted Amazonian splendour, she considered her options. Leaning back on the throne she decided she 'was destined for just such a place not merely for the length of a ball, but for always.'[12] In a moment of delicious triumph, she looked down on Louis and Prince Charles, who were sitting on the steps below her. There was a penniless prince, there was an infant king, while across the borders from France was Ferdinand III, whose wife had just died. The Emperor was an extremely pious man and Mademoiselle had prepared carefully for courtship, burying herself in the works of St Theresa and even pondering taking her vows as a Carmelite. She also let her hair get dirty, declined to powder it, and thought it best to resist the temptation of a *mouche*. 'I had it in mind to marry the Emperor,' La Grande Mademoiselle recalled, 'and was so taken up with the idea that a Prince of Wales became, merely, an object of pity.'[13]

The mother of the object of pity was deeply suspicious, and came over to accuse the triumphant lady of harbouring ambitions for Ferdinand rather than for her son. It seemed to Henrietta Maria that her problems were without end. Not only was Charles conspicuously failing in his amatory duties, but news came from England that the Puritans had broken into her chapel at Whitehall, flung the Rubens into the Thames and destroyed the wafers and the pyx in which they were kept. Her priests had brought her some comfort when they told her that the pyx had been saved by loudly bursting open and soaring to the heavens. The House of Commons, nonetheless, had resolved that it would 'make Prince Charles repent' for having left the country to join his mother amid a throng of papists.[14] A rich wife was ever more essential to him, and Henrietta Maria was determined to force the issue by challenging La Grande Mademoiselle over her intentions regarding the Emperor.

Mademoiselle pleaded innocence, but her mind was indeed made up and the Emperor was to be her prize. The following day her father approached her on the subject, warned her that the Emperor would not make her happy and suggested that she might be more content in England if matters there were ever to improve. Realising that this was a moment of supreme importance, Mademoiselle rose to the occasion. 'I prefer the Emperor,' she told her father. 'I beg you to agree to the marriage. I don't care for youth or gallantry. It is the position I am thinking of, not the person.'[15] For once she was not to have her way. The Emperor married one of his Austrian cousins, thereby ensuring that the comedy of Mademoiselle and Prince Charles was not yet quite played out.

Other distractions arrived in Paris to beguile the boy. While the fractious courtiers around his mother squabbled (at one point Charles was obliged to patch up the threat of a duel between those two natural irreconcilables Prince Rupert and Lord Digby), the Villiers boys passed through the city on their way home from the Grand Tour. The eighteen-year-old Duke of Buckingham had become as polished as he was cynical, and Charles turned eagerly to the companionship offered by the old friend of his nursery days. All three boys had already led lives of extraordinary activity. The teenage Villiers brothers had run away from Cambridge, joined up with Prince Rupert, taken an active part in the siege of Lichfield in Staffordshire, and then enjoyed the magnificent hospitality offered by the great families of Italy in a chain of palaces from Venice to Florence and Rome. Senior members of their entourage feared for the effect they might have on the Prince, and it is clear that the Duke especially, turning his all but neurotically nimble mind to the derision of anything serious – religion, politics, the pomposity revealed in the King's letters to his son – diverted Charles enormously.

Together they explored Paris and learned the ways of young male aristocrats, picking up the argot of the nobility – *amirable* for *admirable* and *chouse* for *chose* – while also observing the quickly changing fashions in cloaks, doublets and hats, and the innumerable colours of stockings with such names as 'dying monkey', 'rejoicing widow' and the delicious 'mortal sin'. Hire shops were available for those who could not afford to keep up with the changes, but, for the aristocrat at least, this whole elaborate display was directed at advertising to the world that he was an *honnête homme*. The French way of doing things was making a profound impression on the teenage Prince, and the idea of the *honnête homme* was to have an influence that never left him. The notion had little to do with honesty and much more to do with a raffish worldly wisdom. The desire to please others ranked high in this code. So, too, did a quick wit, elegance and bearing. Here was a way of behaving with what Madame de Motteville shrewdly called 'that apparent civility practised in society in the midst of hatred and envy.'[16] It was a survivor's code, and Charles was beginning to employ it with adroitness.

Something nonetheless had to be added to make it complete. 'One cannot be an *honnête homme*', wrote an expert, 'unless one is permanently in love,' and by now Charles had acquired his own secret if unconsummated amour.[17] While he was playing laborious court to La Grande Mademoiselle his eye had lighted – as had the look of many others – on the lovely Duchesse de Chatillon, *la divine Bablon*. The Duchesse however had given her heart wholly to the husband with whom she had eloped and Charles soon began to look elsewhere. This was partly in exasperation at the farce he was still obliged to endure in his pursuit of La Grande Mademoiselle. At a ball given in the Palais Royal after Easter, the great lady requested him to dance with Mademoiselle de Guise, he flatly refused and instead led her rival Mademoiselle de Guerchi on to the floor. When he declined to dance with Mademoiselle herself she was deeply offended and complained roundly to Prince Rupert. He, in his turn, tried to make excuses for Charles, pointing to his youth and ignorance, but Mademoiselle was not, for the moment, to be consoled.

There was also a more serious side to Charles's friendship with the Villiers boys, for it was with them that he continued his haphazard education. Reading with Doctors Earle and Duppa, with whom they passed an hour each morning, may on some occasions have seemed a chore, but the young noblemen had with them the great philosopher Thomas Hobbes to tutor them in mathematics. It is clear that Charles himself acquired sufficient enthusiasm for a recondite subject to be able later on to talk intelligently to experts and enjoy chemistry and the 'mechanics of physic'. Nonetheless, his was not an intelligence to be fed by deep reading. As the shrewd and observant Marquis of Halifax was to write years later in his *Character of King Charles II*: 'his wit consisted chiefly in the quickness of apprehension'. Charles had what the Marquis called 'a mechanical head', and it was this that accounted for such interests as 'his inclination to shipping and fortification'. Here, rather than in the classics, was the world that appealed to many of the brightest young minds of the time, and Charles was to acquire enough knowledge of technical subjects such as navigation to display an expertise which the stuffier considered unbecoming in a man of royal blood. It was during these weeks, free from the erstwhile formality of his father's court and the ponderous influence of Hyde, that the youthful Charles made the all-important discovery of how his contemporaries saw the world and joined with them readily. To the end of his life, Charles found Buckingham irresistible and many, many times turned a blind eye to his outrageous behaviour.

It was also obvious to all three youths that France was in a state of mounting political turmoil. The country's long-drawn-out and expensive war against Spain was going badly, and the voices raised against Mazarin were increasingly acrimonious. The aristocracy were resentful of the military reverses, while members of the French Parlement chafed at the limits set to their power. The rich and scholarly lawyers who made up this body longed for that voice in matters of policy which Richelieu had years before denied them. Now the chance to express their resentment had arrived. In May 1648, the *paulette* – the annual fee these men paid the crown for their seats in the Parlement – was due for reassessment. As members gathered in Paris, they drew up far-reaching plans for a say in matters of taxation and the limiting of royal power. The threat to the French monarchy was obvious, and a turbulent populace could easily be encouraged to reinforce it. As Charles and the Villiers boys wandered the streets of Paris they could hear mutterings of complaint as people went about their business or stopped for a moment to watch the street urchins, each armed with a vicious sling, hurling stones into the moat beneath the city wall. In a matter of months, this sling – *la fronde*, as it was called – gave its name to the civil war that would engulf the country for fourteen chaotic years.

Despite such diversions, this was a time of inactivity for Charles. He talked vaguely of seeking employment in Denmark and more enthusiastically of joining the French army in Flanders. This last idea was rapidly quashed as being far too dangerous – almost as bad, indeed, as another notion that was circulating. The gossip among the exiles now had it that Charles was secretly married. Such rumours had already reached the ears of Hyde and the Council before the Prince left Jersey, and they had spoken 'freely to him our opinions of the fatal consequences of it'. Jermyn assured the worried Chancellor 'that there were no such thoughts', adding that 'if it ever should be attempted, he would publicly oppose it'. Hyde was less than convinced. From his Jersey retreat, his view of the Queen and those surrounding her had become increasingly jaundiced. 'They have no opinions but for a day,' he wrote, 'and call it ingenuity not to be peremptory in anything.'[18]

They plotted all the same and, while the Prince was obliged to kick his heels, his mother especially showed that she was determined to take up the reins of power. Henrietta Maria was resolved to maintain the Royalist cause at any price, and eventually she persuaded Mazarin to send an envoy to the Scots Presbyterians who were now holding her husband captive in Newcastle. She then proposed to the King that he follow his original plan and submit to the establishment of an official Presbyterian church in England. In that way he would win himself a Scots army and irreparably divide the squabbling religious sects opposed to him. King Charles refused out of hand. He would not, when it came to the point, betray either his royal authority or the Church of England. For him, this was more than a matter of politics. It was a question of salvation.

To the little court at St Germain such intransigence was infuriating. Henrietta Maria in particular failed to sympathise with it. Was she not the daughter of Henri IV, who had notoriously declared that Paris was worth a mass, changed his beliefs, and thereby won himself a kingdom? She could see no difficulty in appearing to compromise with an uncouth collection of heretics when one could break one's word to them after one had got what one wanted. King Charles nonetheless remained adamant, and the exasperated Scots, having sermonised their captive, argued with him and even gone down on their knees begging him to convert, at last gave up what they saw was a lost cause. They handed the King over to the Parliamentarians and retreated back across their border.

The Parliamentarians themselves however were in a state of dangerous disarray. Not only were they troubled by deep religious divides, the civil war had been ruinously expensive and Parliament itself could no longer afford to pay the army it had raised. Disaffected men moved among the troopers and began to draw up radical plans in preparation for the reign of King Jesus. England must become a republic, a democracy even. It was for 'visible saints' among the godly to inherit the earth and 'share in the lands and estates of gentlemen and rich men'.[19] The Royalist gentry saw themselves faced with the unacceptable options of rule by religious fanatics, by a Parliamentary oligarchy or by the forces of military despotism. They sought allies for their beleaguered cause, and gradually an understanding was built up between the Royalists, moderate English Presbyterians and those among the Scots who sympathised with both.

The Scots sympathisers were headed by the Duke of Hamilton, who was the majority leader in the Scots Parliament. At Hamilton's request, commissioners were sent secretly to Carisbroke Castle on the Isle of Wight, where King Charles was now a prisoner of the Parliamentarians. Both parties eventually agreed to an 'Engagement' by which, in return for permitting the establishment of a Presbyterian church in England for three years, the Engagers would provide the Royalists with an army. When news of this reached France, Henrietta Maria was overjoyed, and a debate at once took place among the members of the Prince's Council. Hyde's known opposition to an alliance with the Scots was overruled, and the Queen eventually gave her consent to the Prince's departure for Scotland, provided only that he could take with him his Anglican priests and such close friends as he wished. Suddenly it seemed that there might be a chance of action for Charles and, at the close of the meeting, 'the Prince's resolution was taken without more ceremony to come into Scotland'.[20] Riders were then despatched from St Germain with messages in which Charles declared himself 'inexpressibly desirous' to be among the Scots in order that he might lead their army and fight for his father's throne.

While the excited youth dreamed of military victories and the salvation of the Royalist cause, other events fuelled the fires of optimism. On 20 April, the Duke of York, who had long been held by Parliament in St James's Palace, was slipped out of England disguised as a girl and taken by a certain Colonel Bampfield to where the Duke's sister and brother-in-law, the Prince and Princess of Orange, were living in The Hague. Soon after the Duke landed, pockets of discontent across England and Wales began to stir, while at the end of the month came further extraordinary good news: part of the Parliamentary fleet stationed off Kent had mutinied, declared for the King and weighed anchor for Holland. It was now imperative that Charles be despatched there to secure the loyalty of these men, and Mazarin, his mind preoccupied with the coming war of the Fronde, gave the Prince permission to leave France. Charles was now the eighteen-year-old saviour of the Royalist cause with a fleet at his disposal and a Scots army to support him.

He sailed for Holland and, on 12 July, dined with his sister Mary and her husband at The Hague. The marriage between the doll-like couple portrayed by Van Dyck was not a happy one. Mary had inherited much of her father's remoteness and cold concern with rank. She did little to ingratiate herself with the Dutch people, with her formidable mother-in-law or with her husband. There were as yet no living children of this marriage, and William was consistently unfaithful. Indeed, much to the concern of those around him, he had shown more interest in being a playboy than in being a prince, and was a twenty-one-year-old who was reckoned to show 'neither determination or prudence'.[21] He was clearly disturbed by these traits in himself and, with the death of his father, was attempting to reform. This resolve coincided with the arrival of his brother-in-law, and much to the concern of his advisers, who warned him against 'getting more deeply involved in the English labyrinth', he raised troops for Charles, chartered and equipped some ships for him, and spent 30,000 francs on purchasing weapons for the Engagers' army.[22] Most valuably of all, he was a young man near in age to Charles and could offer him the personal support he needed.

This last was more to be relied on than the tangle of ambition evident among the mutinous English fleet. Charles had already been forewarned of the problems he would face. Now he had to deal with them at first hand. In particular, he had to cope with the machinations of the Colonel Bampfield who had smuggled his brother across to The Hague. The Colonel considered he had been insufficiently rewarded for this feat. He began to turn the young James against his mother and father, and, 'having a wonderful address to the disposing of men to mutiny', insisted that the English crews give their immediate loyalty to the Duke, who was wholly under his sway.[23] By the time Charles arrived, James had appointed the severely Presbyterian Lord Willoughby of Parham as his Vice Admiral, but this man had never been to sea in his life and the mutinous English sailors began to doubt the wisdom of what they had done.

In order to test their loyalty, Charles despatched his brother to the port at Helvoetsluys to see how he would be received. For the moment at least there appeared to be nothing to worry about, for the mutineers promised to help restore the King to his rights. Having established that he still possessed a navy, Charles had then to show that he was the man to command it. Considerable resolution was called for and, revealing powers of leadership he had never been called on to display before, he immediately cashiered Bampfield and reluctantly confirmed Willoughby's appointment as Vice Admiral. The petulant James was thereby made to understand that it was Charles and not he who was in overall command, and, when the fifteen-year-old boy was very sensibly sent back to The Hague, he sulked, said he was not trusted and built up an animus against his brother that he would nurture for many years.

It was while he was sorting out these problems that Charles had his first known sexual relationship. The girl's name was Lucy Walter, and she was a young Englishwoman in exile. Many people would later discover that they had a vested interest in presenting her to history both as a whore and as Charles's wife. On the strength of their own word, they would make it common knowledge that Lucy had been passed around several eminent aristocrats before she ended up in Charles's bed. For instance, it was said that Algernon Sidney had picked her up in London when she was about fourteen 'and was to have had her for fifty broad pieces', but his regiment was commanded away and he 'missed his bargain.'[24] Despite the fact that Sidney was not even in London at the time, it was said that he (always a man to do another a favour) passed Lucy on to his brother Robert, who was now Chamberlain to Charles's sister in The Hague. What is more certain is that Lucy, born of an impoverished gentry family, was a girl from a broken home blown hither and thither by the winds of war. She probably came with her uncle via Paris to The Hague where, perhaps to preserve some semblance of respectability, she lived under the name of Mrs Barlow. She was of an age with the Prince and, in that high summer of expectation, with Charles the commander of a dubious fleet and shouldering all the glamour and responsibility of a young man apparently about to play a role on the European stage, the two became lovers. Soon afterwards, Lucy found herself pregnant.

The unwitting father now had a fleet to take to sea and a throne to save. Contrary winds bore his ships towards the Yarmouth Roads 'to the great terror and amazement of town and country'. Everything was readied to woo these people to his side. A public statement was drafted assuring all that the Prince's intentions were to restore his father's rights through the help of the Scots Engagers, to maintain the privileges of Parliament, abolish the great burden of taxes under which the people suffered, and disband the loathed Parliamentarian army for which these taxes had been raised. Finally, a general Act of Indemnity was promised ensuring that bygones would be bygones and that the country could return to its old, comfortable ways. The townspeople of Great Yarmouth were sympathetic, but garrisoned Parliamentary soldiers made them wary, and the most they felt they could do was offer provisions to Charles's fleet.

Deprived of a port, the disappointed Prince ordered his men to sail for the Kentish coast where, close to the Royalist garrisons at Deal and Sandown Castle, they could blockade the Thames estuary and deny Parliamentarian London its transports and supplies. It was known that the Parliamentarian squadron anchored in the Thames under the Earl of Warwick was too small to challenge them unaided and now, as they approached the mouth of the river, William Batten, the leader of the original mutiny, sailed out in a valuable warship to join the Prince. Charles welcomed him with a knighthood and appointed him Rear Admiral. It was a measure of the Prince's shrewdness however that he accepted Culpepper's advice and did not fall into the obvious trap of seizing and then confiscating all the rich merchantmen plying their cargoes back and forth along the estuary. To do so would have been to alienate the City grandees whose support for the King was vital. Nonetheless, to turn down easy prizes was certain to disgruntle his men, and Charles compromised by holding one of the vessels captive and promising to release it at a hefty charge.

On 10 August, while his senior officers squabbled over what the fleet was to do, another problem presented itself in the uncouth and dirty form of the Earl of Lauderdale, a representative of the Engagers. The Earl had come to explain, in an accent almost impenetrably thick, that the qualifications Henrietta Maria had placed on her son's involvement with the Scots were not wholly to the Engagers' liking. With Hamilton's army now marching towards England it was, Lauderdale suggested, essential that Charles make for the Firth of Forth at once to show his commitment to his Scots allies. The Prince listened to this advice 'with much gallantry' and a clear desire for action, but Lauderdale suggested that there were some difficulties to be got over first.

It was not acceptable to the Engagers that they should have to co-operate with ultra-Royalists. And then there was the question of Charles's Anglican chaplains. The Prince would see that these men were unacceptable too. Surely it would be altogether more expedient if he submitted to the forms of the Presbyterian church. Charles demurred, but the thirty-year-old Lauderdale with his wild, unwashed red hair hanging down either side of his face, was more than a match for a youth of eighteen. It was imperative that Lauderdale bring a suitably sanitised Prince north of the border and he pressed his case. He insisted that any delay would be fatal, and it was with a degree of relief that he watched the young Charles eventually sign an agreement to worship in the Presbyterian rite while he was with Hamilton's army. Charles felt he had been forced to prevaricate for the survival of his hopes and, in a matter of moments, he made that compromise his father had long refused. He had thereby shown himself the politician he would become.

If Charles had made this concession in order to sail to Scotland, his crew for the moment refused to follow him. The mutineers were turning mutinous again, and there were loud whisperings about throwing Lauderdale overboard. In his now ill-provisioned ships, and with the prospect of his men turning against him, it was time for Charles to show leadership once more. He went up on deck and issued a challenge to the sailors: would they not follow him wherever he went? There was more discussion and some murmurings of agreement as a ketch hoved into view bringing news that Warwick and the Parliamentary fleet were sailing towards them. Charles's men were spoiling for a fight and would not be gainsaid, but no one – including the Prince himself – knew that they were being lured into a pincer-movement. While Warwick bore down on them from the Thames, the six remaining Parliamentarian vessels had set sail from Plymouth.

Charles himself was dancing with excitement and Batten begged him to retire to safety. He would have none of it. He was determined, he said, to 'preserve his honour, which was dearer to him than his life, and at the main-mast on the deck he would take his fortune'.[25] Then, for two days, the Prince's ships and Warwick's ships – the first squadrons of the Royal Navy ever prepared to fight each other – havered, bluffed and waited for battle. But supplies on the Prince's fleet were running low and a return to Holland became essential. Then the lights of the Portsmouth vessels were dimly descried on the nighttime horizon. Batten, wise in the ways of naval warfare, knew the perils of an encounter in the dark and, overruling the fiery Rupert, persuaded the Royalist fleet to sail at once for Helvoetsluys. There, on 4 September, Prince Charles dropped anchor, safe but despairing at the news that greeted him.

The Engagers' army had been routed by Cromwell at Preston. The slaughter was terrible, and the survivors were 'sold for 2s a piece to be carried to new Plantations'.[26] Such a sentence of slavery was designed to put an end to any further Royalist hopes of help from Scotland, while the pitiful fate of the risings in England not only demoralised the King's supporters there but brought Prince Charles himself a measure of personal tragedy. The Villiers boys had left France and joined with Lord Holland in his attempt to seize London. Their little army had been forced prematurely into the field, the city had ignored their appeals and their efforts were brought to a bloody end at a skirmish near Kingston-upon-Thames. There, young Francis Villiers, 'a youth of rare beauty and comeliness of person', was killed by a cowardly blow delivered from behind a hedge.[27] The Prince's plans for his father were in ruins, and although a desperate Lauderdale begged him to come north, Charles refused and turned dejectedly to live in Holland on such charity as his brother-in-law might provide. His first attempt to secure the English throne had ended in dismal failure.

The defeat of their hopes divided Charles's supporters against each other and their rivalries turned venomous. The Prince was surrounded by men who often hated each other more than the enemy and were constantly on the lookout for their own advantage, 'hot brains who have so much in their fancies as how to advance their private fortunes and to compass their ambitions and covetous designs'.[28] It was left to the eighteen-year-old Charles to be the centre of authority and discipline, and at one point he had to interpose personally to prevent a duel between Culpepper and Prince Rupert. 'Great distractions' then flared round the council table as embittered, exiled men blamed each other for their failure. The Prince's navy, meanwhile, 'full of anger, hatred, and disdain', mutinied for pay.[29] To make matters worse, Charles himself fell ill with a mild attack of smallpox, and the strongest about him were left to restore order as best they could.

One of these men was Hyde. Relations between the Prince and his great servant had deteriorated badly during Charles's last days in Jersey, but it had been agreed that Hyde would go to his master if and when Charles ever left France. Now the gout-ridden Hyde had been summoned from the consolations of scholarship – he was at work on his magisterial history of the civil war – and with difficulty had come to Charles's side. Like many other Royalists, his poverty was now 'notorious' and he had written to Jermyn telling him that 'you will easily believe that a man who has not had a boot on these two years – nor in truth hath a boot to put on – cannot in a moment put himself into an equipage for such a journey'.[30] Money was sent to him and eventually, having been robbed on the way by Dutch privateers, Hyde arrived in The Hague. There he set about raising what cash he could to victual the fleet and pay the mutinous crews, while Prince Rupert brought those who remained to order. The English sailors were unwelcome guests all the same. Their blatant privateering had offended the Dutch, and at a hint from the Prince of Orange they made for Ireland, where the forces of Ormonde appeared to provide the Royalists with their last hope of armed support.

The Prince of Orange persuaded Charles himself to stay on at The Hague, and there, having recovered from his illness, he spent Christmas with his family. The turn of the year brought terrible news from England. The New Model Army, after an agonised three days of meeting and prayer at Windsor Castle, had determined to call his father, 'that man of blood', to an account for the 'mischief he had done to his utmost against the Lord's causes and the people'.[31] To ease this process, Cromwell ordered the purging of recalcitrant Members from Parliament and, with the remaining 'Rump' their creature, the Army pressed ahead with the trial of the King. Prince Charles threw himself into hectic but hopeless activity in a last, desperate attempt to save his father's life.

He sought an immediate audience with the Dutch States General and had an aide deliver them a paper which begged their help. The senators were sympathetic and promised to send an ambassador to England to plead his case, but the Parliamentarians refused him an audience until the trial was over. Other appeals were equally unsuccessful. Charles wrote to Mazarin and the Queen Regent saying that the victorious Parliamentarians were 'setting an example dangerous to all other princes'.[32] The French envoy in London was ordered to stir himself but achieved as little as the Dutch. In his desperation, Charles then wrote to Fairfax, expressing his disgust at the idea of regicide, 'the mere thought of which seems so horrible and incredible that is has moved us to address these presents to you, who have now have power, for the last time . . . to testify your fidelity, by reinstating your lawful King, and to restore peace to the kingdom'.[33] The letter had no more effect than the other appeals and merely drew attention to the fact that the Prince's existence provided Parliament with an embarrassing problem. While his letter remained unanswered, a measure was hurried through the House of Commons declaring that 'no person whatsoever should presume to declare Charles Stewart . . . commonly called the Prince of Wales, or any other person, to be King, or chief magistrate, of England and Ireland'.[34]

Nothing more could be done except wait, and it was nearly a week after the execution of the King that Charles had confirmation of his father's death. It came almost by chance and in the form of one of the badly printed gazettes that were the exiled Royalists' chief source of information. Perhaps mercifully, the newspaper reached his chaplain, Dr Goffe, first. The sombre cleric approached the youth who was now his King with the only words that protocol allowed: 'Your Majesty—' His meaning was obvious at once, and Charles burst into tears as the ghastliness of his plight swept over him. He was a son without a father, a king without a throne, a man without a role.

4

The Treaty of Breda

At his brother-in-law's expense, Charles clothed himself in royal mourning purple and then, from his black-draped rooms, despatched letters and ambassadors to the crowned heads of Europe. Surely these people would sympathise with his plight and offer him help to regain his throne. Requests were sent to Portugal and Spain, to the states of Italy and Germany, to the Scandinavian countries, and to Russia. Their success was extremely limited. In Moscow, Lord Culpepper did obeisance before the Czar, listened for two hours while the list of the boyars' titles was read out as protocol demanded and, in return, was loaned 20,000 roubles in corn and furs. The Queen of Sweden sent a quantity of arms, and the Portuguese offered the use of their harbours to Royalist warships. France, involved in the wars of the Fronde, was unable to help, while the replies of lesser rulers expressed polite regret for the execution of Charles I and an embarrassed inability to help his son. The Count of Neuburg, for example, wrote declaring that 'God the Almighty, the righteous judge, will not allow such a criminal deed to go unpunished.'[1] Nonetheless, like other German rulers recently emerged from the devastation caused by the Thirty Years War, the Count was unable to offer anything more than sympathy and righteous indignation.

In England itself, the Rump Parliament set about abolishing the monarchy as 'unnecessary, burdensome and dangerous'.[2] The House of Lords was also swept away, and in 1649 the country was officially declared a commonwealth. Defeated Royalists went home to their estates where a few dreamed up hopeless schemes for returning Charles to his throne, while others consoled themselves by developing a cult around the memory of his father, guided in part by a book called *Eikon Basilike* – 'The Image of the King'. There they could read Charles I's supposed speech from the scaffold, his prayers, and extracts from his private correspondence. Thirty-five editions of *Eikon Basilike* were published within a year of the King's execution, and from such enthusiasms as these might his son draw faint intimations of hope and see glimmerings of a desire for his return.

It was clear nonetheless that effective help would have to be sought elsewhere, and Ireland at first seemed to offer the greatest possibilities. The execution of the King had been greeted there with such horror that the Irish rebels patched up a peace with Ormonde and thereby enabled him to put a fresh Royalist force into the field. At The Hague, all eyes were now turned to Ormonde, but there were some who doubted the wisdom of allying their cause to a largely Roman Catholic army, while all knew that a chronic shortage of money meant that Charles's room for manoeuvre was severely limited. As one Royalist wrote: 'though the King be resolved for Ireland, and desires to be there as soon as may be . . . the want of money is incredible and the debts so great, that I know not how we shall get over these difficulties'.[3] Hyde nonetheless supported the plan for an Irish alliance, as did another great Royalist now arrived at The Hague: James Graham, Marquis of Montrose.

Here was a man whose valour, bearing and accomplishments commanded the admiration of Europe, and whose devotion to the Stuart cause was absolute. 'I never had a passion upon earth so strong as that to do the King, your father, service,' Montrose once told Charles and, in the early days of the civil war, he had raised a Scots army for Charles I and led his savage and ill-disciplined men against the Covenanters and their leader, the fearsome Archibald Campbell, Marquis of Argyll.[4] Fifteen hundred of Argyll's men were slaughtered by Montrose at the Battle of Inverlochy, and so intense was the loathing of these two chiefs that, when Charles I took refuge with the Covenanters and bade Montrose sheath his sword, the Marquis sought refuge on the mainland of Europe. Now he was anxious to raise another Scots army for his new king. Montrose was also determined to advise Charles about the intricacies of Scots politics and save him from the dangers these posed. In particular, he was resolved to warn him against what he saw as the duplicity of the defeated Engagers who had once come to his father's support and to guard him against the wiles of the commissioners sent by Argyll and the Covenanters. This rigidly clerical party now held the reins of power in Scotland, where they inflicted on the people all the miseries of the religious fundamentalism with which they were also threatening the King. Charles's abject submission to the Covenant was their price for offering him the Scottish crown.

Both Hyde and Montrose were absolute in their determination that Charles should never seek to win allies at the cost of surrendering his religious principles and the beliefs for which the Royalists had fought and died. They knew, too, that the Covenanters were only offering the King a semblance of power since, once he was in their hands, he would be no more than a puppet. Charles himself was aware of the justice of this view and, for the moment, placed his hopes in Ireland and Ormonde. Nonetheless, the habit of listening to all who offered him advice and then vacillating between the opinions he received was growing in him and now, while he agreed with Hyde and Montrose, he also inclined his ear to the Machiavellian counsels of his brother-in-law. He was receiving his first and most influential lessons in the art of dissimulation.

Prince William of Orange, roused from his sensual apathy, had clear and bold views about his own future and that of his exiled brother-in-law too. He felt himself to be, like Charles, a prince unfairly at the mercy of his parliament and was resolved to free himself from the States General of Holland. He would then establish the House of Orange as an hereditary monarchy, form an alliance with France and, with a vast army, enlarge his patrimony and intimidate those of his countrymen who opposed him. The love of the rest was clearly desirable, and there seemed no better way of winning this than to show his Calvinist subjects that he had persuaded the King of England to unite with the Covenanting Scots. These men would help Charles get back his throne, and William would in turn gain a loyal and grateful ally. The Covenanters themselves were aware of William's interest and sent emissaries to him. As the young Prince concluded his audience with them he promised to advise Charles to accept the Covenant and, the following day, he assured the Covenanters that he had indeed done so. What William did not confess to was the fact that he had hinted to Charles that he would loan him his notional army to bring England to order and so allow him to renege on any promises falsely made with the Scots.

With these plans in mind, and tempted by the chance of his first real exercise of power, Charles resolved to listen to the commissioners newly arrived from Scotland. He put on every appearance of majesty. At six foot two inches, the King was an impressive figure, and the silver star of the Garter glittering on his breast greatly increased the sense of decorum. He was clean-shaven, and his dark hair was parted in the centre so that it fell easily about his cravat, the locks on the right hand side being slightly longer than those on the left, a fashion he had acquired in France. He greeted the Covenanters with what he hoped was a disarming easiness of manner, but Hyde, who hated all thoughts of an alliance with these men, noted that they entered his master's rooms at the Binnenhof Palace in a manner more becoming ambassadors of a free state than subjects. The great servant then fumed in silence as Robert Baillie, the Covenanters' principal spokesman, told the King that they came 'upon condition of His Majesty's good behaviour, and the observation of the Covenant'.[5]

Charles suavely parried these first hectoring advances and accepted a handsomely bound copy of the Covenant with such disarming grace that even the carping commissioners felt bound to confess that 'His Majesty is of a very sweet and courteous disposition'. Charles was 'one of the most gentle, innocent, well inclined Princes, so far as yet appears'. He was manly, intelligent and careful not to speak too much or too enthusiastically. All this was noted with favour, and it was considered 'a thousand pities' that he was not 'at one' with his Scots subjects in matters of religion, but this could surely be attributed to the 'very evil generation' of courtiers who surrounded him.[6] What was more natural than that a young man should be led astray by people like these?

Such advances were watched with particular distaste by Princess Sophia, the youngest daughter of the Queen of Bohemia, then resident at The Hague. She already knew that the commissioners disliked her, for they had complained that this charming and natural girl was constantly seen at Charles's side even in church. There was little doubt that he was attracted to her and, one evening, he invited her to walk with him in the Voorhout and said to her (knowing that she shared a wide-spread disapproval of his mistress) that she was 'handsomer than Mrs Barlow' and that he hoped to see her some day in England. The Princess Sophia was wise in her generation, and, realising that Charles was 'richly endowed by nature, but not sufficiently so in fortune to allow him to think of marriage', she declined a second invitation for an evening promenade, saying that she was suffering from a corn on her foot.[7]

These days of delicate negotiation at The Hague were soon violently shattered. There now arrived in the city an ambassador from the English Parliament who had been one of the lawyers who drew up the charges against Charles I. The Dutch, naturally enough, received the man with the honours they thought due to him, but hotheads among the Royalist exiles were so exasperated that they broke into the man's house while he was at supper, 'cleaved his head with a broadsword' and quietly departed. The King was 'exceedingly troubled and perplexed' by the brutal stupidity of this act, and the Dutch promptly asked him to leave.[8] Decisions about what to do had rapidly to be made, and it was necessary first to give an answer to the Covenanters. Montrose gave it out as his unhesitating opinion that concessions to any of these men's demands would bring Charles nothing but 'shame and ruin'. Swearing to the Covenant was anathema to all true Royalists, and what the commissioners offered was a mere shadow of power. 'When they demand Your Majesty's consent to all acts establishing their League in all your other kingdoms,' Montrose wrote, 'it is the same thing as if they should desire you to undo you by your own leave and favour.'[9] Charles was obliged to agree, but rather than dismissing the Covenanters out of hand he wrote hinting at some mild points over which they could agree before saying he could not interfere with matters in England and Ireland at their say-so.

The commissioners were furious. 'Our grief for this paper is very great,' wrote one. 'It was much worse than anything we expected; not only the hand of the worst English counsel, but that of James Graham also.'[10] The disgruntled men then returned to Scotland to report to Argyll while Montrose himself, appointed by Charles as his Admiral and Lieutenant-General in Scotland, began collecting arms and men from sympathisers across northern Europe. He was further encouraged by his grateful sovereign's promise that Charles would 'not determine anything' touching the affairs of Scotland 'without having your advice thereupon'.[11] As Montrose then set about his task, Hyde readied himself for Spain in the hope that he might be able to raise funds there. At a stroke, Charles was parted from his two most intelligent and principled advisers, and such isolation would begin to expose his true nature.

He did not, as might have been expected, make straight for Ireland. He sent much of his luggage there but listened once again to Prince William and his wife, and resolved to make a detour into France. Hyde was appalled. He pointed out that his master had no invitation to go there and that the journey would be a waste of time and precious money. What he really feared was that the suggestible King might fall once again under the influence of Henrietta Maria and her advisers, Jermyn especially. Hyde already believed that Jermyn had it in mind 'to procure a speedy meeting between the King and the Queen' at which he would 'engage and tie up the King as much as ever his father was to the counsel of the Queen'.[12] There was nothing Hyde could do to prevent this, and Prince William and his wife were, besides, so insistent that Charles should leave the country that they provided him with a handsome sum of money for the journey. By early June he was on his way. Travelling secretly behind him went Lucy Walter, who on 9 April had become the mother of their son James, the first and most ill-fated of Charles's many bastards.

Charles's party, along with the Prince and Princess of Orange, proceeded through Delft and Rotterdam to Breda where a fête was held in Charles's honour. Then, accompanied only by the Prince and forty of his troops, he proceeded to Antwerp. This was Spanish territory, and although Charles was greeted with every appearance of civility by the Archduke Leopold – and with similar courtesy by the Count of Pignoranda in Brussels – no material help was forthcoming from either. Spain was poor and was being harassed by France, to where the King himself was bound. He eventually arrived at Péronne, where he was met by the Duc de Vendôme, who offered him lodgings and then accompanied him to the French court at Compiègne. There, waiting for him with his mother, was his erstwhile *amie*, La Grande Mademoiselle.

The lady was now a little more favourably inclined towards him. Mazarin and the Queen Regent were convinced of the reality of Charles's Irish hopes, while Jermyn had told her that if she indeed became Charles's wife she could continue to live at the French court while he went off to mend his fortunes. Mademoiselle hinted that she was appalled at the very thought of such unchivalrous conduct. 'I should not be able to refrain from selling all my property and hazarding it to reconquer his realms,' she declared, like a heroine from one of her favourite romances. Nonetheless, as she later confessed, 'the thought frightened me a little because, having been all my life rich and happy, such reflections overwhelmed me'.[13] She needed an excuse to get out of a difficult situation, and religion seemed to provide one. How could she marry a Protestant, she asked Jermyn? 'Religion is a thing one cannot let pass,' she went on, 'and if he cares for me he ought to overcome this difficulty, and I would overcome many on my side.' She was intrigued all the same. 'I am dying to hear him say sweet things to me,' she said, 'for I do not know what it is like, no one ever having dared say them to me; not on account of my rank, for they have frequently been said to queens of our acquaintance, but on account of my character, which is very far removed from *coquetterie*.'[14]

Mademoiselle dressed herself carefully for the meeting with Charles, even having her hair elaborately curled, which was something she was usually averse to. As she then rode out to meet the King at Compiègne, the Queen Regent teased her on her appearance: 'Ah, it is easy to know people who expect their lovers! See how she is got up!'[15] But

Mademoiselle's so-called lover proved once again to be a bitter disappointment. Although he chatted readily – and in French – to the little King Louis, Charles refused to say anything serious about his affairs when pressed, claiming once again that he could not speak Mademoiselle's language. She was profoundly unimpressed. 'From that moment I resolved not to conclude the marriage,' she wrote, 'conceiving a very bad opinion of a King, who, at his age, did not interest himself in his own affairs.'[16]

More embarrassments were to follow when the company sat down to dinner. Among the innumerable dishes prepared was one of ortolans – a great delicacy – to which Charles appeared completely indifferent as he flung himself (in Mademoiselle's phrase) on large plates of beef and mutton. So healthy an appetite was disconcerting, and the great lady later recalled that she was ashamed. When the meal was over, her satiated suitor appeared as dumb as ever. For an agonising quarter of an hour she waited for him to talk. Fearing that he was mute through shyness, she summoned a courtier to join them, and he had no sooner sat down than the two men started conversing with great enthusiasm. Clearly, there were to be no *douceurs* and, when the time came for him to leave, Charles, pointing to his mother's secretary, merely said: 'Monsieur Jermyn, who speaks better French than I, will have told you of my intentions – and of my hopes. I am your most obedient servant.'[17] With that, Charles kissed Mademoiselle's hand and left for St Germain.

Here Lucy Walter was also accommodated, but it is clear that the relationship was beginning to fade. Lucy was now attended (and perhaps more) by Lord Wilmot, and it was in Lord Wilmot's coach that the diarist John Evelyn travelled with Lucy to St Germain in August 1649. The fastidious connoisseur was not favourably impressed, writing that he found Lucy to be a 'brown, beautiful, bold but insipid creature'.[18] Others of Charles's relationships were also under strain, and none more so than that with his mother. The bitter, impoverished Queen was becoming ever more volatile and strident in her demands, and Charles realised he had to free himself from her influence. At nineteen he regarded himself less as a dutiful son than as a king. He was coldly, formally polite to Henrietta Maria, but he made it clear that she was to have no major part in his plans. When she started scenes, he merely said to her that he would always perform his duty towards her with great affection and exactness, but that in his business he must 'obey his own reason and judgement'. On one occasion, he 'did as good as desire her not to trouble herself in his affairs'. With that, he walked out of the room and from then on seemed 'not to desire to be so much in her company as she expected'.[19]

If such moments suggest that Charles was determined to be his own man, his judgement was still prone to youthful immaturity. Nothing shows this more clearly than his continuing friendship with his old nurse, Mrs Wyndham, who was now angling for her husband to be appointed Secretary of State. Hyde and the elderly Lord Cottington, who were at St Germain *en route* for Spain, were appalled at the prospect of having so mediocre a man as Colonel Wyndham admitted to the King's Council. Having listened to the lamentations of the Queen at her son's 'unkindness', Hyde resolved to confront him, but to no avail. He was told that if Wyndham were ignorant of the duties of the Secretary of State then he could quickly learn them, that he was 'a very honest man', that Charles himself had never been able to do anything for him, and 'had not now anything to give him but this place'.[20] The interview was then brought to a close.

Hyde had clearly failed, but others knew that, where plain speaking had not succeeded, wit might work. One day, the venerable Lord Cottingham began telling Charles and the assembled courtiers a long story about a deserving falconer. Charles asked Lord Cottingham what favour he was begging for the man. Having praised the falconer's voice and his ability to read, Cottingham paused and then, with mock earnestness, declared, 'I beseech Your Majesty to make him your chaplain.' A puzzled Charles asked him what he really meant. Bravely preserving his deadpan expression, Cottingham replied that 'The falconer is in all respects as fit to be Your Majesty's chaplain as Colonel Wyndham is to be Secretary of State.'[21] There was an awkward moment of silence before the courtiers burst out laughing and Charles, his face darkening at a joke told against him, turned away in embarrassed anger. The story was repeated to Wyndham, however, and no more was heard of the Colonel's aspirations to the Secretaryship.

If Colonel Wyndham was easily dealt with, the fractures among the members of Charles's Council were altogether more problematic. While those men centred around the Queen favoured an alliance with the Scots Covenanters, the more traditional Royalists, led by Hyde, continued to abhor the idea of treating with the late King's enemies, preferring rather to seek help from the Spanish and the Pope in return for concessions for Roman Catholics. They even toyed with the idea of negotiating with extreme radical groups in England, promising them liberties of conscience that would in fact never be granted. The young 'Swordsmen' in the court fluctuated between whichever party seemed temporarily to have the more influence, while 'in the meantime nothing is settled or acted by sad and serious counsels, but by catches, and on occasion, to the heart breaking of all men that are faithful to the King'.[22] Then news began to filter into France that hopes of help from Ormonde and Ireland were being rapidly and terribly annihilated.

On 2 August 1649, Ormonde's forces were routed by the English at Rathmines, just south of Dublin. Such an Irish army could never be put together again, but now, with Irish resistance irreparably weakened, the English under Cromwell prepared to subdue the land with appalling ferocity. No quarter would be given to those who persisted in offering support to Charles Stuart. On 15 August, bringing with him an army of 8000 foot and 4000 horse, Cromwell arrived as Commander-in-Chief and Lord Lieutenant of Ireland. He made straight for Drogheda, which was the natural place for the shattered Irish troops to rally and regroup. A week later, Cromwell's terrible artillery arrived: eleven siege guns, two eight-inch cannon, two seven-inch cannon, two twenty-four pounders, three calverins and twelve lesser field pieces. The Governor of the town had boasted that he who could take Drogheda could take Hell, and Cromwell, white with battle fury, determined to prove him right. His monstrous artillery was fired at the hapless town, whose walls were soon breached, enabling Cromwell's veterans to enter and slaughter some 3000 soldiers and civilians. The details of the carnage were appalling. Men whose legs had been shot away fought on their stumps. Screaming soldiers were smoked out of the churches, while the Governor himself – once so brave in his defiance – was beaten to death with his own wooden leg by men convinced it contained a cache of gold.

Drogheda was only the first of Cromwell's Irish atrocities, and, while the ravishment of the island continued, Charles's presence there would have been folly. Nonetheless, he hated his 'shameful' but enforced idleness at St Germain. He was hurt by the coldness increasingly shown to him by the French nobility once his novelty value had worn off, and eventually he decided to move back to Jersey. There, it seemed, was a place altogether more conducive to reviewing his plans than fractious St Germain. Approaching winter made a Parliamentarian attack unlikely, while the loyal islanders had proclaimed Charles as their king seventeen days after his father's execution. Besides, the abolition of the English monarchy and the defeat of the Irish meant that Charles was no longer of any use to Mazarin and the Queen Regent. Now they were anxious to get rid of a guest whose own country had put a price on his head and who was being shadowed by an assassin. But there was another reason for leaving St Germain. In her grief and powerlessness, Henrietta Maria had found her church to be the one sure haven where she could nurse her bruised soul and dream of England becoming a part of Catholic Europe. Now she was setting out to convert her children. While she failed to lure Charles towards certain political disaster, the Duke of York might yet be worked on. Charles, realising the threat this posed, resolved to take his younger brother with him to Jersey. On 27 September, he and the Duke set sail from Coutainville. Charles himself took the helm of the flagship, and, although they were pursued by the Parliamentarian fleet, they managed to evade capture and arrived safely in Jersey the following afternoon.

Here the penniless Charles was obliged to maintain what state he could. He reviewed the island's militia, stood godfather to Lady Carteret's daughter and went hunting and visiting until rumours of threats to his life meant that he could not go out alone and unguarded. When Buckingham and his train arrived, Charles created the Duke a Knight of the Garter, while Hopton, Carteret, Jermyn, Culpepper and others were given grants in the still loyal colonies of North America. But lack of money remained a pressing problem. Parcels of royal land on the island were sold, household servants were dismissed and begging letters were written to Royalists on the mainland. Such poverty and inaction were not only humiliating. They contained political dangers too. As one of Charles's circle wrote to tell Ormonde: 'foreign princes begin to look upon him as a person so lazy and careless in his own business that they think it not safe, by contributing to his assistance, to irritate so potent enemies as they fear his rebellious subjects are'.[23] Ormonde himself remained the one seeming support, and hopes of Irish help were not entirely abandoned. Agents were sent to Wales and the West Country to organise bridgeheads for an invasion, and one of the Grooms of the Bedchamber was despatched to Ireland itself to assess the situation there. He returned in December with devastating news. It was Ormonde's opinion that only a military diversion in England could prevent the entire island from falling beneath Cromwell's sword. Help, if it were to come at all, would have to come from the Scots.

Montrose was labouring on Charles's behalf with his customary determination but only moderate success. The Duke of Friesland promised to quarter his men. The Holy Roman Emperor offered to raise Charles's cause at the next meeting of the Diet. The Duke of Courland presented six ships of wheat, and the King of Poland volunteered 4000 soldiers. This was no army of invasion, but exaggerated reports of Montrose's efforts reached the Covenanters, and Argyll was concerned. He knew that the people of Scotland wanted their King, and he saw that his own advantage lay in pleasing them. Argyll therefore persuaded the Scots Parliament to authorise George Winram, the Laird of Libberton, to be sent to Charles in Jersey. There Winram would try to 'extricate' the King from his 'wicked council' and play on his deepening poverty. Winram already knew that Charles had 'not bread both for himself and his servants, and betwixt him and his brother not one English shilling'. A young man 'living in penury, surrounded by his enemies, and not able to live anywhere else in the world unless he would come to Scotland' might easily fall prey to temptation and sign the Covenant for the sake of a throne.[24]

Opinion in Jersey was bitterly divided. The younger Royalists gathered about the Duke of York were appalled by the thought of a compromise with the Covenanters and, rather than allowing Winram to see the King, talked of 'throwing him over the wall'.[25] Jermyn was altogether less adamant. He saw, as he thought, the advantages of siding with Argyll and began to circulate 'with great diligence and care' any report which discredited Montrose. In such an atmosphere as this a firm decision had to be made. Charles would have to choose to put his hopes either in the Covenanters or in Montrose. For the moment he vacillated, trying to be all things to all men, and surveying his options with a wary and increasingly cynical eye. He was learning to prevaricate, but he was also learning that the decisions it fell to him alone to make had to be made in the secret recesses of his mind. He had watched his squabbling courtiers for too long not to know that the advice they offered was tainted with their own interests. He would listen to them and then, even as he practised the art of 'concealing himself and disguising his thoughts', ponder the issues. When he had then weighed up his own advantage, he would act – act not necessarily decisively or crudely, but rather with the subtlety and deviousness of a man keeping his options open.

He resolved to listen to both sides still. After a stormy debate in the Council, Winram was sent back to Scotland with a public letter in which the King accepted Argyll's protestations of loyalty and asked him to send commissioners to meet with him at Breda. He then privately wrote to Montrose assuring him of his continuing support and telling him not to be concerned 'by any reports you may hear as if I were otherwise inclined' to the Covenanters 'than I was before'. He also entreated Montrose 'to go on with your wonted courage' in raising an army. Such a force, after all, had already obliged Argyll to make overtures to Charles. Now its swelling ranks might force him to soften his terms. Montrose had a useful role to play, and 'I will never fail in the effects of that friendship I have promised,' Charles wrote, sealing inside his letter the medal and ribbon of the Order of the Garter.[26] With that, he ordered some new clothes in which to appear before the Covenanters in Breda.

Charles journeyed to that city via Beauvais, where he arrived on 4
March 1650 to find his mother waiting for him. For all their earlier
disagreements there was now an appearance of 'great kindness on both
sides', but its duration was brief. Henrietta Maria had come to Beauvais
to urge her son to make reasonable terms with the Covenanters but, as
an increasingly acrimonious fortnight passed, she saw deeply into her
son's nature and grew alarmed that he might make any concessions and
even sign the Covenant itself. She implored him to do no such thing.
Nor should he abandon Ireland and Ormonde, or forget the efforts of
Montrose. Above all, he should not consent to anything his father would
have viewed with horror. Charles listened politely but maintained a
studied 'indifference' to his mother's pleas. Pragmatism rather than
principle was the key to survival. When he finally parted from her,
Henrietta Maria's face was 'very red with anger', and after Charles had
'put her into her coach he did not stay one moment with her' but turned
sharply away.[27] He was on his own in a hostile world.

By the end of March, Charles had arrived in Breda, where the
commissioners sent by the Scots were invited to an audience in his
bedchamber. There, dressed in the 'embroidered suit' he had ordered
while in Jersey, Charles prepared to treat with these men in his most
gracious manner. He soon found that the severity of the ministers sent
by the all-powerful Presbyterian Kirk to enforce the Covenanters'
demands froze any possibility of compromise. They still insisted that
Charles was to sign the Covenant, institute a rigid Presbyterianism
across all his realms, ratify the Acts of the Scots Parliament, abjure
Ormonde and the Catholics in Ireland, and then 'acknowledge the sin'
of his dealings with Montrose. Indignant Royalists claimed that such
impossible terms were only to be expected 'from brazen-faced rebels
and barbarous brutes'.[28] The King's chaplains then closed around him
and talked in urgent voices of honour and conscience. Jermyn and his
party, on the other hand, urged Charles to pursue his obvious advantage and league with the Covenanters, arguing that it was 'needful
sometimes to hold a candle to the devil'.[29] The Covenanters themselves
meanwhile begged their more extreme members not to press their case
too hard, while Charles himself did nothing. If he held out, Argyll might

offer easier terms. If he waited, Montrose might march to his aid. Nothing could be lost by delay, for Charles, it seemed, had nothing to lose. Only Hyde in distant Spain saw the danger in the situation and wrote that 'where all is lost, we may be cozened of our innocency'.[30]

It was at this dangerous moment that Prince William of Orange arrived in Breda. His position was delicate in the extreme. The Dutch were growing impatient with Charles's presence on their borders and wished him to leave as soon as possible. The Prince, too, was anxious that his brother-in-law should go since the expense of maintaining him in Breda was so great that he had been forced to pledge the city itself in order to support him. William was determined nonetheless that Charles's departure should be to his own political profit. He still wanted him as ally regardless of the cost, and, even while urging in public that the King should not submit himself to the Kirk or allow the affairs of England and Ireland to fall into the hands of the Scots, he was privately suggesting that Charles should make any concessions necessary to securing their support. If needs be he should even swear to the Covenant and observe the Presbyterian form of worship while he was in Scotland. After all, he could repudiate the Scots entirely once he had regained his throne. Charles listened once again to his brother-in-law's advice and then offered the Covenanters terms which he knew were unacceptable. When, as expected, these were rejected, he broke out 'into a great passion and bitter execration' of the commissioners, saying for the benefit of those listening that nothing would induce him to set foot in Scotland if he could not take his chaplains with him.[31] Perhaps such a gesture would make the Scots weaken, but the ministers scowled, saying that they could find only 'lightness and vanity' in him.[32]

In fact they were devastated that the King had not fallen into the temptation they had offered him. 'I can assure you', wrote one exultant Royalist, 'all the Presbyterian party looked last night like drowned rats.'[33] They had apparently lost their prize but, while they considered their plight, Charles reviewed his own. His prospects appeared bleak indeed. He knew that Ireland was falling daily before Cromwell's sword, while Presbyterians in England had sent word that they would rally to his side only if he submitted to the Covenanters. No money could be found to help Montrose raise troops and, indeed, there was little news of Montrose himself. For the moment Charles felt that he could not abandon his great servant for the dubious benefits offered by Argyll, and suddenly it seemed that he did not need to. A private emissary arrived from Argyll promising that, for all the ill-will the Marquis was known to bear him, Montrose would not be sacrificed. If he abandoned his plans to invade Scotland, he would be given 'honourable' employment. An unseen politician altogether more ruthless and adroit than Charles was deftly smoothing the young King's path into temptation.

Reassured by Argyll's promises, Charles sent word to the commissioners that negotiations might be reopened, and they assembled to hear his terms. He would grant all their demands in Scotland. He would assent, if they were ever passed, to Acts of Parliament establishing Presbyterian worship in England and Ireland. He would not however break his word to Ormonde and, in return for the immense concessions he was prepared to make, he insisted that the Covenanters reconcile themselves with the men who had once signed the Engagement with his father, promise him their unquestioned help in regaining his English throne, and assure him of his own safety, honourable treatment and freedom. Still the Scots demurred. They insisted that Charles must renounce Ormonde and repudiate Roman Catholicism entirely. Discussion once again seemed at an end and, in the ensuing silence, Charles listened to the advice pressed on him by others: by Prince William, by the Queen of Sweden, by the Duc de Lorraine, by his attendant lords, by friends such as Buckingham. All urged him to agree to the Scots' terms. All said he could repudiate them later. It seemed that royal survival could be guaranteed only by moral surrender, and Charles's decision was finally made. He would sign the Treaty of Breda and ally himself to the Scots.

There was one other matter still to be decided. Charles now wrote a public letter to Montrose ordering him 'to forbear all future acts of hostility . . . and also, immediately upon the receipt of these our letters, to lay down arms, to disband, and withdraw'.[34] This vital letter never reached him. By the time its bearer arrived in Scotland, Montrose's little army of 2000 men had been destroyed at Corbiesdale and

Montrose himself had been brought to Edinburgh, where it was decreed that he should be hung and quartered, after which his head was to be placed on the Tolbooth and his severed limbs despatched for public display to the major cities of the land. Argyll had got his revenge and now, as the commissioners invited an abject Charles to Scotland, so it seemed that Argyll might have the King in his power too. As he claimed to the Scots Parliament, he had Charles's own word that he was 'no ways sorry that James Graham was defeat, in respect, as he said, he had made that invasion without and contrary to his command'.[35]

The Scots Parliament was jubilant but still not content. The great enemy of the Covenant was dead and the King of England was all but in their hands. Now they would wring from him the last, humiliating drops of concession. As Charles and a large party of his followers, including his chaplain, went aboard ship at Terheiden, they were followed by new commissioners from Scotland bearing new demands. Bad weather set in and the ship was obliged to anchor off Heligoland, where these demands were presented. The Covenanters would make no concessions to the Engagers. Charles was openly to break with Ireland and forbid Roman Catholic practices there. He himself was to take the Covenant and force it on his subjects. Furthermore, he was not to rely on the Scots automatically giving him help to regain his throne. They would do so only when the Kirk and Parliament agreed that such a course was 'lawful and necessary'. The Scots were requiring abject surrender.

A desperate and furious Charles swore that he would agree to none of this and that, rather than going to Scotland, he would land in Protestant Denmark. The row was still raging when his ship dropped anchor in the Spey, but, with the Scottish coastline just visible through a thick mist and with all hope of compromise gone, there appeared to be no option but for the King to submit. Even now he wanted to make it clear that the laws of England took precedence over anything contained in the Covenant, but the commissioners rejected the plea out of hand. Why should they concede such a point when victory was so nearly theirs and the King seemed within an inch of surrender? Anger was useless, protest futile, and thus, in the dank Scots mist, Charles laid his honour in the dust and swore the great oath of the Covenant. 'O my lady,' Hyde wrote to a friend, 'we are making haste out of Christianity and forgetting that there is another court to appear in when we are out of this.'[36]

But Hyde was not present as the young man read the appalling document through. 'I Charles King of Great Britain, France and Ireland', it declared, 'do assure and declare by my solemn oath, in the presence of Almighty God, the searcher of all hearts, my allowance and approbation of the National Covenant and the Solemn League and Covenant above written.' The doctrines of a loathed Presbyterianism had apparently won, 'and I shall observe these in my own practice and family, and shall never make opposition to any of these, nor endeavour any alteration of them'.[37] To agree to such articles was an act of the merest political expediency, and each side knew the depths they had plumbed. Charles's reputation was in tatters, and events would show that it was torn to no purpose. The Covenanters meanwhile realised that they had tricked a young man into signing an agreement he could never honour in his heart. 'Our guiltiness', wrote one, 'was the greater.'[38]

5

A Fading Crown

The depth of Charles's error was obvious the moment he set foot in Scotland. Argyll's followers alone were permitted access to him, and when he was taken to Argyll's house in the Bog of Gicht it was immediately made clear that he must dismiss all the Engagers from his train. Here was a taste of the discomforts to come, but such narrow-mindedness on the part of the Covenanting leaders was not matched by the people whom they tyrannised. The ordinary Scots loved their King. The citizens of Aberdeen lit bonfires in the streets and presented Charles with 1500 Scots pounds, a sum altogether too generous in the view of their Elders, and other towns were told not to follow their example. Guilt and humiliation were to be the order of the day and, to remind him of his sinfulness, the house at which Charles was lodged in Aberdeen offered a commanding view of the severed hand of the ill-fated Montrose, which was now on public display.

The King's party continued its way through Dundee and St Andrews. At the last Charles was required to listen to a four-hour sermon – one of many such performances with which he was to be bludgeoned over the succeeding weeks – and, having attended with every appearance of patience, he agreed to visit the house of the preacher, the Reverend Robert Blair. With instinctive courtesy, the minister's wife ran to fetch the King a chair, but was at once stopped by her husband,

who told her that a healthy young man could perfectly well fetch a chair
for himself. Charles merely smiled at the rudeness, but over the weeks
that smile was to become ever more forced. In the most difficult circumstances he was learning once again what many of his contemporaries
considered to be the all-important art of dissimulation.

Charles's party moved on and 'on the ninth day he came to his own
house at Falkland'. There he stayed, 'having a little park with deer, and
fair hills about it for hunting'.[1] That Falkland was to be no idyll was at
once apparent. Having obliged him to dismiss the Engagers in his
company, the Scots Parliament now resolved to cut down on the
number of Charles's English followers. All but nine were 'voted away',
leaving him only with the Lords Buckingham and Wilmot, Dr Fraser,
three gentlemen, an usher and two servants. These men were allowed
to remain provided that their characters and behaviour met the standards set by the Covenanters. Charles was naturally dismayed to lose so
many friends and tried to remonstrate with Parliament, but his efforts
were to no avail. The prescribed persons were ordered to leave the
country within eight days and, to add insult to injury, the names of Lord
Wilmot and another were added to the list of undesirables.

Only Argyll himself – squinting, remote, his sensuous mouth twisted
into an expression of severe denial – appeared to ease the King's
comfortless state. There was nothing in this of generosity. Argyll was a
figure of commanding intelligence and cunning who, in Hyde's opinion:
'wanted nothing but honesty and courage to be a very extraordinary
man'.[2] He saw clearly that he now stood on slippery ground. The great
mass of the people were weary of the tyranny of the Kirk, and Argyll
was the champion of the Kirk and the chief supporter of the Covenant.
He realised it was essential to his continued security that he win
Charles's confidence and, to this end, he instructed his son to attend
carefully to the young King's needs. His table was to be lavish, he was
to have good horses to ride and, when he appeared in public, he was 'to
want nothing that was due to a great king'.[3] This, in Argyll's view,
included an appropriate wife, and he now made plans to marry Charles
to his own daughter, Lady Anne Campbell. But all of this was being
kind to be cruel, for if Argyll attended to the King's creature comforts,

he was determined to let him have no say in government, prohibiting him from attending meetings of the Council and making sure that he had little contact with ordinary people. As one observer wrote, Charles was 'outwardly served and waited on with all fitting ceremony due to a king, but in his liberty [was] not much above a prisoner, sentinels being set every night about his lodging, few daring to speak freely or privately to him, and spies being set upon his words and actions'.[4]

Thus circumscribed, the King fell victim to the mercies of the Kirk. He was 'not so much as allowed to walk abroad on Sundays', a rigid sabbatarianism being a principal article of the Presbyterian creed.[5] Even his looks and gestures were carefully observed for signs of levity, and instead of card games the King was obliged to sit through innumerable sermons, sometimes as many as six in succession. Argyll, with consummate deceitfulness, suggested that Charles endure all this with good grace. After all, he hinted, if the young man would only 'please these madmen for the present' he would be able to discard them as soon as he regained his throne in England.[6] So welcome was this hope, and so plausible was the way in which Argyll expressed it, that Charles was tempted to be won over by his gaoler. He 'did not only very well like his conversation, but often believed he had a mind to please and gratify him'.[7] Nonetheless, he was not to be duped. When Argyll raised the prospect of his marrying the Lady Anne, Charles deftly replied that 'in common decency' he must consult with his mother first.

While Charles remained a virtual prisoner in Scotland, the Parliamentarians in England were gravely worried by his presence across the border and, in June 1650, Cromwell and Fairfax were appointed to lead an army against the Scots and so remove for ever the Stuart threat. Fairfax considered this an unwarranted invasion of a sovereign country and refused to take up his post. Cromwell was made sole Commander-in-Chief and began to march north with an army of 5000 horse and 10,000 foot. As he reached the border, his artillery commander, George Monck, raised yet another regiment, which was to enter English history as the Coldstream Guards. Thus reinforced, the Parliamentarians marched unopposed into Scotland, keeping to the coast so that they might be constantly provisioned from their ships.

Charles was secretly delighted. He had long realised that his presence in Scotland would draw the Parliamentarians north and he had hopes that an uprising would spread across England in the absence of the army. He had already written to his brother-in-law asking him to land a force in Torbay, telling him that 'all the assistance of the Scots will be vain without such a concurrence as this'.[8] He was to be bitterly disappointed. Prince William was unable to comply with his request, and Royalist sympathisers in England were divided against each other, and even against the King. Charles's taking the Covenant had alienated many of his natural supporters, his treatment of Montrose had offended others, while to them all the Scots were dangerous foreigners with whom they could not bring themselves to form an alliance. As a consequence, England was quiet as Scotland prepared for war.

The Scots army, nominally under the command of the ageing Earl of Leven but actually led by his Lieutenant-General, David Leslie, consisted on paper of 26,000 men. Of this considerable force, many were untrained, while a large number were known Engagers whom the Covenanters were determined should be purged from the army as 'malignants'. Hampered in this way, Leslie's only hope lay in defence, and he dug his soldiers in between Leith and Edinburgh. Charles was as desperate to join them as his captors were to prevent him. They rightly feared that his charm would win the soldiers' hearts and ensure the diminishing of their own influence. They moved the King to Stirling, where to his delight he received an invitation from the army to review them. He rode at once to Leith, and 'his coming bred much joy to the soldiery' – so much indeed that they neglected their ordinary duties and Charles, 'sore against his awen mynd', was ordered to withdraw to Dunfermline.[9] Then, with their hero removed and the English close on their tails, the purging of the 'malignants' began. To the ministers of the Kirk it was self-evidently better to fight one's enemies – even the battle-hardened Cromwell – 'with a handful of elect and godly people, rather than with mighty arms loaden with sin'. As a result, the 'malignants' departed and were replaced by 'ministers' sons, clerks, and such other sanctified creatures'.[10]

Having emasculated their army, the Kirk determined to further humiliate their King. Charles was required to sign a paper expressing his shame and sorrow for all the sins of the house of Stuart: his father's, his mother's, his own. The last were a particular interest, and to ensure his future virtue Charles was made to promise that he would always follow the advice of the Kirk. He refused point-blank to sign the document, and a joint committee of the Kirk and Parliament was sent to make him change his mind. He declined to have anything to do with them. The offended ministers responded by saying that such 'stumbling' on the King's part freed the Scots from their responsibilities towards him and, as a result, they would enter a treaty with Cromwell. This meant that they would hand their prisoner over to his enemies. Charles felt there was nothing he could do but submit once again, and, with Argyll whispering soft words of comfort in his ear, he consented to sign the wretched document.

The declaration was then published along with a proclamation that ordered a day of national repentance for the sins of the King and the country. But such events had brought Charles close to the end of his tether. The 'villainy' of the Kirk party had exasperated him beyond endurance, and he wrote that 'nothing could have confirmed me more to the Church of England than their hypocrisy'.[11] Clearly, Charles was thinking of abandoning the whole Scottish enterprise, for in the same letter he required his agent in Holland to ask the Prince of Orange to send him a boat in which, if needs be, he could return to the altogether more hospitable shores of the continent. A chance meeting a few days later with Dr King, the Dean of Tuam, revealed his true feelings. 'Mr King,' Charles began, 'I have received a very good character of you, and I do therefore give you assurance that, however I am forced by the necessity of my affairs to appear otherwise, I am a true child of the Church of England, and I shall remain firm unto my first principles. Mr King, I am a true Cavalier!' Then, in the momentary pause that followed, Charles's conviction lapsed into bitterness. 'Mr King,' he said, 'the Scots have dealt very ill with me – very ill.'[12]

While Charles was plunged in such painful meditation, the Scots army was readying itself for conflict. Cromwell's force was depleted by disease, and during the following days it was further weakened through a brilliant series of marches and countermarches forced on it by Leslie. On 1 September, Cromwell fell back on Dunbar while Leslie's troops held the heights. Cromwell was now faced with an appalling choice: he could either order a humiliating retreat by sea or lead his men uphill through blinding wind and rain to fight an altogether larger army apparently secure in its tactical advantage. Leslie himself was prepared to sit tight, but this held no appeal to the ministers of the Kirk, who were clamouring for battle 'in as confident terms as if God himself had directed them to declare it'.[13] Leslie was commanded to move his men down the hill.

For Cromwell, there passed a night of decision making. As the hours went by and he resolved at all costs to prevent Charles from marching at the head of a Scots army to reclaim his English throne, so he 'rid . . . through the several regiments by torchlight, upon a little Scots nag, biting his lips till the blood ran down his chin without his perceiving it'.[14] By five in the morning Cromwell's decision had been made. To prevent Charles Stuart from being crowned King of England, he deployed his troops and ordered the attack. In a furious hour's struggle as the dawn rose over the hills, Leslie's horse broke and his rain-saturated infantry laid down their useless guns and fled. Three thousand of them were killed, 10,000 were captured, and the Scottish army that the King of England had so abased himself to win all but evaporated.

To the English, it was clear whose victory this was. Cromwell wrote in his despatch to Parliament that the Battle of Dunbar was 'one of the most signal mercies God hath done for England and His people'.[15] To the defeated Scots, the cause of their rout was equally obvious. As a member of the General Assembly or governing body of the Kirk wrote to Charles, the humiliation of their army was God's judgement 'against you and your family, for which His wrath seems not yet to be turned away'. The letter called for another day of public humiliation, but also probed into the morass of hypocrisy in which Charles and the Scots now found themselves. 'If self-interest and the gaining of a crown have been more in your eye than the advancing of religion and righteousness, it is an iniquity to be repented of and for which your Majesty ought to be humbled.'[16] This last was easily arranged, and Charles wrote a public letter confessing that the defeat of the Covenanting army was indeed a just punishment 'for our sins and those of our House'. Privately, he rejoiced.

The power of the Covenanters would now surely decline and Charles could expect a reaction in his favour. Provided he was circumspect he could free himself from both the Kirk and Argyll. He already knew that the Highlanders were all 'at the King's devotion', while the many Royalists and Engagers in the rest of Scotland would flock to his side.[17] His physician, Dr Fraser, encouraged him in this idea and gave Charles wildly exaggerated hopes. There was, Fraser said, a force of some sixty nobles and over 10,000 men ready to take up arms. Charles was desperate to join them. He arranged with Lord Newburgh, his Lieutenant-General, that on the very day the Kirk had resolved to purge his Horse Guards of 'malignants' the purgers themselves should be captured. The Horse Guards would then set off for Fife where Charles would join them in person. They would take Perth and use the city as their base. Charles would then publish a declaration making clear how ill-used he had been by Argyll and the Covenanters, and would wait for an army to form around him.

He was betrayed by those in whom he put his greatest trust. Charles confided his plan to Buckingham, and this friend of his childhood at once saw the ruin of his own hopes. The erratic Duke had convinced himself that Argyll was his most useful ally and believed that the Covenanters' fall would herald his own. He told Lord Wilmot what the King had in mind, and Wilmot, similarly worried, spilled out the whole matter to Argyll himself before joining Buckingham in the King's bedchamber. There the three men spent several hours in hot dispute, at the end of which a disheartened Charles wearily agreed to give up his plan and send out messengers forbidding the uprising. They arrived too late. As the vengeful Covenanters came to demand that Charles dismiss yet more 'malignants' from his train, the leaders of his army informed him that it was impossible for them to withdraw. Charles knew at once that he must try to escape. Accompanied by a few of his remaining followers he went out into the garden and, 'without any change of clothes or linens more than was on his body', rode so furiously towards

Fife that even the pursuing Buckingham failed to catch up with him.[18]

Charles crossed the Tay at three that afternoon and then, having reached the house of Lord Dudhope, persuaded its owner to join him before riding on to the house of Lord Buchan. With Buchan and Dudhope at his side, Charles arrived at the estate of the Earl of Airlie, where a guard of eighty Highlanders joined him as he set off for Clova. But the Laird was not there to greet him. Night was falling, and men and horses were both exhausted. Shelter was essential, but only the poorest cottage could be found and there, 'laying in a nastie roume, on ane old bolster, above a matte of segges and rushes', Charles was found the next day by the Covenanting soldiers looking 'over-wearied and verey fearfull'.[19] The episode known as the 'Start' was over. Colonel Montgomery, the leader of the Covenanting soldiers, persuaded Charles to go to Huntley Castle, where, the following day, Buckingham arrived with 'a mild and discreet letter' begging the King to return to Perth and promising that, henceforth, he could live in Scotland where he wished.

For all the humiliation it brought, the Start marked an important change in Charles's fortunes. He had proved to the Covenanters that they had gone too far and they, now deeply concerned at their own political future, realised that he was a force to be reckoned with. In return for an apology for 'the late unhappy business' to which he had been persuaded', Charles averred, 'by the wicked counsel of some men who deluded him', he was given a say in public affairs.[20] Indemnity was offered to those who had risen to fight for him, but this entirely sensible move provoked furious opposition from extremists among the Covenanters. They issued a 'Remonstrance' which declared Charles to be a man whose 'whole deportment and private conversation showed a secret enmity to the work of God'.[21] His 'unstraight dealings' were detailed, and the Start showed how devious he was. Any treaties signed with him were sinful documents and imposed no duty on the Scots to return him to his throne.

The more moderate Covenanters passed a 'Resolution' declaring that the 'Remonstrance' was 'contrary to the laws of the kingdom', but they pleaded for understanding in vain. The party was fracturing. The

Remonstrants hated the Resolutioners. The Kirk parted company with Parliament over the issue of 'malignants', and Parliament then claimed it could act independently of the Kirk. A few men went over to Cromwell, but many more joined in the national orgy of hypocrisy which broke out in Scotland as men of all persuasions tripped over each other in their rush to declare an undying devotion to the Covenant and thus to the remains of power. In meeting houses across the land men in sackcloth and ashes willingly knelt to make a public confession of their iniquity, and ministers eagerly accepted their protestations as 'unfeigned'. Only a few were honest enough to be appalled. 'If this was not to mock the All-knowing and All-seeing God to his face,' wrote one, 'then I declare myself not to know what the fearful sin of hypocrisy is.'[22]

It was in this atmosphere that Charles prepared himself for his Scottish coronation. Two days of national fast were ordered: one for the nation's sins, the other for the Stuarts' especial failings. Charles was required to do public penance for his family's errors, and did so without complaint. The weary months among the godly had inured him to deceit. He was no longer the youth who had once declared that he would rather flee to Denmark than agree to the Covenant. Power was all, and no action was too shameful or too ridiculous to achieve it. If the Covenanters required him to go down on his knees then he would go down on his knees, only pausing to murmur with weary irony: 'I think I must repent, too, that ever I was born.'[23]

In this atmosphere it was decided to hold the coronation ceremony that would make Charles the focus of nationalist sentiment. It was performed at Scone on New Year's Day 1651 and was planned with great care. A platform six feet high was built in the church to bear the throne. A canopy of crimson velvet made it yet more splendid, and Charles himself was permitted to wear a rich robe. As the royal procession entered the church, so Argyll bore the heavily pearl-encrusted crown which he would later place on his monarch's head. Other peers bore the gilt spurs and the sword of state, but the Presbyterian bias of the ceremony was evident. There would be no superstitious anointing with oil, and the necessary element of shame and humiliation was provided by one John Middleton, a soldier who, as the price of returning to the flock of the Covenanters, was required to do penance in sackcloth and ashes. There was also a lengthy and lugubrious sermon. This was delivered by the Moderator of the General Assembly, Robert Douglas, who was not a man to pass up an opportunity for dismal reflection. How could he resist on this occasion dilating on the instabilities of earthly kings and the wrongs that had made Scotland's a 'tottering' monarchy? All was sin, all was gloom, for, as Douglas triumphantly concluded, 'a King when he getteth his Crown on his head, should think at the best, it is but a fading crown'.[24]

But that supreme moment of coronation had not yet quite arrived. There were public abasements to endure first. The Covenant documents were read out and, when this was done, Charles, in full view of the Scots nobility, kneeled to sign them. To make his humiliation doubly sure, he was then required to repeat the oath he had been made to sign months before on the ship that had brought him to Scotland. Again, he unhesitatingly did so. With his ignominy thus broadcast, Charles was placed on the chair of state and presented to the people as the 'rightful and undoubted heir'. The congregation shouted 'God save the King!', and he sat down to take the coronation oath by which he promised to maintain the religion and laws of Scotland. Then, kneeling once again and lifting up his hands, Charles swore 'by the Eternal and Mighty God, who liveth and reigneth for ever', that he would 'observe and keep all that is contained in this oath'.[25] His hypocrisy was complete and now he was ready to receive the crown. Argyll placed it on his head as the ministers prayed that it might be purged of ancestral sin. Finally, after yet another sermon and more prayers, Charles returned to the royal palace at Scone. He had performed his part, one of the ministers wrote, 'very seriously and devoutly, so that none doubted of his ingenuity and sincerity'.[26]

The coronation feast with its partridges, calves' heads and twenty-two salmon may have compensated somewhat for the dismal atmosphere of hypocrisy, but, while the guests gorged themselves, Argyll meditated once again his plans for marrying his daughter to his royal master. But Argyll's influence was fading even as Charles's rose, and the Marquis's dynastic fantasies were, in truth, founded on sand.

There was no political advantage for Charles in marrying a Scottish bride. Once established in England the search for an alliance in Europe would be altogether more important to him. Charles was well aware of this. He insisted once again that his mother's consent was essential to his choice of a bride and he despatched a certain Silas Titus to France to win Henrietta Maria over to his view. The Queen responded with uncharacteristic tact. She had no objections in principle, she said to her son's marrying into the Argyll family. There was nothing 'new or extraordinary' about a king marrying one of his subjects, but the marriage that was proposed might rouse jealousy in Scotland, while the English, of course, could not be consulted on the matter at all. It was better in the circumstances, she wrote, 'that the thing remains for a while in the same estate it doth'.[27]

While this delicate negotiation was proceeding, Charles threw his energies into raising a new Scots army with which to expel Cromwell from the land and then regain his throne. The efforts he made amazed all who watched him. The indolent youth so often berated by Hyde was submerged in the man of action. Sir Richard Fanshaw wrote that Charles's 'judgement and activity both in civil and martial affairs' had developed to a degree 'you would not imagine in so few months' growth'. He was now 'the first and forwardest upon every occasion . . . adventuring his person – I pray God not too much – upon every show of danger, riding continually and being up early and late'.[28] Detail obsessed him and charm smoothed his way. The Highland chiefs were required to raise fresh levies. Garrisons were inspected, a multitude of towns was visited and a committee of war was set up. Orders then gave way to diplomacy as Charles negotiated for the inclusion of the Engagers in his affairs. Officially, there was to be no more divisive talk of 'malignants'. Cavalier, Covenanter and Engager were all equally the King's men, and by May 1651 a force of 20,000 had been raised. It was, wrote the Dean of Tuam, an 'abundant matter for joy'. The King's power was 'absolute', wrote the admiring Dean. 'All interests are received, all factions composed, the ambitious defeated, the army cheerful, accomplished, numerous'.[29]

The men rallied at Stirling and, under Leslie's direction, were readied for war. Leslie's tactic was a simple one. Cromwell was short of supplies and far from home. He could be starved into submission. Cromwell himself, realising full well the danger he was in, rose from his sickbed and drew on all the forces of courage and guile that long experience had seasoned in him. He crossed the Forth, advanced through Fife, took Perth after a mere day's siege, and thereby divided the new Scots army in two and cut off its supplies. Now all he had to do was wait while Charles decided which of the courses open to him to take. Each worked to Cromwell's advantage. If the young King retreated into the West Highlands he had virtually admitted defeat. If he risked a battle with Cromwell in Scotland he was pitting his inexperienced men against one of the most ruthless armies in Europe. If he marched into England he was hazarding all on an act of youthful bravado.

Charles resolved to march into England. Argyll tried in vain to dissuade him and retreated, despairing, into private life. Others followed, and the great army so enthusiastically assembled began to melt away. Cromwell set off in eager pursuit of those who remained, fortified by the news he was getting from his remarkable espionage system. In March his agents had captured one Isaac Birkenhead, Charles's messenger to his English friends. Birkenhead had on him a letter containing much information about Charles's preparations, along with some useful names. Arrests were made, secrets were betrayed and more letters were produced. The Parliamentarians now had a complete account of Charles's schemes, the means to crack his secret code and the names of many who professed loyalty to him. About 2000 of these last were arrested as the government put England on a state of alert. The militia was called out, suspected Royalists and Catholics had their houses rendered untenable and were required to hand over their horses and arms. Informers were to be given a third of their victims' estates, while the death penalty would be inflicted on those who deserted to the Scots.

By the time Charles reached the English border his army was reduced to about half its original strength. Few came to replace those who had deserted, and when the King marched on Carlisle and ordered it to surrender he was greeted with silent contempt. Disillusion among his followers was keen, and the shrewdest foresaw tragedy. 'I confess I cannot tell you', wrote one, 'whether our hopes or fears are greatest, but we have one stout argument – despair; for we must either stoutly fight or die.'[30] As the army proceeded south the disillusion mounted. To have any chance of success at all, it was essential that friendly forces rise and rally to the King's cause, but there were telling reasons why the people of England declined to come to his support. Common sense kept many away, for it was obvious that Charles was entering England with the ragged end of an already defeated army. His march was no triumphal progress, and he had no money to win the mercenary to his side. Everybody also knew that the Parliamentarian position was just the reverse of this, for the heavy burden of taxes imposed by the Commonwealth regime was now paying for a large, experienced and victorious force. Those who joined it could expect to be well and regularly paid, and Cromwell could rely on some 50,000 men at arms. But above all the country was weary of war. Nothing but disaster had ever issued from Scotland, the Scots themselves were feared and despised, and the majority of Royalists determined to sit out the bad times rather than join a mission requiring suicidal loyalty.

Buckingham's quick intelligence seized on these last points. The 'unreasonableness' of having Leslie in command was obvious to him. The English gentry could never be expected to serve under a mere Scot. A surprised Charles asked who he could possibly put in Leslie's place. To Buckingham, the answer was obvious and he told the King that he was more than willing to take up the post of his Commander-in-Chief. Charles was lost for words, but Buckingham was not to be discouraged and, the following day, he 'renewed his importunities'. The change he was suggesting, he said, was 'so evidently for the King's service that David Leslie himself would willingly consent to it'.[31] Charles told him he must be joking, but Buckingham asked what was so ridiculous about his proposal. He was promptly told that he was far too young for the post. As ever, he was swift to reply. Henri IV, Charles's own grandfather, had won a famous victory at an even younger age, he said. Charles lost his temper, and Buckingham sulked like a schoolboy. He 'came no more to Council, scarce spoke to the King, and neglected everybody else and himself insomuch as for many days he never put on clean linen nor conversed with anybody'.[32]

Charles himself had more important things to worry about than a petulant friend. At a council of war it had been suggested that the only way to boost morale and win the campaign was for the Royalist troops to march on London, but Leslie opposed the idea. He had throughout the march been 'sad and melancholic', and, when Charles tried to raise his spirits by telling him how 'brave' his men looked, Leslie's true thoughts spilled out and he said dejectedly that the army 'how well so ever it *looked*, would not fight'.[33] Charles did not believe him, but he was persuaded not to make a dash for London and instead pressed south along the Welsh border where once as a boy prince he had stirred the people to a fervour of loyalty. Now he was met with a blank response.

It was decided to send Lord Derby and Major-General Massey back into Lancashire, where both men had influence: Derby as a grandee of the Catholic Cavaliers, and Massey as a leading Presbyterian. Such religious differences ensured that neither achieved success, and Derby himself was routed by a detachment of Parliamentarian troops outside Wigan, where four hundred of his men were taken and he himself was wounded. He was then sheltered by the Roman Catholic Penderel family, tenant farmers at Boscobel House, before making his way back to rejoin his King. But Charles himself had had no greater success. The citizens of Shrewsbury closed their gates against him, while those in Gloucester also resisted his appeal. On 22 August, Charles and his army of about 12,000 men arrived at Worcester. His soldiers had now been on the march for over three weeks and were exhausted. Rest was essential, and 'the faithful city' seemed to provide it. Worcester also had tactical advantages. Cromwell had by now cut off any hope of a Royalist advance towards London, and Worcester appeared to offer a defendable base. The Severn formed a natural protection, the city's fortifications might yet be rebuilt, and to its rear lay Wales, where loyalists might still be found. The Mayor proclaimed Charles from the market cross, but civic pomp barely disguised the desperation of the King's plight. 'For me,' he declared, 'it is a crown or a coffin.'[34]

As his men gladly dressed themselves in the new shoes and stockings provided by the authorities in Worcester, Charles made preparations to recruit more soldiers. All males between sixteen and sixty were commanded to assemble in the fields outside the city. Proclamations were issued promising a general pardon to all save regicides, pay was offered to those who deserted from the Parliamentary cause, and a settling of religious issues by reference to the Covenant was held out. Few indeed were those who appeared, and it was clear that Charles would have to fight his cause with the men he had brought from Scotland. He still pursued his preparations with energy. Labourers were ordered to repair the city's fortifications, supplies were commandeered from the surrounding countryside, the city suburbs were razed to the ground, and the bridge over the Severn was broken to prevent the enemy from crossing it.

The failure to post a sentinel at the bridge was the first of the Royalists' tactical blunders. A Parliamentarian force of nearly 30,000 was by now concentrated in the region, and Cromwell sent his generals Lambert and Fleetwood to cross the Severn and position themselves outside Worcester. They crossed the broken and unguarded bridge by means of a plank, drove back the Royalists who were supposed to be defending it, mended the bridge itself, and then sent 11,000 men across. Charles's first line of defence had already fallen, and by now Cromwell himself had arrived with an army numbering three times that of the King. Many of Charles's leading officers, foreseeing catastrophe, 'appeared utterly dispirited and confounded'. Massey even wished that Charles himself were 'safe in some foreign part'.[35]

By 29 August, Cromwell's forces were in position, but he waited until 3 September – the anniversary of his victory at Dunbar – before he moved in for the kill. His guns commenced their assault, and Charles climbed the stairs of the cathedral tower to survey events through his telescope. As he pointed the lens in the direction of the Severn, he could see the Parliamentarian forces guiding a pontoon up the river, confident that they would be defended by the Cromwellian cavalry who had now come to their support. Charles despatched three hundred Highlanders to oppose them but, as they were repelled, the Parliamentarians installed their pontoon and began to bring their regiments across the river.

Charles himself resolved to attack Cromwell's army to the south-east of the city. Proving his undoubted courage, he achieved a short-lived success. Covered by their artillery, the Royalists surged furiously uphill. Gunfire gave way to push of pike, push of pike to butting with muskets. So venomous was the attack and so great the ardour of the King that, for a moment, the Parliamentarian troops fell back. Now, surely, was the moment for the despondent Leslie to join his master, but the lethargy of despair had swept over him and instead it was Cromwell who at once recrossed the Severn and attacked with such ferocity that the Royalists were driven back. There was now such a panic of disorder that Charles was obliged to crawl through the wheels of an upturned wagon whose oxen lay dead in the path before him. Among his forces, desperation rode hard on chaos. Leslie, stirred to panic, rode about the city 'as one amazed or seeking to fly he knew not whither'.[36] Only Charles appeared to keep his head. Having struggled through the mud under the ox cart, fought his way back into the city and stripped off his armour, he called for a fresh horse. He then rode furiously among his bewildered troops, bellowing at them to stand and fight, and, in wild-eyed ecstasy, crying out: 'I had rather you would shoot me than keep me alive to see the consequences of this fatal day!'[37]

It was too late. The Parliamentary forces were pouring over the pontoon, and neither threats nor entreaties could persuade the Royalists to regroup or even close the city gates. The carnage was terrible. The gutters of Worcester ran with blood, and 'what with the dead bodies of the men and dead horses of the enemy filling the streets, there was such a nastiness that a man could scarcely abide the town'. Many fled, and of these some were so exhausted that, as they lay in the fields around the city, the country people came out, robbed them and then cudgelled them to death. Those of a more resilient streak fled through Kidderminster, where the Puritan minister Richard Baxter, newly gone to bed, was roused by the noise of the Royalist cavalry flying through the town. What he heard was the tumult of desolation, 'and till midnight the bullets flying towards my door and windows, and the sorrowful fugitives hastening for their lives, did tell me the clamatousness of war'.[38] Only when dusk began to veil the carnage did Charles himself resolve to flee, leaving ravaged Worcester by the northern gate, his cause in ruins and his very survival in question.

6

The Fugitive

Charles fled Worcester late on 3 September, 1651, accompanied by a posse of his lords. Defeated and exhausted as he was, he knew that he could not give way to despair and that his survival depended on his keeping his wits about him. He was now a twenty-one-year-old king on the run.

While the lords squabbled about the possibilities of making for Scotland, Charles had already rejected this plan, guessing that so long a journey would expose him to too many dangers. How much better to make for London, where, amid the anonymous poverty of a great city, he could hide himself before slipping away to the mainland of Europe. It was vital that as few people as possible should know about this plan, and Charles confined his secret only to Lord Wilmot, telling him that they would meet up at the Three Cranes, by the Vintry, in Thomas Street. The others of his party in the meantime would have to be persuaded to leave, but, as Charles recalled years after the event, 'though I could not get them to stand by me against the enemy, I could not get rid of them, now I had a mind to it'.[1]

It was not long before they were all lost in the gathering dark. Charles turned to Lord Derby to seek his advice. Shelter was urgently needed, and Derby recalled how he had recently been looked after by the Penderels, tenant farmers at nearby Boscobel House, following his defeat at Wigan. Catholic families such as the Penderels ran a highly efficient underground network for smuggling priests and fugitive believers, and were also intensely loyal to the crown. Charles should make for safety with people such as these. As luck would have it, Charles Giffard, the owner of Boscobel, was riding with the royal party, and he undertook that he and his servant would guide them in that direction, his little house of Whiteladies close by being deemed safer than Boscobel itself. Charles agreed, and his party rode quietly on through Stourbridge, pausing only at a house outside the town for a morsel of bread and meat before arriving near Whiteladies at dawn.

A loud knocking at the gate roused the tenant, George Penderel, from his bed. 'What news from Worcester?' he asked.

'The King is defeated and is here,' came the reply.[2]

The door was opened at once, and Charles was hurried into the hall. The servants were roused, and bread, cheese and sack were brought for the famished King. The brothers Richard and William Penderel were then sent for, and Richard arrived bearing a necessary disguise for the King: 'a course noggen shirt', along with 'breeches of green coarse cloth, and a doeskin, leather doublet'.[3] The Catholic underground was already proving its worth, and Charles was now provided with a pair of much patched stockings and a greasy 'long, white steeple-crowned hat'. The King was being transformed into a labourer, and as Richard Penderel set about cutting his hair – making it short on top but leaving it long at the sides – a pair of shoes was brought for Charles. These were far too tight for so large a man and had to be slashed open. Over the following days, the shoes would cause him excruciating pain.

William Penderel then arrived and was summoned into the royal presence by Lord Derby with the words: 'This is the King. Thou must have a care of him and preserve him as thou didst me.' Both William and Richard swore that they would do so, but it was clear that little could be done while Charles was surrounded by so many of his followers. All save Lord Wilmot were persuaded to take their leave, 'every one shifting for himself. The majority made for Scotland, but there were few who were not captured and executed. Charles's intuition about his own survival was to prove correct.

There was danger all the same. By now the sun was rising and it was essential that Charles be got out of the house. To complete his disguise, he was given a billhook so 'that he might seem busy mending hedges' in nearby Spring Coppice. There, as the rain fell and the Penderels kept an eye open for danger, Charles himself saw a party of local militia riding by. They had already passed Whiteladies, asked after the King and been told that he had journeyed through some time before. The deluded men rode on in pursuit of their quarry, but by now the rain was falling torrentially and not even the thickest corners of Spring Coppice offered shelter. Charles eventually became so hungry and so wet that something had to be done for him, and Richard Penderel's married sister was told to bring a blanket along with 'a mess of milk, eggs, and sugar'.

Charles looked up suspiciously as she approached. 'Good woman,' he said to her, 'can you be faithful to a distressed Cavalier?'

'Yes, sir,' she answered, 'I will die rather than discover you.'[4]

Thus reassured, Charles tucked into the welcome food and was left to the ministrations of the Penderel men. As Catholics used to smuggling priests through a dangerous land, they were well aware of the importance of detail to successful disguise. They now taught Charles how to speak with a local accent and, just as vital for a monarch whose graceful deportment might at any moment give him away, they showed him how to shamble like a labourer or, in the picturesque phrase, 'to order his steps and straight body to a lobbing Jobson's gait'. They also had more bitter lessons to impart. The Penderels had to make clear to Charles that they could not assist his planned flight to London for the simple reason that they knew of no safe houses in which to hide him on the way. Where could he go? The Penderels mentioned a certain Mr Wolfe who lived close to the Severn and had a house with 'hiding holes for priests'. It occurred to Charles that his best plan was now to go there and cross the Severn into Wales 'as being a way that I thought none would suspect my taking'.[5] Wales was a Royalist area and, accompanied only by Richard Penderel, Charles set out under cover of dusk.

The two men had gone only a little way before the white-clad figure of a local miller challenged them: 'Who goes there?'

'Neighbours going home!'

'If you be neighbours, stand!'

They would take no such risk. Richard Penderel bolted up a narrow lane, followed by Charles in his now agonising shoes. 'So we fell a-running,' the King recalled, 'both of us up the lane, as long as we could run, it being very steep and dirty.'[6] Charles eventually persuaded Richard Penderel to 'leap over a hedge and lie still to hear if anybody followed us'. When they were satisfied that they were not being pursued – the miller was a Royalist hiding some of the King's men and was in fact as frightened as they were – Charles and Richard Penderel set off once again for Mr Wolfe's house at Madeley. They arrived there towards midnight.

Old Mr Wolfe was roused from his bed and asked if he would offer to protect 'a person of quality'. He was disinclined, saying 'he would not venture his neck for any man unless it were the King himself'.[7] He was told the truth and his manner changed. He was nonetheless obliged to tell the fugitives that, for all their hopes, his house was no longer safe and that they would have to hide in his barn. Charles and Penderel stayed there throughout the day, and that evening the men discussed their plans. It soon became clear that flight to Wales was no more safe than a journey to London. The Severn was strictly watched and guarded, and the only course of action Wolfe could recommend was that Charles return to the Penderels, making the journey on foot. The disappointed men returned the way they had come but, since they thought it was necessary to avoid coming in contact with the miller again, Charles decided that they should wade the stream that ran his wheel rather than cross the bridge. Penderel at once confessed that he could not swim, adding that the 'scurvy river' was a dangerous one to ford. Charles was not to be put off by such considerations. 'and I, entering the river first, to see whether I could myself go over, who knew how to swim, found it but a little above my middle; and thereupon, taking Richard Penderel by the hand, I helped him over'.[8]

They landed safely on the opposite bank, but Charles's lacerated feet were being sorely chafed by sand from the riverbed trapped in his shoes. He had all along shown himself considerate and courageous, but now, as he and Richard Penderel blundered about in the dark, the pain and hopelessness of the whole enterprise swept over him. For the first and only time on his journey he was overcome by despair. He threw himself on the ground, telling his companion to leave him, and exclaiming that he would rather die than walk another step. His guide mustered all his resources of tact and kindness, 'sometimes promising that the way should be better, and sometimes assuring him that he had but little further to go'.[9] The two men eventually came to Whiteladies, where they learned that Wilmot, escorted by John Penderel, was now safely ensconced at nearby Moseley Hall. They themselves then arrived at Boscobel towards three in the morning, Richard Penderel leaving Charles and his aching feet in the safety of the woods as he went to rouse the inhabitants.

He found that one Colonel William Carlis, a redoubtable Royalist sympathiser, was hiding there. Carlis had been one of the last men to flee Worcester and now, when he was brought out to meet the King, they exchanged a tearful greeting before returning to the house. There Charles was offered 'a posset of thin milk and small beer' by the wife of William Penderel, who lived at Boscobel with her husband. When Charles had bathed his feet, been offered a clean pair of stockings and watched Mrs Penderel dry out his shoes with hot cinders, plans had once again to be made. There was still no question of the King being moved by daylight, and it was decided that he and Carlis should spend the day deep in Boscobel Wood. Carlis had already chosen a tall oak in which he had resolved to hide and now, taking William Penderel's wooden ladder with them, the two men went out with no more comforts for the day than a couple of pillows, some beer, bread and cheese.

As Charles later recalled, 'while we were in this tree, we see soldiers going up and down, in the thicket of the wood, searching for persons escaped'.[10] The danger was clear, but so exhausted was Charles after several nights without proper rest that he fell asleep in Carlis's arms. Eventually, Carlis himself caught a cramp and, fearing that he could no longer support his sleeping monarch's weight (but equally frightened that anything he might say would be overheard by hostile soldiers), he was 'constrained to practise so much incivility as to pinch his Majesty to the end he might awake him to prevent his present danger'.[11] Duly woken, Charles returned with Carlis that evening to the greater safety of Boscobel House.

They found that throughout the day the Penderels had been discreetly helping the Royalist cause. William Penderel and his wife had kept an eye open for Parliamentarian soldiers. Richard Penderel had gone to Wolverhampton to buy little luxuries such as wine and biscuits, while a third brother, Humphrey Penderel, now appeared at Boscobel bearing important but alarming news. He had gone to the local militia headquarters to pay a levy and had there been interrogated by a Parliamentarian colonel. The man knew that Humphrey came from Whiteladies and an intelligence report said that Charles had also been at the house. The Colonel brusquely informed Humphrey of 'the penalty for concealing the King, which was death without mercy', and added that the reward for those giving information which led to Charles's capture 'should be one thousand pounds certain pay'.[12] Humphrey, quite untempted by the reward, prevaricated adroitly. He admitted that a band of Cavaliers had indeed turned up at Whiteladies and that the rumour was that the King was among them, 'but there was no likelihood for him to stay there'. After all, three families shared the house and, as they were all 'at a difference with one another', concealment of the King or anyone else was out of the question. Whiteladies was quite simply not a safe house.

If the Colonel was satisfied, Charles was alarmed. As he sat at his chicken supper, his face darkened. To people such as the Penderels, £1000 was an enormous sum. Colonel Carlis quickly said that 'if it were one hundred thousand pounds, it were to no more purpose'. Loyalty was beyond price and, after a brief moment of doubt, Charles was reassured. After all, Humphrey Penderel had not sold him to his enemies. Then, mentioning that he was anxious to make contact with Wilmot so that he could tell him of the change of plans, Charles prepared to go to bed. For his Sunday dinner, he said, he would like some mutton. With that, he retreated to one of the hiding-places in the house, where he slept 'very incommodiously, with little or no rest, for that the place was not long enough for him'.[13] The following morning he rose early and, with aching limbs and torn feet, hobbled up and down the long gallery.

Charles preserved his humour and continued to win the Penderels with his charm. Nonetheless, his apparently innocent request for mutton had been an embarrassment to them since such a luxury was beyond their means, and, if they went to buy a portion of meat locally, they would surely draw attention to themselves. The only option was to 'make bold with the sheep of someone else'. Carlis went out to find one, slaughtered it, skinned it and brought the carcass back in triumph to Charles. With a smile, the King cut the leg into 'Scotch collops', after which he 'pricked them with the knife point, then called for a frying-pan and butter, and fried the collops himself'.[14]

When breakfast was over, John Penderel came over to Boscobel to see that all was well. For the past few days he had been Wilmot's guide, and he was amazed to find Charles at the house, believing that he was by now safely in Wales. John was at once sent back to Moseley to inform Wilmot of his master's plight, but he arrived at the house only to be told that Wilmot himself had gone. Muttering that they were now all 'undone', Penderel told Thomas Whitgreave, the Catholic owner of Moseley, of Charles's misfortunes. It was clear that urgent action would have to be taken to save the King, and Whitgreave and his priest at once took Penderel over to nearby Bentley Hall, the home of Wilmot's friend and companion-in-arms Colonel Lane. These two friends had by now developed a clever plan for Wilmot's escape. The Colonel's younger sister Jane had acquaintances called Norton who were firm Royalists and lived at Abbots Leigh, close to the great port of Bristol. Mrs Norton was pregnant, and a while before the Battle of Worcester a pass for Jane and a manservant had been obtained so that Jane could ride over and be at her friend's side. What better way could there be of helping a Royalist on the run than to disguise him as Jane's manservant?

Wilmot, for all that the life of a middle-aged bon viveur seemed to be his first and sometimes his only priority, was in fact a deeply loyal man, and he had initially thought that this remarkable opportunity of escape should be offered to the King. Since he now believed that Charles was safe in Wales, he had resolved to take advantage of the scheme for himself and had arranged to leave for Abbots Leigh the following morning. On being informed of the King's plight, he cancelled the plan at once. Charles should leave Boscobel forthwith and make immediately for Moseley Hall. There, Wilmot would join him and the details of the route could be worked out. John Penderel was sent back to Boscobel to fetch the King, who had spent a quiet Sunday at his prayers before taking a book into the secluded garden of the house. A sudden royal nosebleed had provided the only cause for alarm, but that was now staunched and Charles listened eagerly to the plans presented to him.

The King was all for making for Moseley with as small an escort as possible, but the Penderels, wiser in the ways of the underground, suggested that a considerable party might be an advantage were they to be approached by any of the numerous soldiers still combing the area. It was agreed that all the Penderel brothers and another should accompany him, but Charles was adamant in his refusal of their suggestion that he should walk to Moseley. His feet were still excruciatingly tender and the Penderels, realising the justice of what he said, found a wretched saddle for him so that he could ride Humphrey's carthorse to the environs of his next safe house. Then he would indeed have to walk. Surrounded by the Penderels, each of whom was armed with a billhook or pitchfork, Charles set off on what he jokingly complained 'was the heaviest dull jade he ever rode on'.

The quick-witted Humphrey had an apt reply: 'My liege, can you blame the horse to go heavily when he has the weight of three kingdoms on his back?'

If Charles smiled, his expression soon changed. The escort had arrived at the spot from where the King would have to continue his journey on foot. He dismounted and set off as fast as he could. Then he remembered his manners. The Penderels had risked everything for their fugitive monarch and he had said nothing in farewell. Charles turned back and caught up with them.

'My troubles make me forget myself,' he said. 'I thank you all.' Then he stretched out his hand for the Penderels to kiss.[15]

His duty done, Charles stumbled back to join his guides. Soon his approach to Moseley was observed by its owner, Mr Whitgreave, who was on watch in the orchard. So effective was the King's disguise that

Whitgreave recognised him only by his companions, but once Charles was in the house he took him upstairs to see Wilmot. Charles was then shown the Moseley priest-hole. This was a comparatively spacious if dark and airless hideaway, doubly hidden behind the panelled wall of a bedroom and a trapdoor in the cupboard behind this. Over the next few days it would prove its worth and Charles, satisfied that he was as safe as he could reasonably expect, turned to talk with his new hosts. Mr Whitgreave's priest bathed his feet, and Charles grew 'very cheerful and said, if it would please Almighty God to send him once more an army of ten thousand good and loyal soldiers and subjects' he would surely regain his throne.[16]

All the members of Charles's escort save John Penderel had now been ordered home, and the following morning the greater part of the servants at Moseley were sent out of the house on errands. Charles himself was then introduced to old Mrs Whitgreave and, later in the day, watched her as she tended to the wounds and hunger of his erst-while soldiers, now limping back along the public highways to Scotland. It was a pitiful sight, and it was perhaps this, coupled with the fact that he had time on his hands, which suggested to Charles that he offer his hosts an account of his life in Scotland and the events that had led up to the Battle of Worcester.

During his stay at Moseley, Charles also had the opportunity of talking to the family priest, Father John Huddleston. He examined some of his books and papers, in particular the manuscript of *A Short and Plain Way to the Faith and Church*, a Catholic tract written by Huddleston's uncle. He gave every appearance of being impressed. 'I have not seen anything more clear or plain upon this subject!' Charles declared when he had finished reading the tract through. It all seemed so logical, each idea following on from what had gone before. 'The arguments here are drawn from succession and are so conclusive, I do not see how they can be denied,' Charles declared.[17] This was an extraordinary comment for the head of the Anglican Church to make and on any other occasion would have been deeply shocking, but the fugitive in Moseley Hall was in no position to indulge in theological wrangling, even if he cared to. His life depended on the good-will of his

Catholic subjects, and this he could not afford to upset. Gracious manners were his best suit, and they were in evidence again when Charles was shown the chapel. It was, he declared, 'a very pretty place', the altar and its fittings reminding him of a similar arrangement he had once owned himself. Huddleston was charmed. 'Your Majesty is, in some sort, in the same condition with me now – liable to dangers and perils,' he said, adding, 'I hope that God who brought you hither will preserve you here.'

The King was touched and replied: 'If it please God I come to my crown, both you and all your persuasion shall have as much liberty as any of my subjects.'

This was probably sincerely meant, but the chance of Charles ever coming to his crown appeared to be rudely shattered that afternoon when a maid started shouting on the stairs. 'Soldiers! Soldiers are coming!' Boscobel and Whiteladies had already been turned over, and now the troopers were determined to search Moseley Hall. Charles was immediately bundled into the priest-hole as Whitgreave, shrewdly ordering that all the other doors of the house be left open, coolly walked out to greet the search-party. At first he was roughly handled, but he managed to protest that he was in far too poor health to take any part in public life or even hide a fugitive, and the soldiers reluctantly departed. His courage and nerve had saved the King's life, but now it was time for Charles to depart. At midnight Colonel Lane arrived to escort him to his house at Bentley. The first and most frustrating part of Charles's flight was coming to its close. So far he had only been led round in a desperate circle but now, as he passed from the hands of loyal, impoverished Catholics into the care of the Royalist gentry, so he would have to show not only his courage and stamina but his quick-wittedness and his ability to deceive.

Having arrived at Bentley, it was agreed that Charles should set out again for Abbots Leigh at dawn, riding with Jane Lane, her cousin Henry Lascelles and her sister and brother-in-law Mr and Mrs Petre. The Colonel had provided Charles – or 'William Jackson' as he was now called – with the sort of suit and cloak typically worn by a tenant farmer's son, but if the disguise was superficially successful it contained hidden dangers. The King of England knew little of the daily lives of such people as tenant farmers, and the simplest mistakes could arouse suspicion. Even now he presented his arm in the wrong way to help Jane Lane up on to her horse and had to be corrected by the Colonel. Other more serious embarrassments were soon to occur. The party was making for the house of one of the Colonel's friends at Long Marston, a village near Stratford and thus some forty miles from Bentley. All had got off to a fine start until, round midday, the horse that the King and Jane were riding cast a shoe. It was Charles's task as 'William Jackson' to get a new one made. This would mean talking to the local blacksmith while the job was done. The dangers were obvious, but the actor in Charles delighted at the idea and he later perfected the story into a much told anecdote:

> As I was holding my horse's foot, I asked the smith what news. He told me that there was no news that he knew of, since the good news of the beating the rogues the Scots. I asked him if there was none of the English taken that joined with the Scots. He answered that he did not hear that that rogue Charles Stuart was taken; but some of the others, he said, were taken, but not Charles Stuart. I told him, that if that rogue were taken he deserved to be hanged, more than all the rest, for bringing in the Scots. Upon which he said that I spoke like an honest man, and so we parted.[18]

When the party reached Stratford, the Petres left them, and Charles and Jane Lane, accompanied by Lascelles, reached Long Marston. Here 'William Jackson' took his proper place in the kitchen quarters and was immediately required to show his wits again. He was asked to wind the clockwork jack turning the joints on the spit. He fumbled.

'What countryman are you', said the angry cook, 'that you know not how to wind up a jack?'

A smart answer saved the day. 'I am a poor tenant's son of Colonel Lane's in Staffordshire,' Charles said; 'we seldom have roast meat, but when we have, we don't make use of a jack.'[19]

The next day the party arrived at Cirencester, and the following morning set out for Abbots Leigh, where they arrived late in the after-noon. They had passed safely enough through Bristol, but now Jane Lane was required to show her reserves of cunning in order that Charles be preserved from the inevitable cross-questioning he would get if he stayed in the servants' quarters. She told her hostess that 'William Jackson' was ill and asked if he could be put to bed and have his supper brought to him there. An understanding Mrs Norton arranged for this, but although the doctor she sent to examine the patient failed to recognise him, Pope her butler looked at the invalid with some suspicion when he brought in the supper. The following morning Pope again looked 'very earnestly' at Charles's face as both men stood in the hall, and a little while later Charles was approached by a worried Lascelles.

'What shall we do?' the man asked. 'I am afraid Pope knows you, for he says very positively to me that it is you, but I have denied it.'[20]

Charles asked if the butler was an honest man and, on being informed that he was, made a shrewd decision. 'I thought it better to trust him, than to go away leaving . . . suspicion on him,' he recalled. Pope was brought before the King and told the truth.

The delighted butler, who had often seen Charles as a boy and had later served in his father's army, warned the King that there were a few servants in the house who could not be trusted and then added that he would be 'useful to you in anything you will command me'. Charles at once took him into his confidence. He told Pope that he was expecting the arrival of Lord Wilmot the following day, and the horrified butler, knowing that there were those at Abbots Leigh who would certainly recognise the peer, arranged that he would smuggle him into the house by night. When he had done that, he said, he would go to Bristol and see if he could find the King a ship which was sailing for the continent.

Pope was as good as his word. He managed to get Wilmot into Abbots Leigh under the cover of darkness, but he had less success in his search for a ship. Nothing suitable was sailing for a month and it was impos-sible that Charles should lie low in the region for so long. The resourceful Pope made a suggestion. He knew of a family living in the little village of Trent some forty miles away on the borders of Somerset and Dorset. From there enquiries could easily be made at the nearby ports of Lyme Regis, Poole, Portsmouth and Southampton. The family's name was Wyndham and Charles knew them well for Edmund, the elder brother, had married the daughter of his old wet nurse and then gone into exile in France. The Wyndhams were also part of Wilmot's numerous acquaintance, and Pope's suggestion was taken up by both men with enthusiasm. Wilmot would precede the King to Trent and ready the family to receive him. Charles would follow on behind with Lascelles and Jane Lane.

This excellent plan foundered on the most unlooked-for event. Jane Lane's friend Mrs Norton gave birth to a stillborn child. Both decency and caution forbade Jane suddenly leaving Abbots Leigh under these circumstances, yet it was imperative that Charles depart as soon as possible. Once again, his survival was at stake and Charles himself hit upon a melodramatic yet workable solution to the problem. A letter must arrive informing Jane that her father was seriously ill and that her presence was required immediately at Bentley. Who better to deliver such a letter than the loyal and serviceable Pope? The ruse succeeded. The following day Charles set out with Lascelles and Jane Lane, riding first in the direction of Bristol until it was thought safe enough for them to turn south towards Trent. The party broke their journey for the night at Castle Cary, where Wilmot had asked a loyalist of his acquaintance to house them, and, the following morning, they set off for Trent itself. As they neared the house, Charles's relief at being among friends was patent.

'Frank, Frank, how dost thou do?' he cried out as he saw Wyndham waiting for him in the fields.[21]

Charles was hurried into the house, where it was agreed that Lascelles and Jane Lane should depart the following day. Discussion then turned to the question of a ship. Colonel Wyndham had many useful acquaintances, and he contacted a friend in Lyme, a certain Captain Ellesdon who was known to be a devoted Royalist. One of Ellesdon's tenants – a man named Stephen Limbry – was found to be sailing for St Malo the following week, and it was decided that Charles and Wilmot should be hurried on board his ship in the guise of two merchants urgently seeking to recover debts in France. Limbry would pick the two men up from the coast at Charmouth by night.

There remained the question of finding a safe place for Charles to hide while he waited for the longboat. A proclamation had now been issued for the arrest of the King as 'a malicious and dangerous traitor to the peace of the commonwealth'.[22] The fair at nearby Lyme would be buzzing with this news, and the wisest course appeared to be to book a room for Charles at the inn at Charmouth itself. To explain his sudden departure at night would require some versatility, and it was agreed that Wyndham's servant should be sent over to book the room and tell the landlady in the strictest confidence that her guests were a besotted couple who were planning to elope. Wilmot would pose as the prospective bridegroom, a cousin of Wyndham's as the bride, and Charles as their manservant. Charles himself readily agreed to the plan. He had passed the idle time of waiting with nothing better to do than boring holes in gold coins (perhaps for presentation as souvenir medals), and now it seemed he might escape at last. He set out the following morning and arrived at Charmouth just after sunset. Limbry himself arrived an hour later to confirm that his longboat would be off the beach at midnight.

It did not arrive. As dawn rose, the disillusioned and exhausted group huddled on the beach were at a loss as to what to do. Eventually it was decided that Charles and Wyndham should make for Bridport. There they would book a room at the principal inn and wait for Wilmot, who would ride off to see what had happened to Limbry and his boat. Inevitably, all of those involved feared treachery and, for the moment, they were unaware that they had been betrayed by farce.

Limbry had gone home to prepare his sea chest only to be cross-questioned as to his intentions by his wife. She obliged him to admit that he was taking a couple of gentlemen secretly to France, and Mrs Limbry, who had heard the proclamation for Charles's arrest being read out at the Lyme fair that day, at once suspected that her husband was shipping Royalists. She was terrified. The proclamation had made clear that those who offered help to any Royalists would be deemed traitors. And what if one of the passengers were Charles himself? As his wife lost her temper, Limbry slipped upstairs to pack his chest. The desperate Mrs Limbry followed and locked the door on him. She was not going to be left a widow, and as Limbry hammered on the door and demanded to be let out, his wife threatened to scream the house down unless he shut up. Limbry eventually did as he was told.

Charles was now in real danger. Bridport was milling with Parliamentarian soldiers being sent to subjugate his old refuge of Jersey. For all Wyndham's protests, a brave front was the only option and, with the cool recklessness Charles could summon on occasion, he pushed his way through the town and up to the best inn. 'We found the yard very full of soldiers,' he recalled years later. 'I alighted, and taking the horses thought it the best way to go blundering in amongst them, and lead them through the middle of the soldiers into the stable.'[23] For a man who had had no sleep and had passed the night waiting on tenterhooks, this showed exceptional courage and the sort of quick-wittedness Charles was obliged to display again when he was suddenly confronted by the ostler.

'"Sure, Sir," says the ostler, "I know your face?"'

Rather than facing this challenge straight on, Charles decided on a friendly, oblique approach. He asked where the ostler himself came from and a story spilled out about his having once worked in Exeter where he lived in the house of one Mr Potter.

'"Friend, certainly you have seen me then at Mr Potter's, for I served him a good while, above a year,"' replied the King.

'"Oh!" says he, "then I remember you a boy there."'

That clinched the matter and the ostler, his curiosity satisfied, 'desired that we might drink a pot of beer together, which I excused by saying that I must go wait upon my master, and get his dinner ready for him'.[24]

Wyndham had, in fact, already ordered dinner for them all and it had just appeared when Wilmot's servant hurried into the room. Wilmot himself had somehow managed to go to the wrong Bridport inn and had sent his servant to look for the royal party and to tell them to meet him outside the town. They set off at once, unaware that Wilmot, by the merest bad luck, had placed them in the gravest danger.

Once he had seen Charles and Wyndham off from the inn at Charmouth, Wilmot discovered that his horse had lost one of its shoes. As if he were in the most ordinary circumstances, he summoned the ostler and told him to take the mount to the nearest blacksmith. The ostler, who was in fact a Parliamentarian soldier trying to make a few shillings on the side, was a naturally suspicious and imaginative man and he had already managed to convince himself that the inn had had no less a guest the previous night than Charles Stuart. The facts were obvious to him, and a fortune rested on the matter. The 'son of the late tyrant', as the proclamation called him, had disguised himself as a woman and was the so-called eloping bride. What the blacksmith had to tell him only confirmed the ostler's suspicions. The three remaining shoes on the mount he was attending to had all been made in different counties. One of them had definitely been forged in Worcestershire, and that decided it. Charles Stuart was trying to flee the country disguised as a woman and was even now in the area! The ostler eventually went to see his commanding officer.

Captain Macy was clear about his duty and, even as Charles, Wilmot and Colonel Wyndham were meeting together outside the town and resolving to return to Trent, he spurred his horse in the direction of Bridport. Macy missed his quarry by minutes and was unaware that the royal party were now riding across country and had managed to get themselves thoroughly lost. They were in fact in a village called Broadwindsor. There, realising that they would need accommodation for the night, Colonel Wyndham went up to the local innkeeper. As chance would have it, the two men were distantly acquainted, and when Wyndham told the man that he and his friends were more than five miles from home and were therefore liable to be questioned by the authorities, he was given rooms at the top of the house where it was unlikely they would be disturbed.

They were not to enjoy the quiet night they needed. Soldiers on their way to Jersey were milling through the countryside looking for billets. Rooms at the Broadwindsor inn were immediately requisitioned and, as the raucous soldiers settled in, so one of their camp followers gave birth to a child. By now the whole village was in uproar, and the worried elders hurried to the inn to remonstrate with the new mother in the loudest terms. On no account whatsoever would her bastard become a charge on their community! The matter was still being debated at dawn when the soldiers were ordered to fall in and march for the coast.

The sleepless lodgers on the top floor meditated on their plans. With the Parliamentarian army about to take ship for Jersey it would be sheer foolishness to try and find a boat for the King in the area. Charles would have to return to the comparative safety of Trent. There he could wait while Wilmot and his man made for Salisbury, where Wyndham had a trustworthy friend called John Coventry. At Salisbury enquiries could also be made about ships sailing from the coasts of Hampshire and Sussex. With Salisbury only thirty miles away, communication would be relatively easy. The following morning, as the Parliamentarian soldiers marched off to reduce Jersey, Charles and Wyndham slipped back to Trent to await developments.

Charles would have to bide his time at Trent through nineteen long and often dreary days but, even on the first evening of his return, a man came to dinner who was to help change his fortunes. He was one of Hyde's many cousins – also called Edward – and he mentioned that he had recently been in Salisbury where he had happened to meet with one Colonel Robert Phelips, a distinguished Royalist from a great but currently impoverished family. Wyndham knew Phelips's worth and saw that, working in conjunction with his friend John Coventry, much might yet be done. These new recruits to the King's cause met up with Wilmot on 25 September and at once set to work. A boat and a master mariner were hired, and it seemed advisable that Charles should now be asked to move on from Trent to Heale House near Salisbury, the home of the widow of yet another of Hyde's cousins, Mrs Amphillis Hyde.

Charles was less than enthusiastic about the proposal. Time had weighed heavily on his hands over the past few days, and the inevitable reaction to the strain he had been under began to set in. For all his youthful energy, he had lived for weeks with a constant undertow of fear. At any time his whereabouts might have been discovered. A careless word or a lucky Parliamentarian officer could easily have exposed him, and he would have been despatched instantly to public humiliation and death. He had been forced into brief, intense contact with strangers who were prepared to sacrifice all for him and had then been parted from them at a moment's notice. He had been hungry, constantly exhausted and obliged to use his wits with lightning speed. Above all, he had been defeated. He had seen his Scots soldiers trudging igno-miniously back home, the awful human witnesses of the end of his hopes. Now, as he sat once again boring holes in gold coins he resolved that he would not lightly let himself be persuaded into the first scheme for his escape that came to hand. He was determined that his aides should know this. He wished Coventry, Phelips and Wilmot to under-stand that while 'he desired all diligence might be used in providing a vessel' it was necessary 'that they should be ascertained [certain] of a ship before they sent to remove him, so that he might run no more hazards than what of necessity he must'.

The resourceful Phelips suggested that he and his companions again try to persuade Charles to move and then get in contact with one of the most upstanding figures among the local Royalists: Colonel George Gunter of Racton, near Chichester. While Phelips himself rode over to Trent, Wilmot, disguising himself as Mr Barlow (a ruse which convinced virtually none who met him), set out to visit Gunter. The loyal Colonel was not duped for a minute by Wilmot's disguise, but the conversation between the two men suggests the almost religious devo-tion that the idea of monarchy could inspire among Royalists, even in the most bitter days of their fortunes. A sighing Wilmot opened it: 'The King of England, my master, your master and the master of all good Englishmen, is near you and in great distress; can you help us to a boat?'

For all that Gunter had lost his fortune in the King's cause and was now deeply in debt, he looked sad for a moment and then broke out: 'Is he well? Is he safe?'

'Yes.'

'God be blessed.'

Gunter, at least, was a practical man and there was now the matter of finding a boat. He confessed that he was 'little acquainted' with seafaring types but would do everything in his power to find a suitable captain. Wilmot's relief was palpable. He 'was abundantly satisfied' with Gunter's answer and, 'hugging him in his arms', he 'kissed his cheek again and again' before retiring to bed.[25]

Gunter was as good as his word. He made prodigious efforts, and rode great distances, before finally approaching one Francis Mansell of Chichester with his request for a boat. 'I have two special friends of mine', he said, 'who have been involved in a duel, and there is mischief done, and I am obliged to get them off if I can.' Mansell thought briefly and then recalled that there was a friend of his in Brighthelmstone (the present-day Brighton) who might be able to help.

The two men rode off as soon as they could and eventually tracked their man – Nicholas Tettersell – to nearby Shoreham. It was left to Mansell to open the delicate negotiations, this sort of business 'being his affair and trade'. Discussion was protracted, for the suspicious Tettersell sought to drive a hard bargain. He insisted first on knowing who his passengers were, and Mansell told him what he believed to be the truth, namely that the two men were duellists on the run. The Captain seemed to be satisfied with this and then demanded a deposit of £60 for agreeing to have his ship ready to weigh anchor at an hour's notice. Since Gunter did not know how long it would take to bring the King to Brighthelmstone, it was necessary to persuade Tettersell to delay for as long as necessary. A sweetener of £50 guaranteed that he would, 'under pretence of freighting his bark'.

Charles had now to be brought on the last stage of his flight. Phelips had eventually persuaded him to leave Trent for Heale House, and on the morning of Sunday, 12 October he set out to collect him from there. They rode first in the direction of Warnford Down, where they had arranged to meet Wilmot and Gunter. There followed an arduous but uneventful forty-mile ride, at the end of which it was decided that the party would spend the night at the house of Gunter's sister at Hambledon. Here they were served with wine, ale and biscuits before sitting down to supper. They were some way into the meal itself when Gunter's brother-in-law, Thomas Symons, arrived drunk, having 'been all the day playing the good-fellow at an ale-house'.[26]

'This is brave,' he said, looking round at the unexpected company. 'A man can no sooner be out of the way but his house must be taken up with I know not whom.' Blearily recognising Gunter, he asked, 'Is it you?' and then, feeling affable, declared, 'You are welcome, and, as your friends, so they are all.' It was now time to take a good look at these friends, and the drunken Mr Symons made first for the King. 'Here's a Roundhead,' he blurted out, probably basing his judgement on Charles's roughly shorn hair. The tipsy man was slightly surprised to have such a fellow in his house and, looking across at the Colonel, he said: 'I never knew you to keep Roundheads' company before.'

'It's no matter,' Gunter said quickly. 'He is my friend, and I will assure you no dangerous man.'

Symons promptly sat himself down on the chair next to this friend and took him by the hand. Breathing ale fumes all over Charles, he announced: 'Brother Roundhead, for his sake thou art welcome.'

This mistaken identity having been established, it was necessary to continue with it, and Charles played up to the role with his customary aplomb. From time to time, Mr Symons's conversation was enhanced with words more suitable for the company he had been keeping earlier that day. The Roundhead was deeply offended. 'Oh, dear brother,' he complained, 'that is a 'scape; swear not, I beseech you.'

Symons clearly enjoyed feeling superior to this affectation of whining virtue and thought it would be great fun to get the Roundhead drunk. A range of 'strong waters and beer' was brought to the table. Charles was by nature abstemious with alcohol and he certainly did not want to get drunk on this occasion. Whenever Symons looked away, he passed his glass to his neighbour. Ten o'clock came, and it was highly desirable he go to bed. There was another long, hard ride to face the next day, but how could he make his excuse? Colonel Gunter showed the same adroitness at the dinner table that he had earlier shown in arranging larger matters. Looking across at his brother-in-law, he said: 'I wonder how thou couldst judge so right; he is a Roundhead indeed, and if we could get him to bed the house were our own, and we could be merry.'

Symons readily agreed and, while he sat toping with Wilmot, the others went upstairs to sleep.

Their destination the following morning was Brighthelmstone, some forty to fifty miles away. They broke their journey at Houghton, stopping at an inn for bread and beer, along with some ox tongue thoughtfully provided by Gunter from his sister's pantry. They then rode on to Bramber, where, to their horror and surprise, they found the place swarming with Roundhead soldiers newly discharged from guarding the bridge and eager for refreshment. Wilmot, who was probably still suffering from the effects of his companionable night with Mr Symons, suggested they turn back. Gunter would have none of it.

'If we do we are undone,' he said. 'Let us go on boldly and we shall not be suspected.'

'He saith well,' agreed the King.

They passed through Bramber without incident but, on the other side of the village, they were to be severely frightened. A low whistle from Charles made Gunter turn round and he saw to his horror a party of some thirty to forty soldiers charging up the narrow lane behind them. Gunter slackened his pace, the others drew up with him, and the soldiers thundered by with such vehemence 'that we could hardly keep our saddles from them'. The Roundheads 'passed by without any further hurt', and the shaken little party reached Beeding about half an hour later. Here they divided, Gunter making with all speed for Brighthelmstone. There he booked himself into the George, where he was eventually joined by the others. As they sat waiting for Mansell and Captain Tettersell, the King was cheerful, Gunter noted, 'not showing the least sign of fear'.[27]

He was unaware of the dangers swarming around him. Tettersell arrived and had no sooner entered the room then he recognised Charles. He was fully aware of the immense personal risk he had been lured into and turned angrily on Mansell, who eventually managed to convince him that he had acted in good faith. Tettersell fell silent but was still aggrieved. But others too recognised the King. Smith the landlord had been helping himself generously to the alcohol he had brought up for the royal party and suddenly rushed up to Charles, grabbed hold of his hand and kissed it. 'It shall not be said but I have kissed the best man's hand in England,' he blurted out, making things worse by adding, 'God bless you wheresoever you go. I do not doubt, before I die, but to be a lord and my wife a lady.' The incident had its ridiculous side, and Charles was broadminded enough to smile before retreating into a nearby room without saying a word. The horrified Gunter joined him and begged his pardon. He swore that he himself had said nothing and could not conceive how the man knew the King's identity. 'Peace, peace, Colonel,' Charles said, 'the fellow knows me and I him. He was one that belonged to the backstairs of my father. I hope he is an honest fellow.'[28]

With that, Charles returned to the other room and opened the window. He noticed that the wind had veered and pointed this out to Tettersell. Gunter offered the man an extra £10 if he would sail immediately, but the Captain knew perfectly well that they would have to wait for a favourable tide and, still angry at being tricked into danger, was determined to raise his price. He wanted Gunter to insure him for £200 against the loss of his ship. The Colonel argued that this was wholly unreasonable and that a price – a generous price – had already been agreed. Tettersell stood his ground and Gunter was forced to comply. It then occurred to Tettersell that men in so desperate a position would be prepared to pay anything, and he tried his luck again. He required the Colonel's bond for the money. Gunter began to lose his temper, 'saying among other things that there were more boats to be had besides his; and if he would not act, another should'.[29]

Charles saw the danger at once. Tettersell might very well shrug his shoulders and force them to find another ship. He had already prised a handsome sum out of them and there was nothing to stop him now from wriggling out of unwanted danger and even reporting the presence of the King to the authorities. After all, the promised reward of £1000 was a vast sum to such a man. Charles quickly declared that Tettersell was in the right to ask what he did, and the reluctant Gunter gave his bond. Tettersell was assured, and words of genuine loyalty came pouring out. 'Carry them he would, whatsoever came of it.' It was then agreed that the Captain would go and assemble his crew, return to the inn and ride with his passengers to Shoreham. Charles and Wilmot would board the *Surprise* that night. High water was at seven the following morning. Tettersell caught the tide, and, two hours after his boat had set sail,

Parliamentarian soldiers came pouring into Shoreham. They had orders to search for 'a tall, black man, six feet two inches high'.[30] Charles had been on the run for exactly six weeks and had made his last escape by a hairsbreadth.

On board the *Surprise* he chatted knowledgeably to Tettersell about navigation as the ship made for the Isle of Wight. This was not to be their destination – their bearing was merely a blind to confuse those who might be watching from the shore – but the ruse entailed one further, last deception. The crew of four men and a boy had to be given an alibi in case difficult questions were raised when they returned to England. This was easily done. Charles was by now a past master in deception and he went to talk to the crew, silver in hand, telling them that he and his friend were merchants going to collect a debt in Rouen and that they needed to persuade the Captain to change course. Tettersell feigned a reluctant agreement to altering his route, and the matter was settled.

Throughout the night they ran before a northerly wind and shortly before dawn sighted the French coast. As the wind and tide changed, so they dropped anchor just off the tiny harbour of Fécamp, but with sunrise it seemed they might have to face danger yet again. Charles spotted a boat to leeward 'which, by her nimble working, I suspected to be an Ostend privateer'.[31] He at once went down to the cabin to tell Wilmot and suggest to him that, without further ado, they ask the Captain to land them from his cock-boat. In a last, great exercise in persuasion, Charles convinced him to drop both him and Wilmot off. The cock-boat was duly lowered and, as it approached the beach, so one of the crew, a Quaker named Richard Carver, carried an exultant but exhausted Charles to French soil. There he would resume the long, bitter days of his exile.

7

Exile in France

Charles and Wilmot gathered together their energy and found they had just enough money to travel to Rouen. When they arrived in the city their appearance was so disreputable that the proprietor of a local inn made difficulties about hiring them a room, and they were obliged to send to two English merchants and beg for cash and a change of clothes. This was a first, small taste of the poverty and powerlessness that were now to engulf the King. For the moment, the loyal Mr Sambourn and Mr Parker came to their master's aid and, as they were doing so, met up with Charles's old tutor, Dr Earle. In a state of intense excitement, Earle hurried off to the inn and asked a young man whom he took to be a servant where he could find the King. Charles smiled and, as he held out his hand to be kissed, Earle broke down in tears. He was the first man on the continent to see for himself that Charles was safe.

Charles and Wilmot then travelled by way of Fleury towards Paris. They were met outside the city by an agitated Henrietta Maria, who had been obliged to spend wretched weeks worrying about the fate of her eldest son. Although news of his defeat at Worcester had travelled to France with the familiar speed of bad tidings, no one appeared to know what had happened to the King himself and, as the days passed, it seemed to the Queen Mother that his chances of having escaped alive were slim. Now she was confronted by her vagabond son. An ever observant Venetian ambassador wrote that Charles's 'retinue consisted of one gentleman and one valet, and his costume was more calculated to induce laughter than respect; his appearance, in short, being so changed, that the outriders who first came up with him thought he must be one of his own menials'.[1]

For the next few days, Charles answered the questions put to him about his escape with a wealth of improbable stories. Dissimulation had now become second nature to him. While he felt free to vilify the Scots in loud and bitter terms, lies were essential to protect those in England who had risked their lives for him, and Charles was now well practised in deceit. He had received, he said, much help from a highwayman. He had made his way disguised to London where he had lodged in the house of 'a certain woman' who had helped him flee. 'To avoid any risk in quitting London, he wore her clothes, and, with a basket on his head, got down in safety to the waterside, and there continued his voyage.'[2] One of the English spies who were now constantly to trail Charles realised that such stories were just 'romance,' but, as he observed the King spinning his fabrications, he saw Charles's initial irony lapsing into something close to despair. 'He is very sad and sombre,' the spy reported, 'that cheerfulness which, against his nature, he strove to assume at his first coming having lasted but a few days, and he is very silent always.'[3]

It was hardly surprising that Charles should be sunk in gloom. The energy he had put into regaining his crown had been spectacular, and his defeat had been total. The price he had to pay was heavy indeed. He was now an impoverished exile who had abased himself for nothing and whose followers were departing from his side. For such men as these, many of them young like himself and with a life before them, compromise with the Commonwealth seemed preferable to an aimless, hopeless existence abroad. As the loyal Hyde was to declare, 'it is a very hard thing for people who have nothing to do to forbear doing somewhat which they ought not to do'.[4] The conduct of the Queen Mother increased Charles's bitterness, for Henrietta Maria, divisive as always, had become an ever more zealous proselytiser for the Catholic cause.

Her new confessor was an ardent convert to the faith, the French had hinted that her pension was not provided for the relief of heretics, and a number of the exiles about her had agreed to convert. Now she turned her attentions to Charles. She was far too subtle to approach his conversion in a direct way and, convinced as she was that only a conjunction of all the Catholic princes in Europe would restore her son to his throne, she attempted to win him by other means.

Those about the King who still hoped to get help from the Scots urged Charles to show his devotion to Presbyterianism by attending the Huguenot chapel at Charenton. Henrietta Maria encouraged this, knowing that this would separate her son from the Anglican church. However, she believed with a mother's instinct that the Presbyterian form of worship held no appeal for Charles and hoped that, disillusioned and floundering in his faith, he might yet be welcomed into the Catholic fold. The return of Hyde from Spain foiled her plan. The Chancellor was horrified that Charles seemed to be abandoning his Anglican beliefs and he exerted himself with all his considerable powers of persuasion to woo Charles back to the faith of his boyhood. His success deepened Henrietta Maria's contempt for him, and from now on a state of barely concealed warfare existed between the two.

Nor were the troubles caused by Charles's mother confined to matters of religion. A fierce disagreement had broken out between Henrietta Maria and the Duke of York, a petulant seventeen-year-old who was easily persuaded that he was treated with unkindness. Many wanted to remove James from his mother's influence, and he was persuaded to go to Brussels. There his poverty was so great that he was obliged to seek help from his sister in The Hague, but Mary's mother-in-law forbade her to receive him, and it was while he was passing a wretched winter at Rhenen that news came of yet another blow to the Royalist cause. The Prince of Orange had died of smallpox.

Charles was devastated by the loss of an ally so near himself in age and opinion, and he realised that with his brother-in-law's death their plans for a Protestant and Royalist alliance in northern Europe had come to a sudden end. There would be no more whispering of Machiavellian advice from that quarter, and Charles wrote to the superintendent of his sister's household saying: 'because it is impossible for me to tell you in a letter the great affliction and sorrow I have for the loss of my dear brother, the Prince of Orange, I shall leave you to imagining it, and the interest you know I have in it'.[5] But it was not only grief that filled Charles's mind. He was also concerned about the fate of his sister, now the mother of William's male heir. He longed to know with brotherly affection 'how my sister does for her health, and with what discretion she bears her misfortunes; whether my nephew be lusty and strong, whom he is like, and a hundred such questions'.[6] The answers were not all encouraging. Mary was wholly under her mother-in-law's thumb and that lady was now trying to wrest control of the boy for herself on the grounds that Mary was a minor and that her royal birth did not make her sympathetic to the Dutch republicans who, for their part, increasingly saw their interest as lying with the Commonwealth men in England.

Such divisions at home and disappointments abroad were made worse by Charles's continued poverty. Henrietta Maria had welcomed her son with tears of relief, but she could offer him little by way of material comfort. Her allowance was often unpaid, and when Charles asked her for some money with which to buy a shirt she told him that she did not have a sou and, moreover, that if he were going to eat with her and the family, then he would have to pay for his meals. Their first frugal supper opened the account, and the following months would show that Henrietta Maria was determined that it should be paid in full. The result was pitiful. By the middle of 1652 Hyde was writing to a friend, 'it is not possible for you to conceive the miserable and necessitous condition we are in here; no servant having received a penny since I came hither, and what the King gets being not enough to provide him with clothes and meat'.[7] Small amounts of money were sent by faithful Royalists in England, and the wildest hopes were entertained that Prince Rupert would return with his privateering navy rich with booty; but, for the moment, Cardinal de Retz alone came to Charles's aid, borrowing 1500 pistoles from a friend which he then entrusted to Lord Taaffe for the King's assistance.

Taaffe was now drawn into a close and curious relationship with

Charles I and Henrietta Maria, by Daniel Mytens. The love of the royal couple brings peace to the nation.

Five Children of Charles I, artist unknown. Prince Charles is the central figure.

Oliver Cromwell, by Robert Walker. The portrait was painted in 1649, the year of the execution of Charles I.

Edward Hyde, 1st Earl of Clarendon, by Thomas Simon. The medal was struck at the time Hyde was elevated to the peerage.

Archibald Campbell, 1st Marquis of Argyll, by David Scougall. The 'glaed–eyed marquis' was the leader of the Scots Covenanters.

Charles II and William Carlos in the Boscobel Oak, by Isaac Fuller. This is a romanticised image of the most famous episode in Charles's life.

Charles II escaping with Mrs Lane, by Vandergucht.

Charles II in exile, by Adrian Hanneman.

Charles II and Mary of Orange dancing at The Hague, by Janssens. The ball was held on the eve of the Restoration.

Charles II, by Samuel Cooper. An image of Charles restored to his full majesty.

Charles for, with Wilmot living in the cheapest lodgings he could find, it was Taaffe who served as the King's chamberlain, cup-bearer and even, on occasions, his valet. This closeness was all the more remarkable for the fact that, during Charles's absence, Taaffe had become Lucy Walter's lover and the father of her daughter. To Henrietta Maria's disgust, all of them were now living in the Louvre, but it is typical of Charles's attitudes to such matters that, for the moment at least, the situation appeared to give him little cause for concern. His relationship with Lucy had cooled beyond the point of rekindling, while to remain comparatively civil towards the woman meant that he could at least keep in contact with their two-year-old son.

In such circumstances as these it was impossible to maintain appearances. The English royal apartments in the Louvre were pathetically shabby and were rarely visited by people after they had heard the tale of the King's adventures. Charles himself was hard-pressed even to borrow money, while his followers lived in the meanest conditions and were obliged to walk the streets of Paris since they could not afford carriages. Hyde felt this deprivation keenly. He was a man who greatly loved the pleasures of conviviality and the comforts money could buy, but now he was reduced to sharing one meal a day with some half-dozen companions and going without warm clothes. Sometimes the cold in his room was so intense that he could not even hold a pen. The efforts of Jermyn eventually appeared to win a meagre allowance from the French royal family for Charles himself, but this was not regularly or fully paid, and when the money did come in his mother clawed it back to cover the debts he owed her. She urged him to find a rich wife, and Charles reopened his pursuit of La Grande Mademoiselle.

This time his deception was in earnest and the lady was charmed. La Grande Mademoiselle strode into Henrietta Maria's apartments, her hair uncoiffed, to be told that Charles himself looked 'very ridiculous' since his own hair was still roughly cut and his clothes were shabby.[8] The disguise in which he had deceived his enemies nonetheless set the heiress's heart a-flutter. Charles had, she wrote, 'le meilleur migne du monde', and because he could now pour forth *douceurs* in his miraculously improved French she could think of him as genuinely gallant.

How wretchedly life had passed for such a man in Scotland, where no one was allowed to enjoy music and he had been, as he said, furiously bored! Now he was in a civilised country and was longing to dance with his friends.

Spies reported that Charles's time since his return was indeed much given over to 'dancing, balls, and masking', and that he had become 'a great pretender to wit and jesting among the ladies'.[9] Mademoiselle herself had an excellent band of violins, and on a subsequent visit to her – dressed in a borrowed wig to cover his cropped hair – Charles danced exquisitely as her orchestra played. Soon he was visiting her every other day, dropping in at her evening parties especially, just in time for supper. Henrietta Maria urged on the match with her usual heavy-handedness, telling Mademoiselle that if she were really to marry her son then she would be more of a queen than she was now. A wedding between them was bound to speed Charles's restoration to his throne. But a shadow was already beginning to fall across this farce. Ever on the look-out for a powerful king, Mademoiselle was turning her thoughts towards Louis XIV, for all that he was eleven years her junior.

Henrietta Maria, with the insight of a mother and the cunning of the poor, at once divined the depth of the lady's mind. Charles was sent to Mademoiselle's rooms to tell her that his restoration would be twice as sweet for sharing it with her. She, for her part, bluntly told him that he would have a better chance of being restored if he went back to England.

'What!' he exclaimed, 'you would wish me to leave you as soon as I have married you?'

'Yes,' she said, 'for in that case I should be more obliged than I am to take your interests to heart.'[10]

If this was a tactless comment, La Grande Mademoiselle's other objections to Charles were equally insuperable. While some of her friends urged on her the duty of converting him to Catholicism, the rest suggested that her pursuit of the English King was damaging her reputation abroad. Besides, why should she want to marry a man who was so poor that she might end up dying of starvation? Such reasons were persuasive, and Mademoiselle began to turn a deaf ear to her suitor's *douceurs*. Soon she was requesting that the penniless King should not visit her quite so often. The couple did not see each other for three weeks and, when they met again, an exasperated Charles brought the farce to a determined end. In a court where such matters were of supreme importance, he had previously appeared content to sit on a stool beside his *belle amie*. What did his rights as a king matter if he were in love? Now, at their last interview, Charles sat on the proffered chair – a chair with arms. 'He thought he was causing me great humiliation,' La Grande Mademoiselle huffily recorded, 'but he did nothing of the kind.'[11] Charles, she had decided, was a king wholly unworthy of a woman such as she.

For a while Charles returned to pursuing an old flame, *la divine Bablon*. The Comtesse's husband had died in the bloodbath of the Fronde, but, despite the charms of this lovely if avaricious young woman, it was the renewal of that war itself which was to be Charles's more serious concern. Soon after his return to France, the opponents of the crown, led by the Prince de Condé, were joined by the Duc de Lorraine outside Paris. A beleaguered Louis sent Charles a letter asking him to invite the Duc to a parley. Believing that he might be useful, Charles went at once, 'not so much as staying to change his clothes'.[12] For his own reasons the slippery Lorraine withdrew his forces, and the disappointed leaders of the Fronde declared that Charles was responsible for the defection of their ally. They vowed in their anger that he would be 'thrown into the water, bound head and foot'.[13] An angry mob besieged the Louvre and, as the gutters of Paris ran with blood, the English court resolved to flee. Charles rode through the streets with his hand on the door of his mother's coach so that he could protect her from assault. Nonetheless, despite the Amazonian efforts of La Grande Mademoiselle, who by this time had thrown in her lot with Condé, his cause declined. Louis returned to his capital determined deep in his teenage heart never again to endure such insecurity and humiliation as he had recently known. In his relief, he felt that recognition was due to his brother of England for the part he had played in his restoration and, safely installed in the Palais Royal amid 'an abundance of ceremony', Louis thanked Charles for the 'great pains he had taken in labouring the healing up of those sad breaches between his Majesty and his people'.[14]

Such gratitude was not matched by any tangible reward. With Louis returned to his throne, Mazarin resumed the reins of power. He recognised the importance of treating with the powerful England of Oliver Cromwell and knew that in Charles he possessed a useful means of persuading the English to return to the conference table. He therefore kept Charles in poverty and by his side. As a result, the King's spirits became ever more depressed. While his brother James was given permission to ride out and join the French army, winning himself considerable renown, Charles was obliged to look for action where he could. First he sent Lord Norwich to Brussels and The Hague but, as so often, nothing was to come of these overtures. Charles then decided to send Wilmot, newly created Earl of Rochester, as an ambassador to the Holy Roman Emperor. Would the Emperor and the German princes provide a sympathetic ally with money, soldiers or, at worst, an invitation to meet them? Rochester proved a slack ambassador. 'Are you sure that he does not, when he receives any letters, put them in his pocket and forget that he received them?' asked an exasperated Hyde.[15] Despite such dilatoriness, Rochester eventually pleaded his master's case before the Diet at Ratisbon, but the exhausted princes of the Empire, their treasuries emptied by war, could promise only a small subsidy, which was not fully paid, and some of the money that did come in was spent by the ebullient Rochester on 'Christmas plum porridge', mince pies, baked meats and brawn.[16]

It seemed that Charles's best chance lay with the Dutch, although these hopes again were far from assured. The death of Prince William had been followed by a series of events almost as remarkable and shocking as those in England. The European powers looked on amazed as the leaders of the seven provinces, headed by Holland, abolished Prince William's office as Stadholder and held a General Assembly at The Hague at which they repudiated monarchy and centralised government. The management of the army was removed from Orange control, the provinces themselves were given a degree of autonomy, the Orangists were forced underground, and a form of republic was set up in which Holland as the richest of the provinces played a decisive role in the conduct of foreign affairs. It seemed natural that such a state

should wish to ally itself with the English Commonwealth, and overtures were duly made. The meetings that followed were nonetheless
dominated by mutual suspicion and impossible demands. The English,
viscerally jealous of the immense wealth earned for its country by the
Dutch seaborne empire, made preparations for war.

In order to damage Dutch trade, the Rump Parliament had passed a
Navigation Act which forbade the importing of any goods into England
except in English ships or vessels of the country in which those goods
were made. This hit the Dutch hard. Parliament then looked on as other
actions edged the two countries nearer to war. English privateers seized
Dutch vessels on the pretext that they were carrying French goods.
There was constant friction as the English demanded that their right
to the sovereignty of the seas be recognised by a lowering of flags.
The Dutch themselves were not keen for a fight, knowing that their
navy was in poor repair, but by the start of April 1652 shots had
been exchanged between Admiral Blake and Tromp. The war had
unofficially begun.

A delighted Charles saw his opportunity and made overtures to the
Dutch ambassador in Paris, saying he would ask the French for support
and offering to send his own ships to fight in the war. The Dutch were
wary of accepting help from a known Orangist of little international
influence, but when war was officially declared in July Charles came
forward with a host of further promises. He would 'put such places as
Ireland and Scotland into the hands of Holland as would enable them
to torment their enemies'.[17] If the Dutch helped him regain the Scilly
and Channel Islands, he would give them perpetual fishing rights off
the Orkneys. He suggested that the Dutch try to cut off London's
supply of coal by seizing Tynemouth in his name. His would-be allies
remained unmoved, even when he offered them Guernsey, which, he
said, he could easily prise away from Commonwealth rule. Finally,
Charles was led to make the boldest offer he could. 'If the States will
assign me some ships – no more than they think may fitly serve under
my standard – I will engage with my own person with them in the
company of their fleet, and either with God's blessing prevail with them
or perish in the attempt.'[18] The offer was again politely declined.

Two years after the war started, the exhausted parties found themselves desperate for peace, and the long-drawn-out negotiations resulted in a treaty which contained a bitter blow aimed directly at Charles himself. Both sides agreed that they would expel each other's enemies from their soil and never 'grant them any lodging, help, or entertainment'.[19] Charles, in other words, could expect no assistance from the Dutch. In order to make assurance doubly sure, a further clause set down that his sister Mary (whose cold and haughty naivety in political matters had shown her to be at best a hindrance) would never be able to entertain him even on her own property. As a condition of peace the English required that 'no rebel or declared enemy of the republic of England shall be admitted or suffered to abide in any castles, towns, havens, or other privileged or unprivileged places appertaining to any persons, of what dignity or State they may be, within the dominion or jurisdiction of the United Provinces'.[20] The treaty, Hyde declared, 'has struck us dead!'[21]

One by one the borders of Europe were closing against Charles. Holland offered no haven. Denmark followed suit. Sweden signed a commercial treaty with the Commonwealth on similar terms. Portugal was quick to follow. But the most bitter disappointment of all was still to come. In September 1654 Cardinal Mazarin, seeing where the advantage lay for his war-torn country, also signed a commercial treaty with Cromwell. There could be little doubt that a closer relationship would follow and, with it, the permanent expulsion of Charles from the one country where he had so far found a haven.

Hopelessness was deepening around him, and news from home brought no relief. Ireland had been utterly and cruelly subjugated, but for some months past the notion of a revolt in Scotland had seemed to offer comfort. Letters arrived from those leading the Royalist cause there, and Charles replied to them declaring his intention to be with the leaders in person. His restlessness and dissatisfaction were evident. He would 'rather die with his sword in his hand' than 'sit still and dream out his life'.[22] But that, it appeared, was what he was condemned to do. Help from Denmark and Holland was essential to the success of the Scottish plan and this was naturally withheld. Charles's advisers warned him of the danger he risked by returning to Scotland, and their counsels eventually prevailed. In the end, the Scots plan was betrayed, the army of resistance was defeated, and hope in Scotland itself faded completely as the nation submitted to a union with its conqueror.

The news from England was hardly more encouraging. Many of the Cavaliers were reduced to poverty and suffered under legal restraints. It seemed that there was little they could do. 'It breaks my heart', wrote one, 'to be out of action, and to live under a power that is so hateful to me.'[23] But others too were chafing under the new administration, and there were those who began to long for the return of Charles. 'As they had joined in driving out this good young King,' declared a minister in Derby, 'so they must join as one man, hearts and hands, to bring him in again, for till then they must never expect to see good days in England.'[24] For such people as these, the Rump Parliament was becoming ever more unpopular. It was believed by many, especially those in the army, that it had failed in its threefold task of encouraging godliness, overhauling the legal system and framing a satisfactory new constitution. Drastic action was necessary and, on the morning of 20 April 1653, Cromwell went to the House of Commons. After sitting quietly for a while he rose to harangue the members. Inspired by 'the spirit', as some were later to believe, Cromwell told the astounded company that 'the Lord has done with you and has chosen other instruments for the carrying on of his work'.[25] He would, Cromwell declared, 'put an end to your sitting' and then, summoning a soldier to advance on the mace,' the symbol of the authority of the House, he ordered him to 'take away these baubles'.[26] Cromwell was now resolved to enforce a godly dictatorship whose wonders of virtue would scour from men's hearts for ever the desire to see Charles Stuart returned to the throne.

To achieve this, Cromwell called for the election of a parliament which would draft a constitution and then, hopefully, retire. London and the provinces were searched for suitable embodiments of the godly with whom to stock the assembly. The mocking quickly christened the gathering after one of its less conspicuous Members, the London tradesman Praise-God Barebones. But such men, once called, proved themselves unable to control the reins of power. They squabbled over issues none could solve, and a frightened majority of moderates voted to dissolve the House. Having thus admitted defeat, they gathered up the mace once again and delivered it, along with the Parliamentary rolls, into the hands of an amazed Cromwell. Godly dictatorship, he saw, was at an end and, in the absence of a legitimate monarch, other constitutional experiments would have to be tried. Four days after the collapse of the Barebones Parliament, Cromwell accepted a new formula for ruling the country. There would be a limited, single-chamber parliament, a council of State would serve as the Privy Council had once done, while Cromwell himself would be appointed Protector for life, a role roughly corresponding to that once held by the Stuart kings.

A few in England were stirred to revolt, and in September 1653 Charles despatched an aide to investigate the morale of the Cavaliers who were helping to organise resistance. It was a move Hyde was entirely in sympathy with. 'Something', he wrote, 'must be attempted at home by the courage and virtue of those who are weary of the servitude they live under.'[27] He had in mind a concerted uprising. 'If this can be so ordered that in several places at once some considerable attempt may be made the rebels may be distracted, and friends abroad may give more assistance than can be positively undertaken or promised.'[28] A new organisation, the Sealed Knot, existed to translate Hyde's thoughts into deeds.

Charles was enthusiastic about the Knot, going to secret, early-morning meetings with conspirators in the Tuileries or the Jardin Renard, unaware for the moment that he was being spied on by the perfidious Bampfield, who had once organised the escape of the Duke of York. 'The King is as solicitous as you could wish,' Hyde told Rochester, 'and goes himself on his own errands.'[29] Charles suggested that an attempt on London 'would cover all', and he charged the members of the Sealed Knot to appoint leaders and raise funds. His confidence was misplaced. The plot they devised was betrayed and a number of the conspirators were executed, one of them wrongly claiming that Charles himself had authorised the assassination of Cromwell. A second initiative raised nearly a thousand men, but the plan to murder the Protector on his way to chapel was again betrayed and, with the government's espionage system working with remarkable efficiency, the Sealed Knot saw its plans constantly postponed.

So much disappointment was corrosive, at times eating away at Charles's energies until he was left with little but a bitter, monotonous certainty that there was nothing very much he could do. For purposeless months he had been forced to live in the palaces of France, a refugee king in darned linen obliged to scrounge credit for his very survival. Messengers, when they arrived, brought only bad news and expected to be tipped with money he did not have. He had himself done more than any of the fractious, bickering courtiers around him to regain his throne. At a humiliating personal cost he had raised an army, useless though it had been. He had fought a battle and, defeated, barely escaped with his life. Now it was obvious to common sense that his position was hopeless. The princes of Europe had turned their backs on him. He walked in a shadow world of politics. At times he must have known despair, but this was not the natural bias of his mind. There was something too vigorous, too coarse in him for that, and his weakness took other forms. If effort were useless – absurd even – then why bother to make it?

An alarmed Hyde watched the King sliding into apathetic indifference. Charles took little interest in the voluminous correspondence Hyde saw as necessary to maintaining his hopes. 'I do not forget the letters the King should write,' he opined, 'but he never sets himself to that work but on Fridays.'[30] Even then he was not punctual to the job. 'When anything is to be done by the King's own hand we must sometimes be content to wait, he being brought very unwillingly to that task, which vexes me exceedingly.'[31] Such laziness, Hyde believed, was clouding Charles's ability to make sound decisions, and this squandering of his natural ability was depressing to observe. 'By truth itself,' Hyde lamented, 'he hath more judgement and understanding, by many degrees than many who pretend to it, and that is the only thing that breaks my heart, that he makes no more use of it.'[32] Hyde noticed, too, another weakness that would grow over time into a habit that would exasperate all those about him. 'He cannot be severe or sharp in things, or to persons whom he in no degree approves.'[33] Charles was lazy-mindedly trying to be all things to all men.

Hyde was sure that Henrietta Maria was in large part to blame for this. 'All the counsel in the world cannot reform the King while he is with the Queen,' he wrote, and the atmosphere between these two was now poisonous.[34] Hyde had not been afraid to speak his mind and Henrietta Maria's Bourbon pride flared up. She had long detested Hyde for the simple reason that he was her natural superior. Jermyn was ordered to be as obstructive as he could, but the harassed woman was not above making scenes in public. At a court masque, Hyde was sitting beside Ormonde when the Queen entered. She asked 'who that fat man was that sat by the Marquis of Ormonde'.[35] Charles, embarrassed but quick-witted, said that he was 'the naughty man who did all the mischief and set him against his mother'. Those around laughed and even the Queen blushed, but as her faction continued to undermine Hyde's efforts the couple took pains to avoid each other, and the frustrated Chancellor was forced to confess: 'If I did not serve the King for God's sake I would not stay here a day longer.'[36]

Charles tried raillery to diffuse the futile and bitter plotting about him. When the Catholics and the supporters of the Presbyterian Scots joined forces to try and have Hyde removed – the Catholics hoping he might be sacked as a known opponent of their faith, the Presbyterians calling him a 'declared enemy to all their party' – Charles 'made himself very merry with the design' and publicly revealed its absurdity.[37] This did not end the matter. As Hyde recalled, 'both factions continued their implacable malice towards him'.[38] The flimsiest hearsay evidence was gathered together to allege that Hyde was a traitor in Cromwell's pay, and when this was exposed for what it was Charles lost his temper, declaring that the whole business was 'a vain thing . . . false and ridiculous', and that it deserved to 'discredit those who urged it'.[39] So seriously did he take the matter that he issued a declaration which stated that 'the accusation and information against the said Mr Chancellor is a groundless and malicious calumny, and that he is very well satisfied of his constant integrity and fidelity in the service of his father and himself'.[40]

Even this did not put a stop to the rumour-mongering, and Hyde's enemies made one last attempt. It was now said, not without some reason, that an exasperated Hyde had muttered bitterly about the King's laziness and done so in such a manner that he was not fit to sit at the Council table. Hyde was 'wonderfully surprised' at such reports.[41] When it came to a public discussion of the point, he was about to leave the room but Charles forbade him. Ridicule and anger had failed to staunch the flow of poison, and now honesty seemed the best policy. Charles declared that he could well credit that the Chancellor had said what he was alleged to have said. He did 'really believe', he declared, 'that he was himself in fault, and did not enough delight in his business'.[42] That brought the matter to a close, but the ill effects on Charles of this period of enforced idleness were worrying to many. While Hyde was certain that he had evaded the proselytising of the Queen Mother and was 'as firm in his religion as ever his blessed father was', there were other faults.[43] There was a 'want of secrecy' in the exiled court, too much was public knowledge, and the root of this problem was traced to Charles himself. He had not yet learned tight-lipped discretion nor to be comfortable with the loneliness that goes with keeping great secrets. Close advisers complained that 'while the King doth so freely discourse all of his affairs of the greatest secrecy, openly in his bedchamber, it will never be otherwise'.[44]

Other disturbing traits were also beginning to develop in him. Not only was Charles lapsing into a cynical and easy-going readiness to go along with the advice of those who seemed ready to free him from the burden of thought, his sexual appetite was also making people talk. In his vigorous early twenties, frustrated and often depressed, sex offered the King, besides physical release, the pleasures of escape and conquest. Pursuit could convince that he was still alive to excitement, while success might be rewarded with a brief, satiated oblivion. At some time during these months in France, Charles slept with Elizabeth Killigrew, the wife of an Anglo-Irish gentleman, by whom he had a daughter named Charlotte Fitzroy, her surname suggesting her illegitimate paternity. It is probable that he also slept with Lord Byron's widow Eleanor. Meanwhile, Paris itself may have afforded more impersonal forms of comfort. There were *maisons des baigneurs* in the city to which a man could go (assuming he had the money) where 'one was tended and cherished, and could indulge oneself in all the pleasures offered by the luxury and depravity of a great city. The proprietor and all his employees guessed from a glance or a gesture if you wished to preserve your incognito, and all of those who served you knowing perfectly well who you were assumed ignorance of everything about you, even to your name.'[45]

Hyde was hurt and depressed by the damage he felt Charles was doing to himself. 'It is too true and cannot be denied', he wrote, 'that the King is exceedingly fallen in reputation, which cannot be recovered but by some bold attempt. Besides, I must tell you he is so much given to pleasure that if he stay here he will be undone.'[46] But where could he go? There was no real opportunity for making a 'bold attempt' and money, as ever, was a pressing problem. Charles had even been obliged to put his own seal and his brother's Garter medal into hock. The return of Prince Rupert with merely one privateering vessel and a single prize proved that these items would not quickly be redeemed. Rupert's profits were scarcely enough to cover his expenses, and a bitter row broke out between him and Charles when the King sold off the ship's guns to Mazarin for much less than they were worth.

The Cardinal offered Charles 3000 pistoles as a down payment on the guns and promised to settle the balance as soon as the weight and worth of the brass had been ascertained. Such meagre generosity was more than a business deal. Mazarin had now matured his policy towards the Cromwellian Protectorate and realised that his country's future relations with England would have to be conducted around the principle that Charles could no longer be recognised as England's reigning sovereign. Mazarin was therefore anxious to remove him as soon as possible from French territory. Knowing that the King was deeply in debt, he promised to pay off his French creditors, and the advance on the guns was intended as an earnest of his good intentions. To make departure an even more pleasing prospect, Mazarin promised that Charles would regularly receive the small pension granted to him by the French and would be provided with his next six months' money in advance. It was then agreed that the King would quit Paris and make for the Low Countries on 10 July 1654.

There remained the matter of parting from his family. Relationships there had continued to deteriorate. Charles was jealous of the freedom allowed to the Duke of York and the way in which he was distinguishing himself as a soldier. He also had to contend with his mother. Henrietta Maria was now insisting that Charles admit that he had been in the wrong over many matters and was demanding that he confess to having 'used her ill'.[47] This he would not do. Although he was resolved to try and preserve what he called 'a good understanding' with his mother, Charles would not allow her to dominate him, 'nor can I promise to follow any advice she shall give me for the disposal of myself and the conduct of my affairs'.[48]

So much plain speaking resulted in 'hot disputes, between mother and son which, in their turn, led to Charles becoming ever more obstinate as the Queen's temper flared. Even the ubiquitous Commonwealth spy was impressed by the firm way in which he put his foot down. 'For though in appearance he is gentle, familiar, and easy,' the spy reported, 'yet he will not be purmanded [overborne] nor governed by violent humours, such as these are.'[49] This indeed proved to be the case, and Henrietta Maria, unreconciled to her eldest son, set off for Rheims to attend the coronation of her nephew Louis XIV. The rightful King of England in the meantime was obliged to put his clothes and bedding in 'a light cart' and to set off for an uncertain future as a royal remittance man. He was now, Hyde declared, 'as low as to human understanding he can be'.[50]

8

The Wanderer

Charles was immediately made aware of the humiliations and discomforts of rootless exile. When the royal party came to Cambrai, then in Spanish territory, they found the gates of the city closed against them. There were French soldiers in the area, the citizens were wary, and Charles was 'compelled to stay long in the afternoon' before he was allowed to enter.[1] When he was finally let in to Cambrai, the Governor offered him his house, but the Spanish nobility declined to visit him, fearing 'lest their showing any respect to the King in his passage through their country should incense Cromwell against them'.[2] Even a monarch without a throne appeared to pose a threat, and Charles moved on to Mons. There some excited English Royalists tried to convince him that disaffection in England was such that if he now returned he would be certain to regain his throne, but the circumspect Charles told them that he would bide his time until information was more certain and plans more securely laid. He was opposed to any 'desperate or unreasonable attempt' to seize back his power and was determined 'to sit still in such a convenient place as he should find willing to receive him'.[3] In pursuit of this haven, Charles moved on to Namours, Liège and thence to Spa, where he was joined by his sister Mary.

Brother and sister had not seen each other for four years, and a contemporary who watched them embracing with tears of joy declared that Mary's 'tender love and zeal to His Majesty deserves to be written in brass with the point of a diamond'.[4] Her lonely state as a widowed mother forbidden to greet her brother on Orange territory was a constant burden to her, and Mary was determined to make her reunion with Charles as cheerful an occasion as possible. As they settled down to life in Spa, Hyde took charge of the royal household of eighty people and, since the King appeared for once to be in funds, he paid the servants their arrears and tried to ensure that they were well fed and comfortably housed.

When the weather improved, life became a series of *fêtes champêtres*. 'There is not a day or night but there are balls and dancing,' wrote one observer. 'I think the air makes them indefatigable, for they dance the whole afternoon, then go to supper and after they go into the meadows and dance there.' The effect on Charles himself was beneficial, bringing out his natural delight in pleasure after the sour months spent in France. 'None is so much commended as our King,' the observer continued, 'who indeed is grown a lusty and proper person [and] gains affection of all by his affable and free carriage amongst them.'[5] Even the inevitable Cromwellian spy reported back that the royal party was 'as merry as if they had the three kingdoms'.[6] But much of this pleasure was on the surface. If Charles showed a naturally energetic young man's ability to enjoy himself, he was nonetheless concerned about the younger members of his family, his brothers especially.

The Duke of York still appeared to be under the influence of the Colonel Bampfield who had helped him escape from England, and, re-alising now that this shifty individual was a Parliamentarian spy, Charles wrote to his brother telling him not to employ the man in anything important. He also included in his letter a note for his thirteen-year-old brother Henry, Duke of Gloucester. This lively, popular little boy had been allowed to remain behind with his mother in Paris on the condition that he stayed loyal to his Anglican faith and resisted any attempts Henrietta Maria might make to convert him. 'You must attend your book and exercises diligently,' Charles wrote, 'and set some time apart every day to spend . . . with your tutor, to whom you must always show kindness and regard.'[7] For a while his instructions were followed.

When smallpox broke out in Spa, the royal party decided to move on to Aix-la-Chapelle where brother and sister took the waters, received generous presents from the city fathers and attended vespers in the cathedral, where they also viewed the relics, Charles comparing his sword to that of Charlemagne preserved there. Such tourism was diversified with hunting and hawking, and with parties that went on into the early hours. Although the King himself never over-indulged on these occasions, his courtiers did and quarrels broke out. Charles, who always enforced the strictest discipline in the matter of duelling, had to interpose between Rochester and Lord Newburgh, while a Cromwellian spy was woken by the crashing of furniture when a drunken fight broke out between Lord Wentworth and Major Boswell. In the mornings, while these men nursed their hangovers, Charles, accompanied by five or six of his more sober gentlemen, walked through the city to fetch his sister from the waters, his familiar black clothes offset by white silk stockings and his Garter star. Nonetheless, despite his pleasant idling, Cromwell's spy wrote back to his masters saying of Charles that 'for all his dancing, I believe he has a heavy heart'.[8] This was unquestionably so. His was still a rootless exile, and, when the time eventually came for Mary to return to Holland, Charles decided to accompany her as far as Cologne, where he had resolved to live if the citizens would make him welcome.[9]

This proved to be the case. The royal party was greeted with a salute of thirty cannon along with 'many shots of guns and muskets'.[10] Charles and Mary were housed in the delightful house of a Protestant widow, 'full of decent rooms and pleasant gardens'. Two hundred musketeers fired welcoming salvoes at their door, and the city magistrates arrived with speeches of welcome and 'two lusty fodders of wine'.[11] Brother and sister then visited the Jesuit college, and were observed again by the Cromwellian spy as they stood eating grapes and fruit, a matter of some annoyance to the spy himself since by the time he got to the buffet the food had all been eaten. Although the Elector of Cologne – 'a melancholy and peevish man' as Hyde described him – ignored the King, the citizens were so 'civil and conversible' that they helped to pay off Charles's debts.[12] However, when he returned to the city after a festive visit to Düsseldorf and a tearful parting from his sister at Xanten, Charles was to find himself involved in difficulties.

The summer holiday he had so enjoyed had been largely paid for by his sister, and now he had to look to his financial affairs. These were by no means as sound as they might have been. The sum voted by the Diet was irregularly paid and never received in full, while the Emperor's promise of support was empty words. Charles's French pension was likewise only intermittently forwarded to him, and Jermyn felt no compunction about deducting substantial sums from it to reimburse himself for services to the King's cause. Rochester set about coaxing funds from the German princes, but since much of what was obtained was spent on the parchment and couriers required for maintaining contacts with allies in England, the King was forced to retrench. He sold off his expensive hounds, only to be provided with another pack by a thoughtless Royalist. Charles was unable to order new liveries for his servants, and even had to buy himself a cheaper muff than he wanted to protect himself against the bitter winter winds through which he regularly walked around the city. By the spring of the following year, he was significantly in debt.

In these reduced circumstances, Charles passed his time as best he could: hunting hares, swimming in the Rhine, playing cards or a little harpsichord, and learning Italian. Such diversions relieved the monotony, but he still had worrying problems to deal with. Back in Paris his distraught mother was now trying to convert Henry, Duke of Gloucester, to Catholicism. Not only was she convinced that such a tactic was the best means by which she could raise money for the Stuart cause, but the boy had recently seen a short spell of service with the French army and now, returned to Paris, was so enamoured of the military life and so susceptible to the flattery of French courtiers, that he was rapidly becoming 'insupportable to all persons'.[13] Discipline was required, and when the worrying news of his mother's efforts to convert him reached Charles he was so angry that he nearly lost his self-control.

He wrote furiously to his mother: 'if you proceed in this I cannot believe that you either believe or wish my return to England'. Henrietta

Maria's lack of political judgement was gravely worrying. 'Nothing I can ever say or do will make my Protestant subjects believe but that this is done with my consent,' Charles added. Having pointed out her folly to his mother, he then tried to bring emotional pressure to bear. 'Remember', he declared, 'the last words of my dead father, who charged my brother upon his blessing never to change his religion.'[14] Charles's letter to Gloucester himself meanwhile was designed to frighten the boy into submission and show him what harm could be worked by a teenager in his position. 'The letters that come from Paris say that it is the Queen's purpose to do all she can to change your religion, which, if you hearken to her or to anybody else in that matter, you must never think to see England or me again; and whatsoever mischief shall fall on me or my affairs from this time, I must lay all on you, as being the cause of it.'[15] In fact, the frightened boy was as loyal to his religion as he was to his brother and begged his mother not to bully him. 'I will never change my religion,' he declared, 'I beseech your Majesty not to press me further.'[16]

Henrietta Maria remained indifferent. She had already sacked Henry's tutor and sent the child himself to the abbey at Pontoise for instruction in the Catholic faith. Ormonde was despatched to fetch him away as all of Europe looked on. The grandees of the Protectorate were delighted by this humiliating turn of events. Mary of Orange, knowing the force of her mother's personality, expected her to succeed in converting the boy. French Catholics thought her merely ridiculous, remarking that they admired 'the madness of the scheme'.[17] Meanwhile, the sad family quarrel went on but, after being lectured once again by his mother and then left alone to think over what she had said, Henry realised that he had to obey his brother. An hysterical Henrietta Maria turned on him, disowned him, vowed to see his face no more and ordered him to leave her lodgings.

The following morning, still firm to his duty, a tearful Henry begged to be allowed to say farewell. He resolved to kneel in his mother's way as she went to mass, but Henrietta Maria swept by in unregarding callousness, and the boy returned to his rooms to find his bed stripped, his horses turned out of his stables and no food provided for him. Even little Henriette Anne was forbidden to talk to him, and when a last appeal to the Queen failed, Ormonde sold his own diamond studded Garter medal and eventually travelled with the boy to Antwerp. Catholic Europe sneered. The Venetian ambassador in Paris wrote back to his Senate gloatingly informing them that 'the princes of the House of Stuart, having been expelled from the kingdoms of this world, will now submit to banishment from the kingdom of Heaven'.[18] Henrietta Maria, remaining true to her bitter resolve, never saw her son again.

The affair of the Duke of Gloucester was only partly hidden from the predominantly Catholic residents of Cologne, but they did not threaten Charles with expulsion, and, with this crisis over, he turned his attention once again to encouraging uprisings in England. Even under the Protectorate, the country had failed to settle either to godliness or to tranquillity. Known Royalists were returned to Parliament, while the Fifth Monarchists, feeling themselves to be no nearer the New Jerusalem, virulently criticised the Protectorate and called Cromwell a warrior of Antichrist. Religious fervour was raging with extreme intensity, and there now emerged into this fraught and dangerous atmosphere a sect whose ideas were so radical that all were troubled by them. It seemed that members of the Society of Friends – the so-called Quakers – aimed at nothing less than the overthrow of all government and all law.

The rapid growth of the Quaker movement among artisans in the north of England led to the founding of evangelical missions to London and the south that were, in their turn, so successful that by the second half of the 1650s Quakerism was a national movement. It held much – including a genuine and powerful spirituality – to attract its followers. By their insistence on greeting the Christ in all people, the Quakers emphasised a democracy of the spirit which at once took on a radical social edge. In an age when elaborate modes of greeting reflected social hierarchy, the Quakers' refusal to doff their hats was far more than an amiable eccentricity. The distaste for 'hat honour' was a refusal to acknowledge the importance of superior social standing and could be seen as an affront to the gentry as deep as the use of the familiar 'thee' and 'thou' to all without distinction.

Matters came to a head with the behaviour of the Quaker leader James Nayler. When, in 1656, Nayler rode through Bristol on a donkey in what was clearly intended as a re-enactment of the triumphal entry into Jerusalem, the authorities were deeply disturbed. Nayler and his female acolytes were arrested and taken to London where, while Nayler himself was branded, whipped, pilloried, and had his tongue bored, those Members of Parliament who wished to curb Cromwell's tolerant approach to minorities made Nayler's a test case of religious policy. 'Cut this fellow off,' declared one Member, 'and you will destroy the sect.'[19] Although Nayler's life was saved, the following year saw the revival of old legislation allowing for those who did not attend church on Sundays to be heavily fined. It seemed increasingly that the only way to contain mounting chaos in England was to go back to the old forms, the old ways. The New Jerusalem was fading before a longing for the normal and the safe.

Small bands of hot-headed Royalists were also prepared to foment problems for the Protectorate. King Charles's involvement with these men – and more particularly his policy of apparently listening sympathetically to all but openly committing himself to none – was to prove disastrous. The position had already been made difficult by problems of communication and the fact that the Royalists were divided among themselves. During the summer of 1654, the Sealed Knot had been unable to stamp out two pathetic Royalist plots which had been quickly suppressed. Now a splinter group which Charles and his advisers referred to as the 'new council' or the Action Group planned a major uprising for the following spring. Charles threw his weight behind these men but still regarded the Sealed Knot as the principal force in English Royalism. Such confusion was worse confounded by the fact that the new council despised the members of the Sealed Knot for being over-cautious, while members of the Sealed Knot dismissed the new council as zealots embroiled in dangerous fantasy.

In this hopeless situation, the new council intended to go ahead with their plans regardless of the Sealed Knot, who said they would take part in any uprising only if ordered to do so by the King. It was obvious that participation by members of the Sealed Knot was essential to the success of a rebellion, but Charles could hardly order them to go against their carefully considered judgement or hinder the new council in their plans. In the end, he authorised the new council to proceed, but no sooner had he despatched Rochester to command the rising than a member of the Sealed Knot arrived to inform the King that most of the new council's leaders had been arrested and that the uprising had to be called off. Charles again refused to take decisive action. Instead, he sent an agent to London with instructions to mediate between his supporters and then went himself secretly to a freezing, snow-swept Zeeland in order to be ready to sail for England as soon as success was reported.

Disaster was all that ensued. Ludicrous rumours reached him that Yorkshire was in arms, that a string of towns between Exeter and Newcastle had risen, that Fairfax had declared for him and, most ridiculous of all, that Oliver Cromwell was dead. In fact, the little pockets of conspiracy in Leicestershire, Staffordshire and the north collapsed. In the west one Colonel John Penruddock entered Salisbury, but his initiative was soon suppressed by a government keen to make examples of the twelve men it executed. It then imposed military rule across England. The country was divided into eleven districts, each of which was commanded by a major-general who was to be a pattern of godly behaviour and vigorously enforce laws against drunkenness, blasphemy, theatrical performances and so on. Penruddock's revolt having convinced him that he had been in error when he tried to conciliate his enemies, Cromwell was trying once again to enforce the rule of the Saints, declaring that those who attempted to overthrow the Protectorate or were known supporters of Charles would be gaoled or exiled. This was Cromwell's most unpopular experiment. The swelling of the militia it involved was disliked, the 'decimation' tax levied on Royalist sympathisers brought salt to wounds that might have healed, while the poor standing of the major-generals themselves made them widely despised.

To deepen Charles's personal embarrassment, Lucy Walter had now turned up in Cologne with their son and was clearly desperate for money. On 11 January 1655, Charles had signed a warrant providing her with a pension of £415 a year, which was to be paid at Antwerp so as to keep her as far as possible from the court. Four months later, Charles's sister was writing to him saying that Lucy 'thinks of another husband', by which time Lucy herself had settled in The Hague. Charles despatched Lord Taaffe to tell her that he would send her money when he could afford it and also to inform her that she should live somewhere less public since her presence in the Dutch capital was doing harm to his reputation.

Indeed, such was Charles's concern that by the beginning of 1656 he felt obliged to employ Daniel O'Neill – known familiarly as 'Infallible Subtle' – as a secret agent to investigate matters and determine whether he should now insist on having custody of the child. O'Neill uncovered a morass of squalor. 'Every idle action of hers', he wrote of Lucy, 'brings your Majesty upon the stage.' Lucy's affair with the married Thomas Howard (a Cromwellian double-agent) was creating so much scandal among the proper burghers of The Hague that the Orangists wanted her removed as soon as possible. Meanwhile, her maid was blackmailing her by threatening not only to spread the story of her adulterous liaison far and wide, but to tell tales of two self-induced abortions. O'Neill was unsure whether this last rumour was true, but he was horrified when a desperate Lucy suggested to him that they solve the problem of the maid by running a needle through the woman's ear and into her brain while she was asleep. O'Neill managed to put a stop to that, but, when Lucy reminded him that the King had promised her money, he wrote to Charles begging him not to send her any since it was clear that the woman would only fritter it away and then ask for more. He also advised the King that if he were really prepared to recognise young James as his son it would be as well to get the boy away from his mother as quickly as possible. The infant was living in a lewd household and his education had been scandalously neglected. 'He cannot be safe from his mother's intrigues wheresoever he is,' O'Neill declared. 'It is a great pity so pretty a child should be in such hands as hitherto have neglected to teach him to read or to tell twenty though he hath a great deal of wit and a great desire to learn.'[20]

These personal problems took place against a background of deepening poverty. With Charles's pensions still irregularly paid at best, Hyde wrote of 'insupportable debts', and the King was on occasions reduced to a single course at mealtimes, while once, for ten days in succession, he had to do without meat.[21] The sufferings of his followers only made the feeling of hopelessness worse. 'Wonder not at my silence,' wrote the elderly Lord Norwich, 'for I have been dull, lame, cold, out of money, clothes and what not, since that my only coat was not quite burnt off, when it was desperately singed, even to such a degree as I was forced to cut it.'[22] Even Cromwell's spies felt a flicker of pity for these people. 'How they will all live God knows!' wrote one. 'I am sure I do not!'[23] Small incidents deepened the gloom. The King wrote to Anthony Ashley Cooper (a man who would later play an important and controversial role in his life) saying that this brilliant young man would surely realise 'how unsettled all things must be, till I am restored to that which belongs to me, which would restore peace to the nation'.[24] But the small and delicate Cooper, whose subtle mind veered with every change of wind, had for the moment thrown in his lot with the Parliamentary cause and never answered Charles's letter. For the moment, the future clearly lay elsewhere.

Charles's misfortunes were made worse by changes in the international situation. For some years the English government had refused to intervene openly in the war between France and Spain. Both sides regarded Cromwellian England as a strong and useful ally, and in 1655 Cromwell decided to force the issue by taking his own initiative. Declining for the moment to agree an alliance with France, he sent his victorious warships to the West Indies, where they seized Spanish Jamaica. The English court in exile saw a golden opportunity opening before them. Approaches were made to Spain, but the tortuous course of Spanish diplomacy ensured that nothing came of these for some time. The fact that Cromwell refused to hand Jamaica back nonetheless stirred the French to action, and Mazarin sent an envoy to London to negotiate an Anglo-French treaty of friendship. One of its clauses stipulated that Henrietta Maria, as a daughter of the French royal family, should remain in France and that her dangerous eldest son should never again be granted shelter there. With France and Holland thus closed to him, Charles appeared to have lost that most vital of strategic advantages: a Channel port from which to launch any effort he might make to regain his throne.

The coastal towns of the Spanish Netherlands (present-day Belgium) alone remained a possibility, and many of the advisers around the King, including the over-enthusiastic Irish Jesuit Peter Talbot, urged him to travel to Brussels. A secret conversion to Catholicism would, Talbot argued, secure any deal with the Spanish that Charles wished to make. This advice was wisely ignored and, instead, careful preparations were made to impress the haughty Spanish with the dignity of the English cause. Ormonde was despatched to Brussels to give the negotiations the required air of patrician dignity, but they took a long while coming to nothing until the Spanish King, learning that Cromwell was readying yet another powerful fleet, granted his viceroy in the Netherlands leave to treat on his behalf. The Spaniards now made it a condition that Charles should come to Brussels without his counsellors, hoping that a desperate and unadvised young man would be easy to manipulate. Certainly, Charles himself was both wary and anxious to impress the Spaniards. He asked Ormonde to get him a Spanish New Testament so that he could acquire at least a smattering of their language. Knowing too that extreme punctiliousness governed Spanish etiquette, he wrote to Hyde regretting that he did not have with him the older man's guide to the correct forms of address.

Aware of his disadvantages, Charles travelled to Brussels in disguise, but was forced to retire to a nearby village when his presence became known. It took three weeks to frame a treaty, the terms of which showed that the King's experience with the Scots had schooled him in the hard-faced subtleties of international diplomacy. Here was no abject surrender, no weak-kneed concessions to impossible terms. Charles agreed to hand Jamaica back to the Spanish when he regained his throne. He also promised to try and prevent English privateering off the coasts of South America. He agreed to suspend the penal laws against the English Catholics, and to lend Spain warships with which to recover Portugal. In return, the Spaniards offered him 6000 fully paid soldiers who would serve as the core of the King's effort to regain his throne.

These men would be given their orders once his followers had secured an English port where they could land.

It seemed at last that the years in the wilderness might be over, but it soon became apparent that the alliance was riddled with misunderstandings. The Spaniards expected Charles to return to Cologne after the negotiations, from where he would encourage the Royalists to rise up and seize an English port. He would do no such thing. The difficulty and expense of organising anything from Cologne were all too familiar. Instead, determined to wring every possible advantage from the present situation, Charles lingered in Brussels until encouraged to move himself and his court to Bruges, where the Spanish agreed to pay him a pension of 3000 écus a month, his French allowance having now naturally evaporated. Only his household plate and linen remained behind in Cologne as security for his debts. But Bruges, for all its prettiness, proved to be a backwater and it was from there, as he walked beside the modest canals and listened to the persistent pealing of the bells, that Charles was obliged to watch the erosion of his hopes.

Having first spent time living at the home of Thomas Preston, an Irish loyalist, the King moved into an agreeable house in the Rue Haute. From here he could organise the duties great and small expected of a monarch in exile: visiting the English convent, for example, and being made patron of the archery Guilds of St George and St Sebastian. He was also trailed by the inevitable Parliamentarian spies, who sent back exaggerated reports of debauched Royalist life. Bruges was a place of 'fornication, drunkenness and debauchery', they declared.[25] This may have been true for some of the King's courtiers, but Charles himself, sunk in a deepening melancholy as his plans came to nothing, quietly slept with his new mistress, the lovely Catherine Pegge. By her he had an illegitimate daughter who died, and a son who was somewhat unimaginatively named Charles Fitzcharles. Another daughter, Charlotte Fitzroy, was fathered on Elizabeth Killigrew, and Charles also appears to have courted the independent-minded Henrietta Catherine of Orange with a mixture of political intent and genuine admiration. Women of forceful character had now established themselves as his principal erotic choice, and while he bought the Princess such small gifts as he could afford – pairs of gloves from Paris, for example – he wrote to Taaffe boasting that he thought the lady 'the worthiest to be lov'd of all the sex'.[26]

This was not a sentiment that could be applied to Lucy Walter, who was fast sinking into moral and physical decline, undone by the hardships of her insecure existence and the destructive traits in her own temperament. Having made life in The Hague too difficult for herself and those around her, she decided to return to England, taking her son James and his sister with her. Cromwell's agents promptly arrested her, describing her as 'the Wife or Mistress' of the King, and thus a valuable prize.[27] Lucy was kept in prison for two weeks and closely questioned, after which Cromwell decided it would serve his purposes best to release her amid publicity designed to suggest his magnanimity. Having discredited Charles as the 'pious charitable Prince' who squandered his money on such women as this, he ordered that Charles's 'lady of pleasure and the young heir' be freed by his officers, who were to 'set them on the shore in Flanders'. This, it was alleged, was 'no ordinary courtesy', and by the following month Lucy was in Brussels.[28]

The irate and worried King was now determined to wrest his son from Lucy's grasp and he arranged for James and Lucy herself to be lodged in the house of his agent Sir Arthur Slingsby. Slingsby was ordered 'in a quiet and silent way, if it could be, to get the child out of the mother's hands'.[29] This was not a role with which he could be trusted. When Lucy failed to pay for her keep, Slingsby tried to have her arrested. Lucy ran weeping and screaming into the street, clutching James to her bosom. The passers-by were at once on the side of the distressed mother, and Slingsby made matters worse by declaring that he was acting on behalf of the English King. This provoked such an uproar that the Governor of Brussels was forced to intervene and Charles, desperate to avoid a diplomatic incident, could only agree in embarrassment as his erstwhile mistress was found new accommodation in the house of Lord Castlehaven.

Charles employed the stately Ormonde to explain the situation to the Governor of Brussels, and Ormonde's letter, with its references to 'those wild and disgraceful courses' Lucy had taken, suggests how exasperated with her Charles and those nearest to him had become. A tone of strained decency characterised the letter as Ormonde hinted how all concerned in the issue wished that Lucy would quietly disappear. 'Besides the obligation it will be to the King,' he wrote, 'it will also be a great charity to the child, and in the conclusion to the mother, if she shall now at length retire herself to such a way of living as may redeem in some measure the reproach her past ways have brought upon her.' Should Lucy refuse, the penalty would be harsh. 'If she consents not to this,' Ormonde continued with words clearly designed to be repeated in Lucy's ear, 'she will add to all her former follies a most unnatural one in reference to her child, who by her obstinacy will be exposed to all the misery and reproach that must attend her, when neither of them is any further cared for or owned by His Majesty.' Those who helped Lucy in these circumstances would be doing an 'injury' to Charles, and 'supporting' her would be 'in mad disobedience to his pleasure'.[30]

Faced with such bullying as this, an ailing Lucy resolved on a final attack. She vowed that she would publish all Charles's letters to her. The ever useful O'Neill suggested Slingsby get hold of these as quickly as possible, while Charles responded by sending his agent Edward Prodgers to Brussels to remove the boy from his mother's care as deftly as he could. Lucy was well aware of the dangers surrounding her and made yet another public scene when Prodgers tried to spirit the boy away. The contest was too much for her all the same and eventually, exhausted and ill, she submitted to the inevitable and surrendered James to his father, who, in turn, placed him in the care of the newly elevated Baron Crofts of Little Saxham. Henceforth, the boy would be known as James Crofts. To make up for the deficiencies in his education, he was sent to Paris to attend the Jansenist school at Port-Royal. Lucy herself meanwhile, in her last flourish of desperation, followed the boy to France where, some time at the close of 1658 she died 'of a disease incident to her profession'.[31] Her legacy nonetheless remained: a pretty boy who was to be a source of deep anguish to his father.

While attending to these painful personal matters, Charles was also trying to persuade King Philip's representatives in the Spanish

Netherlands – his illegitimate son Juan-José, the formidable diplomat Don Alonso de Cardeñas and the brilliant young soldier the Marquis of Caracena – to fulfil expectations which the terms of his treaty with Spain had never actually guaranteed. For instance, Charles wanted the seaports of the Spanish Netherlands opened to those ships that recognised his authority, for in such ways he could raise money through privateering which would then be used to launch his invasion force. He also wanted to be allowed to muster his own army on the coasts, and he tried to persuade the Spanish to pay for this. Finally, he urged the Spaniards to make the invasion of England so important a priority that they would consider carrying it out even before he had secured an English port where they could land.

The Spaniards were diffident in the face of such youthful ardour. What was a major matter for Charles was a minor consideration for them, and they did not wish to be seen as too closely supporting the Stuart cause since this would hamper any peace they might subsequently be able to negotiate with Cromwell. But reasons other than politics were also persuasive. The Spanish treasury was all but empty and, while King Philip was obliged to dine on rancid meat, his hugely expensive armies were over-extended across many fronts, even as Cromwell's navy destroyed one of the silver fleets that was bringing much-needed bullion from the Americas to Spain. To subsidise Charles to the extent he expected was clearly impossible, and, as he began to assemble his army, military developments made the possibility of employing Spanish soldiers in his attempt to seize his throne ever more remote. A brilliant campaign led by Juan-José and Caracena ensured that the French army was so soundly beaten that the Spanish Netherlands could now be protected by a much reduced force, and the surplus soldiers were sent to fight in Spain's struggle with Portugal. Charles's allies now commanded a much diminished army in the area, and it seemed that he was being outmanoeuvred on every front.

Disappointment only increased his resolution. Charles saw it as ever more essential to muster his own force, and the most obvious supply of men was that band of Royalists fighting as mercenaries in the armies of France. These soldiers included the Duke of York, and when James was commanded to attend the King at Bruges he reluctantly appeared with over a hundred men. In addition, the Irish sent him hundreds of soldiers, and the combined ranks were so swollen by English and Scottish Royalists that by March 1656 Charles had some 2500 men at his disposal. The Duke of York was appointed Lieutenant-General, but the presence of so many soldiers billeted in a foreign country was a logistical nightmare. Frequent difficulties arose. While Hyde was happy to grumble about Spanish incompetence, some English officers falsified the lists of men under their command and pocketed the spare cash that this produced. The local people meanwhile looked on appalled at what they could only think of as the barbaric dress and behaviour of Charles's Scots and Irish soldiers especially. They were quick to blame them for the robbery of a church, and Cromwell's spies concurred with this disapproval. 'Of all the armies in Europe,' wrote one, 'there is none wherein is so much debauchery as in these few forces which the said King hath gotten together.'[32]

Charles at first believed that he should land his motley army in Scotland, either to divert Cromwell away from south-east England where he could then land an invasion force, or as a means of encouraging the Scots themselves to revolt. Juan-José wisely advised against this, and spies reported that there was no enthusiasm for an uprising in Scotland. Cardeñas then suggested assassinating Cromwell himself, but when an agent called Sexby arrived in the Spanish Netherlands and offered his services he proved so unpopular that Charles refused to have anything to do with him. The whole position was becoming exceedingly embarrassing, and to keep up his credit with the Spaniards Charles was required to bluff and lie.

This was the strategy of a desperate man. Charles let it be known that what were in reality the fragmented, disillusioned members of the Royalist underground in England were so well organised that an uprising was sure to take place before the Christmas of 1656. The Spaniards were prepared to believe him and to continue supporting his troops, but when Christmas came and went Charles felt obliged to complain to the Spaniards that it was their fault no uprising had occured and that the soldiers they now promised him were too few for success.

He followed this by asking that the Spaniards pay him immediately for another revolt which was sure to take place the following winter. But by now the Spanish treasury was so depleted that all the Spaniards themselves could do was to continue talking with Charles's advisers in the hope that funds might eventually arrive from Spain. When at last they came, they were wholly inadequate even for the needs of the Spanish army, and Charles sent a resentful memorandum to Juan-José blaming him once again for the failure of the plans to invade England and suggesting that one last attempt be made the following November. Charles himself meanwhile remained in Brussels trying to co-ordinate these efforts, but by now it was clear that even some of the members of the Sealed Knot were double-agents, and it became necessary for the King to lie once again about the probable success of a winter uprising.

But by this time profound changes were again taking place in England itself. Early in 1657, Parliament presented a remonstrance to Cromwell and followed it with the Humble Petition and Advice, which proposed that the Protectorate be made hereditary – that Cromwell should in fact be king. Strong and complex currents had carried men towards this idea. Not just the Protector's failing health and the discovery of plots against his life persuaded them. More and more people had grown resentful of the military regime, fearful of the godly, embittered by the efforts to inflict the New Jerusalem, and tired of continuous experiments with constitutional reform. While the unpolitical many longed for a quiet life, leading Parliamentary intellectuals argued that only a monarchical government – the old form – could bring this about. Even the exiled Hyde could see the soundness of this position. It was the institution of monarchy that the people loved, he believed, the office rather than the man. Cromwell, strong at home and undefeated abroad, seemed the natural as well as the ideal choice. The only question was whether he would accept the title. In the end he refused the name of king – 'a gaudy feather in the cap of authority' as he called it – but accepted the role, believing its adoption to be essential if he were to avoid a wrangling Parliament that might refuse to raise the money and troops he needed to defend the country against any invasion launched by Charles.

There was little real likelihood of this. The chronic lack of means and the cruelty of the preceding winter had already worked their damage on Royalist morale. Rochester had died, while even Buckingham now decided to desert what appeared a hopeless cause, leaving the friend of his boyhood and returning to England, where he married the heiress of General Fairfax. Meanwhile, the exiled King himself could not even find the money to get his washing done. Hyde noted that 'every bit of meat, every drop of drink, all the fire and all the candle that hath been spent' had been acquired on account 'and to get credit for a week or more is no easy matter'.[33] It seemed that only 'some extraordinary act of providence' could redeem the embittered Royalist cause. But for this they would have to wait, because events seemed to be removing all hope.[34] In the summer of 1658, a combined army of the French and the Parliamentarians defeated the Spanish at the Battle of the Dunes. This resulted in Dunkirk being handed over to the victorious English, and Charles, in a state of the bitterest disillusion, retreated close to the Dutch border and it was there, on 10 September 1658, while he was playing tennis at Hoogstraten, that Sir Stephen Fox suddenly approached him with news of the most remarkable kind. A week earlier, on the anniversary of his victory at the Battle of Worcester, Oliver Cromwell had died.

9

'A King! A King!'

The public mourning for Cromwell was ostentatiously royal. A darkened room in Somerset House was opened to the public, and a long procession of the curious filed slowly past an effigy of the Protector that was suitably draped in heavy black velvet. After a decent interval of two months, the black covering was replaced with crimson and the wax image was adorned with a sceptre and crown before being placed upright on the catafalque to be illuminated by the flickering light of five hundred candles. On 23 November 1658, the hearse was borne in procession to Westminster Abbey with a medieval pageantry of hooded mourners, black-draped horses, lowered banners and the slow, funereal beating of military drums. The poet Andrew Marvell wrote that the public wandered like ghosts about the Protector's tomb, blinded with tears. But the reaction of many was, in truth, very different. John Evelyn sardonically recorded that only the dogs wept. Mud was thrown at Cromwell's escutcheon, while the 'graver sort' contemplated 'the happy days approaching'.[1]

Those days were slow to come. It would be nineteen months before Charles was restored to his throne, and for much of that period the outcome of events was extremely doubtful. Certainly, Charles himself was by now too well schooled in adversity to make a dash for his throne, borne on by the fantasy that the people of England would welcome him with acclamations and open arms after the long night of Puritanism. He sought instead to root his aspirations in the more solid ground of a shrewd marriage. Charles renewed his pursuit of Princess Henriette Catherine of Orange. He addressed her a lovesick letter via her formidable mother in which he first made plain that he would prefer to be restored to his kingdom with the help of the Dutch above all other people. He then went on to ask her whether the Princess was free to accept his proposal and enquired how he might most tactfully go about presenting it. The Princess fainted when she was shown the letter and had to be put to bed, but, while her interest in Charles appears to have been genuine, politics ensured that her feelings were disappointed.

The day after his father's death, Richard Cromwell officially succeeded to the Protectorship, and by the end of September 1659 the little court in exile had learned that the greater part of England supported him. General Monck had 'cheerfully proclaimed' Richard as the new Protector in Scotland, while the rulers of Europe were resolved to continue relations with England as before. Such news was devastating, and Hyde recorded that 'the King's condition never appeared so hopeless, so desperate'.[2] Charles refused to despair. Ormonde was despatched to Princess Henriette Catherine's mother with a formal offer of marriage, but this was civilly declined and the rejected suitor had now to endure the darkest days of his exile.

For all the delight at Cromwell's death, the news coming from England told of a country that was settled, quiet and at peace with itself. The Cromwellian dynasty appeared strong, and the tranquillity it brought smothered Royalist hopes of insurrection. Meanwhile, Charles himself had to endure abject poverty. His Spanish allowance had not been paid for four months and the ragged, shiftless King was obliged to sell his plate and eat his meagre daily meal off a plain trencher. Those around him watched as he grew thin and increasingly irritable. 'He has not', declared one courtier, 'the least good nature left.'[3] And it was just such observers who now increased the King's wretchedness. While Charles himself behaved with stoic self-possession, his disillusioned followers descended into riot. One day a serious struggle broke out on a tennis court, and the angry and drunken courtiers were separated only when the Dukes of York and Gloucester interposed. So concerned were they by the incident that they reported it to the King, who summoned the culprits before him that evening. All Charles could do however when the sordid details were made clear was to order the offenders to be locked in their rooms without food, for all the world like naughty little boys. The quarrel was made up the following day and apologies were made, but it was becoming increasingly clear that, as one of Charles's followers declared, 'if we continue longer as we are, we must perish'.[4]

As so often in his life, Charles's fate was changed not by his own efforts but by the activities and circumstances of others. For all that the people of England had quietly accepted Richard Cromwell as their Protector, rifts were widening below the surface of national life. The army was seeking political power and was also insisting that Richard actively promote godliness in the military by choosing pious officers who would attend to the reformation of manners and the protection of peaceful religious minorities. Frequent prayer-meetings suggested that there was a strong current of unrest, and the situation was contained only when Richard summoned a great meeting of the officers at which he stressed his loyalty to their aims and surrendered his control of military matters in most areas save the all-important business of appointing senior personnel. Such difficulties were then compounded by the continuing problem of debt. For all the naval victories won by Cromwell's fleet in its struggle with the Dutch, the war itself had been widely unpopular and ruinously expensive. Spanish privateers threatened British trade, while the navy failed to capture sufficient booty to pay its own costs. Despite heavy taxation, there was a serious shortfall in government revenue and this in turn assured that arrears of pay in the army continued to mount. When public accounts were finally drawn up, it was discovered that the government was over £2 million in debt and that its credit was virtually non-existent. The only resort was to call a session of Parliament which would authorise a massive increase in taxation.

When the disastrous state of the nation's finances was revealed to them, the Members were thrown into confusion. Senior officers in the army demanded that Parliament be dissolved, and when this was refused the military retaliated by rallying round London. Richard was left with a mere two hundred men to stand against the thousands gathered at St James's Palace. His defeat was clear and, while soldiers began looting the wine cellars of Whitehall, Richard himself agreed to the dissolution of Parliament. The embattled Protector was fast becoming 'Tumble-Down Dick' and, at the urging of the army, Parliament voted to pay his debts and pension in return for his signing an agreement by which he promised to retire from public life and live in peaceful seclusion. The experiment of the Protectorate was at an end, but by the summer of 1659 the various sources of discontent in the country were so inflamed that many feared the outbreak of widespread violence.

It was tempting for the little court in exile to exploit such conditions, but Hyde urged extreme caution and hoped that the King would 'not be prevailed with to do any sudden thing'.[5] He believed that the current regime in England would soon collapse and counselled Charles and those about him to refrain from 'hurting themselves upon projects'.[6] Besides they had, he believed, a powerful if unlikely ally waiting in the wings. With great strategic insight, Hyde and some of those close to him had fixed their eyes on General Monck, the commander of the Protectorate forces in Scotland. Here was the man who might yet effect the restoration of the King. It was believed that Monck was 'not absolutely averse to it, neither in his principles nor in his affections'. Quite as importantly, he 'commands, absolutely at his devotion, a better army . . . than there is in England'. Such a figure would have to be handled with extreme care. Monck was 'a sullen man that values himself enough, and must believe that his knowledge and reputation in arms fit him for the title of Highness and office of Protector'. It was essential that he be prevented from launching a personal coup. Gentle persuasion would have to be used 'to show him plainly, and to give him all imaginable security for it, that he shall better fit all his ends, those of honour, power, profit, safety, with the King than in any other way he can take'. As to the means such a man should employ to restore Charles to his throne, those must be entirely chosen by Monck himself. The

King and his courtiers were not to 'boggle' at anything proposed, 'so it oppose the present power'.[7]

Despite such advice, the little court in exile rapidly became implicated in abortive uprisings. Charles was visited in May 1659 by John Mordaunt, an irrepressible Royalist zealot who had now come up with a daring but seemingly workable scheme by which pockets of Royalist sympathisers across the country would rise simultaneously and then co-operate in a massive onslaught on the government. By the middle of June, Mordaunt believed that his forces were ready, and at the close of the month Charles wrote to him assuring him: 'I do therefore resolve that myself or one of my brothers, or both of us will (with God's blessing) be with you as soon as you shall desire.'[8] It seemed that an end to inaction might at last have come, and Charles decided that he would sail from Brittany and cross seas controlled by the Commonwealth navy in order to offer the rebels his personal support.

Familiar problems bedevilled the scheme. Its supporters were over-optimistic and divided among themselves. The sheer number of men involved resulted in a fatal loss of secrecy, and a double-agent was at work. The government acted quickly, arresting known leaders and seizing caches of arms. For the most part the uprisings collapsed in pitiful and frightened muddle. Only Sir George Booth proved himself an effective leader, gaining control of the greater part of Cheshire along with areas of Lancashire. Nonetheless, when the Parliamentary army under John Lambert advanced on him, Booth was obliged to escape disguised as a woman. Foolishly asking an innkeeper for a razorblade, he was reported, arrested, committed to the Tower and charged with treason. Royalist hopes had once again collapsed, and Jermyn wrote that the news from England was now 'not only worse than we looked for, but even as ill as we could have imagined'.[9]

Every attempt to encourage uprisings in England had ended in failure and Charles now resolved on an altogether more ambitious plan. France and Spain were currently concluding a peace treaty, and Charles hoped that by negotiating personally with their representatives he might obtain not only recognition of his status as a legitimate European monarch but their combined aid in helping him to regain his throne.

To achieve this it was essential that he deal personally with Cardinal Mazarin, and Charles wrote to his mother asking for her assistance. Despite the fact that they had not seen each other for five years, Henrietta Maria, who was still deeply upset by her oldest son's behaviour towards the Duke of Gloucester, agreed to do what she could. Ormonde was sent to further the King's appeal, but, when he finally obtained an interview with Mazarin, the Cardinal told him there was nothing he himself could do. He then gave it as his opinion that it would be extremely unwise for Charles to travel to Spain and try to take part in the negotiations. To emphasise his disapproval, he refused to grant him a safe conduct through France.

Nothing daunted, Charles set out for Spain in disguise, taking with him only Lord Digby and O'Neill. The entire trip, which was conducted in a most leisurely manner, took three months. The King went first to La Rochelle, where he waited a week for a favourable wind; then, changing his mind, he decided to travel by public coach into Spain. A worried and angry Hyde received occasional letters from his master describing the excellent food and inns along the road, and hinting at the 'pleasant accidents' he encountered on the way. 'God keep you,' Charles concluded, 'and send you to eat as good mutton as we have every meal.'[10] When the King arrived in Spain, the resident Spanish ambassador greeted him with ostentatious courtesy, kneeling in the road to kiss his hand and escorting him to his lodgings to the salute of guns. However, there was little he could do to help. The presence of Mazarin ensured that only the vaguest promises of assistance were forthcoming, and when Charles himself, in an attempt to appease the great powers, caused consternation in Protestant Europe by attending mass, Hyde had to assure the English Royalists that the King was still loyal to his faith. The gravest concern had been aroused to no purpose, and Charles was finally told that his presence was no longer required and that he should return to his exiled court.

Only a letter from Hyde saved him from despair. His own initiatives had failed to secure him any advantage, but Hyde's powerful insights into the political situation in England were now proving their worth. General Monck had indeed declared for the King and was even, it appeared, readying himself to treat with him. Hyde begged Charles to return as quickly as possible, and the King duly set out. As his journey continued, so strange omens seemed to support his hopes. Ormonde received a letter telling him that in London a three-day-old child had cried out: 'A King! A King! Bring me to the King!' The cry was apparently repeated several times, and when the miraculous infant was given some money and asked 'What would you do with it?' the reply came that it should be given to Charles.[11]

Charles himself hurried on to Colombes, where there was a tearful reunion with his mother and, more importantly, a meeting with his youngest sister, the fourteen-year-old Henriette Anne. The encounter released in Charles a deep and surprising spring of brotherly love. For nearly a decade he had been an exile, living at a distance not only from his country but from his family. His mother had exasperated him, his brothers York and Gloucester were often tiresome, his love affairs had been largely casual or, in the case of Lucy Walter, a painful embarrassment. Now this little girl – thin and with one shoulder higher than the other – brought out all his capacity for affection, and this was a gift that Henriette Anne returned with abundance. The bond that formed between brother and sister became as important to the King's emotional life as it would eventually be to his political fortunes. Here was a member of his family he could confide in with absolute trust. Soon, in the numerous letters they were to exchange, Henriette Anne would be his 'dear dear sister' and he would be begging her not to put too many 'majesties' in her correspondence with him, 'for I do not wish that there should be anything between us but friendship'.[12] Now however, after just a fortnight, they would have to part. Events in England were at last summoning Charles to his throne.

The strained relationship between the recalled Rump Parliament and the army reached its crisis when some of the officers in the force that Lambert had led to victory against Booth addressed a petition to the House of Commons listing their grievances about cash and godliness. When the petition reached Westminster it was read behind closed doors, and, in the atmosphere of conspiracy created, hostility against the militia flared. The army tried to muster further support for its complaints, and the frightened House cashiered the men who had signed the petition. An aggrieved Lambert summoned his troops, and the House was once again occupied by the army. But the unplanned coup left its leaders confused. They had acted in self-defence, and now they appeared to be in charge of the country. They proposed that a Committee of Safety should run the government, and it was while the commission for this was being drawn up that events took yet another wholly unexpected but decisive turn. A letter arrived from Scotland signed by General Monck. In this he utterly condemned the actions of his fellow officers and declared that he and his troops stood for the expelled MPs.

For all that he was still unsure about the role of the monarchy, there was no question in Monck's mind that a return to parliamentary government was essential, and popular opinion was on his side. The London apprentices were expressing vehement opposition to the overthrow of Parliament and launched a petition which by the start of December had been signed by some 20,000 people. The Committee of Safety tried to ban its presentation to the City authorities, but it was carried in triumph through the streets to Guildhall, while the proclamation banning it was read by the leader of a troop of horse from the Exchange. There was uproar. Soldiers were sent in to restore order, but when they were pelted with stones and ice they lost their tempers and fired on the crowd. A few of the protesters were killed, several were wounded, and the following day a coroner declared that the dead youths had been murdered. Large-scale unrest in the capital seemed assured, and as Monck began his slow march southwards, so the greater part of the country declared for parliamentary government. By the time the General arrived in the capital, the young Samuel Pepys was recording in his newly begun diary, 'Boys do now cry "Kiss my Parliament" instead of "Kiss my arse" so great and general contempt is the Rump come to among all men, good and bad.'[13]

Monck wrote to the House demanding that it issue writs for an election within the week and then dissolve. The move was immensely popular. Bonfires blazed across the city (Pepys counted thirty-one of them) and, as church bells rang out in defiant cacophony, people roasted great rumps of beef in a vivid display of their feelings. Someone showed Pepys an illicit Lion and Unicorn painted on the back of a chimney, and now, in the streets, people were beginning to 'talk loud of the king'.[14] Ormonde accurately caught the mood of the country when he wrote to Jermyn telling him that 'the general disposition of the people . . . seems to promise great advantages to the king; four parts of five of the whole people besides the nobility and gentry, being devoted to him'.[15]

Charles himself determined to act with caution and charm, presenting himself in the most favourable possible light, even while trying to ensure that he was gaining his own advantage. Here was the style of the mature man. He wrote to General Monck in a tone at once diplomatic and personal. 'I know too well the power you have to do me good or harm, not to desire you should be my friend,' he declared.[16] Here was a sentence perfectly adjusted to a most delicate situation, and the General resolved to open secret talks. A messenger was sent to Brussels with assurances of Monck's interest and the strongly expressed conviction that Charles should move away from that conspicuously Spanish and Roman Catholic city. The King, along with Hyde and Ormonde, accepted that this was sound advice and so, telling the Spanish that he intended visiting his sister, Charles moved his court to Dutch and Protestant Breda.

It was there that Charles and his Council composed two documents of the greatest interest. The first was a letter to the Speaker, and thus to the House of Commons as a whole. The other was the so-called Declaration of Breda. Both were designed to reassure the nation and re-establish a sense of continuity and tradition. Both documents were also careful to appeal to the contemporary belief that history, rather than being largely a matter of chance and accident, was controlled by the hand of Providence. The forthcoming restoration of the King was to be considered not a man-made matter but an act of God. Faith, reconciliation and tradition were shown as the means of ensuring civil order, and to pave the way for this last Charles offered 'a free and general pardon' to all the enemies of the house of Stuart save those whom Parliament chose to except.[17]

This emphasis on parliamentary authority was carefully insisted upon. 'We do assure you upon our royal word', Charles wrote in his letter to the speaker, 'that none of our predecessors have had a greater esteem for Parliaments than we have, in our judgement, as well as from our obligation.' He went on, 'we do believe them to be so vital a part of the constitution of the kingdom, and so necessary for the government of it we well know that neither Prince nor people can in any tolerable degree be happy without them'. Such words were at best a questionable overstatement. No mention at all was made of the King's traditional prerogative powers, but this was a time for healing rather than division. Members of Parliament had to be courted, and 'therefore you may be confident that we shall always look upon their counsels as the best we can receive, and shall be as tender of their privileges and as careful to preserve and protect them as of that which is most near to ourself and most necessary for our own preservation'.[18]

The country not only asked for peace, it demanded that its King parade before it in material splendour. But, when the Parliamentary Commissioners arrived at Breda, Charles's poverty was still painfully evident. His credit was so bad that it had proved impossible to order new finery, and the Commissioners were shocked to see how shabby Charles was, his clothes 'not being worth 40/- the best of them'.[19] The gift of a chest of sovereigns solved this difficulty, and the King and his immediate family at once summoned tailors. York ordered a suit brightly trimmed with yellow, Gloucester another of grey offset with red ribbons. Charles's courtiers would nearly always be dressed in brilliant pastel shades, but he himself, tall, saturnine and coarse-featured, his hair already slightly greying, knew that such gaudiness was inappropriate to both his looks and his role. Sombre colours suited him best. He had not yet discovered the fashion that he was to make his own – the long, closely fitting and richly embroidered coats that emphasised his height and, in a strange way, his self-contained isolation – but he knew that browns, puces and dark blues were most appropriate for him. Even now, those about him noted that 'the King seems a very sober man'.[20]

Such an image was necessary amid the mass of euphoric people that thronged about him. In addition to his brothers and Princess Mary, various dukes, ambassadors and the Dutch Stadholders came to wish Charles well. Large numbers of his own subjects also arrived to offer their congratulations and squeeze what they could out of the expected royal bounty. Charles received them with that sharp-eyed insight into others' self-interest that had now become second nature to him. His was no innocent gratitude, and the small details of his conduct at this time suggest that for all the general sense of euphoria he was determined to be wary and to give his allegiance to no one group. His bearing suggested that he wanted to be the king of a nation rather than the leader of a faction. Besides, for all the parliamentary overtures he had made in the Treaty of Breda, there remained the matter of his prerogative powers – the exceptional, unique position of the English monarchy itself. Time would show that Charles was not prepared to compromise this in any way at all. Now was not the occasion to make such feelings clear, but deeper than the public acclamation, more powerful and more remote, lay the ancient authority of kingship: Charles's undisputed right to summon, prorogue and dismiss his parliaments, to create peers, bishops and judges, to declare war and make peace, and to embody in himself the majesty of the state.

Even now he hinted at his sovereign independence. When a group of Royalists was granted an audience in his bedroom, he listened to their fervent protestations of loyalty and then asked for wine. He was served, as became a king, on bended knee, and, as he lifted the glass to his lips, he said with cold reserve: 'I drink to your health – for I am now even with you, having done as much for you as you have done for me.' As his visitors then bowed and left, Charles turned to his brother James and said: 'I am out of their debt.'[21] Other more simple and earnest men could be treated in a way that appealed to a streak of royal irony that was not without its cruel side. For all Charles's earnest protestations, a certain Mr Case, an elderly Presbyterian, was concerned about the King's religious beliefs. Had he become a Roman Catholic during his long exile amid the dangers of Europe? There was little point in trying to convince the man in a conversation, and some way altogether different had to be found. Mr Case must be made to feel privileged, allowed to think that he was a man with special insight, special access even to the state of the

royal soul. He was duly hidden in a closet from where he could listen to
His Majesty at prayer. 'O Lord,' the King began, 'since Thou art
pleased to restore me to the throne of my ancestors, grant me a heart
constant with the exercise and protection of the true Protestant religion.
Never may I seek the oppression of those who out of tenderness of their
consciences are not free to conform to outward and indifferent cere-
monies.'[22] A delighted Mr Case found this all very satisfactory. He was
a man invested with privileged knowledge of the great, and he went
back to his concerned companions exulting that 'God hath sent us a
religious King!'

Now it was time to make for The Hague. After a long, uncomfortable
voyage on a *jaght schip* or 'yacht', during which Princess Mary was
severely seasick, seventy-two coaches, each of them pulled by six
thoroughbred horses, carried the royal party towards that beautiful city.
They arrived at eleven in the morning of 16 May, and the glories of
the Mauruitshuis were at once thrown open for Charles's use. Money,
which a few weeks earlier had been so scarce, was now offered to the
King in extraordinary abundance. The Dutch, determined to woo the
monarch they had once shunned, presented him with £70,000, and then
redoubled their bounty by offering him a service of gold plate and a
great bed, its tapestried hangings wrought with gold and silver wire.
The English representatives then stepped forward. The Houses of
Parliament presented their king with £50,000 and their letters, a
humble Sir John Grenville reverently pronouncing the sacred syllables
of the word 'Majesty' which 'not long since was the aversion of varlets
and fanatics'.[23] Nor could the City of London be forgotten. Its representatives sent Charles £10,000 and were rewarded with a gracious
speech in which they were told that the King had always nourished
'a particular affection' for the capital, 'the place of my birth', a point
reinforced when he proceeded to knight the delegates.[24]

In such an atmosphere as this, even the black-gowned representatives
of the Presbyterian church could, for the moment at least, be greeted
with an appearance of generosity. The Elders approached the King with
their familiar gracelessness. 'We have always wished Your Majesty
very well,' they began and then got down at great length to the serious

business of the day. 'We are no enemies to moderate episcopacy,' they declared as a prelude to their convoluted, shame-faced appeal for the sort of toleration they had rarely extended to others. Charles, who had looked such men in the face too often to be other than cynical about their claims, answered with becoming tact. 'I have heard of your good behaviour,' he declared, 'and have no purpose to impose hard conditions on you. I have referred all differences to Parliament.' This was nothing less than the truth, and the Elders, feeling distinctly uncomfortable at the treatment they foresaw, decided on a direct appeal. Would His Majesty desist from using the Prayer Book? If a look of displeasure crossed the King's face, Charles shrewdly converted his anger into a speech designed to appeal to the greater part of those Englishmen listening to him. 'While I give you liberty,' he told the Elders, 'I will not have my own taken from me. I have always used that form of service, which I think the best in the world, and have never discontinued it in places where it is more disliked than I hope it is by you.'[25]

There followed a scene which probed more deeply into the ancient ritual and mystery of kingship. A number of sickly persons came forward to be 'touched' for scrofula, then known as the King's Evil. The symptoms of this disease were vividly noted by a contemporary when he described a young victim as being 'afflicted with a continual running of the most noisome matter in his neck, accompanied often with so great tumours and swellings about his throat, as almost choked him'.[26] It was widely believed that the only cure for such suffering was a touch from the King's own hand. The whole elaborate ceremony that surrounded this process was designed to emphasise the quasi-divine, sacramental powers of true monarchy. Charles, seated on his throne and dressed in his full regalia, was part magician and part priest. Miraculous power flowed through his fingers as doctors led the wretched sufferers before him and bade them kneel as his chaplain solemnly repeated the words: 'He put his hands upon them and healed them.' Charles then leaned forward and stroked the expectant, pleading faces. When he had caressed the last of the supplicants, they once again approached the throne and bowed their heads as Charles hung a gold coin on a blue ribbon about their necks, his chaplain meanwhile intoning, 'This is the true Light who came into the world.' The propaganda value of so strange a ceremony was immense, and it would later be said that during the course of his reign Charles 'touched' some 92,000 people for the King's Evil.

Such public displays were matched by a new and private obsession, the tone of which would colour much of the early part of Charles's reign. The woman was called Barbara Villiers and she had the sort of allure that Charles could not resist. Her slanting, slumberously lidded eyes and pouting mouth would soon make her an icon of Restoration female beauty, while her vivacious personality, so explicit in its appetites, so obviously driven by her libido, roused and challenged Charles in equal measure. Barbara had come to Holland with her husband, the unfortunate Roger Palmer, a man destined to be known merely as one of history's cuckolds. She had already grown bored with him and had also ended an affair with the promiscuous Lord Chesterfield. Now Barbara was looking for a new lover, and she found in Charles a virile, life-bitten man of thirty who could propel her to the very centre of power. Here was a king over whom she could exercise her ferociously domineering personality. How far the affair had developed by the time Charles was ready to leave for England may be judged from the letter he wrote to Palmer thanking him for his gift of £1000. 'You have', Charles wryly declared, 'more title than one to my kindness.'[27] For the moment, Palmer was blissfully unaware of what he meant.

By 23 May, the royal party was ready to depart. Accompanied by his secretary Samuel Pepys, Sir Edward Montagu, the King's 'General at Sea', readied the navy. The King would sail home on the *Naseby*, now hastily renamed the *Royal Charles*. Charles himself, accompanied by his brothers, rode down to Scheveningen, where the shore was blackened with a crowd of some 50,000 people. Welcoming rounds were fired from the ships' cannon, and when the royal party were safely on the deck they were taken to the gilded and tapestry-hung wardroom where lavish refreshments awaited. Pepys, seeing them seated there, declared it to be 'a blessed sight'. There then followed the King's parting from a tearful Princess Mary, 'which done', Pepys recalled 'we weighed anchor, and with a fresh gale and most happy weather, we set sail for England'.[28]

As Pepys continued to watch the King, he was amazed at how 'active and stirring' he was. After so many years of deprivation, Charles's near miraculous restoration tensed his muscles with excitement. Only walking seemed to bring him relief, and he paced the quarter-deck continuously, 'here and there, up and down'.[29] He was too much in the grip of his feelings even to take the ship's tiller, something which at any other time would have given him intense pleasure. Instead, his racing mind went back to the most dangerous days of his life and he began to regale those about him – including Pepys – with the story of his escape after the Battle of Worcester. In the moment of his triumph, Charles's mind went back to the days of hourly fear and lacerated feet, of quickly managed disguises and the quicker use of his wits. The King recalled how he had been forced to act as a serving man, how he had chaffed the blacksmith when Jane Lane's horse had to be reshod, how he had fooled the cook when he bungled the winding of a roasting jack. It was, of course, a marvellous story, and Pepys listened in amazement, his attention only momentarily diverted by the sight of King Charles's spaniels.

By nine in the morning of 25 May the watchman on the *Royal Charles* had sighted the English coast. Another six hours were to pass before the King's party could land, and Charles and his brothers beguiled the time as best they could, feasting on a seaman's breakfast of pork, pease pudding and boiled beef. The King then dressed in a suit of dark-coloured material, the sombreness of which was offset by the brilliant scarlet plume in his hat. Thus attired, he prepared to board the Admiral's barge at three that afternoon and walk on the soil of the land he could at last call his own. To the huge waiting crowd, their shouts almost drowned by the thunderous acclamation of the guns, the King's landing was a moment at once solemn and joyful, and they watched with intense satisfaction as Charles fell to his knees and gave thanks to God for his seemingly miraculous restoration. This was a gesture perfectly suited to the occasion. To the observing many it suggested humility and submission to Providence, but it also hinted at more. The years of rule by the godly had not brought the millennium a jot closer. Men had called themselves saints but had proved themselves all too human when in power. Now the nation had a legitimate king who was God's lieutenant on earth, a sanctified figure granted the ancient and quasi-mystical powers to heal, as well as being the head of a church which was for many the truest embodiment of the nation's Protestantism.

His prayer over, the King rose and walked towards the kneeling figure of General Monck. Bidding his political saviour rise, Charles kissed the man on both his cheeks and, while the mass of the people shouted 'God save the King!', greeted him with the simple, touching word: 'Father!' Then it was the turn of the Mayor of Dover to offer his congratulations. He walked steadily towards Charles, stopped, presented him with his staff and gave him a magnificent leather-bound and gold-tooled Bible. With a perfect sense of tact and drama, Charles accepted the volume, saying: 'It is the thing I love above all things in the world!'[30]

The royal party then moved on to Canterbury, where the difficulties underlying the restoration of the King first became apparent, for it was here that Monck presented Charles with a list of those men whose service he thought merited their being made members of the Privy Council. Folding the paper and putting it in his pocket, Charles told the General that he would always be ready to receive any advice from him 'which will not be prejudicial to my service'.[31] Unfortunately, when Charles came to read Monck's paper, he discovered that it contained the names of some forty Presbyterians or erstwhile rebels and only two Royalists. Since the King was, as he fully realised, still in the power of the General, it was extremely difficult to know what to do and, in the end, it was left to Hyde to handle the important, embarrassing task of disappointing the great man. The royal party then proceeded from Canterbury to Rochester, and on to Deptford, where Charles had the congenial task of watching a hundred young girls, dressed in white with blue headscarves, casting flowers and herbs before his horse. By the afternoon of 29 May – the anniversary of his thirtieth birthday – the King was ready for his triumphal procession into his capital.

Charles entered via Blackheath in an unprecedented display of power and pomp. At St George's Fields the Lord Mayor, accompanied by the Aldermen and the members of the livery companies, presented him with the City sword, while the Headmaster of St Paul's School presented yet another Bible. The seven-hour procession then made its way to Whitehall through streets that were strewn with flowers and hung with tapestries. Along the way from Temple Bar to the Strand ladies sat in the windows and on the balconies, trumpets blared, cannons roared and fountains ran with wine. The whole was a stupendous witness to the national mood of rejoicing noted by the Venetian ambassador. 'The change in the people here is indeed miraculous,' the ambassador wrote back to his Senate; 'the King's name is as much loved, revered and acclaimed as in past years it was detested and abused.'[32]

It was in this mood that the vast crowds flocking the streets first beheld the gilded royal coaches, the gentlemen in doublets of silver cloth, the servants in purple and green, and the 20,000 soldiers. Trumpeters, Lifeguards and heralds swelled these ranks, and even men of such measured intellect as the diarist John Evelyn were swept up in the general euphoria. The restoration of Charles II was, Evelyn declared, a miracle unprecedented since the Jews' return from the Babylonian captivity. The procession in which he took such delight was evidence, he believed, that history and the fate of the nation were in the Lord's hands. 'I stood in the Strand and beheld it,' Evelyn wrote, 'and blessed God.'[33]

The figure all the crowd was aching to see rode into his capital between his brothers. As so often, Charles's appearance was in contrast to the gaudiness about him. He was dressed in a dark suit offset only by the plume in his hat and the blue ribbon of the Garter on his chest. He gave nonetheless every appearance of affability. The ever observant Venetian ambassador wrote of Charles 'raising his eyes to the windows, looking at all, raising his hat to all, and greeting all who with loud shouts and a tremendous noise acclaimed the return of this great Prince, so abounding in virtues and distinguished qualities of every sort'.[34] Many others paid tribute to Charles's bearing, to his tall figure 'so exactly formed that the most curious eye cannot find any error in his shape'. Others again noted his 'quick and sparkling' gaze. Nonetheless, there were elements in the King's appearance that seemed to contradict this seeming joyfulness. Some of these were natural, others the effect of years of deprivation and secret bitterness. Charles's saturnine cast, his black hair and thick black eyebrows gave him an unavoidable hint of gravity and even severity, while those who could observe him closely noted the deep lines running down from his nose, past the ends of his pencil-line moustache, and so to his chin – the care-lines of a man who had often twisted his face in disappointment, suspicion and irony.

Even now, amid the hyperbole of public joy, there was a need for wariness. Although many might think that the wheel of history had at last come full circle, that sovereign power, in Hobbes's words, had passed 'through two usurpers, from the late King to this his son', the crowds of petitioners Charles had faced at The Hague and Monck's list of those men he wished to have preferred all suggested the greed, the rivalry and the partisanship that inevitably encircled a monarch. Charles was fully aware of this. He was too used by experience to be otherwise. That dark, sparkling gaze had seen so much violent change and the deceitfulness of too many men and women to believe that all would remain as joyous as the procession now made the world seem. In Bishop Burnet's words: 'he thinks the world is governed wholly by interests and indeed he has known so much of the baseness of mankind that no wonder if he has hard thoughts of them'.[35]

There were also more subtle reasons for irony. It was surely evident to Charles how small a part he had played in his own restoration. On the occasions when he had exerted himself and tried to regain his crown, the result had always been bloodshed, defeat and death. Now he had been bloodlessly willed into power by his own people, his single contribution having been the adroitness with which he had been able to present himself as the only credible alternative to the repeated failures of the Interregnum regimes. Charles had been restored not because of who he was but because of what he was: his country's legitimate monarch. He had been so long absent from that country however that he appeared in it now as a virtual stranger and as a man who would have to tread carefully if he were going to ensure his survival. There were necessary depths of wariness and even suspicion for the King in his triumph, and these partly justified the impression of the little boy who ran back from the procession to tell his father that Charles was 'a black grim man'.[36]

If there was a certain questioning cast in the King's glance, there were also weaknesses in his personality that in time would seriously threaten his rule. The dangers without were matched by dangers within. Some of these characteristics had already appeared, others would fully emerge only after Charles had taken possession of his crown. Although he was intermittently capable of intense hard work and concentration, Charles was a man who would increasingly show himself as easily distracted and indolent. Hyde had for years nagged him about his reluctance to seize on the details of administration, and even now that the King was thirty he was still prone to lecture him like a lazy schoolboy. Such indolence ran deep and was widely commented on. As Sir John Reresby remarked, Charles 'was not stirring or ambitious, but easy, loved pleasures and seemed chiefly to desire quiet and security for his own time'.[37]

Part of this love of pleasure showed itself in the men with whom Charles surrounded himself. He usually preferred the company of the witty to the wise. While he had the greatest respect for Hyde, for example, his chosen companion as like as not would be Buckingham, now riding incongruously in the procession beside Monck. A relationship that went back to their infancy and had been preserved through adolescence could not be easily cast aside, for all that the Duke was volatile and often deceitful. Indeed, it was precisely the inconsistency of Buckingham and the mercurial fascination of his brilliant, pleasure-loving intellect that was so engaging to Charles and so often objectionable to his subjects. The poet Dryden famously dubbed him 'statesman and buffoon', while Burnet loathed him with undiluted malice, writing of him that 'he was never true either to things or persons, but forsakes every man and departs from every maxim, sometimes out of levity or an unsettledness of fancy and sometimes out of downright falsehood'.[38] From such men as these – along with figures like Buckingham's kinswoman Barbara Palmer – would the Restoration court be made. What few of these people realised however was that below the easily observable personality of the King, running deeper than his indolence, his love of pleasure and his apparent indecisiveness, was an absolute commitment to his own survival. In the end he would baulk at nothing to preserve his throne. The sombrely dressed man riding in triumph along the Strand would never allow himself to be sent on his travels again. He had come into his own, and there he would remain.

The Promised Land

Action now had to be taken to punish and expunge the remaining traces of the old regime. Partly at the prompting of Henrietta Maria, the corpses of Cromwell and two other leading Parliamentarians were dug up and displayed as a repulsive warning of the price of rebellion. Charles himself also insisted that the severest punishment be inflicted on 'the immediate murderers of my father'.[1] Those of the regicides who were still alive suffered the direst penalties. As 1660 came to its close, a series of treason trials took place at which so many were condemned to be hung, drawn and quartered that people living around Charing Cross began to complain that the smell of burning bowels was poisoning the air. Those regicides who escaped paying this ultimate penalty were imprisoned, had their property seized and were paraded annually through the streets of London to suffer the indignities of the vengeful crowd. No mercy would be shown to those who refused to acquiesce in the new regime and Charles, although tolerant by nature, declared that he would use 'all rigour and severity' against those who continued 'to manifest their sedition and dislike of the government, either in action or words.'[2]

The task of re-establishing the monarchy as an effective political power fell largely to Hyde. He remained as magisterial, pompous and indefatigable as ever and now, as Lord Chancellor, his deeply considered conservatism led him to hope that, with the Restoration, the country would return to 'its old good manners, its old good humour and its old good nature'.[3] He was to be increasingly disappointed. The man who so revered traditional forms was appalled by the energies he saw working in the society around him. He thought of the critical and even carping spirit of the younger generation especially as a threat. He lamented what he saw as a lack of discipline, fostered as he believed by the experience of civil war. He disliked the constant 'murmuring' about grievances, and the fact that people seemed so ready to turn against that 'firm and constant obedience' to authority which he thought was the only true foundation of a secure society.[4] Such concerns would be ever more strongly voiced as the England of Charles II sought new modes of expression; but now, as Hyde faced the task of forming a royal administration, he naturally reverted to the old forms.

He saw his principal task as being to restore stability and respect for authority in the state and the church. As Lord Chancellor he would combine these aims under a reverence for the law, but he was careful to reject any publicly acknowledged role as the King's chief minister. All major policy decisions should be seen as coming from Charles himself. Having set these ideas in position, Hyde's next concern was that the King and his ministers should rule in partnership with those of the great and the good with posts at court or in the regions. This was to be rule by the elite, and in constructing such a government Hyde put his greatest emphasis on the Privy Council, which was to be made up from the leading officers of state and the country's wealthiest magnates. He also hoped to strike a balance between those with various competing interests. Charles's brother James and the men who had been his counsellors during the years of exile were appointed to the Privy Council along with other leading Royalists. To these figures were then added such former supporters of Cromwell as Monck, now Captain-General of the armed forces, and a number of leading Presbyterian nobles. The aged and ineffectual Earl of Southampton was made Lord Treasurer, while his son-in-law, the brilliant Anthony Ashley Cooper, was made Chancellor of the Exchequer. This was a wise combination of interests, ability and social prestige, but it was soon found necessary to form an inner ring of advisers, and the influential Committee of Foreign Affairs was set up with Hyde as its dominant member.

There was a host of problems that needed to be solved. Among the chief of these was the need to decommission large parts of the New Model Army. Charles at first offered to take these men into his service, but Parliament, not wishing him to have a substantial military force for which there was no apparent purpose, resolved to reduce the numbers and ensured that this turbulent, dangerous body was finally disbanded with its arrears fully paid and its teeth drawn. An Act of Indemnity and Oblivion was also passed to pardon lesser figures who had sided with the Parliamentarians. Disappointed Royalists unfairly claimed that the Act compensated the King's enemies and ignored his friends, but Charles rewarded those who had helped actively to bring about his restoration, which was surely wise. Monck, for example, was created Earl of Albermarle and given a palace and land worth £9000 a year. Companions in exile like Ormonde were treated with similar generosity, while even those who had led unsuccessful attempts at rebellion during the Interregnum were remembered, General Booth, for example, being made Lord Delamere.

The most difficult question of all was the religious settlement. The Declaration of Breda had referred this matter to Parliament, but debate in the House of Commons was so lengthy and acrimonious – at one point the candles were blown out to bring a halt to the proceedings – that no easy resolution seemed possible. It soon became evident that Charles's hopes of reaching a satisfactory compromise between Anglicans and Presbyterians were far less surely founded than he had supposed. The intransigence of the Presbyterians was especially marked. When Charles offered vacant sees to their leading men they refused them on the ground that the form of episcopacy envisaged was not sufficiently 'primitive', and it was wartime Royalists who eventually filled the greater number of these places, the able, tough-minded Sheldon, for example, being appointed Bishop of London.

To such militant Anglicans as these men a strong monarchy seemed the only solution to the nation's ills. This was not 'a chimerical loyalty', but the result of settled policy. Members of the so-called 'Convention'

Parliament had come up to Westminster 'full of horror at the very thoughts of the past miseries of the civil war and firmly resolved . . . to prevent the like for the future'.[5] They would grant Charles a revenue which they sincerely – if wrongly – believed would be sufficient to cover the usual costs of administering the country. They were determined not to keep him too poor, too dependent or too weak. They were also determined that the restored monarchy should return to power with its prerogatives intact. Charles would be given control of the armed forces, free choice of his advisers and undisputed leadership in matters of foreign policy.

This was far from being naieve altruism, for these men hoped to restore their own fortunes. The constitutional experiments of the Interregnum had increasingly deprived them of what they took to be their hereditary right to a significant say in the affairs of the country. They had come to the painful realisation that, by attacking what they saw as the excesses of the rule of the new King's father, they had actually undermined their own power and then been obliged to look on as people they saw as fanatics experimented with the ever more distasteful rigours of godly rule. The Royalist gentry were now determined to reassert their traditional rights, and a traditional monarchy seemed the best means to guarantee these.

It was not only the strength of the monarchy that concerned these men. The supremacy of the Anglican church was also an essential – indeed, an indivisible – part of their concern with their own stature. They believed that the Anglican church expressed the will of God in its purest form, and the King, as the head of that church, guaranteed the gentry's place in a coherent and hierarchical society. Obedience to such a figure was divinely ordained, and the experience of civil war had shown what chaos ensued when the divine ordinances were not followed. Sectarianism had to be rendered powerless, and such militant Anglicanism would present the King with a number of serious problems. Not only did Charles fail to realise the vehemence of such beliefs, the poor and patchy quality of the information that came to him during his exile had led him to exaggerate the power of Noncomformity in the country. A natural inclination to tolerate religious differences partly inclined him to the famous promise of 'liberty to tender consciences' in the Declaration of Breda, but an altogether more political if misconceived notion also drew him. Charles believed that by extending toleration to Dissenters and Presbyterians he could broaden the base of his support in the country and so perhaps be less dependent on those active members of the Anglican gentry who had 'brought him home in truth'.[6] The first major conflict of the reign was thus already prepared.

Such conflict in the public sphere was accompanied by tragedy in Charles's private life. On 13 September 1660 his younger brother Henry, Duke of Gloucester suddenly died from what everybody had assumed was only a mild attack of smallpox. The King's grief was sincere and painful, for Henry had shown himself to be an attractive and able young man. Such feelings were then curdled by a measure of bitterness when Charles's sister Mary arrived in the country. With her brother now safely established in England, Mary had been insisting that she be rewarded for the succour she had offered her brother during the years of his exile. The price she was demanding was a high one. She expected Charles to throw his weight and influence behind re-establishing the House of Orange as the leading political family in the Netherlands. In particular, she insisted that Charles support her in her campaign to have her son William made Captain-General of the Dutch republic. Charles dutifully wrote in support of her cause but wisely refused at this stage to get further entangled in a diplomatic squabble. A furious Mary now crossed the seas to confront her brother, but she too fell a victim of smallpox. She begged her brother to act as guardian to her son, but by the time Mary died Charles had become embroiled in a situation altogether more troubling.

The Duke of York had presented his brother with the first of the many embarrassments with which he was to litter Charles's reign. His eye had lighted on Hyde's daughter Anne – a plain but witty and clever girl – while she was acting as Maid of Honour to Mary of Orange. Anne became pregnant, a secret marriage was contracted, but this was no sooner concluded than James bitterly regretted what he had done and determined to use his influence to wriggle out of it. His chosen means were slander, innuendo and string-pulling. All of them failed. When

James suggested that others might be the child's father, he could not make the accusations stick. When he tried to get his brother have the marriage annulled by Parliament, Charles refused. There was an important political issue at stake here. James was next in line to the throne, and the child of his *mésalliance* was his heir. Charles recognised that it would seriously threaten royal survival if Parliament were once allowed to have a say in the succession. He therefore insisted that his stubborn, stolid brother abide by the arrangement he had so foolishly made. Charles then tried to do what he could for his Lord Chancellor. Hyde felt himself seriously compromised. He loved his daughter, despised his son-in-law and was deeply upset by their joint folly. He believed his integrity would be impugned by those who did not know the facts, and he felt sure he would be accused of dynastic plotting. Only the King could salvage his honour. Charles offered Hyde a dukedom but, fearing that so great a title would provoke further resentment, on 6 November Hyde took his place on the woolsack as the newly ennobled Earl of Clarendon.

Such events suggested how important it was that the King himself should marry and produce an heir, and secret negotiations towards this end had been proceeding for some time. The Portuguese saw in Charles a valuable ally and had set about winning him over. Francisco de Mello was despatched to England and, having sweetened a number of important courtiers with bribes, he eventually secured a meeting with Charles himself. At this de Mello offered the King of Portugal's daughter and suggested that a fabulous dowry would be forthcoming. Charles listened with interest and then, when de Mello returned to Portugal, turned his ear to the rival Spanish agent as he offered not only the daughter of the ruler of Parma but commercial concessions and a generous price for the repurchase of two possessions captured by Cromwell: Jamaica and Dunkirk. Such international dealing inevitably roused the interest of the French, and Louis XIV (whose repulsive brother was now married to Charles's beloved Henriette Anne) threw his weight behind the Portuguese offer. The Privy Council also resolved on the Portuguese match and, in return for sending Portugal 10,000 men, Charles was promised not only the hand of Catherine of Braganza but trading privileges, the rich cities of Tangier and Bombay, and nearly a third of a million pounds in cash.

It was in such an atmosphere of expectation that Charles held his coronation, an event of dazzling pageantry designed to assert the triumph of the monarchy. The evening before the ceremony itself Charles, much to the delight of his people, led the traditional procession from the Tower of London to Whitehall. Celebrations started the following morning at eight. Once again, the fountains ran with wine as soldiers in red, white and black plumes marched along the railed and gravelled streets. No expense was spared. Clarendon, it was said, 'shone like a diamond', and the robes of one peer were said to have cost £30,000. The horse of state was gorgeously caparisoned with a saddle worked with gold, pearls and a splendid ruby. A further 12,000 jewels decorated the stirrups. Here was the monarchy triumphant, and poets, painters, and architects, historians and preachers spun out ideas that gave the educated public a series of heroic images with which to celebrate Charles's return. The King, entering on his rule in the thirty-first year of his life, was a figure to be compared to Christ entering on his ministry. He was a new David, a new Solomon. His restoration would bring back a state of Eden after the country's collapse into civil war. The Golden Age had returned, and one of the triumphal arches spanning the coronation route predicted a glorious future by showing the expansion of British influence over the world as Charles's navy protected the ever wider expansion of commerce and trade.

Just as elaborate were the preparations made for the coronation ceremony itself. The greater part of the royal regalia had disappeared during the Interregnum and new crowns had to be prepared. Yards of cloth of gold, red velvet and crimson satin were woven to provide the King's robes. Golden, high-heeled shoes were made for him, and in these he towered over the assembled clerics gathered in Westminster Abbey, which was hung with red and blue cloth. The gathered representatives of the European powers were duly impressed, as they were meant to be. England, always something of a mysterious country to many of them, notorious for the execution of its king, and with its language, literature and history little known, was asserting itself as a monarchical power after the aberrant experiments of the Commonwealth. The 'great shout' that went up when the crown was placed on the King's head confirmed this, as did the nobility of England when they swore fealty to Charles by ascending the dais, touching the crown and 'promising by that ceremony to be ever ready to support it, with all their power'.[7]

Such medieval splendour was continued at the great feast held in Westminster Hall. The first course was ushered in by the Earl Marshal, the Lord High Steward and the Lord High Constable, each wearing his coronet and riding a richly bedecked horse. The clerks in charge of the host of scullions wore black satin gowns and velvet caps while, in a final flourish, the King's official champion entered on a white horse and, throwing down his gauntlet, issued the time-honoured challenge: 'If any person of what degree soever, high or low, shall deny or gainsay our Sovereign Lord King Charles the Second . . . here is his champion, who saith that he lieth, and is a false traitor.'[8] Charles was indeed now 'Sovereign Lord' of his country and was possessed, in theory at least, of supreme authority. How far he could exercise this, how far he could enforce his policies, was an altogether different question.

Conflict came to the surface when the newly elected Cavalier Parliament met in 1661. Its Members were if anything more militantly Anglican than those they had replaced, and although a number of Acts were passed in clear support of the King, many others were designed to reinforce the position of the gentry, even at the cost of opposing Charles's wishes. There was trouble from the start. Both the King and Clarendon insisted that the Cavalier House of Commons, as a parliament truly elected under royal warrant, should confirm the legislation passed by its predecessors, the Act of Indemnity especially. Some Members proposed changes that would have reversed previous intentions and punished old enemies, but Charles insisted that the Act be confirmed – it was, he made clear, a point of honour – and eventually he got his way.

The Cavalier Parliament also had to deal with the problem of Charles's finances. For all that their predecessors had resolved to provide the King with what they considered to be an adequate annual income of £1,200,000, their understanding of public finance was confused by their own incompetence – they counted the income from the excise on wine twice – and because the information they worked from was often based on little more than guesswork. Furthermore, the taxes they did allow yielded far less than estimated because of inefficiencies in the methods of collection. As a result, Charles immediately fell into debt, and securing an adequate revenue became and was to remain a pressing matter of survival throughout his reign.

As the King could raise money only in ways approved by Parliament and had lost his income from the abolished prerogative courts, he painted a bleak picture of his plight, telling the Commons that beggary was far worse for kings than for ordinary men. They responded by granting him a benevolence – an extraordinary grant of a year's extra revenue – but while making noises about settling matters for the years to come they agreed only to the imposition of an unpopular hearth tax, which was founded on the belief that the number of hearths in a house was an indication of the owner's wealth. With characteristic over-optimism, the sponsors of the hearth tax Bill claimed that it would bring in a million pounds a year, but in fact it proved extremely difficult to collect and yielded only a fifth of the promised amount.

Much of the rest of the Cavalier Parliament's early legislation reflected a concern with eliminating popular resistance and nullifying the power of Nonconformity. A pathetic event had shown that religious antagonism in the country still posed a threat to peaceful coexistence. Inspired by the scaffold speeches of the regicides, Thomas Venner, a London cooper and the leader of a gathered or non-conformist church, decided with a mere three dozen of his congregation to seize London and impose the rule of the saints. Because the government as yet had an inadequate espionage system, the wrong people were arrested and the fear proliferated that Venner's was but one part of a concerted uprising. A panicking government banned unauthorised meetings and alerted the militia. The gentry arrested any they thought of as dissidents, including nearly 5000 Quakers. When it came to its senses, the Privy Council prohibited more arrests and ordered that most of the London Quakers be released. Nonetheless, the climate of suspicion was such that Charles retained an unusually large force of guards while the fear of rebellion tightened its grip on the country as a whole.

Worried Members passed an Act against tumultous petitioning which outlawed all petitions of over twenty signatures collected without the permission of three JPs, while no petition was to be presented by more than ten persons. Having denied this means of popular protest, similarly repressive measures were adopted in the Licensing Act, which, directed at the enormous amount of pamphleteering which followed the collapse of censorship in 1640, reintroduced statutory control. This was a measure Charles himself was particularly keen to encourage – he twice urged the Commons to hurry its passage – since he had been infuriated by a pamphlet attacking what many considered to be his ingratitude to old supporters.

Legislation was then directed at those who opposed the Anglican church. The Corporation Act was one such measure. Large towns were widely regarded as 'seminaries of faction', places where Nonconformity was rife and the ordinary people politically active. Many such towns were also self-governing and were ruled by an elected corporation whose loyalty to the crown and the church was often felt to be uncertain. Cavalier Members of Parliament wanted to purge such disaffected men outright, but the Lords demanded that the King's voice be heard in any changes that were to be made. The Commons objected, not wishing the monarch to be so directly concerned in the affairs of the localities. The matter was deadlocked until a revised Bill was drafted allowing for the purge to be administered by commissioners. In addition to this sort of surveillance, members of corporations were also required to take the oaths of allegiance and supremacy, repudiate the Covenant, take communion in the Anglican rite at least once a year, and forswear resistance to the crown. By such means as these, the Cavalier Parliament removed Dissenters and Presbyterians from positions of influence in the towns, and did so without extending the powers of the King.

It was legislation in matters of religion itself which revealed the Anglican gentry at their most obdurate. At the start of the session the Cavalier Parliament ordered that all Members should take communion according to the Anglican rite – a Congregationalist MP who refused was suspended – and decreed that the Covenant should be burned by the common hangman. The Act for the Security of the King's Person then restored the church to the position it had enjoyed before the civil war. Nothing less than the old order in its purest form would do, and the question arose of what would happen to Charles's desire to keep moderate Presbyterians allied to it. He tried urgently to have this matter debated and resolved elsewhere, first calling the Savoy Conference, which foundered, and then summoning Convocation – the church's representative assembly – to discuss the issue.

Led by Sheldon, Convocation proved obdurate, while Parliament would not accept the Presbyterians' proposed changes to the Prayer Book. The Members then bluntly told the King that if he opposed their will then they might reject 'the bill intended for the enlarging of his revenue'. Charles refused to give way before such blackmail, but attempts at compromise were futile and his first attempt to extend 'liberty to tender consciences' was virtually at an end when some 1800 ministers were ejected from their livings. The Anglican victory, now so nearly complete, was made yet more secure when in 1664 and 1665 fears of unrest again surfaced and Parliament passed the first Conventicle Act, which forbade meetings of five or more persons 'under the colour or pretence of any exercise of religion', and then voted through the Five Mile Act, which forbade preachers and teachers who refused to comply with the Act of Uniformity to come within five miles of any parish where they had once ministered.

The result of this legislation in religious matters – widely but unfairly named the Clarendon Code – was a change in English life so profound that its effects were to last for 250 years. By passing a comprehensive series of laws, Parliament ensured that Anglicanism became the focus for spiritual, social and political conservatism in the country. The Church of England, led by its bishops and served by its priests and deacons, was strong and united in conforming to an agreed body of doctrine and the use of a single Prayer Book. Consensus had been achieved. At the same time, the Anglican establishment, with the monarch as its Supreme Governor, held the monopoly of privilege.

Only those who conformed to its beliefs and rites could hold public office. An alliance had thus been formed between parson and squire which would bring order and subservience to this world and emasculate the fanaticism of the godly searching after a New Jerusalem. In communities across the land, the manor house and the vicarage stood four square for established privilege and social order. The church – in outward appearance at least – had triumphed over the chapel, and the Anglican gentry had secured an influence they would not willingly forgo.[9]

If the passage of such legislation suggests the poor quality of Charles's management of the House of Commons, his personal prestige was also in decline. The euphoria surrounding the months of the Restoration was quickly turning sour as disillusion deepened. Charles's conduct during the passage of the recent religious legislation had irritated his natural supporters among the Anglican gentry while offering the Dissenters nothing but disappointment. When he tried to limit the effects of the new laws by proposing a Declaration of Indulgence, the measure failed to win assent in the Lords. This once again suggested the very real limits to the King's authority while, at the same time, raising doubts about Charles's religious commitment. An old and fearful spectre had been raised. 'That which shocks most people . . . is the favourable mention of Roman Catholics,' declared Henry Bennet, a subtle and efficient newcomer to the royal circle, a protégé of Barbara Palmer's and a man possessed of the invaluable 'art of observing the King's temper'.

This was a skill the overbearing Clarendon rarely chose to exercise, and it was Clarendon who was largely responsible for another project that was to contribute to Charles's unpopularity: the sale of Dunkirk. This had been one of the great prizes of Cromwell's foreign policy and one particularly valued in Francophobic England since it was the first toehold the nation had possessed in France since the loss of Calais in the distant reign of Mary Tudor. Dunkirk nonetheless was difficult to defend, of little immediate use and extremely expensive to maintain, especially at a time when public revenues were strained. Clarendon eagerly set about selling the port to Louis XIV, but when a public already exasperated by the new taxation heard of the deal they were bitterly angry.

Such causes for complaint were compounded by something alto-gether less familiar: the reputation that Charles and his circle were acquiring for debauchery and sexual excess. As early as September 1661 the broad-minded Pepys was confiding to his diary that 'at court things are in very ill condition, there being so much emulation [envy], poverty, and the vices of swearing, drinking and whoring, that I do not know what will be the end of it but confusion'. Certainly, the country was by now vivid with salacious gossip. The prevalence of syphilis in court circles was a matter of rumour and concern, while the heavy gambling there also provoked comment. Public drunkenness among the courtiers likewise caused ripples of outrage that became waves by the time they reached the provinces. When a crowd of young bucks who were known to be among the King's friends dined at a Bow Street tavern, a drunken Sir Charles Sedley went out on to the balcony to preach a mock sermon. The crowd pelted him with mud and stones, and these missiles were returned with equal enthusiasm until the watch arrived. Sedley himself was arrested, tried, imprisoned and bound over to keep the peace, but this did not put an end to the matter. Pepys was told that the whole incident had been played out in the nude with Sedley himself posturing obscenely. By the time the story reached Oxford, it was said that all the diners had been drunk, while the prurient in Flintshire heard that even the waitresses – all six of them – had been naked. There were those who pursed their lips and muttered that this was just the sort of behaviour that could be expected from a court that favoured French tutors, long wigs and make-up.

It was Charles's own and very public enjoyment of pleasure that caused the greatest concern. Not since the days of Henry VIII had royal promiscuity been so evident. His restoration released in Charles a deep vein of sensuality that in time became obsessive. With power came opportunities for sexual gratification on an unprecedented scale, and these were eagerly seized. Lord Halifax was no doubt correct when he wrote that Charles's 'inclinations to love were the effects of good health and a good constitution', but there was little indeed that was 'seraphic' about them and much that threatened royal authority.[10] Legends about the size of Charles's penis – the poet Rochester declared that it was as long as his sceptre – might have had a clubbable jocularity about them, but the coarsening effect of a salacious court was widely feared.

Pepys, who was certainly no prude, came to believe that the conversation of the King's friends was 'so base and sordid that it makes the ears of the very gentlemen of the backstairs to tingle', and he was deeply troubled to think that the King was 'at the command of any woman like a slave'.[11] Along with many others of Charles's subjects, Pepys gave the matter a great deal of consideration, deciding eventually, despite the evidence of numerous royal bastards, that Charles was essentially a fondler of women. 'The King', he wrote, 'doth spend most of his time in feeling and kissing them naked all over their bodies in bed – and contents himself, without doing the other thing, but as he finds himself inclined; but this lechery will never leave him.'[12] It was all rather troubling especially as it seemed, somehow, to be rather unEnglish too. Pepys thought it was surely necessary to have 'at least a show of religion in the government' – after all, 'sobriety . . . is so fixed in the nature of the common Englishman that it will not out of him'. But it was not only the sexual frankness of the King that was feared. Quite as threatening (if not more so) to many was the open display of sexual pleasure by the women of his court. The conventions were being torn to shreds and left men feeling vulnerable and exposed. The idea that women might drink, gamble and 'talk filth'ly' with 'more extravagance than any man' was disturbing.[13] The fear ran deep, and Barbara Palmer in particular – ambitious, avaricious and openly domineering – was soon loathed as a force in politics that was quite outside the experience of many.

Charles was so casual about his visits to Barbara that even his guards commented when he came back through the palace gates at all hours having visited the woman Evelyn described as 'the curse of our nation'. Pepys, on the other hand, was not always so censorious. Barbara was, after all, a sexual icon in an age when men were expected to be openly libidinous and frank in their enjoyment of pleasure. Indeed, Barbara Palmer seems to have exerted a strong if ambivalent hold over Pepys. He hankered after a picture of her and eventually bought a print. He

recorded erotic dreams about her. He saw her smocks and linen petticoats, all rich with lace at the bottom, drying in the Privy Garden at
Whitehall and wrote that 'it did me good to look upon them'. When his
employer's maid brought him salacious gossip about Barbara, Pepys was
so excited that he made a pass at the girl herself and became so roused
'that I spent in my breeches'.[14]

Pepys was nonetheless aware of Barbara's baleful influence over
Charles, and feared it for being so conspicuously public. Barbara had
given birth to a daughter during February 1661, and although her erstwhile lover Lord Chesterfield was widely considered to be the father,
Charles eventually recognised little Anne as his own daughter, largely
so that she could be advantageously married. The mother meanwhile
ingratiated herself with the King in the face of considerable opposition.
The Dowager Duchess of Richmond ended a scene by saying that she
hoped the lecherous-eyed Barbara would end up like Jane Shore, the
notorious mistress of Edward IV who had died poor, her body
thrown on a dunghill. Clarendon, Barbara's kinsman by his first wife,
could barely bring himself to name her, referring to her merely as 'that
woman'. There was also an unpleasant scene when three masked men,
probably courtiers, accosted Barbara in St James's Park, berated her
with foul language and sent her back terrified to her apartments.

Charles remained indifferent to the damaging criticism raging about
him. To recognise Barbara's place as *maîtresse en titre* – as well as to give
status to any children he might father by her – he determined to
have her husband, the cuckolded Roger Palmer, raised to the Irish
peerage with a title that would be passed on through Barbara's children
alone. This was an openly cruel insult, but the choice of an Irish peerage
suggests that Charles knew very well that he could expect opposition
from Clarendon, whose power as Lord Chancellor did not extend to
Ireland. Charles ordered his Secretary of State to 'prepare a warrant for
Mr Roger Palmer to be "barron of Limbericke" and Earl of Castlemaine
. . . and let me have it before dinner'.[15] There was no gainsaying such a
command, and it was as the Countess of Castlemaine that, in the spring
of 1662, Barbara gave birth to the King's son. The boy was later baptised
Charles at St Margaret's, Westminster, but the christening itself led to

a furious row with Roger Palmer, now a Roman Catholic, and, when Barbara stormed out of his house with every item of value she could seize, he retreated to France in high dudgeon. The newly elevated Lady Castlemaine was pleased to have got rid of a nuisance, but suddenly she faced something altogether more dangerous: a rival.

It was into the bearpit of the Restoration court that Charles was now to introduce his future wife. Few women could have been more un-prepared or more unsuitable. At twenty-three, Catherine of Braganza had led so sheltered a life that she was utterly unused to the ways of the world. An intense and even neurotic Catholic piety governed her days, and one of the few expeditions she had so far made outside her Portuguese palace was to pray at a local shrine when she heard of her forthcoming marriage. Thus prepared, she made the long and stormy crossing to England accompanied by a retinue of confessors, barbers, perfumiers, a deaf duenna, and 'six frights' of ladies-in-waiting whose hideous farthingales and straitlaced attitudes would soon cause considerable embarrassment. On disembarking, the timid little Princess asked for a cup of tea, but this still rare commodity being unavailable, she had to make do with a mug of small beer. Her appearance did not greatly impress, Evelyn writing of a woman 'low of stature, pretty shaped, languishing and excellent eyes, her teeth wronging her mouth by sticking a little too far out, for the rest sweet and lovely enough'.[16] It was Catherine's hair, however, widely swept back from the sides of her head, that particularly astonished the King. 'Gentlemen,' he is supposed to have said, 'you have brought me a bat.'[17]

The Princess, of course, was Catholic, and careful preparations had been made for Charles's marriage to her. The Portuguese ambassador had rightly assured the King that Catherine, although devoted to her beliefs, 'was totally without that meddling and activity in her nature which many times made those of that religion troublesome'.[18] Public proprieties had nonetheless to be preserved. Clarendon insisted that Charles emphasise his Protestant credentials by arriving at Portsmouth to greet his new Queen with an Anglican bishop at his side. It was agreed that a brief and secret Catholic ceremony would be held in deference to Catherine's sensibilities, but that a public, Protestant service was essential. This last was held in the Great Chamber of the house of the Governor of Portsmouth, the royal couple sitting on two railed-off thrones to keep them apart from the crowd in the room. After the ceremony, in Portuguese fashion, the blue-ribbon loveknots were cut from Catherine's dress and distributed among members of the congregation, but the wedding night itself was not a success. The sea journey had upset the Queen's menstrual cycle, and Charles, tired from his own journey, wrote that 'it was happy for the honour of the nation that I was not put to the consummation of the marriage last night, for I was so sleepy'.[19]

For the moment at least Charles was determined to be charitable to his inexperienced little bride. She was clearly so anxious to please and appeared to have fallen under his spell already. He wrote to Clarendon, 'if I have any skill in physiognomy, which I think I have, she must be as good a woman as was ever born'.[20] Such goodness was to be tested almost at once. Back in Portugal, the Queen's mother had warned Catherine about Lady Castlemaine and told her never to allow the woman's name to be mentioned in her presence. The Countess, pregnant with the King's child, was not to be so easily put off. With blazing effrontery she demanded that her lying-in take place at Hampton Court, where Charles and Catherine were on their honeymoon. The King would not allow that, but his mistress was far from admitting defeat and played her hand in a manner wholly typical.

Court gossip had made clear that the King regarded the straitlaced virgins that surrounded his wife as an undesirable foreign influence over her. They did not understand English ways. They would not sleep in a bed that had ever been occupied by a man, and particularly objected to the English habit of urinating in public, complaining 'that they cannot stir abroad without seeing in every corner great beastly English pricks battering against every wall'.[21] Clearly, these women would have to go, along with their attitudes. So far, only the Countess of Suffolk had been suggested as an English Lady of the Queen's Bedchamber, and Castlemaine saw her chance. In a series of terrible scenes, violent-eyed, screaming and tearful, she so played on the King's guilt and so wore down his resistance that her name was eventually placed at the top of the list of appointees.

To Charles's amazement his docile little Queen flared in Latin outrage, striking the loathed name through and telling him that he could send her back to Portugal if he insisted on appointing the Countess to her household. The King tried to calm her down, uttering transparent lies about his affair with Castlemaine being over, a thing of the past. It was not over, as Catherine knew perfectly well, and a few days later Charles's mistress had persuaded him to slip her in among the other ladies due to be presented to the Queen. As the royal hand was extended for Castlemaine to kiss, so one of the farthingaled 'frights' leaned towards Catherine's ear and told her who the kneeling woman was. The hand flinched back. There were tears, a nosebleed, and the Queen was carried from the room in fits.

It was left to Clarendon to sort it all out. With someone else to do his dirty work for him, Charles stood firmly on the remains of his dignity. In a stiff interview with the Lord Chancellor, he told him that he felt honour bound to support Castlemaine, the mother of his new child, and that it was his wife's duty simply to submit and obey. If she did not, he added with a desperate and defiant lack of logic, he would take any number of mistresses to insult her. Clarendon set about his task. There were tears, and then another interview as the great embodiment of the law in England pleaded with the slighted Queen to appoint to her bedchamber a woman whom they both, for different reasons, hated. A furious Catherine vowed to return to Portugal at once. Clarendon informed her that she could not leave the country without the King's permission. He then suggested to Charles that the King let the matter rest for a few days. When husband and wife at last met, the shouting match echoed down the corridors of Hampton Court. There followed days of crying for the Queen and a sullen refusal even to look her husband in the eye. But Charles, for his part, was beginning to change. His wife had the spirit that excited him. He was guilty and he felt ashamed. Although he was determined to have his way – Catherine would indeed eventually submit – his feelings for his wife now ran deeper than he had previously expected.

Castlemaine had obtained her post at the cost of the King's beginning to experience a certain tenderness for his wife, but the Countess wanted a lot more than a position in the Queen's household. It was true that her role as Lady of the Bedchamber gave her a cachet. It allowed her to be gratingly attentive as she accompanied the ever more lonely Catherine to her numerous devotions, but this was not enough. The Countess wanted a frank and open admission of her role as *maîtresse en titre*. She wanted rooms in Whitehall, and by April 1663 she had got them. They at once became the focus for all her concerns. The besotted King came there for his obvious pleasures, and raised no objections when his domineering mistress entertained others. Perhaps her promiscuous appetites stimulated his. Among the known names, Castlemaine entertained Sir Charles Berkeley, James Hamilton, Lord Sandwich and Harry Jermyn's lascivious young nephew. Even the King's first illegitimate child, James Crofts, now turned thirteen and, judging from Samuel Cooper's miniature, an irresistibly pretty little boy, found his way to her door. James already had a mistress of his own, but the ever observant Pepys noted that the Duke of Monmouth, as the lad was soon to be known, 'doth hang much upon my Lady Castlemaine and is always with her'.[22]

The children the King had sired by Castlemaine were always available for the devoted father to fondle, and, when children palled, there were the delights of the Countess's table, which even the French ambassador praised. The King spent more and more time in his mistress's apartments, as it was intended he should. Pepys, for all his fascination with the woman, was appalled. He confided to his diary that 'my Lady Castlemaine rules him, who hath all the tricks of Aretin* that are to be practised to give pleasure – in which he is too able, having a large ——; but that which is the unhappiest is that, as the Italian proverb says, *Cazzo dritto non vuolt consiglio*'.**[23] The result was both obvious and disastrous. Charles's political judgement was being blinded by lust. 'If any of the sober councillors give him good advice', Pepys wrote, 'and move him to anything that is to his good and honour, the other part, which are his counsellors of pleasure, take him when he is with my Lady Castlemaine and in a humour of delight and then persuade him

* Pietro Aretino, the renaissance erotic writer.
** A man with an erection heeds no advice.

that he ought not to listen to the advice of those old dotards.'[24]

Among the 'old dotards' was Clarendon. Knowing that the Chancellor loathed her, Castlemaine returned his feelings with visceral hatred. She said she hoped to see his head on a stake. Failing this, she determined to surround him with enemies. Bennet and the Lord Digby were among her principal means of attack, and she encouraged them to criticise financial and religious policy as Bennet in particular rose in royal esteem, eventually becoming Secretary of State and taking rooms in Whitehall that gave him direct access to the King. But Charles became decreasingly interested in the day-to-day affairs of government as he fell victim to his obsession for Castlemaine. Clarendon was grieved. 'The worst is', he wrote to Ormonde, 'the King is as discomposed as ever, and looks as little after his business, which breaks my heart and makes me and other of your friends weary of our lives.' Charles ceased to visit his Chancellor at his home, and Bennet took over much of the direction of foreign policy.

But, even while Castlemaine was luring Charles towards potentially grave political danger, her influence was on the wane. She was pregnant through much of 1663 (the child, Henry Palmer, was born in September and was only belatedly recognised by Charles), while a rival attraction had appeared at court in the delicious shape of the fifteen-year-old Frances Stuart. Even Henriette Anne, who had known her in Paris, described Frances as 'the prettiest girl in the world and one of the best fitted of any I know to adorn a court'.[25] Certainly *la belle Stuart*, as she was widely called, was everything that Castlemaine was not. Frances was petite, naive and rather stupid. She preferred building card houses to talking politics and, for all that she was easily susceptible to flattery and flirtation, was wholly, infuriatingly chaste. Charles was deeply stirred, and soon the couple were embracing and fondling in public.

Pepys was once again fascinated from afar and wrote that *la belle Stuart* was 'the greatest beauty I ever saw I think in my life; and if ever woman can, doth exceed my Lady Castlemaine . . . nor do I wonder if the King changes, which I verily believe is the reason for his coldness to my Lady Castlemaine'.[26] Soon, the object of this fascination would be modelling for Britannia on the British coinage, a role her image occupied for nearly three centuries. Nonetheless, Castlemaine was not to be abashed and was too shrewd to fight. Instead, she appeared as Frances's friend, her older confidante, the woman who invited her to the parties where the King was sure to be. At one of these she determined to inflame Charles's desires by staging an imaginary lesbian tableau for his delight. Castlemaine and Frances went through a mock marriage and proceeded to play the bedroom scene in front of the court. Castlemaine was the husband, and only on the King's approach ceded her place, inviting him to lie with Frances, who would not, however, allow the sport to go too far. Charles remained hopelessly attached.

The autumn of 1663 saw a real and altogether more painful bedroom scene. Catherine of Braganza fell seriously ill. Charles was at her bedside, pity and guilt struggling in him while he watched and listened as his wife's mind began to wander and she voiced one of her most deeply seated fears. She thought she had been delivered of a 'very ugly boy'.

'No, it's a very pretty boy,' Charles answered, with all the tenderness he could muster. He continued to listen as Catherine talked again of the child, then of the children – three of them.

'How are the children?' she asked.[27]

The question touched on one of the most painful issues of the Restoration. Try as they might, the royal couple could not conceive an heir to the throne and so lighten for themselves the dark days that were now approaching.

The Horsemen of the Apocalypse

W hen Charles looked beyond the shores of his kingdom he was aware of the existence of three continental powers. Of these, Spain had once been the mightiest but was now in a state of accelerating decay. The Spanish empire comprised vast tracts of South America along with significant parts of Europe, but the effort of ruling possessions so varied and widespread placed an intolerable strain on the country's resources. Exhaustion and deepening poverty led to such humiliations as the loss of the Northern Netherlands after eight decades of war, along with an increasing dependence on outsiders who had the will and the expertise to run the faltering Spanish economy. Such national decline was grotesquely symbolised by Spain's royal family. When Philip IV died in 1665, he was succeeded to the throne by his son, Carlos II, the imbecile victim of in-breeding and that hereditary Habsburg misfortune whereby his lower jaw was so prominent that his teeth did not meet on the rare occasions when he shut his mouth. The rulers of Europe looked on with the eager eyes of birds of prey, believing such a king could not long survive and that, on his death, the carcass of his territories could be fought over for the choicest morsels.

France, on the other hand, presented the wholly contrasting view of a strong, wealthy and ambitious country headed by a young and able ruler. Soon after the death of Cardinal Mazarin in 1661, the twenty-two-year-old Louis XIV announced to his astonished ministers that he was taking up the reins of power himself. Few kings were better suited to the manifold tasks of absolutism. Louis had received the most thorough training from his masters and was extremely hard-working – unlike Charles, he spent long hours at his desk mastering the immense quantities of information he insisted on being provided with. He was also a man of iron resolve and limitless ambition who revelled in the glory of battle. *La gloire*, indeed, was the aim of all Louis' policies, and to this end he set about establishing an immense army and a revitalised French navy so that he could pursue his plan of securing his borders against the Habsburgs and the Holy Roman Emperor, while simultaneously advancing his territorial claims in areas that he declared were his rightful inheritance.

As his reign progressed, Louis not only provided an example of an active and ambitious king. For some he was the alluring image of absolutism. Like Charles, he had seen his country plunged into civil war and had known the dangers and humiliation of flight, open disloyalty and the shrewd questions posed by a Parlement anxious to limit royal power. Unlike the King of England, however, Louis ruled from a throne no longer surrounded by those who would challenge his will. Louis could choose his policies and ministers without constantly looking over his shoulder or tempering his ambition in the pursuit of supplies. Able to demand unquestioning obedience, the Sun King would become, amid the fabulous ceremonial of Versailles, a monarch wholly absolved from subordination to any human authority.

Holland provided an altogether different challenge. Here was a federal republic of seven provinces which had freed themselves first from Spanish domination and then from the threat of absolutism embodied in their principal aristocratic family, the House of Orange. Leadership followed financial power, and the dominant influence in the country was wielded by the formidable Jan de Witt, Grand Pensionary of the province of Holland, whose great commercial cities – Amsterdam especially – provided over half the nation's revenue. Such riches ensured that Holland and de Witt himself exerted a deciding influence over the country's governing body, the States General, and were thus major players on the European stage.

The wealth of Holland was founded on commerce. The Dutch had built up enormous resources of capital, and Amsterdam was the world's money market. The Dutch had, in addition, secured for themselves a substantial mercantile empire in Africa and the East especially, and were also the continent's principal carriers, a great system of rivers and canals ensuring that their storehouses were easily available to the vast quantity of shipping on which their business relied. Manufacturing little themselves, the Dutch grew prosperous on services, and other nations, the English especially, observed them with a jealous eye. Sir William Petty voiced the familiar complaint. 'Do they not work the sugars of the west?' he asked, 'the timber and iron of the Baltic? the lead, tin and wool of England? the hemp of Russia? the yarns and dyeing stuffs of Turkey?' History pointed to the obvious lesson: 'in all the ancient states and empires, those who had the shipping had the wealth'.[1] The same was true in the 1660s.

At the time of the Restoration, England was behindhand in such matters. As the reign developed, English merchants would gather to themselves immense riches as they ranged the world for silks and spices, mahogany or 'speckled wood', tobacco, sugar and a comprehensive range of staple products, along with such exotica as tortoiseshell, singing birds, chocolate and cucumbers. Many were also to profit from the repulsive trade in African slaves, but in 1660 the prospect was sluggish. The great trading associations of the Elizabethan and early Stuart eras – the Merchant and Greenland Adventurers, the Levant, Africa and East India Companies – were variously suffering from debt, fraud and zealous foreign competition. Even the herring in British waters were being fished and marketed by others.

Nonetheless, it was widely understood that trade 'conduces more to a universal monarchy than either arms or territories' and, because the regulation of foreign trade fell within the prerogative powers of the crown, strenuous royal efforts were made to improve matters. The privileges of the older trading companies were confirmed and new companies were established, while a series of Navigation Acts passed from 1660 onwards reformulated the policies set out in their predecessors. Their aims were, in the words of the first of the new Acts, 'the increase of shipping and encouragement of the navigation of this nation'.[2] Open conflict with Dutch rivals was inevitable, and was welcomed by the younger members of the court of Charles II, those gathered around the Duke of York, the country's Lord High Admiral, especially. Most of these men were young, and all of them were ambitious. The naval officers thought hungrily of prizes and promotion, while the ministers favourable to James saw in a war with the Dutch the opportunity to displace such staid, senior advisers as Clarendon who, increasingly crippled with gout, was one of the few who stood opposed to hostilities.

In the circle gathered about James, violence was seen as the way to wealth, and public policy became a mask for private ambition. Such ambitions were then honed by contempt for the Dutch republican form of government. It was argued that, because the Dutch had no substantial aristocracy to provide them with natural leaders, they were without that sense of honour and courage which was so essential to the successful conduct of war. As a result, an English victory would be quick and decisive, Dutch merchants would shrink away from the collapsing republic, and Holland would dwindle as England triumphed. Such views were to be exposed as riddled with the errors of arrogance, as well as an ignorance of the poor state of the navy's preparations. Nobody was more aware of the latter than Samuel Pepys, Clerk of the Acts at the Admiralty. As he confided to his diary in 1664: 'all the news now is what will become of the Dutch business, whether war or peace. We all seem to desire it, as thinking ourselves to have advantages at present over them; but for my part I dread it.'[3]

Charles himself at first affected indifference to his brother's plans for a war against the Dutch, but, in a way that was to become typical of his rule, gradually began to pursue what appeared as two different and conflicting policies. On the one hand, he gave his public assent to the idea of trying to negotiate with the Dutch and so reaching an amicable settlement. While doing this, however, he was also increasingly attracted to the idea of war. Subtle pressure was applied to him to manipulate his natural laziness, and the figure of Sir Charles Berkeley was particularly influential. Attached to the circles of both Castlemaine and the Duke of York, Berkeley was well positioned to win Charles's confidence. He suggested to him that, by encouraging a trade war with the Dutch, the King would greatly increase his revenues and so begin to free himself from dependence on Parliament. Such a policy had a natural appeal, but it is symptomatic of Charles's frequently confused style of leadership that, rather than initiating or authorising these ideas himself, he allowed his courtiers and junior ministers to follow their own initiatives. In such ways as these, the country lurched towards war.

While James and his colleagues tried to influence Charles in the direction of open conflict, the King's ambassador in the Netherlands, Sir George Downing, started to put diplomatic pressure on the Dutch, exhorting trade concessions, trying to turn the mass of the people against their rulers, and seeking to denigrate de Witt especially. His motives, while complementing those of the courtiers, were nonetheless different. While James and his followers revelled in the idea of war and what they saw as the increase in royal wealth and influence that would stem from it, Downing's chief concern was to increase the wealth of the nation at large. Labouring day and night to master the mass of detail this involved, he had a prophetic vision of Britain as a triumphant mercantile state, and his efforts were furthered by English acts of aggression. Sporadic fighting broke out in the winter of 1663–4 on the West African coast where forts belonging to the Dutch East India Company were destroyed, and also in America where the New Netherlands were seized. When de Witt refused to appease these assaults and, instead, resolved to return his enemy's behaviour in kind, the English started to attack Dutch trading vessels.

James and his companions, believing that war was now inevitable, began to prepare both Parliament and the City to back their policies. They skilfully persuaded a Parliamentary committee to produce figures which suggested that the losses resulting from the Dutch competition were so great that hostile action was necessary for the 'honour, safety and future wealth of the country'.[4] Subsidies totalling £3,750,000 were

voted by the close of October 1665, but, as always, these proved difficult to collect and the shortfall was disastrous not only for the long-term
conduct of the war itself but for the career of Clarendon, who obstinately refused to implement changes in the administration of the
treasury which might have increased revenues. In the depths of the
forthcoming hostilities lay the seeds of momentous change.

James set about his preparations, exhilarated by the fact that he was
an admiral leading his fleet into a new type of naval warfare. He and the
circle of men around him not only stood to gain wealth and personal
prestige by engaging with the Dutch, they were also at the leading edge
of Restoration technology and tactics. Prior to Cromwell's naval wars,
battle fleets in the Northern European seas had mostly been made up
from converted merchant vessels which were lightly armed and
constructed. As a result they were intensely vulnerable. The days of
such vessels had now passed and, in their place, came 'great ships',
massive in size and bristling with ninety to a hundred guns. It was
essential that such ships be extensively and regularly refitted, and that
naval dockyards, architects and ordnance offices be run to the highest
standards of efficiency. Here was naval warfare on a new scale, and the
expense was staggering.

The cost of maintaining the navy even in peacetime was a prodigious
£500,000 a year, a sum which was never fully covered from public
revenues and which resulted in an accumulating and eventually
crippling debt. The exhaustion of the navy's credit was a constant
problem and led to the most desperate expedients. Because its adminis-
trators rarely had ample ready cash they usually had to secure supplies
at excessive prices. Sometimes money was so tight that crews could not
be paid off, while on other occasions ships had to be put out of commission because repairs were too expensive. Such was the distress of the
men working in the yards themselves that the rope-makers staged a
mass walk-out in the summer of 1665, and unpaid labourers in
Portsmouth were evicted from their lodgings to live on the streets,
where some of them perished from starvation.

It was against this distressing background that James started readying
his navy for battle. He had ninety-eight men-of-war at his disposal,

including three 'great ships' or 'first rates', eleven 'second rates', fifteen 'third rates', thirty-two 'fourth rates', eleven 'fifth rates' and an assortment of merchantmen, fireships and tenders. By 23 March 1665, daily meetings of his flag officers were taking place aboard the *Royal Charles*, and it was agreed that the war could be swiftly won by luring the Dutch into the open seas and engaging them as early as possible in a setpiece battle. As far as tactics were concerned, the principal objective was to get to the windward of the enemy and then take out Dutch vessels either by gunfire or by capturing them, boarding them or forcing them on to a shoal. A fleet sailing to windward could bear down and attack with ease. Its gunners would not be troubled by smoke, while such a position also allowed for the safe release of the dreaded fireships which, floating towards the enemy, threatened terrible havoc.

The ordinary seamen who were to fight the battle bore the brunt of the navy's financial shortfall, having to endure bad food and irregular pay. Worst of all, many were the victims of barbarous recruiting methods, the press-gangs especially. Any man with any experience of the sea might be called upon to fight. Men aboard homeward-bound merchantmen were 'impressed'. Men and even boys were seized as they plied their wherries on the Thames, while officials in coastal counties rounded up such men as they could find and left tickets in the cottages of others which presented the stark alternatives of naval service or gaol. So urgent was the need for men that farmers were pulled from their fields, and men as old as seventy were rounded up only to be declared unfit for service and sent home penniless. Ragged, sick and inexperienced, some of them no more than children, crews made up in such a manner were said to be fit only for rats.

By Sunday, 28 May, it was known that the Dutch fleet had set sail. Downing's espionage system had provided James with vital information, and the Lord High Admiral knew from this that the Dutch were under orders to attack, though their commander, Jacob van Obdam, was an ill man and an uninspiring leader who was unwilling to use the latest tactics and unable to unite the fractious men he led. To prepare for an engagement on the open seas, James ordered his fleet to sail for Southwold Bay. There the opposing fleets caught up with each other and moved ever closer as the breezes changed and permitted James to obtain the desired windward position. By four in the morning of 3 June, the fleets were off Lowestoft in 'a fine chasing gale'.[5] Aboard the English ships – the White fleet in the van, the Blue in the rear, and the heavily armed Red in the centre – each man was at his allotted place. The captains and the sailing masters stood on the poop decks to give their orders. The lieutenants and the master-gunners readied themselves to fire. Midshipmen stood by the yards listening for the sailing-masters' commands. Down in the bilges, carpenters and their crews prepared to make temporary repairs to the ships, while the chaplains and the surgeons waited in the cockpits to attend to the dead and dying.

The lines of ships at first passed each other three times, exchanging shots, but it was only by the afternoon that James was able to bear down on the Dutch and break their formation. Now the Dutch and the English flagships – *De Eendracht* and the *Royal Charles* – engaged each other in broadsides, while the captains aboard the other vessels plied their gunners hard for two hours. The noise was heard even in London, 'so that all men being alarmed with it, and in a dreadful suspense of the event which we knew was then deciding, everyone went following the sound as his fancy led him; and, leaving the town almost empty, some took towards the Park, some across the River, others down to it, all seeking the noise in the depth of silence'.[6] Meanwhile, thick gunsmoke palled the engagement off Lowestoft, and, as visibility was reduced, so, in a frightening tangle of masts and rigging, ships drifted where they would. The losses mounted and reached their terrible climax as shots tore into *De Eendracht*'s magazine, causing an explosion in which Obdam and 400 of his men were killed. There was no Dutch officer to take overall command, and the Dutch vessels tangled hopelessly with each other as English fireships bore down on them. Six thousand Dutch sailors were killed or captured, and seventeen of their men-of-war were burned, taken or sunk. The remainder prepared to flee.

The English had lost merely a single ship and now readied themselves to give chase, but a famous victory melted away through sheer dishonesty and incompetence. One of James's more disreputable friends, a certain Henry Brouncker, had seen the deaths of so many of his companions that he had lost all stomach for a fight. As his ship pressed the fleeing Dutch, he came up on deck with what he claimed were the Duke's orders to slacken sail. The captain obeyed without verifying the command and the rest of the fleet followed suit. In such a way was James's plan to get between the Dutch and their coast foiled, and the courageous de Witt seized the one opportunity of rallying his demoralised forces. He boarded the Dutch vessel furthest out from the shore and stayed aboard her until the tide returned her to her port. Once landed, he ordered courts martial, appointed a new commander at sea, and oversaw the rebuilding and re-equipping of the Dutch fleet. The English had fatally lost the opportunity of obliterating their enemy, and a continuance of the war was inevitable.

A frustrated James returned to the court, where Charles, concerned about the physical danger the heir had placed himself in, refused to allow him to sail in another sea-battle. The Earl of Sandwich was appointed in his place, and it was Sandwich who, in August 1665, led the disastrous expedition to attack the Dutch merchantmen harboured in the neutral port of Bergen. Enormous wealth was promised since the prizes were the rich fleets returning from Smyrna and the Indies, but riches were not the only consideration. Danish help had been enlisted, for a war between the Dutch and the Danes would close the Baltic to Dutch trade, thereby compounding the damage it was hoped to inflict by destroying the spice fleet. Nonetheless, this elaborate scheme collapsed when the English fleet sailed into Bergen and was immediately bombarded from the shore. After three hours the English were forced to retire and the Dutch sailed home in triumph.

The humiliation at Bergen not only wounded national pride. Sandwich's fleet had been more than usually ill-provisioned, and the reason for this was a clear indication of a natural disaster now raging at home. There had been a chronic shortage of food, water, beer and clothing on board the English ships because the providers of such staples had either died or left London for fear of the Plague. It was said, probably with as much prejudice as precision, that the scourge had come from the Levant and entered London in bales of Dutch merchandise. What is more certain is that the Plague was bubonic in form, was brought by rats, circulated by fleas and spread among humans by infected breath. The speed with which the contagion multiplied was terrifying. Forty-three deaths were notified in May 1665. By the following month 600 had died. In sweltering July, thousands were expiring, and when the epidemic peaked in September 30,000 deaths were reported. The bare statistics give no indication of the daily horrors endured.

While the King and his court retreated first to Salisbury and thence to Oxford (where their lewd behaviour caused consternation among town and gown alike) fearful Londoners were obliged to live and die amid constant suffering. Because there were no adequate hospitals for the sick, victims were isolated in their houses. Most of those affected were among the poor, and since the poor often lived in crowded tene- ments, the presence of one sufferer could bring certain death to as many as six families. So great was the scale of the epidemic that there was not enough lime to pick the corpses clean, and the innumerable shallow pits that were dug were invariably covered with crows and ravens glutting themselves on an unprecedented feast.

The authorities issued regulations, hoping to stem catastrophe by prudence. Public meetings were severely restricted and, when they were held, 'fires in moveable pans are to be used . . . and disinfectants are to be burnt thereon'. Pets and domestic animals were banned from the streets, and no more public houses were licensed 'than are absolutely necessary'. Huts and sheds were erected as makeshift pest houses. Wednesdays and Fridays were to be 'strictly' given over to fasting and public prayers. Finally, 'collections are to be made for the relief of the poor in infected places'.[7] Such measures may have helped limit the spread of the contagion, but its virulence demanded other approaches. Examiners were appointed in each parish to find out which houses were infected, and heads of households were expected to report to these people any swellings or blotches they noticed on their family members. Condemned houses were shut up, marked with a red cross a foot high, and guarded by watchmen night and day so that none could enter or leave. The local constables were to supply such food and other neces- saries as were required, and when death finally came the bodies were carted away and given a night burial that neither friends nor family were allowed to attend. The deserted houses were then placed in quarantine for a month.

The public's response to the catastrophe varied between piety and profanity, heroism and the meanest forms of self-seeking baseness. Houses daubed with the pathetic legend 'Lord have mercy on us' nestled side by side with those where 'tippling and whoring' wore out the days and nights. So-called plague nurses stole from the dead and dying while, on occasions, the suffering was relieved by grotesque comedy. One death cart carried away a bagpiper who was insensible from drink. Eventually he awoke, and, when he began blearily to play his pipes among the corpses, he was taken for the devil himself. Although the President of the Royal College of Physicians fled the capital, more modest doctors laboured with immense courage and an almost complete lack of science as they sought to cure the sick by recommending saline solutions, sweating and covering over 'the stomach with a palister, to guard it against corrosive effluvia'.[8] There were parish dignitaries who also conducted themselves with exemplary rectitude. While many of the wealthy quitted London, the staunchly Protestant merchant Sir Edmund Berry Godfrey, dressed in his black wig and hat with a gold band, stayed on to oversee mass burials and prosecute grave robbers. So conspicuous was the public service of this excellent man with his long-drawn face and stooping gait that the crowds grew to respect and love him, and King Charles, when the Plague was over, rewarded Godfrey with 800 ounces of gold plate.

The autumn of 1665 saw the retreat of the Plague but, as the new year approached, the war with the Dutch entered a new and dreadful phase. The Dutch had already shown themselves determined to take the initiative, for de Witt realised that the survival of his regime largely depended on his own inspiring leadership in the struggle with the English. Summoning extraordinary energy and personal courage, he resolved to sail with the Dutch fleet as its commander in all but name and to rely for practical advice on one of the greatest of his admirals, Michiel de Ruyter. His ambitious plans consisted not only of provoking a decisive battle at sea but of then sailing up the Thames estuary and sinking block ships in its main channels, thereby rendering access to the Port of London all but impossible. His first attempt, made in October 1665, failed, but so lamentable was the state of the English fleet that it did not dare to sortie out and engage with the enemy. Instead, its ships rocked at their anchorages, and the frustrated Dutch were reluctantly obliged to sail for home.

The next and bloodiest stage of the Dutch wars was partly brought about by events on the wider European stage. With the death of King Philip IV of Spain, the struggle between the English and the Dutch broadened into a matter of European strategy involving the ambitions of Louis XIV. The French King had already signed a treaty with the Dutch and now, as Louis sought to wrest important parts of the Spanish Netherlands from Spanish control, so he looked to de Witt as a vital ally. The defeat of the Dutch off Lowestoft had shown that the Dutch navy was far from invincible, and what Louis most feared was that another English victory would see de Witt replaced by the leaders of the House of Orange while the country itself became merely an English protectorate. Support for de Witt thus became a French priority, and Louis reluctantly entered the naval war while telling his admiral that the conservation of his fledgling fleet must be his chief concern.

Louis' decision to enter the war was very unpopular at the French court, Charles's sister Henriette Anne (or Madame, as her marriage now entitled her to be called) strongly opposing it for personal reasons, while others resented the Sun King's going to the support of a mere bourgeois republic. So adroit a politician was Louis that he turned even this criticism to his long-term advantage, encouraging Henriette Anne to continue writing to her brother so that he could covertly signal how reluctant he was to be warring on the English at all. A diplomatic line of communication was thereby set up with Madame at its centre which would in time prove itself to be of the utmost importance. Meanwhile, as war approached, Louis ordered his fleet to sail from Toulon. Such was the poor state of English information-gathering that Charles and his Council believed that the French were about to enter the Channel when in fact they had just arrived off Lisbon, where the French King ordered them to wait, pending the outcome of the first engagements between the English and the Dutch.

Such misinformation was to have the most serious consequences. The Privy Council decided that their only possible tactic was to divide the fleet, sending Prince Rupert with twenty ships to engage with the elusive French while Albermarle (the erstwhile General Monck) was despatched to cover the Thames estuary. But Albermarle not only had a depleted navy. There were those at court who resented the presence of an erstwhile Parliamentarian at the head of the fleet, and Albermarle was to come to believe that he did not even have the full-hearted support of all his officers. Certainly, when the great Dutch navy of eighty-four ships hoved into view there were those who counselled him not to fight. Albermarle brushed their objections aside with characteristic contempt and, on 31 May 1666, hoisted his sails for the most bloody of all the naval battles with the Dutch.

He headed for the enemy fleet anchored off Ostend and bore down on their rear. The Dutch Admiral, Cornelis Tromp, engaged with superior gunpower and forced Albermarle to go about as his fellow Dutch admirals, de Ruyter and Evertsen, joined the battle and sandwiched the English between two lines of fire. Sir William Berkeley was killed aboard the *Swiftsure*, while on the *Henry* Sir John Harman, his sails and rigging on fire, launched a broadside which killed Evertsen. The *Swiftsure*, the *Seven Oaks* and the *Loyal George* were all lost as Albermarle tried unsuccessfully to break the enemy line. Only at dusk did the fleets part to spend the night on necessary repairs.

The following morning, Albermarle gained the advantage of the wind with great difficulty but found he did not have sufficient ships to risk an attack and made instead for the English coast. The Dutch pursued him through the night, and by the following afternoon Rupert's fleet was seen returning from the Channel. Albermarle and Rupert resolved on a joint attack to be launched the following morning, hazarding their fifty-eight ships against the Dutch fleet of seventy-eight. There was prolonged firing during which a few English ships broke through the Dutch line. Sir Christopher Myngs distinguished himself with extraordinary courage when, surrounded by the enemy, he continued to give his orders even though part of his throat had been shot away and he was obliged to plug his windpipe with his fingers. Then a bullet through the neck brought his life to an end. By this time the main Dutch effort was concentrated on the *Royal Charles* and the *Royal James*. The rigging of both great ships was wrecked, the crews were exhausted, and only a sudden fog saved the English from annihilation. They had lost two admirals and twenty ships, while some 8000 men had been killed, wounded or taken prisoner. The Dutch had merely lost some half-dozen ships and 2000 men but, despite the carnage of what became known as the Four Days' Battle, no strategic advantage whatsoever had been achieved by either side.

The recrimination in England was bitter. Albermarle criticised the conduct of his captains, while he himself was blamed for underesti-mating the Dutch. Senior figures were berated for failing to order Rupert's swift return from his fool's errand of chasing after the French. Rupert himself was accused of lacking leadership, and the necessary hard questions were asked about the abysmal quality of English naval intelligence. The English dockyards nonetheless excelled themselves with the speed with which they refitted the damaged ships, and a mere six days later the fleet was ready to sail once more. Albermarle and Rupert manoeuvred close in-shore along the Dutch coast, hungry for prizes and revenge. A privateering raid on the island of Terschelling was mooted, and when Sir Robert Holmes reached there he found a vast flotilla of closely packed Dutch merchant vessels riding carelessly at anchor. The English launched their fireships at once, and in what became known as 'Holmes'' Bonfire some 170 Dutch ships were destroyed, £1 million of damage was inflicted, and a serious depression hit the Amsterdam trade.

The euphoria this produced was short-lived, for now, after war and plague, came a third catastrophe for England. The Great Fire of London began at 2 a.m. on Sunday, 2 September 1666, in the house of one Thomas Farrinor, a baker in Pudding Lane. However it was caused, Farrinor's shop was soon ablaze and, since London was tinder dry after a long hot summer, the fire rapidly spread, fanned by an easterly wind. The cheek-by-jowl confusion of timber-framed houses and inns, their yards littered with straw, provided ready kindling, and with burning embers blowing about the streets a conflagration began. Londoners were used to such incidents – fires were a fact of life – and they had taken little notice of the King's efforts to improve things. Six months earlier, Charles had written to the City authorities warning them of the dangers and pointing out the potential catastrophe lurking in narrow streets. Royal authority was given to the City fathers to pull such buildings down, but nothing was done. The usual precautions had always seemed good enough, and now, as the water-pumps were trundled along the cobbled streets, a peeved Lord Mayor, angry at being called from his bed, stared at the blaze and contemptuously declared that 'a woman might piss it out'.

Soon the blaze had carried the flames down Thames Street, and a burning arc of devastation raged along Fish Street Hill, Lombard Street and on to the Royal Exchange. The flames devoured all in their way as they raced towards London Bridge, where a third of the ramshackle buildings perched upon it were destroyed before the southward progress of the fire was stopped. The largest of the City's pumping machines was soon wrecked, and John Evelyn looked on appalled as the flames raged through 'churches, public halls, exchange, hospitals, monuments and ornaments, leaping after a prodigious manner from house to house and street to street'.[9] Still the authorities failed to take the necessary extreme measures. In theory they should have pulled down houses and made breaks too wide for the flames to leap. The Mayor and the Corporation knew that they were obliged to bear the cost of rebuilding properties so destroyed, and only royal authority could absolve them of their responsibilities. By dawn, that permission had been given, but by now the fire was raging westwards towards the Guildhall and St Paul's, reducing familiar landmarks to rubble.

King Charles behaved with exemplary concern and authority. He gave orders to be rowed in the royal barge from Whitehall to Queenhithe so that he could gain some personal knowledge of the scale of the catastrophe. Realising that it fell to him to take exceptional initiatives, he put himself in some personal danger as he urged the people to pull down houses. A special committee of the Privy Council was set up at Ely House from where, under the direction of the Duke of York and others, it was ordered that fire posts be set up and allowances be paid to those who manned them. Charles sent in his own troops to help clear the wooden wharves along the Fleet river. Trained bands from the surrounding counties were summoned to control the swelling, desperate crowds hurrying out of the inferno with such possessions as they could save. Many of these people were making for the open spaces of Moorfields and Spitalfields, where makeshift camps were established as the exhausted tens of thousands lay on the ground 'like herded beasts'.[10] Supplies of ships' biscuits were doled out to them, only to prove inedible.

Still the fire raged on. Cheap Street was ablaze. The great halls of the livery companies were reduced to ashes. The flames engulfed St Mary-le-Bow, and Bow bells fell molten to the ground. The heat was now so intense that terrible and unexpected catastrophes occurred. Huge fire-balls rolled with awful destruction and, drawing the air to themselves, created vacuums of such a scale that spires and ancient walls imploded, destroyed by an invisible power few if any understood. It was as if Doomsday had come and the wrath of God had been released – released, as some muttered, to punish the sins of the court. Human agency could do little, but still the King continued to set what example he could. He rode hither and thither across his wretched capital, his face black with soot, his clothes drenched with water and sweat. A purse of a hundred guineas hung from his shoulder and was emptied to encourage those who were striving with might and main. When his own hands were needed, Charles leaped from his horse and passed water buckets along the chain, toiling, as an observer noted, like 'a poor labourer'. Prayers and fasting were ordered, but no pleas to heaven could stop the flames as they rushed towards old St Paul's and fed on its timbers until the melting roof collapsed and the lead cascaded down Ludgate Hill.

By 6 September, when the fire had finally burned itself out, the task of reckoning up the destruction began. Two surveyors were appointed and came up with horrifying figures. Of the 450 acres within the City walls a mere 67 remained untouched. Over 13,000 houses had been destroyed, eighty-nine churches had been reduced to rubble, the halls of forty-four livery companies had had their splendours reduced to ash, and four bridges had collapsed. Over 100,000 people faced the prospect of a cruel and homeless winter. One of the great medieval cities of Europe lay in ruins, and it was estimated that £10,000,000 would be needed to rebuild it.

Charles played a major part in the reconstruction. He had already acquired a taste for building. His attempts to rebuild the palace of Whitehall had foundered through lack of money, but he had resolved on constructing a new palace at Greenwich, and now the devastation caused by the Great Fire stimulated the town planner in him. He appointed a Privy Council committee to oversee the work. He urged the City fathers to strive for 'the beauty, ornament, and convenience' of the new London.[11] He followed closely on a map the proposals for widening and straightening existing streets, made numerous suggestions, and above all encouraged the use of brick rather than flammable wood. Grand designs for remodelling the City around a logical sequence of straight, intersecting thoroughfares foundered, but Charles had in Sir Christopher Wren an architect of genius. If Wren's contribution to the rebuilding of London has sometimes been exaggerated, he nonetheless provided the City with some of its most beautiful parish churches and the baroque masterpiece that is St Paul's Cathedral. That vast structure – its rhetoric perfectly adapted to grand ceremonial functions, and its dome one of the supreme achievements of European architecture – remains the most massive if not the most lovable witness to the artistic flowering of the Restoration.

The process of rebuilding London was agonisingly slow, despite the proud legend on the Monument that 'three short years complete that which was considered the work of an age'. The long-drawn-out suffering meanwhile deepened the resentment and suspicion that the Fire had given rise to. Demoralised Londoners were left looking for explanations of the woes that had fallen on them, although Charles had taken the earliest opportunity to reassure them. Riding out on 6 September 1666, he told the crowds that the Fire was not the result of a plot but was simply due to the hand of God. Many refused to accept this. They sought a moral explanation for what had happened and, as they did so, the bitter religious divides in the country widened dangerously. The Quakers were certain that the Fire was a righteous punishment visited on a city that had so conspicuously persecuted them. Others feared that it was the work of extreme sectarian groups, but by far the greater part of this unjustified suspicion was directed to an old and traditional enemy. The Great Fire could only have been the work of Roman Catholics seeking to undermine the confidence and prosperity of a virtuous, Protestant people. The poison of bigotry, wrung from fear, flowed through national life with a new vehemence, and soon anti-popery would become the most dangerous of the nation's neuroses.

Across the North Sea, meanwhile, the Dutch had their own views on the origins of the Great Fire of London. It was God's revenge for the burning of their fleet by the English. A pamphlet gloatingly described how the 'proud and self-satisfied city' of London had not enjoyed this national triumph for long, for the Lord of Hosts 'with His wind threw down all the remaining buildings, beautiful palaces and shops of the rich merchants which were swallowed up and destroyed'.[12] Now, the Dutch believed, the damage wrought by the Almighty could be made worse by the hand of man. They sent a secret agent to reconnoitre the English coast and the approaches to the great naval dockyard at Chatham especially, and by the summer of 1667 the situation appeared particularly propitious for an attack. Chronic financial difficulties had obliged the English to keep their fleet at anchor. Supplies voted by Parliament had been used of necessity to help clear the mountain of accumulated naval debt, and there was no money left to pay contractors and victuallers in readiness for fresh initiatives. Even supplies for repairs had run out, and unpaid workers had downed their tools and gone elsewhere. What cash there was the authorities spent on comparatively small-scale defences such as the great chain, guarded by gun batteries, which was stretched as a barrier across the Medway.

The Dutch were now well prepared to realise their long-nurtured dream of a raid deep into English waters. The work of their spies had familiarised them with the complex channels of the Medway, and they timed their sailing so that they could take advantage of a spring tide. Once launched, their fleet was divided, the larger part being sent to cruise the mouth of the Thames while a squadron of seventeen warships and twenty-four auxiliaries was despatched up the Medway. Immediate panic ensued. Neither Gravesend nor Tilbury were adequately defended, while at Chatham itself Albermarle discovered that neither ammunition nor boats were available. Defending the great chain at once became his principal concern, but here again incompetence and low morale were working their effects. Albermarle eventually managed to have some lesser ships scuttled on either side of his last line of defence, thereby narrowing access to the river, but he soon discovered not only that the defensive batteries which supposedly covered the chain were manned by amateurs but that the oak mountings on the guns themselves had been stolen and the cheap planks used to replace them so flimsy that the gun-wheels sank into the mud after each firing. The greater part of the English fleet, lying at Chatham and poorly manned, could not be defended from an enemy attack.

Mutiny compounded the incompetence. As the Dutch sailed up the river, unpaid, disillusioned seamen and dockyard workers stood idly by. The crew of the *Unity*, the frigate guarding the chain, deserted. The Dutch then released the first of their fireships and, as it broke through, crews from other guardships and even the *Royal Charles* itself surrendered. More Dutch fireships destroyed the *Royal Oak*, the *Loyal London* and the *Royal James*. Albermarle's cannon returned merely ineffective fire as the triumphant Dutch wrought deepening disaster. Only when the last of their fireships had been sent in did they retire, using merely 'a sorry boat and six men' to tow away the greatest of all their prizes: the English flagship, the *Royal Charles*.[13] As the thick smoke spiralled into the sky, the national humiliation was complete. In John Evelyn's words, it was 'a dreadful spectacle as ever Englishman saw and a dishonour never to be wiped off'.[14]

While the rejoicing Dutch struck medals and presented their admirals with golden cups, recrimination in England was bitter. The angry voices of the disfranchised many were loud in the London streets. It was clear where the fault lay. The national humiliation was a direct result of the 'debauchery and drunkenness at court', but then again 'no better could be expected when the Popish and profane party are in such credit'.[15] This heady brew of sex and sectarianism yeasted ever more violently in the popular mind, and street politics became acrimonious. Underlying it all was a deep-seated fear that England would fall a prey to the twin foreign evils of popery and tyranny. Pepys heard the complaints and noted in his diary 'how the people do cry out . . . that we are bought and sold and governed by the papists and that we are betrayed by the people about the King and shall be delivered up to the French'.[16]

Parliamentarians were equally bitter, and what could not be said in the House was sometimes confided to paper. The Restoration saw the widespread and often illicit circulation of biting political satires, either in surreptitious printings or as manuscripts that were secretly copied out at home. Pepys collected these avidly and wrote of one that 'it made my heart ache to read it, it being too sharp, and so true'.[17] Andrew Marvell, now Member of Parliament for Hull, was one of the bitterest and liveliest of these satirists, and his 'Last Instructions to a Painter' offers a vivid picture of the sleazy grandees and placemen attached to the Court. Castlemaine is attacked with particular savagery, Marvell creating a salacious cartoon image of her chasing a well-hung groom, washing down his smelly body and then tickling him between the toes before returning to the presumably more hygienic delights of Henry Jermyn.

When people thought about the court of Charles II, this is what many of them imagined. Marvell captured the feelings of horror and outrage that the most intelligent people felt, but, significantly, he did not attack the King himself. The role, if not the man, still commanded the most profound respect. For Marvell, the corrupt courtiers and the self-seeking placemen are spots blemishing the brilliant sun of royalty. How much happier the nation would be if the King were advised by honourable men – by members of Marvell's own Country party – all of them true patriots, public spirited and incorruptible. The language of a profound political divide was here being formed, and for Marvell it was the gentry of the Country party alone who could oppose the corruption of the court faction – that 'race of Drunkards, Pimps, and Fools'.[18]

In such a frenetic atmosphere as this wild rumours circulated that

Charles had abdicated and fled. There was a run on the banks, and people bitterly compared Cromwell's successes at sea with the present defeat. A swiftly negotiated peace appeared the only option and was strongly urged by Clarendon. 'Although peace can be bought at too high a price,' he wrote, 'it would suit us highly in the circumstances and we are not in a position to decline. Peace is needed to calm the people's minds, and would free the King from a burden which he is finding hard to bear.' The English negotiators were instructed to be conciliatory in their approach, and the Peace of Breda eventually confirmed Dutch claims to West Africa and Surinam, while the English retained possession of New York, New Jersey and New Delaware. Dutch ships would lower their flags to English vessels in the Channel only. Nonetheless, national pride was not entirely salvaged and a scapegoat still had to be found.

To most people, the victim was obvious. An angry mob, sore from what they viewed as the humiliation of the sale of Dunkirk, had already pulled up the trees and smashed the windows of Clarendon's palatial house in Piccadilly, thereby showing where the popular mind at least laid the blame for the recent defeat. But the Chancellor had more immediately powerful enemies at court. Younger men such as his rival Henry Bennet, now Earl of Arlington, and Buckingham's protégé Thomas Clifford, along with Thomas Osborne and Sir William Coventry, the newly appointed Joint Commissioner of the Treasury, all saw the Chancellor's fall as expedient to their own rise. They found a natural ally in Castlemaine, who proceeded vehemently to nag the King on their behalf. In particular she was concerned that her kinsman, the Duke of Buckingham, recently sent to the Tower for his outspoken attacks on Charles, should be reinstated in the royal favour. She approached the King with so bold a front that he flew into a temper and called her a whore who had no business meddling in affairs that did not concern her. She responded by telling Charles that he was a fool who did not know who his true friends were. The couple did not speak for four days, but the King eventually relented and Buckingham was released, enabling him actively to promote the careers of his clients who sought Clarendon's fall.

Castlemaine had got her way, but she was not the only female thorn in the royal flesh. Frances Stuart had refused to succumb to Charles's will and, in April 1667, she returned his presents and eloped with the Duke of Richmond. So much for royal favour, the delights of a long pursuit, the placing of the girl's image on every coin in every purse in the realm. Charles's disappointment and fury boiled over in a letter to his sister. 'You may think me ill-natured,' he wrote, 'but if you consider how hard a thing 'tis to swallow an injury done by a person I have had so much tenderness for, you will in some degree [understand] the resentment I use towards her.'[19] The 'resentment' was clear to many, as was the fact that his passions were clouding his judgement. The observant were scornful. Pepys believed that the King was increasingly governed by wine, woman and rogues. The story leaked out that, on the night of the burning of the English fleet, Charles had supped with Castlemaine and the new Duchess of Monmouth and that, while the nation's sea defences burned to ruins, he had frittered his time away chasing a moth about the room. For moralists, the lessons were clear. Plague, fire and war were judgements from heaven against 'our prodigious ingratitude, burning lusts, dissolute court, profane and abominable lives'. England was a new Egypt, a second Sodom.

The sacrifice of an unpopular minister might yet appease the national mood. Besides, the weight of Charles's own resentment against Clarendon was beginning to chafe. Entering now on middle age, the King found his Chancellor's familiar shortcomings – his natural assumption of moral superiority and censoriousness, his disapproval of younger men, and his hostility to innovation – increasingly irksome. The fact that Clarendon was so often right was no more attractive. But Clarendon was an ageing man. He no longer had the energy fully to discharge the responsibilities he had jealously gathered to himself. More dangerously, he was generally unpopular not only in court circles and among the general public, but in Parliament too. It was increasingly plain that he regarded the House of Commons as an institution to be kept strictly within bounds, and some even accused him of having said that its only use was to raise money for politics it had no right to meddle with. By late August 1667, Charles believed that the Commons was planning to impeach Clarendon, and he made it known that he wished him to resign. Clarendon refused, rightly pointing out that he had committed no crime. At the end of the month however, as pressure mounted, an aide was sent to collect his seals of office.

The victory of Clarendon's enemies was still incomplete. Castlemaine might be exultant and sycophantic courtiers declare that only now could Charles be truly called a king. Buckingham however was resolved on Clarendon's total destruction, and he worked subtly on Charles until the King's resentment against his oldest and most loyal servant became so bitter that he ordered that charges should be prepared against him. By the close of October, the Commons had appointed a committee to consider how an impeachment might be drawn up. Buckingham assured the King that only Clarendon's death would appease the angry House, and the list of offences was prepared. The greater part of these amounted to no more than hearsay accusations and complaints against the Chancellor's undoubted high-handedness and avariciousness. The House of Commons nonetheless voted them forward, and it was only the Lords which stood firm, despite vehement campaigning from Buckingham and the King himself.

But Charles had gone too far to retreat. His political survival was at stake and he leaked to Clarendon a plan whereby Parliament would be prorogued and a court of twenty-four hostile peers appointed to hear the accusations of treason levelled against him. The legal mind could see that these were trumped-up charges, but the legal mind was power-less in its own defence. A last meeting with the King, a meeting at which Clarendon foolishly lectured Charles on the pernicious influence of Castlemaine, neither proved the great servant's guilt nor revealed his master's pity. Clarendon at last recognised that his life was in peril and that flight was his only course. As he left Whitehall on his way to France – where he would complete his great history of the civil war – a triumphant Castlemaine, arrayed only in her nightdress, stood 'joying herself at the old man's going away'. It was said that Clarendon himself looked up at the woman who had done so much to destroy him and declared: 'O madam, is it you? Pray remember that if you live, you will grow old.'[20] With the great representative of conservatism thus shamefully discarded, Charles would have to seek for new ways to rule, new ways to ensure his survival.

The Grand Design

The fall of Clarendon broke the mould of English politics and ushered in a new period of deviousness, deceit and mounting suspicion. In time the effects of this would seep across the whole country, poisoning the euphoria with which Charles had been welcomed back to his throne. The problems were felt first, and most poignantly, in his own family.

For all that his brother's marriage to Anne Hyde had long ago lost its intimacy and James himself had guiltily pursued a train of women, the Duke felt honour-bound to defend his father-in-law. He pressed Charles to allow the old man to return to the country, and the King replied that, while he would take no offence at any kindnesses offered to him, Clarendon would not be allowed to come home. Charles himself had been at pains to indicate his displeasure with others who supported his erstwhile Lord Chancellor, and he had been particularly severe towards the bench of bishops, who had virtually to a man seen Clarendon as the defender of the Anglican constitution. In response, the bishops of Winchester and Rochester were told to leave the court, while the powerful Sheldon was removed from the Council and informed that the King no longer wished to hear him preach. Such moves inevitably caused concern, and as worried conservatives began to group themselves around the Duke so a 'kind of inward distance' grew up between him and Charles.[1]

What his allies took for rectitude in James was in fact a form of rigidity. He was not a completely foolish man. He was brave and energetic, but he had a craving for authoritarian certainties which he increasingly felt could be satisfied only by submitting himself to the Catholic church. His experiences on the continent had fed this propensity and, lacking his brother's guile and pragmatism, he had allowed his conscience to rub itself sore. At the time of the Restoration it was whispered that James was 'a professed friend to the Catholics', and his home life encouraged this interest.[2] Anne Hyde may no longer have interested him sexually – she had taken refuge in comfort-eating and troubled corpulence – but the power of her character was not to be gainsaid and she too was turning to Rome, dying in March 1671 a professed Catholic. By the close of the 1660s James was approaching a religious crisis and he later dated his conversion to 1669. He continued to attend Anglican services for another seven years, growing increasingly restive and guilty as he did so. His secret feelings had nonetheless to be hidden as best they could because, in the absence of a legitimate heir, James was the successor to the Protestant English throne.

While the Queen's infertility made James an important man, it brought only misery to Catherine herself. The corridors of her husband's palaces echoed to the sounds of his bastards at play while she was obliged to endure a succession of miscarriages. Early in May 1668, she was delivered of a stillborn child and Charles, as ever confiding his most personal thoughts to Henriette Anne, told her that he was 'troubled'. There was only one consolation to be drawn. ' 'Tis evident she was with child, which I will not deny to you till now I did fear she was not capable of.'[3] The following year the signs of a second pregnancy were eagerly watched by the King, the court and the country at large. Pepys recorded in his diary that he had had a glimpse of Catherine in the white apron of an expectant mother. A delighted Madame was again bombarded with details. 'She missed *those*', Charles told her, referring to Catherine's periods, 'almost, if not altogether, twice.' The poor Queen was again terrified that she might miscarry and had to batten on what comfort she could. 'The midwives who have searched her say that her matrix [womb] is very close, though it be a little low,' Charles told his sister. 'She has now and then some little shows of *them*, but in so little quantity as it only confirms the most knowing women here that there is a fair conception.'[4] Such hopes were once more frustrated in June 1669, and Charles himself gave up believing that his wife would ever conceive again.

The disappointed father had, nonetheless, the responsibilities of a king, and offering comfort had to give way to shaping a policy. While whispering abounded – there was vague talk of a remarriage in the event of the Queen's death, and more dangerous gossip that Monmouth was either legitimate or could be pronounced so – Charles took a brief but active interest in a legal solution to his problem. The House of Lords was currently preoccupied with the Roos case. Lord Roos had already obtained a church divorce in order to separate himself from his unfaithful wife and bastardise her children. Now he sought a civil measure which would permit him to remarry. In defiance of the greater number of his bishops, Charles helped the Bill through the Lords, re-alising that it might in the last resort provide the precedent for his own remarriage if he divorced Catherine for infertility. So tendentious an interest roused not only the opposition of the clergy. The royal mistresses were worried for their livelihoods, while the Duke of York feared for his position as heir. In the end, Charles did not take advantage of the Lords' ruling, preferring instead to remain by his Queen and to stand firmly by the natural rights of his brother.

Among those who had encouraged Charles's interest in the Roos case was Buckingham, whose mercurial mind had now taken a fancy to political power. As ever, his ideas were wildly impractical. His solution to the problem of the Queen, for example, was rumoured to be having her kidnapped if she refused to retreat in decent shame behind the walls of a nunnery. His interests went further, however, than separating the King from his wife. Buckingham fomented the differences between Charles and his brother and then, wishing to extend his range, severely threatened the already strained relationship between the King and the Commons. Buckingham appeared to get his way because of the lifelong friendship he had enjoyed with Charles, nurtured by the Duke's wit. Buckingham was exciting company, and here was a particularly dangerous form of influence for, as contemporaries recognised, 'there is no way to rule the King but by briskness [wit], which the Duke of Buckingham hath above all other men'.[5]

Buckingham knew that to build up his political strength he had to establish his own placemen by ousting those of others. Sometimes personal vendettas helped in this. The assertive if highly efficient Treasury Commissioner William Coventry, a personal aide of James's, was dismissed from his office, having foolishly challenged Buckingham to a duel. A campaign was also launched against Ormonde. Buckingham craved the office of Lord Lieutenant of Ireland, saying that the work could be done by a deputy. Ormonde was naturally concerned, but was given assurances by the King that he could 'rest confident of his justice and favour to me'.[6] This was a lie. Buckingham cornered Charles at a 'merry party', insisted once again on Ormonde's removal and got his way. The callous treatment of so fine a man as Ormonde says much about Charles's methods, as does the fact that he then appointed a nonentity to Ireland and thereby deceived Buckingham of his hopes.

Charles felt he needed his friend all the same, and he believed that Buckingham had a particular influence among the 'factious'. It was partly because of this that Charles now encouraged the Duke to urge on the House an old but most unpopular idea. In February 1668, Charles asked Parliament to find 'some course to get a better union and composure in the minds of my Protestant subjects'.[7] He was looking, in other words, to establish that degree of religious toleration he had failed to win at the time of his restoration. Free now of Clarendon, Charles had no wish to be dependent on others, and, by gaining the active support of his Noncomformist subjects, he might yet liberate himself from the all-mastering influence of the Anglican establishment. He wished increasingly to live by his prerogative powers.

Buckingham proceeded to campaign with such obvious indiscretion that Sheldon got wind of his plans and organised a counter-attack. The Bishop showed the skill of a practised politician. Much was made of small disturbances committed by Dissenters, while the baleful influence of 'conventicles' or small, private prayer meetings was loudly insisted upon. These last, it was said, were hotbeds of sedition. Buckingham had undertaken to manage the House, but his aides or 'undertakers' so overplayed their hand that not only were the King's hopes heavily defeated but a Parliamentary backlash was built up among those calling themselves 'friends to the Constitution in Church and State'. These men were determined to resist innovation, but as yet they were not hostile to Charles himself, declaring that 'the King, if he pleases, may take a right measure of our temper . . . and leave off creating the undertakers, who persuade him that the generality of the kingdom and of our House too is inclined to a toleration'.[8]

Nor was the House any more inclined to tolerating equality and union with the Scots. Charles's principal servant in Scotland was the Earl of Lauderdale, a man extraordinary for combining extravagance and coarseness of manner with wide scholarship – he had mastered Latin, Hebrew and Greek – along with a genuine Scots nationalism. He and his wife, the formidable Bess, Countess of Dysart, spent furiously on their court, but as 'a man very national and truly the honour of our Scots' Lauderdale saw it as his responsibility to win Charles over with the idea that Scotland might be 'a citadel for his Majesty's service'.[9] Lauderdale aimed to achieve this new and closer relationship by righting the wrongs of the repressed and suffering Scots people who would then gratefully accede to union with England and become firm supporters of the royal prerogative. Charles himself, lured by tales of the large Scots army that would be at his disposal, recommended the idea of union to the House of Commons but met with an angry response. The expectations of equality the Scots held were wholly unacceptable to the Commons and, faced with vehement opposition, Charles lost interest in the idea of union altogether. Increasingly exasperated by opposition to his religious and domestic policy, he prorogued Parliament.

Disappointment with the conduct of foreign affairs also soured Charles's attitude towards Parliament. The disastrous conclusion of the Dutch Wars had convinced the King that he should never again let himself be involved against the united powers of France and Holland,

and he was now determined to try and break the alliance between these two countries and assert his prerogative powers in the shaping of foreign policy. Formidable difficulties stood in the way. The Dutch were grateful for the French help they had received and wanted to ensure its continuance, while an open agreement with Catholic France was offensive to every fibre of the true Protestant Englishman. Such people's interest in foreign affairs pointed them in the direction of profitable trading links with Spain, France's traditional enemy. Indeed, a treaty had recently been signed with Spain in which a secret clause stipulated that neither country would go to the help of the other's enemies. Practical and diplomatic reasons thus barred an open alliance with France, but it is an indication of the way in which Charles's mind was working that he now wrote privately to Louis XIV promising that the deal being negotiated with Spain was 'only a simple treaty of commerce which would in no circumstances be prejudicial to France'.[10] The King was once again trying to be all things to all men, and with the underhandedness that was now second nature to him, he assured Louis that he would spend the next year trying to negotiate a close agreement with him. The conduct of foreign policy was, after all, a central element of the royal prerogative.

This delicate play of deceit was thrown into confusion by Louis' territorial ambitions. Louis himself was to write a few years later that 'my dominant passion is certainly the love of glory', and it was in pursuit of *la gloire* that he now marched into the Spanish Netherlands and laid claim to them in the name of his wife.[11] His easy success startled Europe and, realising the diplomatic advantage this gave him, Louis reined back his enthusiastic generals and opened negotiations with the rulers of the Holy Roman Empire, Holland and England. Each of them, Louis believed, had their reasons to want him as an ally. Charles had certainly hinted as much, and the Protestant Marquis de Ruvigny was despatched to London to negotiate an agreement. For England, an open alliance with France was still out of the question, but neutrality could be bought at a price. Charles, urged on by Buckingham, asked for a French subsidy, a share in French conquests and commercial privileges. The French, believing this to be exorbitant, returned a dusty answer, and

Charles's first attempt to ally himself with the most thrusting state in Europe failed.

He did not give up. At a meeting of the Committee of Foreign Affairs held on 1 January 1668, Charles decided on an altogether more subtle approach to France. In order to bring an end to the war in the Spanish Netherlands without offending the French themselves, he suggested that England accept a hint given by the Dutch and ally with Holland to put pressure on Spain, obliging it thereby to accept the terms Louis had offered. Buckingham's rival, Arlington, a cautious, experienced diplomat, Protestant in his sympathies and personally dependent on the royal bounty to support his lifestyle, headed these negotiations. Agreements were reached over the combined use of force, a secret clause confirmed that the allies would turn on France itself if Louis reneged on his promises, and, with the inclusion of Sweden in the treaty, it appeared that Charles was now a leading player in a Protestant Triple Alliance. In other words, he had become a force to be reckoned with in Europe and Louis would have to take notice of him. Charles wrote to his sister to make sure that he did. 'I believe you will be a little surprised at the treaty I have concluded with the States [General],' he declared. He assured her that he had entered on it only to help Louis make peace and that 'I have done nothing to prejudice France in the agreement.' Besides, what else could he have done? He had tried to make friendly overtures to Louis but 'finding my propositions to France received so cold an answer, which in effect was as good as a refusal, I thought I had no other way to secure myself'.[12]

Having publicly declared his Protestant credentials, Charles believed he could turn to Parliament in the expectation of a generous supply. 'I lie under great debts contracted in the last war,' he told the Members, 'but now the posture of our neighbours abroad, and the consequence of the new alliance will oblige me, for our security, to set out a considerable fleet to sea this summer.' There were fortifications to be looked at as well, and 'besides, I must build more great ships'.[13] The House was far from impressed. Members were still troubled by the King's attack on the Anglican establishment and were busying themselves in an examination of the costs and causes of England's defeat at the hands of the

Dutch. They were in no mood to be generous and feared that any additional money they might offer would be used for purposes other than they intended. Charles grew increasingly impatient. He wrote to his sister saying that 'the Parliament goes on very slowly in their money, but they advance something every day'.[14] Eventually they agreed to supply the King with an insignificant £300,000, which would be raised mainly by taxes on French wines and spirits. They then made their opinions of Charles's religious policies clear by moving the second reading of a Bill against conventicles which provided for the distraining of the goods of those dissenters who attended them.

It was during this frustrating period for the King, with an obstructive Parliament prorogued, that Charles's new policies began to crystallise. He was at last determined to take a decisive role in the leadership of his country, and all his efforts would be directed towards increasing royal authority by freeing himself from the restraints placed on him by the Anglican church and Parliament. Caution, compromise and consensus had not led to the creation of a great and powerful European figure, and Charles was clearly resolved to become this. The reserves of energy and enthusiasm on which he drew were matched only by the subtlety of his guile and the depths of his deceit.

His ideas also involved enormous personal risks. Charles would try to free himself from the Anglican gentry and win the support of Catholics and Nonconformists by offering them toleration. He would try to boost his international role – and also guard his back – by forming a secret alliance with France. Last, but by no means least, he would reopen the war against the Dutch. Success in battle would expunge the recent sense of national humiliation. The esteem and power Charles gained would enable him to install his nephew, the young William of Orange, as the sovereign Prince of Holland and thus a powerful ally. Most alluringly of all, victory at sea would produce prizes, vastly increase English maritime trade and augment the customs revenue, thereby at last freeing Charles from what he saw as his humiliating financial dependence on a parliament.

Such ambitions formed the first part of the so-called Grand Design, allies and enemies the second. To help secure these last, Charles leaked to Louis the secret clause in the Triple Alliance whereby its signatories had agreed to unite against France in the event of Louis reneging on his promises to Spain. By so doing, Charles signalled to the French King the true direction of his interests. He was not a Protestant potentate but a useful friend, someone worth taking notice of. Negotiations were opened in April 1668, but Charles proved so difficult to pin down that they eventually came to nothing. This was just what he hoped. Such international dealing was not to be principally a matter for diplomats. The King of England wanted to conduct affairs in his own person and Louis willingly concurred. After all, what had the most astute King in Europe to lose by dealing directly with one of the least practised and most lazy?

It was agreed that Henriette Anne would provide the ideal medium for a secret correspondence. Louis was prepared to accept her as 'the natural bond of union between us' and also because, by employing such a person, international secrets would not become the automatic possession of Charles's ministers.[15] As for Charles himself, the sister whom he loved and who had been the recipient of the most intimate details of his married life would now be the go-between for his political ambitions. He repeatedly urged the utmost discretion on her. 'I must again conjure you', he wrote, 'that the whole matter be an absolute secret, otherwise we will never compass the aim we end at.'[16] Henriette Anne was delighted to accept such a role, seeing it as a means of immersing herself in something other than the details of her unhappy marriage while also boosting her adored brother's prestige. 'Your glory and profit will coincide in this design,' she wrote of the forthcoming war with the Dutch. 'What is there more glorious and more profitable than to extend the confines of your kingdom beyond the sea and become supreme in commerce, which is what your people most passionately desire and what will probably never occur so long as the Republic of Holland exists.'[17] Most of the elements of contemporary royal ambition are here: glory, territory, a patriarchal concern for the people, a contempt for democracy and a relish for family fixing. All that is absent is a sense of naked greed.

It was this last that provided both Charles and Louis with their real reason for war. The Dutch were fabulously rich, wealthier per head than either the English or the French. The world's bullion flowed along Amsterdam's canals and was hoarded there in the world's largest bank, which by 1670 could boast deposits of nearly five million florins. The city's Exchange dealt in stocks and shares on an unprecedented scale, and envious observers could berate the Dutch as 'the people who absorb nearly all the profits of trade in all parts of the world and leave only a very small portion to the other nations'.[18] This last was the crux of the problem. It was believed by most economists that the world's wealth consisted of bullion, that this was of a more or less fixed quantity, and that the only way of increasing a nation's share was to use the machinery of government to grab it. In the last resort, this meant war. For all the immense and successful efforts he had made to boost French industry, Louis himself subscribed to this notion, and he was now preparing to seize a large portion of Dutch wealth with a huge navy and an unprecedented army of 119,000 officers and men. These were trained, in part, by one Colonel Martinet.

The advantages to Charles of such a powerful ally were more evident than the risks, for he was playing an extremely dangerous game. The alliance, when it became known, could only prove abhorrent to the greater part of his people, while the underlying reason for engaging in it at all – the unashamed augmenting of royal power at the expense of the church and Parliament – was all too terribly reminiscent of the years of his father's personal rule. Charles had no substantial military forces of his own to defend him from his people's wrath, nor was there any guarantee that a politician so astute and ruthless as Louis would stick by him once the King of England had served his use. Some means had therefore to be found of placing the most powerful man in Europe under an obligation, and it was this difficulty that gave rise to the most extraordinary of all the terms agreed by the two kings: at a time suitable to Charles himself, and in return for a French subsidy and the promise of armed support, Charles would declare his conversion to the Catholic church.

It does little credit to Charles's deviousness to suggest that there was anything sincere about this. It is true that at home he was surrounded by Catholics and crypto-Catholics, but he was fully aware of the enormous weight of public opposition to their beliefs. It may also be true (the single source for the story is unreliable) that, on the anniversary of the feast of the conversion of St Paul, a haggard and tearful Charles confessed to his brother and a small circle of James's friends that he was troubled at being unable openly 'to profess the faith in which he believed'.[19] However, Charles's Scots coronation had shown him to be a skilful actor on such occasions as these and he had since had time to hone his craft. He was certainly not bought by Louis, for the offered subsidy was small. Nor did he necessarily see the Catholic church as the indispensable support of a powerful monarchy. The King of Sweden, after all, was a Protestant. There remains only one answer: Charles was indulging in a form of blackmail. If matters in England turned dangerously sour, Charles could announce his conversion to Roman Catholicism, and King Louis of France – *le roi très chrétien* – would be obliged to come to his support for the honour and security of Catholic Europe. It was a question of survival. In the last resort, Charles the grandson of Henri IV knew that England, quite as much as Paris, was worth a mass.

By May 1670, the intricate and hard-fought negotiations for the Grand Alliance were all but complete and it remained only to sign the deal. What better cover was there for so secret an undertaking than an elaborate state visit from Charles's sister, Henriette Anne? It was over nine years since he had last seen her – their relationship had been kept alive entirely by correspondence – and Charles's excitement was clear. It had been arranged that the royal couple should meet at Dover, but Charles arrived too early and had to return to London, from where he took a ship, hoping to rendezvous with Henriette Anne at sea. The winds were against him, however, and he was obliged to return to Dover. There he greeted his sister's arrival seated in the royal barge.

The cold May rain failed to damp the pleasure of the reunion, a pleasure made all the more intense on Henriette Anne's part by the fact that she had only with the greatest difficulty persuaded her wretched husband to let her travel at all. Now she revealed her charm. The royal couple embraced with a show of deep affection. There were parties at sea at which Henriette Anne showed herself 'fearless and bold' as she worked her way along 'the edges of the ships'.[20] There was a visit to Canterbury and a play and a ballet to attend. Her brother showered presents upon her and, for all the state of his finances, gave her a thousand crowns to build a chapel in memory of their mother, who had recently died. Only one disappointment marred Charles's pleasure. There was in his sister's train an attractive, baby-faced lady-in-waiting called Louise de Kéroualle. The King was determined to have her, but Henriette Anne put a stop to the hoped-for intimacy. She was, she said, responsible to the young girl's parents and Louise's honour was a sacred trust.

Meanwhile, the real diplomatic work of the visit was concluded. The Treaty of Dover provided the groundwork for an alliance between England and France, and was based, on Charles's part at least, on undiluted cynicism. The treaty provided Charles with the sum of two million livres tournois and declared that 'the lord king of Great Britain, being convinced of the truth of the Catholic religion', had 'resolved to declare it and reconcile himself with the Church of Rome as soon as the welfare of his kingdom will permit'.[21] The timing of this declaration was left to Charles himself, but to protect him from the all but inevitable consequences of so rash an act – assuming that he was ever foolish enough to commit it – Louis would provide him with 6000 footsoldiers at his own expense. The fifth clause then laid bare the real reason why the two kings had woven this intricate web of hypocrisy. It declared that Charles and Louis would make war on the Dutch States General in order 'to reduce the power of a nation which has so often rendered itself odious by extreme ingratitude to its own founders'.[22] A thin smoke-screen of moral justification was raised in this way to hide the naked rivalry and sheer greed that were the true reason for hostilities. The treaty was signed on 22 May 1670 and, as the ink dried, there remained to Charles only the delicate business of bamboozling the greater number of his closest ministers.

Arlington and the tough-minded, domineering Treasury Commissioner Thomas Clifford – both of whom were to die confessed Catholics – had already signed the treaty and were thus fully aware of

what their master was up to. Charles nonetheless thought it necessary
to bring Buckingham, Lauderdale and Ashley into his scheme and, in
order to fool them, a second bogus treaty – a treaty *simule* – was
prepared. This made no mention whatsoever of the King's alleged
conversion to the Catholic faith, and at the close of the year the fraud-
ulent document was signed by the five advisers closest to him: Clifford,
Arlington, Buckingham, Ashley and Lauderdale. The initials of these
men made up the word Cabal – a word suggesting intrigue and underhand dealing – but the very fact that three of those included were not
privy to the full range of Charles's deviousness suggests that the
acronym has a neatness which does scant justice to the divisions and the
lack of trust that truly marked their relationship. This was precisely
what Charles intended. 'When rogues fall out,' he once declared, 'the
master is like then to know the truth.'[23]

Henriette Anne's business was now concluded and the time came for
her to depart. Charles was visibly moved. Even the French ambassador
felt obliged to report his surprise that so wily and manipulative a man
should be capable of such deep feeling as he watched brother and sister
embrace and then turn from each other no fewer than three times. But
this display of feeling concealed a deeper pathos, for Henriette Anne
was now seriously ill. Throughout her stay in England she had lived on
little more than sips of milk and had easily grown tired. On returning
home she sent her brother 'the firste letter I have ever write in inglis',
declaring 'how much I am your frind'.[24] By 29 June she was so ill that
she took to her bed where, amid the appalling anguish inflicted by
the poisoning of an already perforated duodenal ulcer, she died the
following day. 'Do you believe in God?' Abbé Bossuet asked her in her
last moments. 'With all my heart,' she is supposed to have replied, but
according to the English envoy who was present her final thoughts
were all of her brother. 'I have loved him better than life itself,' she
whispered, 'and now my only regret in dying is to be leaving him.'[25]

Charles's grief prostrated him for days, and when he finally roused
himself it was to complete the business his sister had played so large a
part in bringing about. Raising money was the first essential. When the
Commons reassembled in October 1670, Members were informed that

the King was £1,300,000 in debt on his ordinary revenue, which was designed to cover his household expenses and the day-to-day costs of the country's administration. In addition, he needed £800,000 for the navy. So urgent was the need for money that Charles took the unusual step of summoning the Commons to Whitehall, where he told the assembled Members that he felt the threat of danger from the French was so considerable that money for the defence of the realm must be their prime consideration. They responded with a variety of suggestions. A land tax was considered. A proposal to tax playhouses was put forward but met with strenuous opposition. Eventually, Bills of supply were passed, while a tax on profits and income raised £350,000 for the navy. Nonetheless, when Charles adjourned the House of Commons a Bill imposing import duties was lost and the King himself, determined not to summon the Members again before the declaration of war on the Dutch had been launched, resorted to extraordinary and dangerous methods of raising cash.

It had long been the government's practice to borrow money, often at exorbitant rates of interest, from the City bankers. To secure these loans, the government pledged its forthcoming tax revenues, which were then paid directly to the bankers. If these so-called 'orders in course' were not paid then the money saved would become available to the Treasury for other purposes. The temptation to raise funds in this underhand way proved irresistible, and Charles issued instructions for what became known as the Stop of the Exchequer. The effects, naturally enough, were disastrous, the usually temperate John Evelyn declaring that the Stop was 'an action which not only lost the hearts of his subjects, and ruined many widows and orphans, whose stocks were lent him, but the reputation of the Exchequer forever'.[26] At least two major banks were indeed severely hurt, rich and poor alike suffered, while the long-term effects on Charles's credit were so damaging that he himself was later obliged to confess that the Stop had been a 'false step'.[27]

Equally insidious were the effects of the second move Charles now made in the effort to secure his position. On 15 March 1672 he issued a Declaration of Indulgence which suspended the penal laws against religious minorities and allowed Catholics to hold mass in private houses and Dissenters to worship in public provided authorised sites were used and the presiding ministers were licensed. Charles's public motives for this move appeared liberal and benign. He had issued the Declaration, he said, 'for the quieting of the minds of our good subjects' and 'for inviting strangers in this conjecture to come and live under us'.[28] His methods and his supposed intentions were nonetheless regarded with the deepest suspicion.

Were not Catholics at court legion? It was known that Castlemaine had converted, and the beliefs of the Duke of York were a matter of concern to all. It was clear to many that the issuing of the Declaration of Indulgence was 'a deep popish design' heralding the coming of the Antichrist, and such fears mingled with the gravest reservations about the methods Charles had employed to get his way.[29] He had acted out of what he called 'that supreme power in ecclesiastical matters which is not only inherent in us, but hath been declared and recognised to be so by several statutes and Acts of Parliament'.[30] There were many who disagreed with this. The judges claimed that Charles was using powers he did not in fact possess, while many less qualified people raised their voices in alarm. The Venetian ambassador declared that it was 'incredible how much excitement the measure causes all over the country'.[31] There were those who nonetheless supported Charles's move. Among the chief of these was Ashley, who saw the Declaration as a means of broadening the appeal of Protestantism. As a result, among the showers of honours now rained on the Cabal, Ashley was created Earl of Shaftesbury, the title under which he would later do his most important work.

As for Charles himself, he seemed to be approaching the acme of his power. He had concluded a secret treaty with the most mighty King in Europe and his personal safety seemed guaranteed. His long-treasured project of religious toleration appeared to have come to fruition by his passing a Declaration of Indulgence which would ensure that the disaffected minorities in his kingdom gave him their support. By the Stop on the Exchequer he had raised large sums of money without having to resort to Parliament. All of this had been achieved by what Charles believed to be the legitimate use of his prerogative powers. Now he was about to exercise these in one final and decisive way by declaring war on the Dutch. As he waited for hostilities to begin, he seemed to some observers at least to be the most 'absolutely powerful' monarch England had known since the time of the Norman Conquest.[32]

The King at Play

As Charles waited for war there was much to divert his leisure hours. He had entered now on his forties and remained a vigorously active man. For all his nights of pleasure, he often rose as early as five in the morning, when he would pace the royal parks with his long, fast stride as he made his way to swim in his private canal or row a boat down the river. Often he would be accompanied by the pert little spaniels that have since come to bear his name.

To a man burdened with secrets, involved in the high and devious dealings of international politics and aware all the time of the hostility and criticism of those who surrounded him, these loyal pets could do no wrong. Lavish cushions were ordered for them. When Charles himself was unable to exercise them a liveried royal dog-walker took them out and was generously rewarded for his pains. The dogs were allowed to sleep on the King's bed, where they were even known to litter. There were nonetheless dangers for those who dared to approach them too closely. One eager Royalist bent down to stroke their heads and was at once rewarded with a sharp nip. 'God Bless Your Majesty,' the poor man called out, 'but God damn your dogs!'[1] Charles himself smiled with that ironic affability which had by now become the carapace of an altogether more reserved and private man.

Walking, swimming and rowing were only three among the many

forms of physical exercise in which the King took pleasure. He played croquet and bowls in St James's Park, and succumbed so enthusiastically to the Restoration craze for pall mall – a game in which a ball was propelled by a mallet through a raised hoop – that he had a 1500-foot pall-mall alley constructed in that part of London which still bears its name. The surface was covered with cockle-shells spread by a man who delighted in the title of the King's Cockle-Strewer. Tennis – or more correctly 'real' or royal tennis – remained a firm favourite. Indeed, for many years the game was the King's 'usual physic', and Charles played so energetically that he once lost four and a half pounds in a single match.[2] So avid was he that the ancient tennis court at Hampton Court was repaired soon after the Restoration, while others were built at Whitehall and Windsor. These courts were provided with expensive day-beds on which Charles could relax after an invigorating game, while the facilities also included monogrammed towels that were bought at ten shillings a pair.

Fishing suited the King's more sedentary moods, while he could also enjoy shooting in the royal pheasantry or in the elaborate duck decoy (complete with a chain of pools fed by the Thames) that he had built in St James's Park. Charles was also an expert horseman, a fact which gave much pleasure to that most skilled of equestrians, the Duke of Newcastle, his old tutor. 'No man makes a horse go better,' Newcastle wrote, adding that he had sometimes seen horses previously unridden submit to Charles's control, 'which is the quintessence of the art'.[3] The royal mews was a thriving concern where great sums were spent on providing for the well-being of scores of horses, and in one year £1000 was spent on hay alone.

No fewer than sixty of these mounts were hunters, and for many years Charles enjoyed the thrill of the chase. At his restoration, the King, who had been embarrassed during the years of his exile by the gift of a pack of hunting hounds, eagerly restocked the royal parks and forests with deer. New Forest, Sherwood Forest, Windsor Forest, Waltham Forest, Enfield Chase, all at various times echoed to the cries of royal hunting parties, and severe penalties were imposed on those who dared to kill a deer unless under royal warrant. But, for all this enthusiasm for the chase, the interest in horses most keenly associated with Charles remains flat-racing. Newmarket soon became the focus of his delight in the sport of kings. Here, two or three times a year – and for visits that often lasted several weeks – Charles put aside any interest in other royal business. Here was a place for pleasure and relaxation, the tone of which often called forth carping comments. On 19 October 1671, the ubiquitous Evelyn 'lodged this night at Newmarket, where I found the jolly blades, racing, dancing, feasting, and revelling, more resembling a luxurious and abandoned rout than a Christian court'.[4] To house these festivities, Charles bought (although never fully paid for) Audley End, and later had Wren build him a palace in Newmarket itself which proved, nonetheless, to be an unsuccessful design which Evelyn considered ugly and Charles found uncomfortable since the ceilings were too low for so tall a man.

Once arrived at Newmarket, Charles took a keen interest in all details of the sport. He was perfectly happy to talk to the jockeys and even to dine with them. He discussed weights, heats and the breeding of stud horses. He donated a royal plate as a prize, and watched training from a little pavilion on a nearby hill or even while on horseback himself. His opinions on the technicalities of racing were genuinely appreciated, and his own skill as a jockey was remarkable – especially for a man of his age and height. When in his middle forties, Charles still felt himself able to compete in the heats, and in 1675 he gained the plate he had himself donated, winning it purely on the strength of his 'good horsemanship'.[5] One permanent memorial of these occasions still remains: the Rowley Mile at Newmarket was named after the King's most famous stallion, whose prodigious powers at stud were such that the equal prowess of Charles himself led to his being nicknamed 'Old Rowley'.

The most lasting testimony to this affable side of Charles is the particular pleasure of Londoners, for it was Charles who opened St James's Park to the public. Here, as he walked or played games, the King could be seen and even approached by his people, an apparently 'merry monarch' delighting in the things they took pleasure in and unencumbered by an excessive formality which throughout his life ran contrary to his deepest instincts. Such a note of public benevolence was enhanced by Charles's practical and aesthetic interests. The Park was not only to be for public use, it was to be beautiful too. In line with his taste for all things French, Charles consulted with the great Le Nôtre when planning the avenues of trees, the ornamental lakes and the canal which provided so welcome a respite amid stuffy and unhealthy London.

Here too the curious could enjoy looking at the King's collection of exotic birds, which included a pair of pelicans from Astrakhan that a bemused Evelyn described as looking like something 'between a stork and a swan'.[6] Birdcage Walk still recalls the existence of this royal aviary, just as Storey's Gate memorialises its keeper. But it was not only grand projects that concerned the King. His intense, practical curiosity was easily stirred by all aspects of planting parks and gardens, and one of the most delightful pictures of the Restoration period shows the royal gardener, Mr Rose, presenting Charles with the first pineapple to be grown in England. Dorney Court, the home of Lady Castlemaine's estranged husband's family, provides the background to this charming scene.

It also hints at darker truths, for Castlemaine herself was now coming to personify all that the ordinary people of England most loathed and feared about the profligate Restoration Court. It seemed that Castlemaine's ambition and her greed, her sexual excesses and her desire for power knew no bounds. Every incident involving her corroded respect and increased mistrust. Her ostentatious conversion to Roman Catholicism enhanced the aura of suspicion, and even Charles's deeply Catholic Queen was far from pleased by her church's gaining so conspicuous a follower. Catherine made it clear that she did not appreciate Lady Castlemaine's attendance at mass in her chapel, but Charles himself made light of his wife's objections with his usual wit, saying, 'as for the souls of ladies, I never meddle with *those*'. To some highly placed in the Anglican church the loss of the King's *maîtresse en titre* was almost a cause for celebration. 'If the church of Rome has got by her no more than the church of England has lost,' declared the future Bishop of Norwich, 'the matter is not much.'[7]

Such sarcasm often seemed the best way of dealing with the woman. When Castlemaine gave birth to Charles's son George at Oxford in 1665, some undergraduates pinned a note in Latin to her door which was soon translated into a memorably obscene couplet which exactly evoked the anger and disgust with which her sexual licence and political ambitions were viewed:

The reason why she is not duck'd?
Because by Caesar she is fuck'd.[8]

Castlemaine's interest in high politics was particularly worrying. For example, she forcibly intervened when Charles felt obliged to send Buckingham to the Tower for the attacks that the extravagant Duke had made upon him. There was no question of Buckingham's kinswoman humbly begging for his release. She told Charles what she expected him to do and, in blazing anger, he responded, calling her a whore who meddled in matters that were no business of hers. She was not to be silenced by a display of wrath that would have made others cower. She knew her influence over the King, knew that for all his black anger, his creased brows and concentrated, furious eyes, he was in his deepest nature willingly subservient to her and that she could lead him in whatever direction she chose. Summoning up all the power of her natural and terrible gift for histrionics, Castlemaine yelled at the King, telling him that he was a fool and that he trusted his business to incompetents rather than to able men like Buckingham. The couple did not speak for three or four days, but Charles – as Castlemaine knew he would – eventually gave way and ordered Buckingham to be released.

Castlemaine's belief in her power over the King reached paranoid proportions when she determined to have him recognise the paternity of the child she was bearing by the dissolute Henry Jermyn. Once again she stormed into the royal presence to demand Charles's compliance with her wishes. The child was to be christened in the royal chapel at Whitehall, she declared. If Charles refused, she would bring the baby to court and smash it down on the marble floor in front of him. It was in vain that Charles complained that they had not slept with each other for months past and that he could not therefore possibly be the father. 'God damn me! but you shall own it!' came the hysterical response.[9] The jealous, wounded King looked on abashed as his mistress triumphed over him. She demanded his absolute submission. She told him she would publish his letters to her. She made him kneel before her and beg forgivenesss. She threatened to 'bring all his bastards to his closet door'.[10] She insisted that he recognise any child she bore regardless of who the father really was. Charles, in horrified weakness, listened, grovelled and appeared to consent, but deep within him a steely sense of self-preservation forbade him becoming an absolute fool. Matters quietened down and he refused to acknowledge the child. Then he sought comfort elsewhere.

Among the many duties of Will Chiffinch, page to His Majesty's Bedchamber, was that of acting as Charles's procurer-general. Casual women could easily be smuggled up the backstairs of Whitehall. More public affairs could also be pursued, and Charles sought relief in a host of women. The catalogue of his amours includes both some of the great ladies of the court – the Countess of Falmouth and the Countess of Kildare among them – along with one of the Queen's Maids of Honour, Winifred Wells, whose attractions included the 'carriage of a goddess and the physiognomy of a dreamy sheep'.[11] Even clergymen's daughters such as Mrs Jane Roberts succumbed, only to die 'with a great sense of her former ill life'.[12] Mrs Knight, 'who sung incomparably, and doubtless has the greatest reach of any Englishwoman', beguiled Evelyn with her voice and Charles with her body.[13] The pretty dancer Moll Davis, 'the most impertinent slut in the world', was easily spirited away from the Duke of York's Theatre, 'the King being in love with her; and a house is taken for her and furnishing and she hath a ring given her already, worth £600'.[14] Such conquests helped dampen but did not quench Charles's passion for the imperious Castlemaine. Pepys noted that the King was 'as weary of her as is possible, and would give anything to remove her; but he is so weak in his passion that he dare not do it'.[15] All he could manage was a compromise. He moved her out of Whitehall into Berkshire House, where she lived until mounting debts obliged her to sell the property and build a smaller one in the grounds.

Her own conquests, meanwhile, continued to multiply. Many of these were conspicuously public. Passing the dramatist William Wycherly in Pall Mall, Castlemaine called out coarsely after him and

Wycherly, roused by the prospect, replied in kind, followed her and started a relationship which was declared to all the world when he dedicated his first play, *Love in a Wood*, to her. The future Duke of Marlborough – handsome, virile and twenty-one – willingly pursued a relationship which he knew would enrich him. When Castlemaine gave him £5000 he refused ostentatiously to squander the money in the expected manner and instead, with a characteristically chilling lack of romance, invested it in an annuity. Charles's only comment on the young man's behaviour was the wryly contemptuous: 'I forgive you, for you do it for your bread.'[16]

Nor were writers and young officers Castlemaine's only prey. She had a developed taste for rough trade (Marvell, as we have seen, had already imagined her seducing a sweaty groom) and now she briefly took up with a rope-dancer called Jacob Hall. She had her portrait painted with him at her side, and even provided him with a salary.[17] Other stories altogether more revolting may be apocryphal, but they suggest the atmosphere that Castlemaine had now created about her. When the body of Bishop Robert Braybrooke was exhumed nearly three hundred years after his death in 1440, the corpse was found to be in a remarkable state of preservation. A bemused Lord Coleraine looked on one day as 'a lady as she seemed to be of great quality, being attended there with a gentleman and two or three gentlewomen, desired to see this body and to be left alone by it for a while'. The lady was Castlemaine, and what Coleraine discovered when he eventually returned to the grave is best told in his own words. He found the good bishop's corpse 'served like a Turkish eunuch, and dismembered of as much of the privitee as the lady could get into her mouth to bite'. As the horrified man went on to say: 'Bishop Braybrooke was thus more despoiled by a kind lady in a quarter of an hour, than by the teeth of time for almost three centuries.'[18]

As the King's passion for Castlemaine slowly cooled, so her avariciousness grew. Her spending was riotous and she realised that at thirty she should start preparing for her old age. She wanted titles and she got them. In 1670 she was created Countess of Southampton, Duchess of Cleveland and Baroness Nonesuch. With this last honour went the grant of Nonesuch House, Henry VIII's fantastic renaissance palace, which the newly elevated mistress stripped of all that could be sold and then allowed to fall into a state of abject decay. But even the looting of a palace was not sufficient for Castlemaine's needs. In a court addicted to gambling her debts multiplied furiously (in one day she lost £20,000), even as Charles tried to bail her out. He gave her a pension of £4,700 a year from Post Office revenues. The Privy Purse seemed permanently open to her, and soon she was receiving upwards of £30,000 a year. Only in 1676 did this reckless extravagance finally come to an end when Castlemaine retreated with her pregnant fifteen-year-old daughter to Paris, from where she continued to bombard Charles with exasperating letters.

One place where the harassed King could occasionally find refuge was on his yachts. The youth who had taken the helm of the *Black Proud Eagle* had not lost his taste for the sea and now, restored to the throne, Charles had not only refitted the boat in which he made his escape from Brighthelmstone and renamed it the *Royal Escape* but had been presented by the Dutch East India Company with a copy of the yacht that had brought him in triumph from Breda to Delft. The *Mary* as this boat was known was appraised by the expert eye of Pepys, who declared her to be 'one of the finest things that ever I saw for neatness and room in so small a vessel'.[19] Soon the Pett brothers were copying and trying to improve on this original, building yachts for the nobility and filling them – after the manner of the King – with feather beds and damask hangings, gilt leather state rooms and the necessary pewter chamber pots. For all their warlike appearance (some of these yachts were provided with eight guns) they were especially suited to racing, and Charles became as enthusiastic about this form of sport as he was about racing horses. Once again, it was not only the exhilaration that won his interest but technical matters as well. Charles became something of an authority on 'the philosophy of shipping', an interest which some disparaged as being beneath him. Charles, wrote Bishop Burnet, 'understood navigation well: but above all he knew the architecture of ships so perfectly, that in that respect he was exact rather more than became a prince'.[20]

Charles's interest in naval architecture points to the practical bent of his mind. Evelyn recorded how he spent time discussing a new type of yacht varnish with him, but the range of the great diarist's interest in the arts and sciences – Evelyn aspired to be, in the Restoration phrase, a 'virtuoso' – was something that he willingly laid before his monarch. A pleasing acquaintanceship resulted. Evelyn had a warm but qualified regard for a king who was 'debonair' and 'easy of access, not bloody or cruel'. He respected Charles's royal bearing, saying that his voice was 'great' and that he was 'proper of person, every motion became him'. He took pleasure in Charles's 'particular talent in telling stories and facetious passages', while he also warmed to a man who, like him, 'loved planting' and 'building'.[21]

Evelyn had published books on both of these subjects and was delighted when, 'being casually in the Privy Gallery at Whitehall, his Majesty gave me thanks (before divers lords and noblemen) for my book of *Architecture* and *Sylva*.'*[22] With that easy courtesy and interest in practical matters which was so characteristic of Charles, he told Evelyn that his books were 'the best designed and useful for the matter and subject . . . that he had seen'. That such a compliment was more than royal graciousness is suggested by the little scene that followed. Charles commanded Evelyn 'to follow him alone to one of the windows' where 'he asked me if I had any paper about me unwritten and a crayon'. By chance Evelyn had both of these and, offering them to Charles, watched as the King laid the paper out on a stool and then 'with his own hands designed me the plot for the future building of Whitehall, together with the rooms of state, and other particulars'.[23] The connoisseur was obliged to confess the the royal draught was 'not so accurately done', but he was nonetheless determined to preserve it as a 'rarity'.

Evelyn was also responsible for introducing to Charles a man who was greatly to beautify a number of the royal palaces with his exquisite woodcarving. Evelyn had found Grinling Gibbons working as a solitary and sober young man in rural obscurity. He was carving a relief version of a great painting by Tintoretto when the connoisseur encountered him and marvelled at the one hundred human figures the piece contained

* *Sylva* was Evelyn's treatise on planting woodlands.

and the splendidly ornate frame, of which he wrote that there was 'nothing even in nature so tender, and delicate as the flowers and festoons about it'.[24] Here was a master English craftsman at work, a genius who must be presented to the King. In due time, Evelyn 'begged of his Majesty that he would give me leave to bring him and his work to Whitehall, for that I would adventure my reputation with his Majesty that he had never seen anything to approach it, and that he would be exceedingly pleased, and employ him'.[25] The 'excellent piece of carving' was in due course brought to Whitehall, where it was placed in the chambers appointed to Evelyn's father-in-law, Sir Richard Brown. Evelyn asked Charles if he would care to have the piece brought to him but Charles's response says much about his naturally easy manner. 'No says the King; show me the way, I'll go to Sir Richard's chamber.' Charles was delighted by what he saw. 'No sooner was he entered, and cast his eye on the work but he was astonished at the curiosity of it, and having considered it a long time, and discoursed with Mr Gibbon, whom I brought to kiss his hand; he commanded it should be immediately carried to the Queen's side to show her Majesty.'[26]

The path to royal patronage was not to be a smooth one. As the Queen began looking at Gibbons's work, so one Madame de Boord, 'a French pedling woman . . . that used to bring petticoats and bands and baubles out of France to the Ladies', began to find fault with the work 'which she understood no more than an ass or monkey'. Catherine of Braganza nonetheless chose to listen to the opinion of this woman rather than Evelyn's own and, much to his annoyance, his protégé was obliged to return with his work to his cottage. Other means would clearly have to be found to promote the work of so talented a man, and in the small, intimate community of Restoration artists and intellectuals this was easily done, 'Mr Wren faithfully promising me to employ him for the future; I having bespoke his Majesty also for his work at Windsor which my friend Mr May (the architect there) was going to alter and repair universally'.[27]

Charles took a considerable personal interest in this last project. He had the grounds of the castle beautified with fountains, while his engineer, Sir Samuel Morland, was also commanded to construct a pump which could raise water from the Thames and then send it out in a jet some sixty feet high. Inside the castle itself many medieval features were stripped out to make room for works by such artists as the Italian fresco painter Antonio Verrio. Great painted figures now swirled about the walls and ceilings in allegorical fantasy as the King pursued his daily round: dining publicly in the Presence Chamber or talking to any 'person of quality as well as our servants and others' in the royal with-drawing room.[28] Here too he could also indulge his taste for music. Although the ballet made him restive and the occasional masques that were performed had nothing of the lavish splendour seen at Whitehall in the days of his father, instrumental music invariably delighted Charles. Once again, French tastes led the way, but Charles's most important contribution to the patronage of English music lay in his having Henry Purcell among the Children of the Chapel Royal and then commissioning works from him when, as a young man, Purcell's genius as a composer was revealed. Charles later appointed him organist at Westminster Abbey and then, in 1682, to the post of Composer in Ordinary.

The music-loving Evelyn described Purcell as being 'esteemed the best composer of any Englishman hitherto', while another interest he shared with Charles was painting.[29] A pleasant passage in his diary describes an evening he and the King spent with Samuel Cooper, the great miniaturist of the age. Evelyn had been summoned to the King's private apartments where he found Charles sitting still (something he invariably disliked) as Cooper set about 'crayoning of his face and head, to make the stamps by, for the new milled money'. Evelyn 'had the honour to hold the candle whilst it was doing', candlelight being preferred to daylight 'for the better finding out of the shadows'. Evelyn was required to entertain the King as he posed and he did so by talking to him 'about several things related to painting and graving'.[30]

Cooper meanwhile worked on, and a miniature he painted of Charles in 1665 is one of the most acute likenesses of him remaining. The tiny ivory dish exactly captures many of the King's salient characteristics. The panoply of his Garter robes conveys a feeling of luxury and power, but the distant look in the wary, intelligent eyes suggests the life-bitten cynicism of a ruler constantly looking beyond the immediate scene about him to detect the hidden, selfish motives of men. To this extent the face had something of the qualities of a mask, something at once fixed and evasive. Contemporaries were intrigued but baffled. 'Those who knew his face fixed their eyes there,' Halifax wrote in his *Character* of the King, 'and thought it of more importance to see than to hear what he said.' He went on to explain that 'his face was little a blab as most men's, yet though it could not be called a prattling face it would sometimes tell tales to a good observer'. This was far from being a cold face. Even though Evelyn could describe Charles's countenance as 'fierce', Cooper was fully aware of the sensuality which was as fundamental to Charles's make-up as his desire for power. The heavy eyebrows do indeed suggest a man whose frown was to be feared, but the large thick nose and heavy cleft chin speak of a man acutely aware of the physical side of life, even as his full lips – once dismissed as 'ugly' in his boyhood – speak of a much practised, moist sexuality. Here was a compelling but not a handsome face, as Charles himself was fully aware. 'Odd's fish,' he once declared as he looked at a portrait of himself, 'I am an ugly fellow!'[31]

Cooper shows the royal face beginning to grow puffy, the deep lines around the nose and mouth suggesting softness and self-indulgence. These were characteristics which large parts of the nation abhorred, and Evelyn was no more blind to them than Cooper. He was painfully aware of 'many great imperfections' in Charles. He deplored a life which 'passed to luxury and intolerable expense'.[32] He abhorred the fact that the King was 'addicted to women' and he was pained by the way in which he easily changed and deceived his ministers. He was also critical of Charles's 'much affecting the French fashion', and no incident in the reign more ludicrously reflects the rivalry between Charles and Louis XIV than what has become known as the incident of the Persian Vest.

After the catastrophe of the Great Fire of London in 1666 and the consequent baleful effect on English trade, Charles decided that the court should set an example by putting aside expensive French fashions, 'changing doublet, stiff collar, bands and cloak etc. into a comely vest, after the Persian mode with girdle or sash, and shoestrings and garters, into buckles, of which some were set with precious stones, resolving never to alter it'.[33] Evelyn loyally praised the outfit for its 'comeliness and usefulness', and when the Queen's birthday was celebrated in November a hundred courtiers appeared dressed in the required garment. A number of these people had wagered the King that he would not persist with his resolution, but it was not inconstancy alone that made Charles change his mind. When news of the fashion in England reached France, Louis found the whole business so absurd that he decided to dress his footmen in the new manner of the English court, and although Charles tried for a short time to brazen matters out he was eventually obliged to yield before the stronger influence and revert to the styles of dress favoured by the French.

Evelyn's hopes that royal extravagance might be curtailed came to nothing, while a visit to the King's library obliged him to realise that despite Charles's interest in matters artistic and scientific he was no great reader, no profound scholar. Evelyn managed to gain access to the library at Whitehall while Charles himself was staying at Windsor, and he began investigating 'with expectation of finding some curiosities'.[34] He was to be disappointed. 'Though there were about a thousand volumes, there were few of any great importance, or which I had not perused before.' Here was no working library but rather the place where the royal patron stored those volumes which had been presented to him. What Evelyn found were a 'few histories, some travels, and French books, abundance of maps and sea-charts: entertainments, and pomps; buildings, and pieces relating to the navy'. His eye was caught by some medieval illuminated manuscripts but the three or four 'entire days' he spent 'locked up and alone amongst these books' only confirmed him in his disappointment.

The King's collection of pictures housed near by was altogether more interesting to him and, along with the Raphaels and the Titians, he was particularly impressed by a picture of Mary Magdalene and the risen Christ by Hans Holbein, a work in which he had never seen 'so much reverence and kind of heavenly astonishment'.[35] While he was looking at these rarities, Evelyn also took the opportunity to explore Charles's collection of 'curious clocks, watches and pendules of exquisite work'. Charles was, indeed, extremely fond of timepieces (this was a great age of English clock-making) even if these lovely instruments in their ebonised and polished cases rarely struck the hours in unison. Here were rarities which gave witness once again to Charles's interest in technology, and it was partly this that persuaded him into the most important act of patronage in his reign: the founding of the Royal Society.

The Royal Society was incorporated under a charter granted by Charles on 15 July 1662, and his genuine interest in scientific matters led to research and debate becoming fashionable among the nobility and gentry. Charles employed one of his gentlemen ushers to convey his enquiries to the Society and probed the members as to why sensitive plants flinched and contracted when touched, and why ants' eggs were sometimes bigger than the ants themselves. He arranged for a laboratory to be built in his palace at Whitehall where experiments could be conducted before him or he could investigate problems for himself. He took a keen interest in all the inventions that the Society patented, presented it with curiosities, and throughout his life provided members with the venison traditionally eaten at their anniversary dinner. What Charles was encouraging in such ways was a profound change in the manner in which the elite looked at the world. Such people were no longer content to stare at nature with passive fatalism and to interpret its workings strictly according to the texts of such ancient philosophers as Aristotle. Propagandists like Bishop Burnet were quick to proclaim a bloodless and deeply civilising revolution which could only work to the benefit of mankind. 'The truth is', Burnet wrote, 'a spirit of learning came in with the Restoration, and the laity as well as the clergy were possessed with a generous emulation of surpassing one another in all kinds of knowledge.' As he went on to add: 'mathematics and the new philosophy were in great esteem'.[36]

This was an understandable overstatement since the foundations of the new science had in fact been laid at the start of the century by 'natural philosophers' such as Francis Bacon. Bacon's *New Atlantis* offered a picture of an admirably organised social and political world

Andrew Marvell, artist unknown. Marvell was the MP for Hull and a great satirist of Restoration life.

John Evelyn, by Robert Nanteuil. Evelyn was a 'virtuoso' – a lover of the arts and sciences – as well as a friend to the King.

Samuel Pepys, by John Hayls. His Diary is an incomparable record of Restoration life while his work for the Navy was of prime importance to the Dutch Wars.

John Wilmot, Earl of Rochester, artist unknown. The wreath of fame honours a monkey, an image typical of Rochester's sardonic view of Restoration manners.

Above Catherine of Braganza, by Dirk Stoop. Charles's self-effacing queen. 'Gentlemen', he is supposed to have declared on first seeing her, 'you have brought me a bat!'
Above right Barbara Palmer, Duchess of Cleveland, artist unknown. Charles's most infamous mistress poses with her son in a manner more often used for the Virgin Mary.

Below left Frances Stuart, Duchess of Richmond and Lennox, by William Wissing. She modelled for Britannia on the nation's coinage.
Below right Louise de Keroualle, Duchess of Portsmouth, by Pierre Mignard. Charles's beloved 'Fubbs' and the balm of his old age.

Nell Gwynn, by Sir Peter Lely (?). The *gamine* orange seller models as Venus.

Below left Hortense Mancini, Duchess of Mazarin, artist unknown. Charles II was only one episode in her remarkable lifestory.
Below right Henriette Anne, Duchess of Orleans, artist unknown. Charles's beloved sister and his only real confidante.

George Villiers, 2nd Duke of Buckingham, by Sir Peter Lely. Charles's oldest friend and a man so mercurial that he seemed to be 'not one, but all mankind's epitome'.

The other members of the Cabal.
Top left Thomas Clifford, 1st Baron Clifford of Chudleigh, artist unknown.
Top right Henry Bennet, 1st Earl of Arlington, artist unknown.
Above left Anthony Ashley Cooper, 1st Earl of Shaftesbury, artist unknown.
Above right John Maitland, 1st Duke of Lauderdale, Jacob Huysmans.

Titus Oates, by Robert White. The evil genius of the Popish Plot.

George Savile, 1st Marquis of Halifax, by Mary Beale. Halifax was a shrewd commentator on Charles and Restoration politics, the original 'trimmer'.

James II and Anne Hyde, by Sir Peter Lely. Charles's brother was briefly to succeed him as king.

Charles II in 1685, by John Riley. 'Old age and experience hand in hand', an image of Charles at the time of the Popish Plot.

William III, artist unknown. The figurehead both of the Dutch House of Orange and England's Glorious Revolution.

where 'Solomon's House' provided the means of mastery over the natural world for the benefit of all people. Gresham College in London had encouraged experiments in science as early as the 1580s, and much useful work had already been done at the University of Oxford. In the years preceding the Restoration, Evelyn had dreamed up a project for a small college where researchers could investigate horticulture, medicine and chemistry. 'The promotion of experimental knowledge shall be the principal end of the institution,' he wrote, and it was with the formation of the Royal Society itself that this dream seemed on the point of fulfilment.[37] To Thomas Sprat, writing his *History of the Royal Society* as early as 1663, it appeared that the advance of rational knowledge was the true means of promoting genuine Christian community and establishing what he called 'the peaceable calmness of men's judgements'.[38]

Sprat's work suggests that the Royal Society was already observing the satellites of Jupiter and investigating meteorology, geography and horticulture, as well as undertaking various projects intended for national security, including studies in ballistics and analyses of saltpetre. The regular publication of research was a crucial part of the Society's early achievement and, if the initial hopes of its founders were not immediately realised, the record of its success was remarkable indeed. The group of scholars and gentlemen amateurs incorporated by Charles included Robert Hooke, Robert Boyle and above all Sir Isaac Newton. Through the discoveries of these men especially, it became possible to view the universe as acting in all places and at all times according to consistent and verifiable rules or natural laws. King Charles's place as the promoter and supporter of these men (though their experiments occasionally raised a wry royal smile) is memorable not just in the history of the nation but in the universal history of ideas.

One of the principal projects of the Royal Society was a reformation of the way in which people used the English language. Sprat wrote of his desire for 'a close, naked, natural way of speaking; positive expressions; clear senses; a native easiness; bringing all things as near the mathematical plainness as they can; and preferring the language of artisans, countrymen, and merchants before that of wits and scholars'.[39] Such a purging and purifying of the language was also seen as desirable by a number of men of letters, among them John Dryden, the man who was to become Charles's Poet Laureate. Dryden rejoiced in what he believed was the new and sprightly elegance of polite conversation and saw that this was mirrored in the great Restoration vogue for social comedy. He attributed the success of both to Charles himself. 'If any ask me', he wrote, 'whence it is that our conversation is so much refined, I must freely, and without flattery, ascribe it to the court, and in it, particularly to the King, whose example gives a law to it.' Charles's intelligent ease of manner had freed the English from their 'natural reservedness' and 'loosened them from their stiff forms of conversation'.[40]

The great flowering of Restoration comedy reflected this. Charles himself took a keen interest in such matters, even suggesting plots to authors and approving or criticising drafts of scenes they wrote. The aristocrats about him followed suit, and while some of the greatest literature of the period owes little to their influence – Milton's *Paradise Lost* and Bunyan's *Pilgrim's Progress* are Restoration works drawing on a Puritan ethos – much of the most characteristic writing of the period in poetry, prose and drama is to be associated with that group of gentlemen gathered about the court who have come to be known as the Restoration 'Wits'. These young men, highly intelligent, critical and dissipated, burning out their energies in a round of neurotic hedonism, included the playwright Sir George Etheredge, Charles Sackville, Sir Charles Sedley of the drunken Covent Garden incident, and, above all, the greatest and most tragic of Restoration libertines, John Wilmot, Earl of Rochester.

Contemporaries noticed that Rochester had 'a brightness in his wit to which none could arrive, and was not destitute of natural modesty till the court corrupted him'.[41] That corruption took the form of 'drunkenness relieved by lechery', but there was in Rochester's manic pursuit of self-destruction a terrible sense of the vulgarity and trivial meaninglessness of a world in which the spiritual had apparently evaporated to leave only vanity and foolishness behind. Underlying the best of his satire, polished as it was by the twin influences of Horace and Boileau, lies an appalling sense of debased and squandered energies. Restoration England, and London in particular, are revealed as tarnished and tawdry places. Even the instinctual pleasures of sex have become corrupted. Boundless desires are cherished by 'whiffling fools', and in a poem like 'Signor Dildo', in which the eponymous hero is chased up Pall Mall by voracious royal ladies, there is a distressing sense of human waste, a sense of tragic futility which found its greatest expression in *A Satyr Against Reason and Mankind*. Here rational, wilful man is trapped in his torturing contradictions until:

> Old age and experience hand in hand,
> Lead him to death, and make him understand,
> After a search so painful and so long,
> That all his life he has been in the wrong.
> Huddled in dirt the reasoning engine lies,
> Who was so proud, so witty, and so wise.[42]

So brightly if briefly did Rochester's comet flare across the Restoration horizon that playwrights especially were irresistibly drawn to him as a model for that most characteristic of Restoration comic figures: the stage rake. The catalogue of these men, culminating in Dorimant, the 'exquisite fiend' of Etheredge's *The Man of Mode*, and Horner in Wycherly's *The Country Wife*, suggests how vividly engaged with its time Restoration comedy was. This was a trait Charles encouraged by two decisions made early on in his reign. In 1660 he granted patents to Thomas Killigrew and Sir William Davenant which stipulated not only that they should be permitted to build a playhouse each and form companies for them but that, from henceforth, only women should be allowed to play women's roles so that plays might 'be esteemed not only harmless delights but useful and instructive representations of human life'.[43]

The result was the formation of the King's Players and the Duke of York's Players, who acted at the King's Theatre, Drury Lane and at the theatre designed by Wren in Dorset Gardens respectively. Performances were held in the afternoons and the houses were packed with the fashionable, with 'sparks', gallants, 'naughty women' and gentlewomen masked 'like a covered dish' to give their lovers an 'appetite'.[44] The more expensive parts of the buildings were luxuriously appointed with green baize and gilt leather seats, while at the front of the theatre, facing the reeking, ogling, pulsating audience, stood the 'orange girls', loaded baskets on their arms, smiling winningly under the eagle eye of Mrs Mary Meggs or 'Orange Moll', the bawdy doyenne of the front-of-house. One of these girls was to become Charles's most famous mistress.

It was generally believed that Nell Gwynn was born in Coal Yard Alley, a slum to the east of Drury Lane. It is possible that her father was one Thomas Gwynn, a Welsh fruit-seller, and more certain that Nell, her mother and her sister Rose lived in destitute circumstances. As a child, Nell had been sent out to sell fish and had later worked as a serving girl in a brothel near Drury Lane. Such experiences had made her street-wise, uninhibited and well able to fend for herself with a delicious combination of coquetry and hard-headedness. She was a natural actress in a world where she knew that her comfort and sometimes even her survival depended on her being able to please men. By 1663, aged just thirteen, she had found employment as one of the orange girls at the King's Theatre.

The theatre provided Nell, already ravishingly gamine, with the opportunity to display the full range of her talents. She became the mistress of the leading actor Charles Hart, a great-nephew of Shakespeare, and under his tutelage made a swift transition from the stalls to the stage itself. Hart taught her to act, John Lacy taught her to dance, and by 1665 Nell Gwynn was the house's principal actress. Her performance in comic parts, mad scenes and travesty roles was irresistible. That avid theatre-goer and connoisseur of female beauty Samuel Pepys was utterly enchanted by her. At the beginning of March 1667, he saw her play the role of Florimell in Dryden's *The Maiden Queen*, and he wrote that 'so great a performance of a comical part was never, I believe, in the world before as Nell doth this, both as a mad girl and then, most and best of all, when she comes in as a young gallant; and hath the notions and carriage of a spark the most that ever I saw any man have'.[45]

Nor was it only Nell's acting that attracted Pepys. She was gloriously, rousingly common, 'a bold merry slut' who with raucous laughter and a quick, dirty tongue could charm and control the host of her would-be admirers. Going backstage one day, Pepys encountered Nell with another actress named Rebecca Marshall and was shocked and thrilled by their earthiness: 'but Lord, their confidence', he wrote in his diary, 'and how many men to hover about them as soon as they come off the stage, and how confident they are in their talk'.[46] He saw her again during the May Day festivities of 1667 as she watched the garlanded milkmaids dancing down the London streets and he recalled her 'standing at her lodging door in Drury Lane in her mock-sleeves and bodice, looking upon one – she seemed a mighty pretty creature'.[47]

She seemed so to Charles too. By 1667, Castlemaine's termagant rages were becoming ever more insupportable. Contrast being the spur to his desires, Charles began to take a keen interest in this girl of the streets and to woo her before the world. His opportunity to introduce himself came one afternoon when he and his brother found themselves sitting in a box adjacent to Nell, who was currently being squired by a certain Mr Villiers. Charles inveigled his way into the conversation and at the end of the play demanded that Nell and her companion join him for supper. The Duke of York was ordered to beguile Mr Villiers while Charles paid his attentions to Nell herself. Everything seemed to be proceeding satisfactorily until the bill came and Charles and his brother found that they had no money with which to pay it. The hapless Villiers was obliged to settle the account while Nell, with that tart and unin- hibited wit that made her so desirable, declared: 'Odds fish but this is the poorest company that ever I was in before at a tavern.'

By the start of 1668, Charles had sent 'several times' for Nell, and two years later had moved her into a house in Lincoln's Inn Fields. There, on 8 May 1670, she bore her first child by the King, and the following year, when she was again pregnant, he moved her into altogether more prestigious lodgings at 79 Pall Mall. The gardens of this house backed on to St James's Park, and so careless of public interest in his affairs was Charles that he had a bank built by the garden wall so that Nell could climb up it and enjoy intimate chats with him. Evelyn was appalled when he overheard 'a familiar discourse between the King and Mrs

Nelly . . . she looking out of her garden on a terrace at the top of the
wall, and the King standing on the green walk under it'.[48] Inside the
house itself, Charles could enjoy a more intimate relationship with his
mistress, attending the musical parties she soon learned to throw,
watching her in her loosely fitting, naturally flowing dresses, or
enjoying her naked – the ravishing little gamine Venus painted by Sir
Peter Lely, ivory skinned, plump breasted, reclined and open to love.
Here indeed was a respite from the politically ambitious Castlemaine,
for Nell, much to the relief of Charles and the nation which watched the
affair, soon realised that she had few interests in this area. Popular
versifiers were quick to celebrate the fact:

> Hard by Pall Mall lives a wench call'd Nell.
> King Charles the Second he kept her.
> She hath got a trick to handle his prick
> But never lays hands on his sceptre.[49]

Nell was also too shrewd openly to declare war on her rivals, while
Charles was far too promiscuous to forgo them. He had not forgotten
the sheepish charms of the lady-in-waiting who had accompanied his
sister to Dover and, free now of Henriette Anne's disapproval, he could
pursue Louise de Kéroualle with all the resources and status of a king.
He would need both, for Louise was both poor and ambitious.
Buckingham was sent to attend Henriette Anne's funeral and begin his
master's courtship. As so often, he brought to the latter task his own
particular brand of irresponsibility. It was Charles's plan that Louise
should be given the post of a maid-of-honour to Queen Catherine, but
when the time came for Buckingham to have a confidential word with
the girl he filled her head with rumours she could not resist. He told her
that Charles's marriage was nearing its end and hinted that a new Queen
of England would have eventually to be found. Louise listened, her
distressed circumstances fuelling her naive imaginings.

The death of Henriette Anne also deprived her of her protector, and
coming from a family that was as long on genealogy as it was short of
cash Louise knew that she would have to take decisive action if she were

to secure herself position and wealth. She believed that these were her natural right, and she was sufficiently calculating to play a shrewd game to achieve them. She had one great advantage. Louise de Kéroualle was regarded by contemporaries as being extraordinarily beautiful. She had fair skin, dark hair and what Evelyn called a 'childish simple baby face'.[50] These gifts she enhanced by affecting the manner of the most refined ladies at Louis XIV's court. She was, in the phrase of the day, a *précieuse*. Nothing in her behaviour was natural or spontaneous, but so accustomed had she become to whispering elegant banalities with a frail and languid voice, to pouting, sighing and limply reclining like a heroine from a romance, that she appeared to be indeed what she had sought to become. But beneath this mannered veneer there remained a poor and haughty woman who was obliged to make her own way in the world and whose developed interest in beautiful things – in all the luxuries of the royal life – was matched by a keen knowledge of their cash value.

Charles's court watched with ever increasing amazement as an infatuated King pursued a woman who would not yield. While the English laid bets on how long she would resist, the French became increasingly concerned. They felt they could have found no better spy than this beguiling woman if they wished to be privy to Charles's most intimate thoughts, but, as the French ambassador was obliged to confess, Charles had not yet 'been to see her in her own room, as rumour keeps saying that he has'.[51] It was over six months before the vapid, calculating beauty allowed the King to visit her in the lavish apartments provided for her in Whitehall, but once permission was given he came morning and night to see that her every wish was provided for.

Matters appeared to be continuing in this way until the autumn of 1671 when, at a dinner at the French embassy, Louise suddenly felt overcome with nausea. Unable to attribute this misfortune to their own food, the jubilant French assumed that Louise must be pregnant. Louis XIV was hastily informed of the good news, and his minister wrote back to say that 'the King was greatly pleased to hear in what manner Mademoiselle Kéroualle suffered the other day'. The French had been concerned over the past months, and now Louis declared himself 'anxious to be informed of what may grow out of this situation'.[52] Nothing, of course, did come to pass, and the more influential of her countrymen about her began to put pressure on Louise. She was urged to surrender her honour for the glory of her country.

The French ambassador felt obliged to have a confidential word with her on the matter, while the charming and worldly-wise Saint-Evremond brought his considerable literary talents to the problem, gently suggesting to Louise that the pleasures of self-love were unhealthy – immoral even – compared to the undoubted benefits of surrender. 'So let yourself go into the delights of temptation instead of listening to your pride.'[53] All of this was to no avail, and those about the King resolved on decisive action. Lady Arlington told Louise in no uncertain terms that she faced the stark contrast of becoming either the latest royal mistress or a cheerless, secluded nun. Having frankly delivered herself of her opinion, Lady Arlington then proceeded to act with all the ruthless savoir-faire of a heroine from a Restoration comedy.

She went to consult with the French ambassador, and together they devised a plan. Autumn was coming and the King was due to attend the races at Newmarket. What could be more natural than for the Arlingtons to entertain him at their magnificent house near by? The ambassador would surely accept an invitation too, and the Arlingtons would, of course, be delighted if he brought Louise with him. The ubiquitous Evelyn observed events. Charles, he noted, came frequently to the Arlingtons' house, 'and after eating he passes several hours with Mademoiselle Kéroualle'. The King was clearly 'solicitous' to please her, and 'those small attentions which denote a great passion were lavished on her; and she showed by her expressions of gratitude that she was not insensible to the kindness of a great king'. As Evelyn then wrote: 'we hope she will so behave that the attachment will be durable and exclude every other'.[54]

While Evelyn hoped for an end to royal promiscuity, the French ambassador hoped for richer rewards and continued to exert pressure on Louise. He told her that she should 'skilfully handle the regard the King has for her'.[55] She was not to tire him by discussing business or annoy him by ridiculing his friends. She was, in other words, to play the part of the perfect mistress and 'let him find his pleasure exclusively in her company'. Lady Arlington meanwhile contrived to be both more imaginative and more down to earth. The bedding of Charles and Louise was now her principal objective, and what could not be achieved in private might yet be effected before the eyes of all. Since they were in the country, why should they not play country games? What could be more delightful than a mock rustic wedding? Pressured by those around her, Louise felt obliged to consent. Evening came. A chamber was luxuriously prepared, and Louise was laid out on the bed and loosened her garters as the laughing courtiers looked on. Then, as the bridegroom appeared and got into the bed beside her, so the audience discreetly withdrew to allow the couple to consummate their union. Nine months later Louise gave birth to a boy whom Charles eventually recognised and created Duke of Richmond.

Having lost her honour, Louise felt obliged to establish her respectability. She faced an uphill struggle in both the court and the country at large. The people of England loathed her. She was haughty, she was Catholic and she was French. She had, besides, an all but un-pronounceable name and it was as 'Mrs Carwell' that they chose to berate her. They looked on appalled as a still besotted Charles lavished gifts upon her with an abundance even Castlemaine had never known. Louise was given forty splendid rooms in Whitehall. These were furnished in French taste, hung with Gobelin tapestries and pictures from Versailles, and then littered with lacquer cabinets and prodigious quantities of silver. Nor was this all she won. Louise hankered after a pearl necklace worth some £8000 and she got it. She longed for a pair of earrings being sold by Lady Northumberland for £3000. She got those too. The Exchequer seemed ever open to her delicate, avaricious hands. Licences sold to wine merchants provided her with an annual revenue of £10,000. Charles gave her an annuity of £8600, a gift of £11,000, while in 1681 she deigned to accept some £22,952. Louise needed such sums to support her reckless gambling – she was known to place 5000 guineas on a single throw – but there was much angry muttering over the 'chargeable ladies about the court'.[56]

Louise now had money beyond her early impoverished imaginings, but another great desire had also to be satisfied. She was desperate to acquire status. An infatuated Charles could deny his 'Fubbs' nothing, and Louis XIV was petitioned so that she could be given English citizenship. Louise was then created Duchess of Portsmouth and given the additional titles of Countess of Fareham and Baroness Petersfield. Nell Gwynn was deeply offended but knew that laughter was the best revenge. The cockney woman constantly made the great French mistress look ridiculous. When Louise went into ostentatious mourning for the Chevalier de Rohan (to whom she was in no way related), Nell appeared at court the following day dressed entirely in black. On being asked the reason for this she exclaimed: 'Why, have you not heard, my loss in the death of the Cham of Tartary? I was exactly the same relation to the Cham as the Duchess of Portsmouth was to the Chevalier de Rohan.' When her barbs upset Louise she called her 'the weeping willow', and constantly drew attention to the fact that the newly enno-bled Duchess's social and moral pretensions were hardly appropriate for a kept woman. When Louise tried to fight back, her attempts invari-ably misfired. On one occasion Nell appeared at the court in an uncharacteristically lavish dress and jewellery.

'Nelly, you are grown rich, I believe, by your dress,' Louise declared. 'Why, woman, you are fine enough to be a queen.'

Nell, with the instant wit of the street, replied: 'You are entirely right, Madam, and I am whore enough to be a duchess.'

It was only the ennobling of Louise's son that seriously riled Nell, and one day she turned sharply to Charles and said: 'Even Barbara's brats were not made duke until they were twelve or thirteen, but this French spy's son is ennobled when little more than an infant in arms!'

Charles himself, with typical diffidence, declined to involve himself in what could become an embarrassing confrontation, and Nell was obliged to pursue other means to achieve her ends. It was said that once, when the King visited her at her house in Pall Mall, she called out to her eldest boy, 'Come here, you little bastard, and say hello to your father!'

The apparent coarseness of the language displeased the King and he asked her not to use the word 'bastard'.

'Your Majesty has given me no other name to call him by,' came the quick reply, and the little boy soon received the titles of Baron Headington and Earl of Burford, and in 1684 Duke of St Albans.

There were more serious matters to attend to, all the same. At the start of November 1670, another foreign visitor appeared at the court. His bearing and interests were very different to those of the over-stimulated decadents who habitually surrounded Charles, for his nephew, William of Orange, was a practical and resolute twenty-year-old, and 'a most extreme hopeful Prince'.[57] To the English ambassador in The Hague he appeared to be full of 'good plain sense', hard-working and un-dissipated. William hated swearing as much as he loved hunting, and invariably went to bed at ten o'clock rather than revelling in excess. Evelyn declared that the young Prince had 'a manly, courageous, wise countenance', and Charles himself was determined to treat this important young ally generously.[58]

Lavish apartments were provided for William, a state ball was thrown for him, and hunting expeditions, race meetings and visits to the theatre were also arranged. Only Buckingham, irresistibly drawn to corrupting anything good, succeeded in making the young man look mildly ridicu-lous. He threw a dinner party for Prince William, got him drunk and watched with considerable pleasure as the now unsteady youth lurched towards the private quarters of the maids of honour. This was the sort of minor lapse that brought a wry smile to Charles's face, but if he declared himself 'much satisfied with the parts of the Prince of Orange', he detected other and more forbidding qualities in him. William was both a 'passionate' Dutchman and a Protestant.[59] Above all, he was an example of that heroic resolve which would be shown by the nation with which Charles was now about to go to war.

14

The Tightening Net

Excuses to clothe a war of naked aggression had to be found, but these were thin indeed. For all that Charles wrote of 'having received many wrongs and indignities from the States General of the United Provinces', when it came to listing these they amounted to no more than the attacks suffered by English settlers in Surinam, difficulties encountered by the Merchant Adventurers, and such trivial matters as the issue by the Dutch of a medal deemed to be insulting, the weaving of a tapestry celebrating their victory in the Medway, and the fact that they were now offering guided tours over the *Royal Charles*, which they had captured in that encounter.[1]

Something more substantial had to be found, and Charles reverted to the ancient principle that the crown of England claimed sovereignty of the seas and expected this to be recognised by the salutes of foreign ships. A test case was deliberately staged. Lady Temple was due to join her husband in The Hague, where he was serving as the English ambassador. A tiny yacht called the *Merlin* had been hired to transport her, and Captain Crow was given orders to sail past the Dutch fleet during the passage and demand a salute from them. If the Dutch refused then Crow was to open fire and continue his assault until their flag was shot away. The valiant Crow achieved this all but impossible task, but when the Dutch Admiral came aboard the *Merlin* to find out why his fleet had been attacked by a mere yacht the absurdity of the position became manifest. Crow declined to arrest the Admiral or to continue firing, and for this entirely reasonable course he was, on his return to England, sent to the Tower.

Other opening skirmishes were equally ignominious. It was decided that privateering raids on Dutch merchant vessels were now appropriate, but the chief of these was badly mishandled. Sir Robert Holmes swooped down on the Dutch convoy returning from Smyrna only to have two of his own ships badly holed as most of the rich enemy merchantmen sailed blithely away. While such incidents were irksome to the Dutch themselves, their manifest failure was a spur to Charles's aggression. With all the crooked logic of bigotry he had now persuaded himself that it was his enemies who were the real aggressors and that it was his patriotic duty to destroy them. As the Venetian ambassador wrote: 'the King is convinced that the hatred of the Dutch for England is hereditary, that it increased because of trade, and became implacable owing to the pretensions of the United Provinces'.[2]

Inspired by such ideas, Charles took an intense interest in the preparations for war. He paid two visits to Nore off Chatham, where the Duke of York was readying the fleet. Here, as the supreme commander of the allied navy, James was to be joined by the forces supplied by the French under their vice-admiral, D'Estrées. The Dutch were resolved to attack before this reconnoitre should take place, and to this end de Ruyter cruised the seas between Southwold Bay and North Foreland. Having failed to encounter the rival fleet, he then entered the Channel but, held back by fog and contrary winds, he had to make for the Flemish coast while his enemies prepared for the attack. Their combined forces appeared to give them a considerable advantage in terms of men and *matériel*. Ninety-eight warships, 6000 guns and 34,000 sailors were surely more than a match for the seventy-five ships, 4500 guns and 20,000 men sent out by the Dutch.

Understanding that morale and co-operation were as important as firepower, Louis XIV issued D'Estrées with instructions which drew his attention to the need to be solicitous about saluting English ships. After all, the English claimed sovereignty of the seas. Nonetheless,

Louis also impressed on D'Estrées his duty to enhance his nation's *gloire* by surpassing the allies where possible in both courage and expertise. Rivalry thus underlay the mask of friendship, and this was soon to harden to mutual mistrust. Meanwhile there was a war to win and, having despatched his orders to his seaborne forces, Louis readied the greatest army in Europe to destroy the Dutch on land. He was now in his element. 'I have decided,' he declared, 'that it is more advantageous and more to my glory to attack four places . . . simultaneously and to command in person at all four.'[3]

In a campaign of devastating efficiency, Louis marched his forces through Liège and Cologne, and, by the start of June, was receiving the surrender of terrified Dutch cities: Arnhem, Amersfoort, Utrecht. An embattled William of Orange was obliged to fall back on Holland itself, while the panic-ridden burghers, believing they faced outright destruction, resolved to secure themselves behind the floodwaters of their breached dikes and then to sue for peace. These last efforts were in vain. Louis treated the Dutch delegation with contempt while Charles, recognising that the generous terms offered him by William were a transparent attempt to break the English alliance with France, refused to listen. He knew very well that the triumphant Louis could dictate what terms he would and he was determined to support the stronger power. Nonetheless, it occurred to Charles that there were certain advantages to be gained if he could persuade his young nephew to betray his country's apparently lost cause and then set him up as a puppet king.

Charles could hope to succeed in realising this last wish only if he won an outright victory at sea, but English plans for the naval campaign were neither novel in content nor effective in execution. Believing that they could rely solely on their superior forces, the allies thought they could obliterate the Dutch navy and then blockade the enemy coast. Such confidence was misplaced. As they put in to water at Southwold Bay, so two divisions of the Dutch navy, sailing line abreast, bore down on them. Taking advantage of the tide and hurriedly bringing their vast battleships into fighting formation, the English and French navies prepared to engage. Crippling confusion was the only result. The French misread the signals flown from James's ship and, instead of concentrating about him, moved south while the English themselves headed north. As a consequence, the divided fleet was involved in two separate actions. De Ruyter moved in on James's vessels in the knowledge that the fate of his nation depended on his success. The *Royal James* was set on fire and sunk, and, while many of her struggling men were saved, Lord Sandwich, the Admiral of the Blue, tried to escape in an overcrowded rowing boat which capsized, leaving him to drown. The following day brought no greater success for the allies. For all James's desire to continue with the action, the inexperienced French navy could only slowly draw itself up into battle formation, and by the time it had done so the weather had deteriorated to such an extent that the fleet was obliged to make for the coast.

The losses in this futile encounter were appalling. It was estimated that English casualties amounted to some 2500 men and, although both sides claimed victory, it was clear that the Dutch had narrowly won the strategic advantage. The English had been prevented from gaining mastery of the North Sea and were therefore in no position to make a landing on the Dutch coast. Evelyn was suitably dismissive of the whole vainglorious episode, writing that it showed 'the folly of hazarding so brave a fleet, and losing so many good men, for no provocation but that the Hollanders exceeded us in industry, and in all things but envy'.[4] Intelligent people in England were refusing to be duped by the war, while Charles's great plans for a ringing naval victory that would make him rich, powerful and free from the influence of Parliament were ignominiously evaporating.

In order to salvage what he could from the situation, he sent Buckingham and Arlington on a diplomatic mission to Holland. There, the experience of military defeat had wrought a profound political change. The humiliated Dutch people needed scapegoats and the de Witt brothers, the leaders of the republican party, were chosen. Johan de Witt was attacked in the street by youths as he returned from a government meeting and was so badly wounded that he was obliged to take to his bed for a month, after which he wrote to the States surrendering all his offices. On the same day that de Witt was attacked, William of Orange was declared Stadholder in Dordrecht, and other major Dutch cities followed suit. It seemed that the hereditary ambitions of the House of Orange were at last being fulfilled and Charles was determined to take advantage of this dramatic turn of events. He became ever more firmly convinced that he might be able to conclude a profitable peace with his nephew. Clearly believing that he could browbeat a young man who, he thought, would want to hold on to power at any price, he resolved on harsh and excessive terms. He wanted to be paid a vast war indemnity. He demanded an annual payment of £10,000 for the right of the Dutch to fish herring in English waters. The money Charles had been unable to seize by war he might yet obtain through peace but, in addition to looking after his financial needs, he was also determined to secure an important if junior ally who would surely understand the obligation he was under and willingly submit to the King's tutelage.

William would do no such thing. On his visit to England he had formed a shrewd idea of his raffish uncle's integrity, and the experience of war had hardened his own resolve. He was determined neither to betray his country nor to show a base gratitude to Charles and his French ally. Buckingham and Arlington soon discovered the calibre of the young man they had been sent to negotiate with. William told them frankly that he did not believe that it was in England's best interests to continue its alliance with France. When Buckingham told him that his patriotism was wholly misplaced since his country was clearly lost, a surly William refused to reply and Buckingham lost his temper: 'It is lost. Do you not see it is lost?'

'It is indeed in great danger,' William calmly replied, 'but there is a sure way never to see it lost, and that is to die in the last ditch.'[5]

This was hardly the sort of attitude understood in the Restoration court, and Charles grew increasingly angry at such intransigence. In order to force his nephew to submit he made it clear to him that he was determined to continue with the war and pointed out that William himself would have to bear the responsibility for the series of Dutch defeats that would inevitably ensue. William refused to be blackmailed in so obvious a manner, and he also ignored Charles's cynical suggestion that the excessive financial demands the English were making would so weaken the republican merchants and shipowners that William's position as Stadholder would be all the stronger. Events had confirmed him in his determination to be his own man. Although William was deeply shocked when the still angry Dutch murdered the de Witt brothers, he was contemptuous when Charles tried to use the assassination to his own advantage. William received a letter in which his cynical uncle told him that if he continued with an unpopular war then he was sure to meet the same fate as the de Witts. He replied with icy disdain. 'Don't imagine that your threats to have me torn in pieces by the people frighten me very much,' he wrote; 'I am not in the least bit faint-hearted by nature.'[6]

This was perfectly true, but if William was no coward, he was no naive hero either. He could play the international game with an adroitness and guile that were more than a match for Charles. While Buckingham and Arlington moved on to negotiate with Louis, desperate to secure his promise that he would not conclude a separate peace with the Dutch, William began a propaganda campaign in England by which he hoped not only to isolate his bellicose uncle from the growing number of those about him who counselled peace but to persuade the English people themselves that it was the French Catholics rather than the decent Dutch who were their real enemies. The campaign was handled with great efficiency, and a net of duplicity and suspicion was being drawn around Charles in which he would soon be hopelessly entangled.

The Commons only drew this net tighter. Charles was eventually obliged to call a session of Parliament in February 1673 to ask for funds, but before he did so he took a number of steps which showed that he wished to continue with his unpopular war. Eight new regiments were raised to provide a force which he could land on the Dutch coast, while he also kept the fleet in commission over the winter, thereby saving himself the expense of paying off his sailors. Having made his intentions clear, Charles then turned to those members of the Cabal who were still enthusiastic in his support. Clifford, newly appointed Lord Treasurer, threw his energies into controlling expenditure, while Anthony Ashley Cooper, newly created Lord Chancellor, was assigned the role of Charles's official parliamentary spokesman. With his aides in place, Charles opened the session of 1673 with a speech of patent dishonesty.

He suggested that it was sheer magnanimity which had led him to prorogue Parliament for so long. He had not wished to trouble Members with a call to vote him supplies until these became absolutely necessary. Having declared that his futile war had been waged for the 'interest as well as the honour of the nation', he then justified his Declaration of Indulgence by saying that it was his way of 'securing peace at home when I had war abroad'.[7] Members would understand that the concessions granted to Roman Catholics were considerably less than those given to Dissenters, just as Members who were worried about the new regiments he had raised would surely appreciate that these men had been commissioned purely as a task force for a foreign invasion and not to enforce the King's rights at home. Having attempted to lead the Commons by the nose, Charles then asked for a vote of supply.

There followed Shaftesbury's defence of the King's policies. Charles listened as this tiny, frail, brilliant orator – uninformed as he was of the secret terms of the Treaty of Dover – waxed lyrical about Charles's love for Protestantism and his patriotic hatred of the Dutch. Warming to his theme, Shaftesbury presented a lurid picture of the republican Dutch as 'the common enemy to all monarchies'. Englishmen in particular knew the horrors that sprang from such a form of government and would surely feel themselves morally bound to oppose them. Having raised this ghost, Shaftesbury then turned his attention to the enormous wealth the Dutch had earned themselves by trade. Fear and jealousy were, he knew, powerful persuaders. The ambitious Dutch, he asserted, aimed at nothing less than the establishment of a 'universal empire as great as Rome'. So monstrous was Dutch ambition that even now, in defeat, they would not accept the terms of peace offered to them, and everybody would surely see that it was a duty to destroy them now that they were down. If, after this, he warned, 'you suffer them to get up, let this be remembered, the States of Holland are England's eternal enemy, both by interest and inclination'.[8]

Having raised the temperature, Shaftesbury launched into the daring but specious argument by which he hoped to convince his listeners that it was the House of Commons who had urged the King to declare war. Had not their Address of 1664 called for action against the Dutch? This was true, although the Address had made no mention of hostilities. Shaftesbury brushed over this. ''Tis your war,' he proclaimed. 'The King took his measures from you, and they were just and right ones.' It was clear to him that loyal Englishmen nurtured in their hearts a deep loathing for all things Dutch and that they longed with a true Roman fortitude to destroy the enemy. 'Delenda est Carthago,' he declared in the words of Cato – 'Carthage', the enemy of Rome, 'must be destroyed.' Then, as he approached the climax of his speech, his cynical manipulation reached its height. Back in 1668, Parliament had voted money for Charles to enter into a Triple Alliance with the Dutch and the Swedes in order to check the ambitions of Louis XIV. That agreement had been broken, Charles had sided with the French and waged war on the Dutch, but now, as Shaftesbury turned to ask for supply, so he called for a new Triple Alliance: 'a Triple Alliance of King, Parliament and people, may it never be dissolved'.[9]

The Commons was not impressed. MPs were in no mood to have their judgement blinded by firework displays of rhetoric. Abjuring enthusiasm, they stuck to detail. They had, as they believed, legitimate grievances and saw Shaftesbury as the originator of these. Thirty-six seats in the House had become vacant during the period of prorogation and Shaftesbury had personally issued writs for elections to fill them. No fewer than eight of these vacant seats were in Dorset, where his family had interests, and there were those in the House who believed that he had used this to ensure that Members sympathetic to the court were returned. The House proceeded to unseat all thirty-six of these new MPs and then declared that the right to issue writs for elections rested with it alone.

Having established this point, the opposition proceeded with considerable finesse and a degree of organisation which enabled them to outmanoeuvre Shaftesbury's attempts to influence them. The Members had a particularly difficult problem to face. For all that they loathed the Dutch war, they were bitterly angry at the attempts William of Orange had made to flood the country with propaganda and subvert

the nation to his views. Charles himself had made strenuous efforts to
limit the flow of this material, arresting two suspected Dutch agents
who had been sent to England to promote the campaign. Persons and
cargoes entering the country were thoroughly searched (it was believed
by some that seditious literature was entering the country in barrels of
butter destined for the Spanish embassy), while a proclamation was
issued against 'licentious talking' on affairs of state. Charles also
enforced laws against unlicensed presses and, in a move that was indica-
tive of events to come, sought ways in which the newly fashionable
London coffee-houses might be regulated. It was in these places especially that men met to discuss the affairs of the day and to read and
circulate the pamphlets and satires that were so influential in shaping
public opinion. This accumulation of measures pointed to the gravity
of the situation, and it was the view of respected and experienced
Members of Parliament that it behoved them to vote Charles a supply
for war when the enemy was so conspicuously tampering with his
prerogatives by trying to influence the loyalty of his people. Seventy
thousand pounds a month for eighteen months was voted to Charles,
but with the most stringent conditions attached, because MPs were
determined to force the King to back down on the issue that concerned
them most of all: his Declaration of Indulgence.

They had a two-fold objection to this. The first of these was legal and
constitutional. Charles had attempted to enforce religious tolerance by
proclamation and had thereby overridden Acts of Parliament. This the
Members neither could nor would allow, but for all their indignation
they resolved to express themselves in firm though modest language.
'We find ourselves bound in duty to inform your Majesty', they
declared, 'that penal statutes in matters ecclesiastical cannot be
suspended but by Act of Parliament.'[10] Charles saw that the money
he so urgently needed depended on his assuaging this grievance but
he refused at first completely to climb down. He tried to insist that he
did indeed have prerogative powers in ecclesiastical matters but
tempered this claim by recognising that he did not have the right to
suspend statutes. The Commons was not impressed and told him that
he had been misinformed. Not content with this, it then went on to vote

unanimously for the preparation of an address requiring Charles to act against the growth of popery.

By doing this Members were making it clear that they remained deeply worried about the King's alliance with Catholic France, and that they were concerned about the number of Catholics who had recently received civil and military offices. Above all, they were indicating that they were determined to protect their Anglican church, their Anglican constitution and their Anglican culture. To this end they framed a Test Bill. The comprehensive harshness of its terms suggests the intransigence of the Members' convictions. Anybody wishing to take public office, use the courts, adopt a child or act as an executor was now required not only to take the oaths of allegiance and supremacy, and to receive communion according to the Anglican rite, they were also obliged explicitly to deny the central mystery of the Catholic mass. They were, in the words of the Bill itself, to 'declare that I believe that there is not any Transubstantiation in the sacrament of the Lord's Supper, or in the elements of Bread and Wine at or after the consecration thereof by any person whatsoever'.[11]

While a cornered Charles tried unsuccessfully to set the Lords against the Commons in an effort to quash the Bill, the MPs themselves obstinately clung to their as yet incomplete draft of a Bill for supply. They knew perfectly well that if they forwarded this to the Upper House it would be passed and would receive the royal assent, and that Charles, once the money was in his pocket, would prorogue Parliament. Representatives of the Court party pleaded in vain that the immediate vote of supply was essential if the Dutch were to be finally and roundly defeated. They were told in their turn that the redress of grievances must precede the grant. This was an old principle, a constitutional tradition, and it served the Commons well in its attempt to suppress all forms of religious toleration.

Charles, devious in his anger, resolved to play his trump card. If a resolute Commons insisted on passing such wholly unacceptable legislation as the Test Bill then he would, quite simply, dissolve Parliament. After all, the coffers of France were deep and Louis was still in need of an ally at sea. The French ambassador was summoned, but as his conference with the King proceeded a dismayed Charles saw his hopes evaporate and his powers diminish in a way more humiliating than he had ever imagined. The ambassador informed him that Louis was not in a position to provide the huge sums of money Charles needed. He would have to go back to the Commons and accede to its desires in order to gain a supply. If this meant accepting the Test Bill, so be it. The ambassador also made clear that the French King expected Charles's continuing support. The money he had already been given would now have to be earned. The position was degrading in the extreme. The King of England was no longer able to dissolve his Parliament at will and was obliged to take his orders from both France and the Commons. The Charles who had once believed that he could, by the use of his prerogative powers, shine among the monarchs of Europe, had been outmanoeuvred by his Parliament and eclipsed by the Sun King. As he made his devastating climbdown – cancelling his Declaration of Indulgence and giving his consent to the Test Act – public rejoicing erupted in the streets of London. The Anglican majority had got their way and legalised intolerance was now a fact of life.

The immediate effect of the Test Act was to convince many people that there was spiritual wickedness in high places. The Duke of York, unable to square his conscience with his ambitions, resigned his post as Lord High Admiral. The Roman Catholicism of the heir apparent was now openly acknowledged, and it was Prince Rupert who took command as Charles's navy prepared once again for war. The plan of campaign was straightforward if difficult to achieve, and was throughout bedevilled by crippling problems. It was decided that the combined English and French fleet would seek out de Ruyter and either defeat or blockade him so that Charles's army could land safely on the coast of Zeeland, where it would join up with the French.

Apathy, ill-discipline and rivalry soon worked their baleful effects. Buckingham (of all people) was put in charge of Charles's newly recruited army, but the Duke had little interest in his post and discipline so far collapsed that his soldiers rioted when they were stripped of their bright new coats which were needed elsewhere. Buckingham's incompetence was such that Charles was eventually obliged to replace him with General Schomberg, seconded from the French army, but he and the imperiously egocentric Rupert at once fell into a mutual loathing so intense that Rupert actually ordered his ship to fire on Schomberg when, contrary to what Rupert regarded as the rule, the French General raised a flag at his masthead as he was sailing to meet his men. These difficulties disappeared only once it became evident that the campaign was doomed from the start and that the English army of invasion was not destined to leave its quarters at Yarmouth, where the drunken soldiers whiled away their time 'buried in sloth and a super-fluity of food'.[12]

Separated from one rival, Rupert proceeded to make more enemies among his own men. He believed that the Duke of York was secretly using his influence behind his back and he quarrelled with those officers whom he believed to be James's protégés. Rupert's suspicions were not without foundation, but quite as dangerous to the long-term running of the campaign was his being constantly exasperated by the stream of orders sent to him by Charles, clearly at the Duke's behest. Many of these orders inhibited Rupert from exercising proper command and he was eventually obliged to write to the King asking him either to 'give me his positive directions, or else leave the way of it to my management'.[13] The appeal had no effect, and a series of missed opportunities convinced Rupert that he was admiral of a campaign almost certainly doomed to failure.

In order to save face, Rupert started to blame the French for every-thing that went wrong, and so public and acrimonious did his criticisms become that they had an important effect in turning anti-French feel-ing at home into outright hostility. When de Ruyter eventually sailed out to sea, Rupert put the French in the van but they were easily over-come and their seamanship was so poor that there was a long delay before they could regroup and come to Rupert's aid. They behaved, he sneered, 'as well as could be expected'.[14] These and subsequent early engagements were inconsequential, but delays in refitting and re-manning the ships were so prolonged that Charles, interfering once again, considered it was too late in the season and too dangerous to attack de Ruyter 'within the banks' of his anchorage in the Schooneveld.

By so doing he ensured that the naval campaign had no decisive outcome.

Meanwhile, the rivalry between the allied navies was coming to a
head. It seemed that the entire English fleet – officers and men alike –
devoted their energy to disparaging the French. The bitter accounts
they wrote up circulated in the taverns and coffee-houses of London,
and Anglo-French relations became so fractious that it was clear that
the naval alliance had irretrievably broken down. Charles, it seemed,
was only mildly exaggerating when he claimed that he and his brother
were the sole English friends the French had remaining to them. It
was now believed by everyone else that the French were cowardly or
treacherous, or both. It was said that they had deliberately allowed the
English to bear the brunt of battle. They had failed to respond to signals.
They could not take commonsense initiatives. They had squandered the
chance of victory. These fires of recrimination were sedulously fanned
by Rupert as he laid the charge of failure at D'Estrées' door and then
used one of the French Admiral's officers to incriminate him further.
The upshot was the widespread belief in England that the French were
acting under secret orders which were aimed at protecting their own
vessels while exposing the English to the maximum of danger. In such
ways the French, rather than the Dutch, became identified as the
national enemy.

William of Orange's propaganda campaign served only to deepen the
mood of contempt. The nation at large was already concerned that, as
Louis XIV's military ambitions spread ever wider across Europe, so
he was obliging Charles to be 'in league with him against all the
world'.[15] The alliance was becoming ever more costly but, as the Dutch
propaganda wildly pointed out, it had altogether more sinister under-
tones. Was it not a conspiracy, a 'design', to establish Catholicism and
arbitrary government in Britain? As pamphlets such as *England's
Appeal* circulated widely, deep-rooted fears began to take on paranoid
proportions. The liberties of a virtuous Protestant people, it seemed,
were being menaced by the foreigners their King had chosen as his allies.

It was in this atmosphere that Parliament reconvened. Charles
urgently asked the Members for a vote of supply, 'the safety and honour

of the nation requiring it', and then referred to the Dutch propaganda campaign as 'the artifices of their enemies'.[16] Once again he employed Shaftesbury to attack the Dutch as ruthless competitors 'who sucked in with their milk an inveterate hatred to England'. Then he waited to see what would happen. Those who opposed the court, those 'few plain, country gentlemen who, though rude and unmannerly [unpolished], had as good hearts as the best of their fellow Members', knew that a failure to grant supply would make it seem that the Commons was responsible for any ill-effects that might ensue. They knew, besides, that foreign affairs fell within the royal prerogative and believed that since Charles had started the war he alone could finish it. Subtle means and a subtle speaker would have to be found to persuade him to this course, and in Sir William Coventry they found both.

In two superbly argued speeches, Coventry destroyed Charles's public arguments for the war. He showed first that Louis was both an unnatural ally and an unreliable one. 'The French interest', he declared, 'is to keep us from being masters of the sea – the French have pursued that interest well.'[17] To achieve this end the French followed their own devious agenda and broke treaties at will. An alliance with such a people was impossible. Coventry then set about demolishing the economic arguments that had persuaded Charles to fight the Dutch. He asserted that mere aggression – international robbery with violence – was no way of increasing wealth in a sophisticated and civilised world. Such an approach might work in 'barbarous countries' but was simply too crude to be effective in Europe. 'What probability is there,' he asked, looking round the House, 'if we beat the Hollander, that we shall get all trade?' A smash-and-grab raid, however grandiosely executed, was no substitute for 'industry and parsimony'. What was needed was competition, competitive pricing, 'under-selling'.[18]

Coventry's speech reveals the growing sophistication of economic thought in England, just as his final proposal suggested that Parliamentary techniques were becoming altogether more polished too. There was no question in his mind that the right to wage war did indeed belong to the King alone, and that right he was not prepared directly to attack. Instead he would oblige Charles to conclude his war by measures altogether more oblique. The Commons, he declared, would vote the King another supply if it judged that Dutch aggression made this absolutely necessary. Coventry was already well aware that the Dutch were prepared to conclude a peace on reasonable terms, but he reinforced his position by insisting that money would be forthcoming only if the spiritual security of the nation were assured. The cost of supply, he declared, would be Charles's protecting England from the menace of popery.

Coventry's was a performance brilliant and subtle enough to outmanoeuvre the King, and an irritated Charles felt that he had no option but to prorogue Parliament so as to give Members time to think again and 'recollect themselves'.[19] They would do no such thing, and when the House reassembled at the start of 1674 Charles was once more driven to a humiliating climbdown. With barefaced effrontery he denied that there was any covert agreement between him and the French, any 'articles of dangerous consequence'.[20] The secret Treaty of Dover would remain a secret still,* but even so shameless an actor as Charles was unable to play his part with his usual aplomb. He mumbled his way through what to many seemed an incoherent speech while fumbling with his notes.

It was all to no avail. Charles had been comprehensively outflanked, and at the start of February he was obliged to conclude a peace with the Dutch. His gains were pathetic when compared to his hopes, and his losses were substantial. The Dutch agreed to salute the English flag, but they did not recognise Charles's sovereignty of the seas. They agreed to pay him a war indemnity, but clawed most of the money back to cover his debts to the House of Orange. They quietly settled the problems in Surinam, but would make no concessions where their pocket was concerned. They refused to pay for the right to fish the North Sea, and Charles was in no position to enforce the debt. He had been outmanoeuvred on every front. The war had brought him no glory, and the disruption of trade had greatly reduced his revenue. He had tried to base

---

* It was not actually exposed until 1830, when it was printed by the historian Lingard.

his support on something other and broader than the Anglican church and had been forced to concede the Test Act. He had allied himself to the most powerful Catholic King in Europe and fanned in his own people the dangerous fires of anti-popery. He had asserted his prerogative powers in the hope of freeing himself from Parliamentary control, only to find that the House of Commons had outwitted him and that the nation now feared the spread of arbitrary rule.

Nor, when Charles turned to his closest advisers, could he draw much comfort from them. The Cabal, riddled with mutual antipathies, had fractured beyond repair. The passing of the Test Act obliged Clifford to resign his offices and he died soon afterwards. Arlington and Buckingham, having indulged in heated mutual recrimination, were now irreconcilable, and Arlington himself resigned in September 1674. Most damagingly of all, the subtle-minded and resentful Shaftesbury (probably aware of how he had been deceived over the Treaty of Dover) had been dismissed as Lord Chancellor and was making overtures to the leaders of the opposition, the Country party. A demoralised impotence in government was the inevitable result. As the Venetian ambassador wrote: 'the King calls a cabinet council for the purpose of not listening to it; and the ministers hold forth in it so as not to be understood'.[21] This was no less than the truth, and new ways would have to be found if Charles and the monarchy itself were to survive as an effective source of power.

15

Politics and Parties

Charles's apparent salvation appeared in the form of a harsh and hard-working Yorkshireman called Sir Thomas Osborne. When he was created Lord Treasurer in succession to Clifford, most people assumed that Osborne's appointment was a short-term measure. He was acknowledged principally as an administrator who did the greater part of Buckingham's work for him, but this little-known, corpse-pale bureaucrat was soon to reveal himself as a man of outstanding ability. His experiences as Treasurer of the navy had convinced him of the importance of regularising public finances, and he now brought his immense flair for accountancy to Charles's assistance in order that the King might have a sufficient revenue to be as independent of Parliament as possible. To secure the royal credit, Osborne arranged that £77,000 a year be paid in interest to the bankers who had suffered after the Stop of the Exchequer. He then bargained with them for lower interest rates on loans, and considerably increased the revenues derived from the hearth tax and the excise. As a result, it was possible not only to pay off old royal debts but to increase Charles's income by more than £100,000 a year. The delighted King made Osborne a Privy Councillor, created him a viscount in 1673 and then the following year, pandering to the man's inordinate love of rank and title, made him Earl of Danby.

The new peer's financial efficiency was underscored by domestic policies that were clear and pragmatic. Once he had become established, Danby told Charles frankly that he would never become 'great or rich' until he consented to 'fall into the humours of the people'.[1] Since the nation was becoming ever more stridently anti-Catholic, the King should not pursue measures that antagonised them. Danby argued that there was no advantage to be gained from the alliance with Louis XIV and that rather than developing a relationship which raised the twin terrors of popery and arbitrary government, Charles should see William of Orange as the nation's natural confederate. He was guided in this partly by his own Protestantism. Danby was a convinced and committed Anglican who, morally opposed to toleration, believed that the political interest of the crown was best served in spiritual matters by the bench of bishops. There was the solid, conventional foundation on which Charles might rear the edifice of royal rule.

To this end Danby carefully nursed the sympathies of Parliament. Early in 1675 he issued proclamations in Charles's name reinforcing the laws against conventicles, or illicit prayer meetings, and imposing the most stringent penalties not only on those Englishmen entering Catholic orders but even on those who attended mass in such once safe places as the chapels of foreign embassies. These public gestures were then reinforced by secret sweeteners. Dutch money flowed into the country to be used as bribes and, along with those offices that were at his disposal, was distributed by Danby's avaricious and manipulative hand to Members of Parliament who were known to be sympathetic to his aims or at least willing to be silent. The House of Commons itself met on 13 April 1675, after an interval of nearly fourteen months. The Members found Charles in a gratingly conciliatory mood as he tried to impress them with the new direction of his policy. Had his actions against Dissenters and Catholics not shown his zeal for the Church of England 'from which I will never depart'?[2] What more could he do to secure the Anglican establishment and right those unfortunate mis-understandings on spiritual matters which had risen solely from the designs of ill-intentioned advisers? Surely Members would now grant him supply for the navy. But the Commons was not so easily won over.

In a series of moves which showed clearly how concerned it remained about the intentions and conduct of royal policy, it insisted that Charles recall the troops he had offered to France. Then it turned to his advisers.

Lauderdale, the only member of the Cabal to survive with his power intact, was accused of actions that merited impeachment. It was clear to worried Members that Lauderdale was part of a conspiracy to promote absolutist government. His high-handed actions in Scotland (where he ruled with a rod of iron) proved this. First of all it was believed he had said that royal edicts had the force of law, thereby implying that Charles's Declaration of Indulgence had been issued legitimately. To make matters worse, he had then played a significant part in raising a large Scots army which, he asserted, could be used anywhere in the realm for imposing toleration. Charles refused to give way to such pressure and the Commons, denied the impeachment of one of his servants, turned to another.

Angry leaders of the Country party asserted that the methods by which Danby had increased royal revenues violated ancient practices and placed too much power in his hands. Now he too was claiming that royal proclamations were superior to old laws. These accusations again lacked substance and had to be dropped when they got bogged down in a mass of technical detail, but even greater confusion broke out when a second request for the recall of British soldiers serving abroad was made, this time to a Grand Committee of the House. On discovering that the vote on the matter was equally divided, Members fell to fighting, spitting and pulling off each other's wigs. Swords were drawn by some, while others put their feet on the mace, which was currently placed (as the procedures of a Grand Committee required) under the Speaker's table. Only when the Speaker himself eventually retrieved it was order restored, but it was by now clear that Members so inflamed would not take kindly to a proposed new piece of legislation that was dear to both Charles's and Danby's hearts.

Both men had been quick to see the danger posed by an increasingly articulate Parliamentary opposition. They were determined to stifle this and they resolved to use their enemies' techniques against them. To this end they framed an addition to the Test Act in the form of an oath that was to be taken by all holders of public office, including Members of Parliament. The oath required men to swear first that 'it is not lawful on any pretence whatsoever to take up arms against the King' or those acting for him. To this entirely reasonable demand was then added a sentence whose serpent-like subtlety appeared to reinforce the status quo while actually ensuring the suppression of criticism. An applicant for public office was now required to swear that he would not 'endeavour any alteration of the Protestant religion, now established in the Church of England, nor will I endeavour any alteration in the government in church or state as it is by law established'.[3] Here was the sting in the tail. Any opposition to the King could be construed as a violation of this oath and a reason for dismissal. What Charles and Danby wanted was a gagging Act and a compliant Parliament of High Anglican sympathies.

Shaftesbury saw through the design at once and fought tooth and nail in the Lords against it, thereby revealing the new drift of his sympathies. Just as Danby had advised the King to listen to the temper of the nation when framing his policies, so Shaftesbury also relied on his instinctive understanding of public opinion to lead an opposition that sought to curtail the powers of the crown and vest authority in Parliament. As the newly prorogued Members trooped back to the shires and Charles himself reluctantly abandoned his additions to the Test Act, it was becoming clear that a profound change was slowly establishing itself at Westminster. Adversarial politics was being born and, along with it, political parties. By so conspicuously seeking an alliance of crown and church, Danby had laid the foundations of what would become the Tory party, even as his opponents began to coalesce into what would eventually be known as the Whigs.

Many among the latter believed that Charles and Danby had covert designs on the constitution and that the public needed to be alerted to what they saw as their Catholic and absolutist sympathies. Andrew Marvell for example, Member of Parliament for Hull and veteran of so many profound constitutional changes, set about composing *An Account of the Growth of Popery and Arbitrary Government in England*. This pamphlet rehearsed many of the fears that gripped the nation. All the ills England had suffered over the past ten years, Marvell asserted, could be attributed to one mysterious and sinister cause. Louis XIV, the Papacy and the Jesuits were united in supporting 'the popish conspirators' who were at that very moment plotting the country's slide into tyranny and superstition. 'There has now for divers years a design been carried on,' Marvell wrote, 'to change the lawful government of England into an absolute tyranny, and to convert the established Protestant religion into downright Popery.'[4]

The actions of eminent personalities lent credence to these fears, none more so than those of the Duke of York. James's surrender of his post as Lord High Admiral had made his Catholic sympathies clear to all, but far more worrying was the fact that, after his first wife's death in 1671, he had been looking for, and had eventually found, a new and Catholic spouse. James was clearly hoping for a male heir who, brought up in his adopted faith, would take precedence over his two Protestant daughters, Mary and Anne. The greater part of the nation was appalled by the prospect. It seemed that the throne of England would very likely pass into the hands of Antichrist, and neither James nor Charles himself did anything to allay these fears, seeing the Duke's marriage as a purely dynastic matter and regarding criticism of it as an invasion of the prerogative.

They were concerned, nonetheless, to get the matter arranged as quickly as possible so that they could present an inevitably hostile Parliament with a *fait accompli*. Various candidates were considered, Charles making sure that he took the upper hand in the decision-making since, as he told James, his brother had already made a fool of himself once in matrimonial matters. The awkward situation clearly ruled out any English bride and appeared to restrict the field to three foreign ladies: an Austrian archduchess who found a better match in the Holy Roman Emperor, a Princess of Würtemberg whom Charles objected to for political reasons, and the Princess of Neuberg, whom James objected to because she was ugly. It seemed that the choice was becoming severely restricted when news came that two further candidates – both of them princesses of Modena – were available. The raven-haired Mary Beatrice in particular was just fifteen and was a choice made all the more desirable by the fact that she had strong French connections. These would be reinforced by generous payments from Louis XIV if she were ever to marry into the English royal family.

A proxy marriage between Mary and James was speedily arranged, and when word leaked out that the heir apparent was now wedded with 'the daughter of the Pope' the nation burst into uproar. Images of the Pope were burned across the country, while there were desperate mutterings about what Charles himself should do to solve his barren marriage. The question of the succession became all-important, and while some hoped that Charles would divorce his Queen, remarry and so produce a legitimate heir, others looked to the eldest and most attractive of his bastards, James, Duke of Monmouth. This insignificant twenty-three-year-old now began to take on something of the appearance of a national hero, the people's darling. Monmouth was an extraordinarily handsome young man and his peccadilloes could surely be put down to the hot blood of his youth. Did it count against him that he had been involved in the attack on Sir John Coventry when, that wit having made a joke about the King's taste for young actresses, he was rewarded by having his nose slit? Honour, after all, was paramount. What matter that Monmouth had taken part in the murder of a beadle, and that his way of life was vain, shallow and libertine? He would mature. Charles had pardoned his crimes, and the youth's weaknesses were not without glamour. Besides, he had a wealthy, Protestant, British wife. Above all, he was an openly avowed Protestant himself. Might ways not be found of making him king if James were excluded from the succession?

The Duke himself continued to narrow and harden his views on all political and religious matters. He would not abandon his Catholicism, for all that he knew such a move would restore him to popular favour. He would not, for reasons obvious enough, change his view on legitimate Catholic succession to the English throne. He even declared that the accession of Elizabeth I (a bastard in Catholic eyes) had been nothing less than a usurpation which had brought with it a deplorable growth of Parliamentary power. This, likewise, was increasingly anathema to James, who treasured even more earnestly ideas of an absolutist monarchy in the French manner. It was partly for this reason that he continued to urge pro-French policies on his brother, despite the fact that he was no longer formally a member of the administration.

Indeed, it was James who was largely responsible for encouraging Charles's renewed overtures to Louis XIV and thereby involving him in an international situation that was so complex and so delicate that the King would have to call on all his resources of guile to survive. Charles's principal need was, inevitably, for money, but he was also aware that a secret alliance with the French would not only free him from Parliamentary constraints but allow him to ignore those of his advisers who were urging him to ally himself to William of Orange. William's agents were still actively promoting his cause in England and Louis was well aware of this. By providing Charles with adequate funds he realised that he could at one and the same time insist on a further prorogation of Parliament, persuade Charles to turn a deaf ear to those who counselled a Dutch alliance and ensure a measure of English neutrality in the conflicts now engulfing Europe. This situation was made all the more pleasing to Louis by the fact that Charles himself once again insisted on conducting the negotiations for the subsidy agreement. As so often, his dislike of detailed paperwork and his natural laziness ensured that he concluded a less satisfactory deal than he might have done.

With an agreement advantageous to his master signed, the French ambassador, Henri de Ruvigny, happily retired from one of the most demanding and exasperating posts in the French diplomatic service. His successor was provided with instructions which show how clearly and in what detail Louis XIV understood the conduct of affairs in England. The new ambassador was told that the country 'may, properly considered, be reduced to the King, the Duke of York, the royal ministers, and "l'esprit de la nation en général"'.[5] It was clear to the French at least that Charles was not master in his own house and that, of his ministers, Lauderdale was most in his confidence while Buckingham retained his influence, despite being out of office. Danby was seen as a brilliant if arrogant economist, while among Charles's mistresses Louise de Kéroualle had particularly upset the French by allying herself to Danby, who could loosen the purse-strings to provide for her innumerable wants. This was a cause for some disappointment since the French had liberally supplied Louise with diamonds, honours and other presents. The situation was to be monitored but, in the meantime, the new ambassador was also to keep a close eye on another beautiful and avaricious woman who had recently come into royal favour.

In 1675, Hortense Mancini, Duchesse Mazarin, arrived in London dressed as a man and looking for a fortune. Her life had already been colourful in the extreme. As a niece of Cardinal Mazarin she was rich and important, and while blessed with a fair measure of her family's remarkable intellect she also had a freedom of spirit and an originality that none could control. These last were her salvation, for Hortense had been married at just fifteen to Charles de la Porte de la Meilleraye, newly created Duc Mazarin, only to find that this scrupulously correct young gentleman was in fact a hopeless schizophrenic.

Her new husband forbade Hortense company, English company especially. He insisted that she spend the greater part of her time at prayer. He refused to allow her to eat in front of men. He searched their bedroom for evil spirits. Having failed to find them, he set out to reform the world. He told Louis XIV that he was an emissary from the angel Gabriel come to tell him to sever relations with his mistress. The King blandly informed him that the angel Gabriel had already told him that the Duc himself was mad. The disappointed lunatic withdrew and, having failed to reform the public world, turned to art instead. He took hammer, chisel and scissors to the fabulous collections housed in the Palais Mazarin. Marble genitalia and voluptuously tinted breasts littered the gallery floor as his tearful curator begged him to cease his sacrilege. Then the Duc turned once again to his wife. He took her to remote Brittany where no lascivious male eye could gloat upon her beauty. Hortense responded by having a passionate affair with the sixteen-year-old Sidonie de Courcelles. She found herself immured in a convent with her friend as a result. After letting rats loose in the dormitories and failing to escape by climbing through a chimney, Hortense was eventually returned to the Palais Mazarin, where she discovered that the greater part of her fortune had been squandered by her husband on litigation. She fled to Italy and then, having conceived an illegitimate child, returned to Paris only to find that her husband now thought he was a tulip and insisted on being watered by his servants every day.

Enough was enough, and Hortense retreated to Chambéry, where she developed a taste for philosophical study. Guided by her lover and tutor – a man who masqueraded under the title of the Abbé Saint-Réal – Louise published her memoirs and thereby became an international celebrity. Among her many English readers was the Duke of Buckingham and, as he turned the pages of her remarkable story, it occurred to him that Hortense Mancini was just the woman to lure Charles away from the dangerous delights of Louise de Kéroualle. He suggested that she come to London and he hired a house for her in Covent Garden.

Hortense was clever, she was worldy-wise and she was now sumptu- ously thirty. Even de Ruvigny was bowled over by her presence. 'I never saw anyone who so well defies the power of time and vice to disfigure,' he wrote. Hortense had that deep-grained beauty which is of the bone and of the spirit. 'At the age of fifty,' de Ruvigny continued, 'she will have the satisfaction of thinking, when she looks at her mirror, that she is as lovely as she ever was in her life.'[6] The connoisseur of female beauty nonetheless gave way before the diplomat. De Ruvigny saw how adroitly Hortense had persuaded the besotted English King to pay her an allowance of £4000 a year. He noted how Charles busied himself about her alimony arrangements and the return of the jewels she had left in France. De Ruvigny's successor was warned that she might use her influence against Louis, and it was recommended that he suggest to Hortense that in general terms at least the French were solicitous for her welfare, even though her demands on them were grossly unjust.

Having charmed the King, Hortense proceeded to charm London. She did so by an inescapably attractive combination of high culture and utter heedlessness. The brightest socialites of the day longed to shine in her presence. French and English wits – Saint-Evremond, du Gramont and Buckingham – sparred and danced around her, and when men seemed dull there were ladies in the court to flirt with too. Castlemaine's daughter, Lady Sussex, was a particular friend. They fenced together in St James's Park wearing only their dressing-gowns. De Courtin, the new French ambassador, scrupulously recorded Hortense's taste for 'special relationships', and wrote back to Paris informing Louis that the King of England paid court to her openly. 'He gives every appearance of being devoted to her during the day,' he wrote, 'but reserves the right to spend the night with anyone he pleases.'[7] As often as not that person was Hortense. Having endured the tedious business of being ceremoniously put to bed, Charles would wait until the palace was quiet and the servants had gone away before getting up, dressing himself and slipping off to his mistress's apartments.

By the middle of 1676, the keen-eyed de Courtin was reporting back that Louise de Kéroualle was eclipsed and he suggested that it might even be advisable to send her home. It was worryingly clear that the jilted mistress was handling her grief with an unbecoming honesty. She cried a lot, she contracted a disfiguring eye infection, she was pale, she was thin, she was pregnant. Pity and professionalism mingled in the ambassador's mind, and he was moved to stay up with Louise through the night to console and advise. 'I never saw so sad or more touching a sight,' he told Louis, who remained singularly unimpressed.[8] Then tears gave way to tactics. For all that Hortense Mancini showed her up as languid and vulgar, Charles's little Fubbs was fond of her King and was determined to hold on to her fortune.

Louise began to court the alien, hated Duchesse. She chatted to charm, and Hortense, secure in herself, unneedy but shrewd, condescended to listen with half an ear. Then she blithely invited Louise to ride in her carriage. Louise's health improved and, with her health, her looks. De Courtin noted the change. Knowing that the international situation might in part depend upon the flush that had now returned to her cheeks, he told Louise that his master Louis XIV attached the greatest importance to her services. She blossomed in the Sun King's favour, and as de Courtin himself handed on his post to Paul Barrillon, so he informed his plump and sly successor that he should be ready to dance attendance on Louise whenever she desired it. Barrillon took the hint and was soon writing back to Louis to inform him that 'I have no doubt that the King talks everything over with her and that she is able to draw him to her way of thinking."[9] But the ambassador was wrong. His over-enthusiastic imagination had mixed business and pleasure in a way that Charles himself had long ago learned not to do. Nonetheless, as Hortense Mancini began a brief affair with the visiting Prince of Monaco, Charles's affections slowly returned to his Fubbs as an erring husband might return to the habitual intimacies of his wife.

While Charles played, Danby toiled. It was now clear that the management of the fractious Commons was a major consideration, and to this end Danby circulated members of the Court party with letters requiring them to attend Westminster punctiliously. Danby hoped in this way to secure a majority because, despite his efforts at reforming the nation's finances, he needed to raise £1,000,000 to fund the royal revenue. The opposition would not countenance so vast a sum, and when they refused to grant Charles a supply he promptly prorogued Parliament and indicated his intense displeasure by refusing to make the customary closing speech. He then turned to Louis in the expectation of a subsidy. But the French King was not minded readily to honour his promises. Further negotiations had to take place, and it was these, combined with Danby's suggestion that Charles approach William of Orange, that eventually persuaded Louis to open his coffers. Gradually it was becoming clear to Charles that, caught between these two shrewd managers of European power politics, he might play a double game.

Charles had already obtained French permission to act as a mediator between the warring states and had sent his emissaries to the interminable peace conference being held at Nijmegen. Now he instructed some of these men to continue cementing his alliance with the French while turning a blind eye to the efforts made by Danby and Sir William Temple particularly to court the Prince of Orange. With the prevaricating guile that had long ago become characteristic of him, Charles was once again trying to be all things to all men. The results of such duplicity were desperately dangerous, particularly to Charles himself. If he had hopes of being the arbiter of a European peace, he now became the victim of the parties he hoped to reconcile. Both Louis and William of Orange attempted to take the direction of English foreign policy into their own hands and fought as viciously and as expensively for influence over the court and Parliament as they did for territory on the killing-fields of Europe. These last, it seemed, were rapidly falling into Louis' hands. Fortress after fortress surrendered to him until, with his defeat of William at Cassel, it seemed that the entire Spanish Netherlands might be his.

The people of England looked on with increasing terror as the forces of Catholic absolutism advanced with seeming invincibility. Realising that his victories would confirm Parliamentary support for the Dutch, Louis offered Charles subsidies for yet another prorogation of Parliament. Charles knew that a recess of over two years was tantamount to a dissolution and that a dissolution raised the appalling spectre of elections. He declined the French offer. A furious Louis chose to see the influence of Danby in this and became so concerned at what he believed was the scale of that influence at Westminster that he began to scatter bribes with a liberal hand.

The Duke of York continued to urge Charles in the direction of the French, while Danby exercised all his ingenuity to persuade his master that an alliance with the Dutch was essential to his interests. Debt and his own financial acumen provided Danby's most powerful arguments. He managed to convince the King that it was not possible to live on a French subsidy, while also persuading a reluctant Commons to vote Charles £600,000 for the refurbishment of the navy. This last was a particularly impressive feat since many Members were convinced that Charles had no intention of using the money for the purposes they had stipulated. To underline their suspicions, they refused to grant him a full supply until he had publicly concluded an alliance with the Dutch. Charles was furious. His bland assurance that 'upon the word of a King . . . you shall not repent any trust you repose in me' had gone unheeded and he felt that the Members were now encroaching on his prerogative powers to make peace or war at will.[10] Did they not realise that such conduct would encourage foreign rulers to believe that it was not with the King of England that they should negotiate but with his the House?

Furious at being cornered in this way, Charles prorogued the house, confident that he would receive a generous reward from the French for doing so. Ralph Montague, his ambassador in Paris, had already suggested to him that sums considerably in excess of those Parliament might grant would be available, and Charles decided to handle the talks himself. Once again his negotiations with the French ambassador were conducted with the lack of attention to detail so characteristic of him and he secured a poor deal. When a horrified Danby eventually discovered what was going on he tried to rectify matters as best he could. He did not dare to attack the agreement itself but tried instead to bargain for a better price. He had little success, while the correspondence his efforts involved would soon have disastrous consequences for him personally. As for Charles himself, he now had money and, true to his own duplicity, he began to make overtures to the Dutch. Wrongly believing that it would give him considerable influence over William of Orange – 'this little man' as he chose to call him – Charles agreed to the Prince's marriage to James's elder daughter, Princess Mary.[11]

'The Prince, like a hasty lover, came post from Harwich to Newmarket,' wrote Sir William Temple. There he continued to play the role of an infatuated young man with considerable aplomb for he saw that there was political advantage in it. Charles and James approached him the moment he arrived and suggested that they get down to business at once. William declined, insisting that he must see his beautiful bride before talking politics. When he was presented to Mary, William found her to be a tall, naive chatterbox of just fifteen who was currently hopelessly in love with Frances Apsley, her 'dearest, dearest dear Aurelia', the beautiful daughter of one of the Duke of York's attendants.[12] Mary was clearly not yet ready for a man, and her unprepossessing Prince was a particularly unwelcome sight to her. William was thin, severe and humourless. He spoke with an ugly, guttural accent. He had little idea of fashion and, worst of all, unlike the periwigged courtiers of England, he wore his own lank hair.

The unlikely suitor continued to parade his feelings. They had mastered him, he claimed. It was quite impossible to discuss international treaties before his personal happiness was settled. The delay was making him deeply discontented. One evening, Sir William Temple 'found him in the worst humour I ever saw him'. Realising that his services were called for, the shrewd and cultivated diplomat listened as the Prince poured out his heart, saying that 'he regretted that he had ever come into England and resolved that he would stay but two days longer, and then be gone, if the King continued in his mind of treating upon the peace before he was married'. Love alone would decide if Charles and William 'should live henceforth, either as the greatest friends or the greatest enemies'.[13]

The following day, Temple had an urgent meeting with the King. He begged Charles to think of all the great consequences that hung upon the marriage. Charles wryly agreed to the match prior to negotiations, accepting that he would have to trust William. He was reasonably sure there was nothing to worry about for he rather prided himself on the skill he supposed he had to judge men's characters from their looks, 'and if I am not deceived in the Prince's face, he is the honestest man in the world, and I will trust him, and he shall have his wife'. Temple was despatched to tell James 'that it is a thing I am resolved on'. Charles was clearly anxious all the same, and as Temple left he muttered to himself: 'Odds fish, he must consent.'[14] The haughty Duke was eventually made to comply and, with the marriage agreed, Charles thought it became him to have a man-to-man talk with the groom. 'Nephew,' he began, 'it is not good for a man to be alone, I will give you a helpmate.' Then the King added what he really wanted to say. 'Remember, love and war do not agree very well together.' The bellicose William listened politely and, since he had got what he wanted, wrote to the States General asking them to despatch £40,000 worth of jewels as a wedding present.

While the public celebrations were suitably lavish, the private feelings of most of those involved were far from joyful. It was a disconsolate little group that gathered in Mary's bedchamber at nine o'clock on 4 November 1677 to solemnise the marriage. Mary was tearful, William frowning, while the Duke of York was clearly sad at the prospect of losing his daughter. The Bishop of London officiated, and when the service was at an end the time came for the couple to be put to bed. By now both parties were reluctant, so reluctant indeed that William would not take off his underpants. Charles decided that a little avuncular advice was called for. Perhaps the Prince should fully undress. After all, it was his wedding night. And what would the bride think? William, with that leaden lack of romanticism that was second nature to him, made it clear he did not really care. Since he and his wife would be living together for a long time, he said, she would have to get used to his habits, and it was his habit to wear his underpants in bed. There was nothing more to be done but for Charles himself to draw the curtains round the bed, saying with ghastly jocularity: 'Now, Nephew, to your work! Hey! Saint George for England!'[15]

By the evening of the following day, as the people of England lit bonfires to celebrate both the Protestant marriage of their little Princess and the Protestant jubilee of Guy Fawkes night, it was becoming evident that the gauche and surly Prince of Orange wished to return to his continental wars. After all, he had won himself not just a bride but an ally whom he hoped to draw into his conflicts, thereby restoring the morale of his people, defending his territories and forcing the French into a strategic retreat. Meanwhile, as the French ambassador made his master's extreme irritation clear to Charles, the King himself set about trying to smooth the waters. Louis would understand that the Dutch marriage had been entered into for the best of reasons. It would prove to the English people that Charles had no intention whatsoever of submitting his country to the sort of Catholic and absolutist monarchy Louis himself had established in France. Nor was this the only advantage of the match. Charles believed that William was now securely under his thumb, while Charles himself had every intention of remaining on the best of terms with France. For his part, Louis was infuriated by such second-rate slipperiness. His opinion hardened that Charles was personally and politically weak, easily led, duplicitous, and blown hither and thither by forces he could not control. The exasperated autocrat knew nonetheless that fury was a crude weapon and that it was Charles's very weaknesses that ensured he could be manipulated. Charles he would have to coexist with, but the Protestant Danby was another matter. When Louis discovered that the Lord Treasurer could not be bought, he decided that he must go, and the French ambassador was ordered to make overtures to the Parliamentary opposition. Then Louis stopped paying Charles his subsidy.

When Parliament reconvened at the start of 1678, it was clear that the French ambassador (assisted in his efforts by the adept and experienced de Ruvigny) had done his work well. Charles was once again in an all too familiar impasse. He was a penniless monarch manipulated by his allies and obliged to face a hostile Commons. That hostility took a subtle form. Opposition MPs did not directly oppose the preparations for war but contented themselves with ensuring that their consent was conditional on the most galling of terms. In particular, they began to trespass on the fringes of the King's prerogatives by insisting that he inform them fully of the terms he made with foreign rulers. Publicly the King was angry, privately he was extremely anxious. He rebuked the Commons and then wrote urgently to Louis begging him to tie him to France with a treaty that would guarantee an annual subsidy of £600,000.

Louise merely pursued his wars. Ypres fell to him and Ghent surrendered. The encroaching Catholic menace created ever greater alarm in England, and, while Charles tried to quieten this by sending a small force to Ostend and recruiting an army of 30,000 men, public opinion refused to be appeased as it realised how easy it was for Charles to raise an army which he could use to establish his will at home. Opposition MPs became more deeply suspicious of the King's motives than ever and Charles turned to Louis once again. Even now he hoped to snatch something from an abject surrender. His bargaining counter was the impressive force of 30,000 men. Both he and Danby were convinced that Parliament so wanted them to disband these troops that it would willingly vote a supply. Louis too would welcome the disappearance of such an army and would likewise pay Charles his subsidy. Showing the deviousness of the truly desperate, Charles was hoping that he might be paid on both sides.

Only at the very close of this intricate game, when the warring armies had finally concluded the Treaty of Nijmegen, did Charles realise that Louis had no intention whatsoever of paying him the subsidy he had promised. Faced with a yawning chasm of debt, the King and Danby took the gambler's option and continued to throw good money after that which they had lost. Parliament had voted £380,000 for disbanding the forces Charles had raised. The money was used for keeping those forces in being. Every scrap of credit had been employed, and the cost of main-taining the army rose to over £750,000. Meanwhile, the very existence of a standing army made it clear to many that Charles was intending to impose arbitrary rule by force of arms. Parliament refused outright to increase his permanent revenue, and still the expenses mounted. Danby's accounting skills had availed Charles nothing. As the treasury continued to pay out, so it became clear that the master of public finances had been reduced to the economies of the casino, and soon the royal accounts were £2,500,000 in the red.

A harassed Charles turned his back on business and left the conduct of public affairs to Danby. He resumed his usual routine, and it was while he was walking through the outer gallery at Whitehall on his way to his morning stroll that he was accosted by a man bearing a letter. Charles read it as he descended the staircase and then, as he approached the entrance to St James's Park, he called the messenger to him and asked him to explain what was going on. The man, Christopher Kirkby, told him that there was a plot against the King's life and that he might well be in danger that very morning.

'How?' Charles asked.

'By shot,' Kirkby replied.[16]

Charles refused to be intimidated but told Kirkby that he would see him alone in his bedchamber on his return.

16

The Popish Conspirators

Engedland in the summer of 1678 was ripe for a conspiracy. For months past worried men and women had been glancing up at the skies where the planets were foretelling calamity. There had been no fewer than three eclipses of the sun and two of the moon, while early in the previous year a comet with a flaming tail had warned of 'frenzies, inflammations and new infirmities' along with 'troubles from great men and nobles'.[1] This tumult in the heavens was matched by suspicion on the streets. There had been too many humiliations, too many troubles. Plague, fire and war had left the people demoralised, and their fear bred monsters. Often those monsters took the form of Catholics in general and Jesuits in particular. For all that such people were a tiny and declining section of the population, here was the enemy within, the insidious power that would bring a virtuous Protestant nation to its knees.

The old arguments against popish rites were rehearsed over and over again. 'I despise such a ridiculous and nonsensical religion,' declared Lord Russell. 'A piece of wafer, broken betwixt a priest's fingers, to be our Saviour!' He then drove his point home with a telling and lurid detail: 'what becomes of it when eaten', he said, 'and taken down, you know'.[2] To such disgust with superstition was added a fear of the political implications of Catholicism. 'From popery came the notion of a standing army and arbitrary power,' declared Sir Henry Capel. 'Formerly the crown of Spain, and now France, supports this root of popery amongst us; but lay popery flat, and there's an end of arbitrary government.'[3] Such thinking engendered hysteria which was then fanned to a white heat by the efforts of the pamphleteers. Horrible imaginings gripped the nation. 'Casting your eye towards Smithfield,' declared one writer, 'imagine you see your father, or your mother, or some of your nearest and dearest relations, tied to a stake in the midst of flames, when with eyes lifted up to heaven, they scream and cry out to that God for whose cause they die, which was a frequent spectacle the last time popery reigned amongst us.'[4]

Only a Protestant monarchy could save the people from such a holocaust, and it was against this background that Charles agreed to his meeting with Christopher Kirkby, the man who had unexpectedly accosted him on the palace stairs. He returned from his walk in St James's Park and asked Kirkby what he knew about the alleged plot to assassinate him. Kirkby told him that two Roman Catholics – a Benedictine named Thomas Pickering and a Jesuit lay-brother called John Grove – had vowed to shoot him. If they failed, the King would be poisoned by his wife's doctor, Sir George Wakeman. A sceptical Charles asked Kirkby who had informed him of this and Kirkby, having said that he had a reliable source, was told to produce him between eight and nine that evening.

Kirkby's informant was a sadly crazed churchman of Puritan sympathies called Israel Tonge. Early in his life Tonge had shown some academic promise, having been a fellow of his Oxford college and received his doctorate of Divinity. The years following the Restoration were a lean time for him all the same and he had had to get by as best he could until, in 1666, he was presented with the living of St Mary Stayning in the City of London. Three months later Tonge's hopes and his livelihood were destroyed in the Great Fire, and with the loss of these came the loss of his reason too. Tonge was now convinced that the Jesuits had not only started the Great Fire itself but were furiously plotting the downfall of the nation at large. To prove his point he began a translation of a work called *Jesuits' Morals*, but his style was so leaden

that his publisher realised he had a failure on his hands and cancelled
the work before the third turgid volume appeared. Such a disappointment only confirmed Tonge in his lunacy, and he was working on an
extravagant History of the Jesuits when there shuffled into his life a man
who was prepared to confirm all his craziest fears.

Titus Oates was a conman of genius, a psychopath whose fantasies
were as ugly as his body. People looked at him with disgust. 'His brow
was low,' wrote one fascinated contemporary, 'his eyes small and sunk
deep in his head; his face was flat, compressed in the middle so as to look
like a dish or discus; on each side were prominent ruddy cheeks, his nose
was snub, his mouth in the very centre of his face, for his chin was almost
equal in size to the rest of his face.'[5] This unprepossessing face was
forever bowed over Oates's chest, and when he spoke it was with a
grating, wailing, sing-song voice. Soon every ear in the country would
be turned to listen to him, but for the moment Oates was still struggling
with his disappointments.

He had been educated first at Westminster and then at Merchant
Taylors, from which he was expelled. Somehow he managed to get into
Gonville and Caius College, Cambridge, for where he was also expelled.
Oates transferred to St John's and then, despite going down without a
degree, took holy orders and was presented with a living in Kent from
which he was promptly dismissed. A brief, dishonourable period as a
naval chaplain followed but, having been once again dismissed, Oates
hung about the seedier edges of the Catholic community in London,
made his first acquaintance with Israel Tonge, and was then appointed
a chaplain to the Earl of Norwich. A mere three months passed before
he was fired, after which Oates converted to Roman Catholicism and
eventually attracted the attention of the English Provincial of the
Society of Jesus. He was promptly sent to the English College at
Valladolid from where, once again, he was expelled when it was discovered that his educational qualifications were insufficient for the courses
in the priesthood offered there. Oates returned to England and, having
inveigled himself into Jesuit circles once again, was sent to the Catholic
boarding school at St Omers. There the boys bullied him mercilessly.
On one occasion they broke a pan over his head, and an embittered Oates

was left struggling with his elementary Latin as he lusted after his tormentors' ripening bodies. Predictably, in June 1678, he was expelled from the school and he returned to London with a festering hatred of all things Jesuitical.

Oates now met up again with Israel Tonge. With the calculation of the seasoned conman, he fed the struggling cleric with carefully selected morsels of information about the Jesuits both in England and abroad. An ecstatic Tonge asked him to write down all he knew, and at the start of August 1678 Oates appeared at Tonge's lodgings with a brief account of a Catholic conspiracy to kill King Charles and raise a rebellion across his lands. Tonge himself, Oates suggested, was one of the chief figures the enemy wished to destroy, and, having thus whetted his victim's appetite, Oates folded up his document, put it in his pocket and left Tonge to his imaginings. These needed further fuelling and, a few days later, Oates's first brief statement had been elaborated into forty-three numbered paragraphs which he cunningly left for Tonge 'under the wainscot at the farther end of Sir Richard Barker's gallery in his house at the Barbican'.[6] An enthralled Tonge decided that the King must be shown this material as soon as possible, and his friend Christopher Kirkby seemed the ideal go-between because he was slightly acquainted with Charles through their mutual interest in the transactions of the Royal Society.

Now, at eight o'clock on 13 August 1678, as Tonge climbed the stairs to the Red Room at Whitehall, it seemed that he would at last be listened to as the saviour of the nation. He was ushered into the royal presence where he read out the most important of Oates's accusations and then handed over the rest for Charles to inspect. The lazy King said he was far too busy to peruse the document and asked Tonge to précis its contents. The crazed cleric told him that after his assassination Charles's three kingdoms of England, Scotland and Ireland would be raised in rebellion against the Catholic James, at which point they would be crushed by an invading French army. Catholicism would then reign triumphant. Charles was not inclined to believe this sorry farago of nonsense, but he was wary nonetheless since 'among so many particulars he did not know but there might be some truth'.[7] He decided he would let Danby sift it out for him. He himself was off to Windsor and, having dismissed Kirkby and Tonge, he commanded a Gentleman of the Bedchamber to deliver the papers they had brought to Danby's lodgings in the Cockpit.

As Danby read through the papers, noting their strange combination of fantasy and detail, he was no more convinced of their truth than Charles had been. It was clear to him that no legal action could be taken on evidence as insufficient as this, but he could not wholly ignore the matter and he gave Tonge to understand that he would need more facts. Oates enthusiastically supplied these, but still there was too little to go on, and it was only when Danby suggested that the government intercept the alleged conspirators' correspondence that Oates felt obliged to forge five incriminating letters and address them to the Duke of York's Jesuit confessor. Incompetence ensured that the letters were not intercepted, and when the confessor received them he handed them over to James himself. The Duke decided that the forgeries were part of a campaign launched by the Parliamentary opposition to discredit his fellow Catholics, and he insisted that the matter be investigated by the Privy Council. What might once have been a farce was set to become a tragedy.

But by now the real conspirators were locked in mutual mistrust. Matters had proceeded with alarming speed, the greatest in the land were closely involved and Tonge feared that Oates would desert him and so leave him alone, ridiculous and vulnerable. If only he could get Oates to swear the truth of his allegations before a magistrate then all might yet be well. By 6 September he had so far prevailed on Oates to agree to this, and the magistrate chosen was none other than Sir Edmund Berry Godfrey, the stalwart local hero of the Great Plague. Realising the terrible implications of what the men before him claimed they knew, Godfrey reluctantly took their depositions on oath. Then, as Oates continued to manufacture evidence against the Catholics, the Council resolved to investigate the whole matter. An exasperated Charles opened the proceedings, outlined his dealings with Tonge and ordered the five fake letters to be produced. They were rapidly dismissed by all present as 'a counterfeit matter', and when Tonge himself was then ushered in he proved himself such a rambling and unsatisfactory witness that Charles brought the meeting to a close and rode off in relief to Newmarket. This natural reaction was to prove a tactical blunder, for that afternoon, while Charles and the Duke of York were at the races, Titus Oates was summoned to give his evidence before the mostly weak and inexperienced Councillors still remaining at Windsor.

This was Oates's first moment of triumph. He had at last been called into the arena of high politics. His shambling, shifty days were behind him. The great of the land inclined their ears and he tickled them with masterly assurance. First, he willingly gave his evidence on oath and then, summoning all the powers of his fluent and revolting voice, he canted about Catholic plots and traitors, seasoning his imaginings with the convincing, salty grains of minor fact. For two or three hours he parried questions and roused suspicions until the Council began to grow impressed by 'his prodigious memory, confidence and unexpected answers at several turns'.[8] Even the forged letters proved no bar to Oates's testimony. When they were folded up and shown him a line at a time he could easily identify who had written them (hardly a remarkable achievement since he had faked the correspondence himself) and when he was asked why the handwriting was so markedly different to that usually employed by the supposed authors, he airily answered that Jesuits always disguised their script in such ways. The Council, 'strangely perplexed', listened with increasing credulity 'and began to apprehend that there was some dangerous mischief contrived against His Majesty'.[9] Its members found themselves unable to resist Oates's story that Charles himself would be murdered, that London would be burned a second time, and that 20,000 Catholics would rise up as one man and slit the throats of 100,000 Protestants. The Jesuits Oates named were rounded up that night, while Charles, at the Council's request, hastened back from the races.

As he took the Council chair the following morning Charles was determined not to give way to fear and unreason. Steadiness was essential amid hysteria, and he would not proceed against the Jesuits Oates had named 'unless the proofs against them were very clear'.[10] When

Oates himself was brought before him Charles quickly caught him out on small points of detail, but luck for the moment was on Oates's side. The Council began to question him about the involvement in the so-called plot of one Edward Coleman, a Catholic convert and secretary first to the Duke and then to the Duchess of York. For all that he did not even know the man, Oates was now in his element and he 'testified much touching the activity and concern of Mr Coleman in these matters, and particularly of his corresponding with Mr La Chaise, confessor of the French King'. Oates then added that if Coleman's papers were 'well looked into there would appear that which might cost him his neck'.[11]

While the Jesuits named by Oates were brought before the Council and acquitted themselves with aplomb, a search was made for Coleman's papers. It would take time to go through these, time that an impatient Charles thought might be better spent at Newmarket, and he returned to the races having told the French ambassador that 'he did not believe the accusations had any foundation in truth' and that Oates himself was 'a wicked man'.[12] Others too were revolted by him. James called him a rascal, while Evelyn wrote that he was 'a bold man, and in my thoughts furiously indiscreet'.[13] Nonetheless, all that Oates had alleged needed to be investigated with what Charles himself called 'great circumspection', for he knew that 'what should herein be omitted at the Council Board will infallibly be taken up at the House of Commons'.[14]

This was the last thing Charles wanted, but events now conspired to force the so-called Popish Plot to the centre of public attention. First came the revelations contained in Coleman's letters. Coleman himself was a foolish, over-enthusiastic man who had earlier carried on a corre-spondence with eminent people abroad about restoring the Roman Catholic faith to England. He wrote loosely of 'the great design' by which he and his co-religionists would 'undermine the intrigues of that company of merchants who trade for the Parliament and the religion', adding that he longed 'to establish . . . the associated Catholics in every place'. He wrote to Père La Chaise, Louis XIV's confessor, asking for money for Charles which he believed would make the King 'afterwards perform all that His Most Christian Majesty can ask of him'.[15] The letters nonetheless made it clear that Coleman took a dim view of what he considered to be Charles's debauchery and that he regarded the Duke of York as an altogether more worthy ruler of the country. Indeed, the letters suggest that Coleman had some vague idea of establishing a relationship between France and James comparable to that which Charles had already secretly negotiated for himself. The sheer grandeur of such a design was part of its allure for Coleman, and his vanity exposed his folly. 'We have here a mighty work upon our hands,' he told La Chaise, 'no less than the conversion of three kingdoms, and by that perhaps the subduing of a pestilent heresy which has domineered over a greater part of this northern world a long time.'[16]

Charles still refused to be drawn into a tempest of bigotry and suspicion. He was reluctant to have the arrested Jesuits tried and 'their blood taken in a case so improbable'. He sought the advice of the High Court judges in the matter who ruled that the single testimony of Oates was insufficient to count against the men. Charles was trying to proceed in as measured a manner as he could but then, on 23 October, and with the House of Commons now in session, there came the great turning point of the Popish Plot: the murdered body of Sir Edmund Berry Godfrey was found on a patch of waste land below Primrose Hill. He was fully dressed, his face was in the mud, and he had been transfixed with his own sword. There was an immediate outburst of national hysteria, despite the fact that no culprits were ever found.* The arrest of the Jesuits named by Oates had already raised public suspicion, and an Order in Council given on 30 September for the disarming of all papists further fuelled the fires. Although his testimony to the Council was supposed to be confidential, it is possible that Oates himself had been talking loosely, and wild accounts of his evidence were circulating in the newspapers. It was becoming clear to people that the King and his Council knew something, and the murder of Godfrey made clear what that was. The Jesuits had hatched a plan to bring the country to its knees, and the murder of so good a man as Sir Edmund was but the first example of the terror these evil men hoped to inflict.

* The murder and its motive remain shrouded in mystery to this day.

The Commons was seething with suspicion, and Charles tried to calm them by briefly mentioning 'a design' on his life said to be the work of the Jesuits; but 'I shall forbear any opinion,' he added, 'lest I may seem to say too much or too little.' He was determined, he said, to 'leave the matter to the law'.[17] But by now such deft circumspection was out of place. Members of Parliament had caught the contagion of the nation and were the spokesmen of its fears. They felt it was imperative to take precautions. They scoured the vaults under the House of Commons as they looked for gunpowder, sentinels were set at the doors, buildings in the neighbourhood were searched for arms, the Savoy was ransacked as men looked for hundreds of thousands of pounds of 'plot money', while even M. Choqueux's nearby firework shop became an object of suspicion. There were dangers all around, and Members began to consider means for 'the better preservation and safety of His Majesty's person'. They begged Charles to banish all papists from a radius of twenty miles around London. Defensive chains were then placed across the capital's streets, and committees were set up to investigate Godfrey's murder, Coleman's letters and the Plot in general. Parliament had taken over the exposure of treason, and Oates himself was now summoned to the Bar of the House.

He perjured himself with all the fluent malice of which he was capable. As his sing-song voice echoed round the chamber, so he told of Jesuit commissions appointing officers to a popish army and then naming ministers to a popish government. A great swathe of the Catholic aristocracy and gentry had already been suborned to these dastardly ends, and Oates's horrified listeners reacted with increasing panic. They sent for the Lord Chief Justice, they barred the doors of the House, they asked for warrants for the arrest of the Catholic peers, and by early the next morning five of these unfortunate men were immured in the Gatehouse prison. Meanwhile Oates continued subtly to play on the nation's fears. While a vast procession of Londoners escorted the corpse of Sir Edmund Berry Godfrey to his grave, he testified to the Lords and, as he came to a close, 'humbly desired that he might have a guard, in regard it is late and dark, and that he goeth in danger'.[18] The triumphant conman was duly escorted to his lodgings, while the duped Commons voted unanimously that they were 'of opinion that there hath been and still is a damnable and hellish plot contrived and carried on by the popish recusants for the assassinating and murdering of the King, and for subverting the government, and rooting out and destroying the Protestant religion'.[19] The momentum of hysteria seemed unstoppable, and further revelations increased its fury.

Knowledge of the contents of Coleman's letters in particular 'made as much noise in and about London, and . . . all over the nation, as if the very cabinet of Hell had been laid open'.[20] The letters inevitably turned public attention to Coleman's erstwhile employer, the Catholic Duke of York. Shaftesbury, riding high on the current of the times, put forward a motion that James be removed from the King's presence and councils, and on 3 November the government capitulated to his demands. James was duly barred from 'all courses where any affairs of the nation were agitated', and as Charles issued a proclamation ordering papists to retire to their homes, gossip and wishful-thinking ran wild. It was now said that the Duke of Monmouth had been declared legitimate and people drank healths to him, to Charles and to Shaftesbury 'as the only true pillars of our safety'.[21]

Such excitement was made worse by the fact that Godfrey's murderers had still not been found, but now a new informer appeared in the corrupt shape of William Bedloe to tell the Lords that he knew for sure that the good magistrate had been murdered by the Jesuits in the Queen's own house. The all too Catholic royal family was clearly implicated in the Plot and hysteria approached crisis point. Men were frightened lest they talked unguardedly in the streets. The trained bands patrolled the City of London. There were fears that the papists might poison the water supply. There was a great whispering about priest-holes, about the discovery of popish books and chalices, and about priests flooding off every ship that disembarked at an English port. Mysterious 'night riders' were glimpsed from Wiltshire to Yorkshire, while 'a great body of men both horse and foot' apparently glimpsed on the Isle of Purbeck started rumours of a French invasion.[22]

Charles himself was one of the very few people in the country not to be swept up in the mounting hysteria, but the inclusion of the Queen in the conspirators' fantasies roused him to a rare display of anger. He knew that Catherine was, as he said, 'a weak woman, and had some disagreeable humours', but he was also sure that she 'was not capable of a wicked thing; and considering his faultiness towards her in other things he thought it a horrid thing to abandon her'.[23] Nor would he. He sent for Oates and, with two secretaries present, closely cross-questioned him about the Queen's connections with the Society of Jesus. Oates claimed that he had seen letters from leading Jesuits thanking Catherine for a gift of £4000, but it was only when Oates himself requested a second interview that he began to spin his most egregious fantasies. Desperate to prove himself an informer altogether superior to his rival Bedloe, he now said that he knew the Queen had privately told the Jesuits that she would no longer tolerate Charles's numerous affairs 'but would revenge the violation of her bed'.[24] The £4000 mentioned earlier (and now stepped up to £5000) was apparently the fee to be paid for the royal murder.

These were the allegations of a desperate lunatic, and Charles was determined to prove them false. Oates was given a comprehensive grilling by the Privy Council and was then hurried straight to Somerset House under guard. If Oates had such an intimate knowledge of the Queen's home and of the conversations she was supposed to have had there, he would surely be able to point out the room in which they took place. He could not. He blundered about the galleries, the staircases and the garden. He muttered about some large folding doors, but eventually had to confess defeat. A furious Charles ordered him to be taken under guard to Whitehall where he was to be kept in close confinement.

Bedloe in the meantime took the opportunity to peddle his own story about the Queen's perfidy to a horrified House of Commons. When he had given his evidence, Oates was once again summoned to the chamber, where he complained bitterly of the treatment he had recently received at the King's hands. Members petitioned Charles to lessen some of the restrictions on him and, relieved by the trust apparently placed in him, Oates muttered the infamous words: 'I do accuse the Queen for conspiring the death of the King.'[25] In the atmosphere of neurotic suspicion he had created, Oates's mumbled phrase was more resonant than a shout, and the Commons agreed to ask for the Lords' support in requesting the King to banish Catherine and her household from London. The Lords would not countenance such an absurdity, and even the Commons came to its senses, Members' minds now focused by the public execution of Edward Coleman, the one certain traitor so far unearthed.

A subject accused of treason in the seventeenth century faced the horrors of a show trial, and Coleman was no exception. He was palpably guilty of the most heinous offences but, true to the judicial standards of the day, he was allowed no defence counsel, no list of the jurymen, no indication of the witnesses ranged against him, and no copy of the indictment. His judge, Sir William Scroggs, the Chief Justice of King's Bench, was a repellent and intrusive man who ensured that Coleman's conviction was a foregone conclusion. The trial nonetheless left many people shaken, for the evidence seemed to lay bare their deepest fears. Coleman's letters suggested that the Catholic Duke of York – a 'heady, violent and bloody' man in Shaftesbury's phrase – would not hesitate to re-establish the Catholic church in England by force. Suspicions against him mounted and James was now, in the words of a contemporary pamphlet, 'the bigoted Popish Duke, who, by the assistance of the Lord Lauderdale's Scotch Army, the forces in Ireland and those in France, hopes to bring all back to Rome'.[26] The nervous authorities believed that a Catholic blood-letting might appease this mood, and the Catholic priests arrested months before on Oates's evidence were hurried before the dreadful Scroggs, who voiced the national fear when he pointed to the innocent men in the dock and declared: 'They eat their God, they kill their King, and saint the murderer!'[27] Only one verdict could be returned in these circumstances, and when the compliant jury had done their work, Scroggs commended them for their efforts saying: 'You have done, gentlemen, like very good Christians; that is to say, very good Protestants.'[28]

While the country reeled under the revelations of Oates and Bedloe, two altogether more powerful conspirators were also at work. At the height of the spurious popish menace, Charles renewed his secret negotiations with Louis XIV and Catholic France. Two difficulties stood in his way. First, he had still failed to disband his standing army, and secondly Louis continued to nurture a deep distaste for Danby, whose role in Charles's earlier attempts to obtain a French subsidy irked him. Now he wished to have him removed from office, and the chosen instrument of his design was the erstwhile English ambassador in Paris, Ralph Montague.

Montague was extensively aware of Charles's involvement with the French and also nurtured professional grievances against both Danby and Charles himself. He believed that Danby had cheated him of a promised advancement, while letters written to him by Charles's erstwhile mistress Lady Castlemaine suggested that Montague had made disparaging remarks about the King. When Montague came over to England without permission to defend himself, Charles's reaction was to dismiss him from his embassy and bar him from the Privy Council. In such ways as these, both Danby and Charles had made an enemy of the man who had handled their incriminating correspondence with the King of France, and Montague was now determined to have his revenge. He went to call on Barrillon, the French ambassador in London, and, in return for the promise of a substantial reward, agreed to make public Danby's incriminating letters to Louis XIV. Louis himself then agreed to expose what he considered to be the true aims of Danby's policies and, in particular, the supposedly arbitrary purposes for which he had raised Charles's standing army. With this design in place, Montague succeeded in having himself elected as a Member of Parliament for Northampton, thus providing himself with a platform from which he could expose both his King and the country's chief minister.

When news of this plot reached Charles he took immediate action. He gave orders that Montague's papers should be seized, hoping thereby not only to suppress the dangerous information these contained but to prepare from the evidence they provided a case against Montague which would prove beyond doubt that the ambassador had been in contact with the papal nuncio in Paris. This last would be sufficient grounds to organise a treason trial, and as anti-Catholic hysteria raged through the country so Montague could be offered as a sacrificial victim whose public execution would prove how keen Charles was to preserve the security of the Anglican church. The plan failed abysmally. The House of Commons had already set itself up as the chief prosecutor of the Catholic menace and now ordered that selected items from Montague's letters be produced and read before it.

Two letters from Danby to the King of France appeared to prove his complicity in a treasonable design and so secured his downfall. A horrified Commons heard how Charles's chief minister had agreed with Louis that 'the King expects to have six millions of livres yearly for three years . . . because it will be two or three years before he can hope to find his parliament in humour to give him supplies'.[29] It was constitutionally impossible to accuse the King of a misdemeanour since he could do no wrong, but it was evident that Charles's closest adviser was, on his own initiative, bypassing Parliament and making overtures to the enemy. Articles of impeachment were at once drawn up against him and, in addition to his being a traitor, it was now clear to many that the High Anglican Danby was actually a man of the popish persuasion who had done his best to suppress evidence about the horrors of the Popish Plot. He had, besides, freely lined his own pockets and those of his followers from public funds.

Such difficulties placed Charles in a dangerous and thoroughly compromising position. For all that Danby had failed to manage the House of Commons in such a way as to prevent the Country opposition from monopolising the investigation of the Popish Plot, the King still needed his chief minister's economic skills if he was to repair his own finances. He also believed, with good reason, that if he sacrificed Danby then the aggrieved minister would have little compunction in using his knowledge of Charles's negotiations with France to blackmail him. Danby was both useless and indispensable, and it seemed that only a combination of deviousness and daring would ensure that Charles survived this crisis. He took the one approach apparently open to him and stooped to conquer. He made secret overtures to a group of Country MPs led by Denzil Holles, for it seemed that these men alone offered a way out. Promising more than they could actually deliver, they told the

King that they would be content if Danby quietly resigned and that they would then vote him a supply for the disbanding of his private army provided that he dissolved the current Parliament and summoned a new one without delay. Charles felt he had no option but to collude with those who had opposed him. At the end of December Parliament was prorogued, and early in the following year was dissolved by proclamation. Under such ignominious circumstances as these Charles brought to a close that Parliament which, eighteen years before, had welcomed him back as the saviour and rightful King of a confused and bewildered people.

New ways of ruling had now to be found, and the months of crisis that followed brought out qualities of ruthless determination, political ability and sheer guile which Charles had only intermittently shown before. One of his first responsibilities was to respond to the problems posed by his brother. On Danby's advice he ordered James to leave the country and then, having told him that under no circumstances should he seek exile in France, he issued a statement denying that he himself had ever married any woman save the Queen, thereby trying to quash once and for all the rumours that Monmouth was legitimate. Having tried to settle the matter of the succession, Charles then turned to his erstwhile minister. But Danby was now an apparently spent force in English politics and, as part of the sweeping changes Charles felt he was obliged to make, he insisted on his resignation. He nonetheless tried to exercise mercy, granting Danby not only a pardon but a substantial pension too. The newly reconvened House of Commons was furious at such a display of royal clemency and held no fewer than eighteen virulent debates on the impeachment which resulted in Charles being obliged to incarcerate Danby in the Tower. The concession was perhaps a wise one, but Charles obstinately refused a complete climbdown. He withdrew Danby's pension but told the Commons firmly that his pardon must stand.

This showed the direction of the King's policies. The royal right to pardon was a prerogative power, and in the crisis swirling about him Charles was determined that the royal prerogative should be defended at all costs and used with the utmost of his skill to ensure his survival.

The strain took its toll and the more observant noted that the pressure Charles was under was obliging him to change as a man. He seemed more withdrawn than before, and more inscrutable. 'His conduct is so secret and impenetrable', Barrillon wrote back to France, 'that even the most skilful observers are misled.'[30]

This indeed was to prove the case. In order to pursue his policies and combat the mounting hostility of the Whigs, Charles had to establish his credibility as firmly as he could. Although the court might have seemed the most obvious place to look for allies, he was sufficiently shrewd to realise that the dissatisfaction of many of the peers ensured that the aristocracy were shifting, dangerous sands. The absence of supply had meant that drastic economies were necessary, and there were disaffected courtiers who now made overtures to the Whigs or showed a significant loyalty to James. Many others were mistrustful. After all, everyone knew how Charles had abandoned ministers such as Clarendon and jettisoned such policies as the Declaration of Indulgence when these ran into difficulties. Nonetheless, if the Tory party were to present a viable alternative to the well-organised and articulate Whigs it was essential that Charles rally behind him those of the nobility, gentry, townsfolk and substantial farmers who formed his natural constituency. Many of these men were proud of long family traditions of loyalty to the crown, a loyalty which seemed to reflect well on their own prestige and rectitude. Many also saw the crown in quasi-mystical terms, and Tory propaganda would soon skilfully exploit these beliefs. Such notions were bolstered, as always, by the Anglican church. The clergy feared that any weakening of royal authority would damage their own, and Sheldon had left them a legacy which emphasised how important it was that squire and parson should be as one in their support of the King. Here were the surest foundations of Tory support, and it was these men who remained naturally loyal to Charles.

To convince the waverers among them Charles continued to make important changes in the structure of government. Not only had a new Parliament been elected, but now a new Privy Council was formed as well. It was essential to take public steps to avoid Whig criticism of the crown's desire for arbitrary rule, and, to present the appearance at least of consultation, Charles remodelled the Council, giving half its thirty seats to senior office holders and the remaining to peers and commoners 'whose known abilities, interest and esteem in the nation' would place them above suspicion of 'either mistaking or betraying the true interests of the kingdom, and consequently of advising ill'.[31] No single minister would have undue sway, no Cabal would manipulate in secret. Among the leading figures appointed were Essex, who had command of the royal finances, Clarendon's able son Lawrence Hyde, Sunderland, who was put in charge of foreign affairs, the shrewd and nimble-minded Halifax, and Shaftesbury, who was appointed Lord President. An appearance of tradition, probity and balance had thus been achieved and, having been achieved, could be safely ignored as Charles pursued his own determined way.

That he was being adroit rather than conciliatory was clear from his promotion of Shaftesbury. By appointing his leading opponent to the Council Charles created a sensation which confirmed for the gullible that he was prepared to listen to a range of opinions, but he was also playing his familiar double game. It was just possible that Shaftesbury's loyalty could be bought by high office but, if it were not, then the fact that Shaftesbury had accepted the Presidency would surely diminish his standing among the more committed and zealous of the Whigs. It was a clever move, but it was not clever enough. Shaftesbury soon realised that he had been offered only a simulacrum of power and he had, besides, his own agenda. For some time now he had been busying himself with the Commons' reports into its investigation of the Popish Plot. From this tangle of lies and suspicion, fear and confusion, he would prepare his case for the greatest crisis of Charles's reign: the attempt to exclude the Catholic James, Duke of York, from the succession to the English throne.

Late in March Shaftesbury gave an indication of his policy. He dwelt on the seemingly inevitable connection between Roman Catholicism and absolute kingship. A month later he launched his attack itself when the Commons was asked to vote on a resolution that 'the Duke of York being a Papist, and the hopes of his coming as such to the Crown, have given the greatest countenance and encouragement to the present conspiracies and designs of the Papists against the King and the Protestant Religion'.[32] Charles reacted with prompt, Machiavellian guile. He suggested compromises, limitations to James's power if he were to succeed, which had the principal merit of being so complex and so inconsistent that he hoped the House would be kept talking for days. Charles was not acting out of personal loyalty to his brother, however, for long experience of James had convinced him that he was a fool. When James had remonstrated with him for walking so openly in St James's Park, Charles had turned to him and, with a light smile of contempt, had said: 'I am sure no man in England will take away my life to make you king.' More prophetically, he was to tell William of Orange that if James were indeed to succeed to the throne then his 'turbulent and excessive temperament' would ensure that he did not stay seated upon it for more than four years.[33]

What motivated Charles in opposing Exclusion was his absolute conviction that such matters lay within the royal prerogative and that under no circumstances whatsoever should they be tampered with by Parliament. While he might have shared his brother's opinion that Members of this particular Parliament were 'so many young spaniels that run and bark at every lark that springs', he knew that unlike his own servile little pets these men had teeth that could inflict real damage.[34] They had ideas that were novel and deeply dangerous. They were determined to limit his authority and they believed in their own. The debates over Danby's pardon had already illustrated this. As one hot-head Whig had declared, 'if they confirmed this pardon to Lord Danby, they made the King absolute', and the consequences of this were clear. 'What difference was there between that and arbitrary power?'[35] It was essential to such men that they believed that they could 'win the King to a good will and liking of what we shall do', for they were the representatives of the people (or at least that very small number of people who had the vote) and 'the foundation of Government is in the People's hearts'.[36]

Shaftesbury himself was perfectly clear about this revolutionary idea – he was to relish his sobriquet 'the tribune of the people' – but he also believed he enjoyed a psychological advantage over the King. He thought that Charles was weak and swayable, and that, despite all his protestations to the contrary, he would be quite prepared to accept the Exclusion of his brother should circumstances force him to it. He was relying on Charles's known limitations, unaware that the most powerful weapons in the royal arsenal were the invisible ones of Charles's unshakeable belief in his prerogative powers and the guile, determination and energy he could employ to defend these. When, on 11 May, Parliament voted on a resolution for a Bill to be brought in 'to disable the Duke of York to inherit the Imperial Crown of the Realm', he knew that he would have to ready these weapons and ensure his political survival by rising above his hostile Commons and fractious Council.[37]

It was already clear to him that he was facing a concerted and well-organised opposition. An important aspect of Shaftesbury's political brilliance was that he could recognise the implications of the new world of power politics opening up before him. Not only was he an able if arrogant manager of his party, he recognised that public opinion and, with this, the nation's growing political consciousness were essential factors in his campaign. He was determined to nurture the atmosphere in which he hoped he could thrive, and to this end he resolved to use the chances presented to him by the continuing turmoil of the Popish Plot. In particular, he wanted to hurry forward the trial of the five peers allegedly involved in that and to secure the conviction of Sir George Wakeman, the Catholic former physician to the Queen who had allegedly been suborned to poison Charles. The intricate details of Danby's position also required a resolution, and if these three matters were to proceed to their climax while Parliament was sitting Charles knew that he faced a complexity of crises which might well bring out the most compromising revelations and so give rise to a situation he could never hope to control. He therefore made the one move open to him and, while Lords and Commons squabbled over whether Danby's case should precede the trial of the peers or vice versa, he prorogued Parliament, ironically announcing his regret that its disagreements had disappointed the great hopes he had placed in it.

The new and inexperienced Parliament had, by its own terms, achieved very little. Only one piece of legislation had actually been

passed, but the unintended consequences of this were to prove
profound indeed. In its attempt to limit the crown's prerogative powers,
the Commons had turned its attention to Charles's right to imprison his
subjects by royal warrant. The issue proved both tortuous and
contentious, and the primary objective was soon smothered in a wealth
of detail. It was in dealing with aspects of this last that there passed on
to the statute book an Act which was to become a cornerstone of British
liberty. It had long been customary for arrested persons to be granted a
writ of habeas corpus so that they might be brought bodily before a
judge or a court to have the charges against them investigated. Great
difficulties had recently been made over the granting of such writs,
however, the lawyers lining their capacious pockets with disputes over
such niceties as to whether courts other than King's Bench had the right
to issue writs of habeas corpus, and whether in certain cases one writ
was sufficient to cover all the eventualities. Parliament was resolved to
tidy up these abuses, even if it could achieve no more, and quietly,
almost unregarded, 31 Chas II slipped into law and confirmed that no
English subject should endure delay in being granted a writ of habeas
corpus. Even Charles himself had reason to be pleased at this apparently minor achievement, for it appeared to give him some shield
for protecting both Danby and the five Catholic peers so arbitrarily
imprisoned by Parliament itself.

But habeas corpus seemed a trivial matter compared to the trial of the
Queen's physician, Sir George Wakeman. Israel Tonge's earliest accusations had involved this man in the plot to murder Charles and his
fantasies had subsequently been taken up with enthusiasm not only by
Oates and Bedloe but by a third false witness, Miles Prance. The
attempt by these men to ruin Catherine's reputation was a tactical error
on several fronts. Even though she was a Catholic, Catherine herself was
held in considerable esteem both by powerful members of the establishment and by the public at large. She was not ostentatious, meddling
and extravagant as Henrietta Maria had been, but was a dignified and
evidently good woman who tried her best to fit herself to the life and
ways of her adopted country and was not loud in her complaints about
her husband's numerous infidelities. Such behaviour helped her greatly

when her alleged involvement in the Popish Plot was investigated by the House of Lords, while her qualities were such as to make Charles himself feel both guilty and protective.

There were those who nonetheless wished Charles to divorce his barren Queen, but since the best that the Whig opposition could hope from such a move was the production of a Protestant heir rather than an excuse for diminishing the powers of the crown itself, many looked forward to the possibility of convicting Catherine of criminal charges which would then make it appear that the Catholic menace was firmly rooted in the court. Stirred not only by honour and shame but by a recognition of the political difficulties he would face if Catherine were ever to be seriously threatened, Charles involved himself personally in the trial of her physician. He intervened in the organisation of Wakeman's defence, and the usual form of a show trial for treason was stood on its head. Moves were made to ensure that key defence witnesses attended the trial (by convention they could not be sub-poenaed), while Wakeman himself was given details of the case mounted against him. The repellent Scroggs was also encouraged to use his heavy-handed and intrusive conduct of trials to bring about the required verdict. He harassed and obstructed Oates and the other pros-ecution witnesses, and in his summing up made it clear that he expected an acquittal for Wakeman. This he duly achieved, and it seemed just possible that the high tide of popish hysteria might now at last be on the turn.

With Parliament again prorogued, Charles once more reopened nego-tiations with Louis XIV. Despite his past experience, he still prided himself on his ability to strike a deal with the most subtle diplomat in Europe, but if his handling of matters at home had so far been deft, his four summer meetings with Barrillon proved him an amateur in matters of tactics and guile. It is just possible that the edge of Charles's mind was blunted by fatigue and a serious forthcoming illness, but he acquitted himself poorly indeed. He was, anyway, negotiating from a position of weakness since it suited Louis' purposes to keep a troubled England out of European affairs.

It seems that Charles greatly exaggerated the extent of those troubles – exaggerated his weakness – and thereby appeared as an over-enthusiastically supine supplicant for French aid who might be cheaply fobbed off. Barrillon played on this. He made it clear to Charles that he had to earn Louis' confidence if he was to regain his support, while Charles himself could do little more than explain England's anti-French policies as the machinations of Danby, ask for a vast supply and then plead for Louis to trust him. Barrillon was confident that he had the upper hand and he hectored Charles with all the force of his master's authority. If Parliament reassembled, no French money would be forthcoming. Previous agreements were to be honoured to the letter. An anxious Charles realised that he was cutting himself off from potential support at home before he had guaranteed assistance from abroad, and he made the most abject promises of obedience before being offered a pitiful 500,000 livres. Nothing of substance had been achieved, for Charles had nothing of substance to offer, and now, humiliated and ill, he took to his bed.

He was suffering from what was probably an acute form of malarial fever, and he was eventually treated with quinine, a cure in which he had himself taken a great interest, being 'the most inquisitive King in the whole world who is also the greatest patron of empirics'.[38] He had encouraged a nervous Robert Talbot to experiment with quinine, despite the entrenched opposition of the conservative medical establishment. Now, as quinine and malaria fought their battle in his shivering and sweaty body, so the counsellors in Charles's crowded sickroom peered at him anxiously, concerned for his health and even more for that of the constitution. Charles was a famously fit man, but he was fifty and in obvious danger of dying. Suddenly the question of the succession was no longer a hypothetical issue but a problem that might at any moment become an urgent practical matter. What should be done about the heir presumptive, James, Duke of York? Was the nation prepared to accept a Catholic king, or would the demand be for Exclusion and for the Whigs' principal candidate, the ostentatiously Protestant Duke of Monmouth?

Monmouth was popular, and recent events were making him more so. He had considerable influence in the army, and troubles in Scotland gave him a chance to shine. The perpetually fractious Covenanters were in revolt, and when their beliefs were attacked by Archbishop Sharp, he was dragged from his coach and torn to pieces in front of his own daughter. The Covenanters then defeated the government's forces, and Monmouth was despatched north as Captain-General of a new army. In the eyes of many Englishmen at least he acquitted himself marvellously. He routed the enemy at Bothwell Brig and then showed clemency in victory. Here was a true Protestant hero: brave, patriotic and merciful, open and honourable, the very antithesis indeed of the underhand and murderous papists. Now, as his father lay desperately ill, some of Monmouth's fellow officers sounded the rank and file of the army and canvassed their opinion on the succession should the King die. In this extremely tense situation, the Council sent word to James informing him that his brother was ill and then, a day later, forwarded a request that he should return to England at once. By 2 September, he had duly arrived, but by this time the worst of Charles's fever was over, he was convalescing and had been presented with a crisis which his new-found health required him to resolve at once. As he dined off mutton and partridges, regained his strength and even began to hanker after the delights of Newmarket once again, so he decided to distance the rival claimants to his throne. He sent James to take charge of affairs in Scotland (where the Test Act did not apply) and exiled Monmouth to Holland, having suspended him from most of his offices for what he promised would be a brief period only.

Having settled that problem, Charles then turned his attention to Shaftesbury. During the King's illness, the Lord President of the Council had been actively campaigning against James's return, and Charles now dismissed him for his impertinence. This was a bold move since Shaftesbury, as Charles must surely have anticipated, threw his energies into the Whig cause with ever greater enthusiasm, hoping thereby to force Exclusion on the country and permanently circumscribe the power of the monarchy. Circumstances, personalities and his own political adroitness seemed to favour him as the currents of national opinion battered ever more furiously against the rock of Charles's determination to preserve his prerogative powers.

First, Monmouth made an unauthorised and loudly acclaimed return from exile, his ambitions encouraged by the welcome he received and by his belief that his ever indulgent father would forgive him for anything he did. In this last he was sadly deluded. Charles, to his intense surprise, refused even to grant him an interview and, instead, deprived him of his remaining offices. Altogether more worrying than an errant, illegitimate son however was a new twist in the web of conspiracy being spun by those out to make trouble for its own sake. A certain Thomas Dangerfield now appeared on the scene claiming to have discovered a plot against the King's life launched by Shaftesbury and the Whigs. When this failed to convince, Dangerfield turned the supposed conspiracy on its head and swore that the whole farrago of lies and invention was actually a Catholic plot designed to undo the nation. The involvement of James in this and the secrets that Dangerfield was consequently privy to made the whole Meal Tub Plot as it was called a genuine threat to Charles, but, while he still kept Parliament prorogued, he faced other dangers too.

Clear thinking was quite as menacing to him as substanceless conspiracy, and at the highest intellectual level the Whigs were now beginning to formulate those notions which Shaftesbury's secretary, the great philosopher John Locke, was later to embody in his *Two Treatises of Government*. When he expounded his ideas in their mature form, Locke would claim that the true basis of the body politic was not a hereditary monarchy but the agreement of all to abide by the will of the majority. In such a world as this, an established, impartial legal system would keep the propertied classes (the true focus of Locke's interest) secure in their possessions, while a separate legislative power – a parliament – would promulgate laws and show itself subject to the majority will by exposing itself to the periodic criticism of the electorate. In this new vision, the prerogative powers of the monarchy that Charles was fighting so hard to maintain were not the hereditary arsenal of the divinely sanctioned Stuart family but a power a prince might use merely on those rarest of occasions when exceptional matters could not be determined by any other authority. In the Whigs' view, a parliament of the landed gentry would be sovereign and the King, no longer an autocrat, would have to content himself by occasionally being called upon to be an umpire.

Locke's ideas would prove as profoundly influential as the discoveries of Newton. Meanwhile, Whig organisation and Whig propaganda ensured the widespread popularity of their cause. If Charles had hoped to silence Shaftesbury by proroguing Parliament and thereby depriving him of a platform he was sadly disappointed. Petitions were organised across the country asking that Parliament should be allowed to reassemble at the beginning of 1680. Proclamations against such 'tumultuous and seditious' petitioning failed to stem the tide, and the energy with which Shaftesbury encouraged his supporters ensured that Exclusion remained at the forefront of everybody's mind. To guarantee this, Shaftesbury and his party organisers took politics to the streets, where a vigorous and feisty propaganda campaign kept alive the anxieties aroused by the Popish Plot.

Every means was used to persuade the people that a Catholic king was a threat to their lives, to their liberties and, where they had it, to their property. Men were hired to 'ball' the Whig cause in the coffee-houses, where the tables were 'continually spread with the noisome excrements of diseased and laxative scribblers'.[39] Contemporaries wrote how satires 'swarm in every street' and 'pass from friend to friend'. Whig clubs proliferated, and when men tired of reading or listening to propaganda they could turn to gamble with playing cards luridly illustrated with the goriest and most sinister scenes of popish treason. Even when the card games were over and people made for home they could not escape the all-pervasive Whig message. Printed material was given out on the streets or thrown into carriages, and offered now a ballad and now a cartoon. The most notorious offered both. 'The Raree Show' was an illustrated poem which showed a two-headed Charles, half Protestant and half papist, as a pedlar hawking his peep-show (his Parliament) across the land in order to raise money or subsidies.

Meanwhile, plays performed at Southwark fair shocked the illiterate multitude by showing the Pope seducing a nun, while the great Pope-burning processions that took place in the middle of November turned politics to mardi-gras. To announce the arrival of the procession, a bellman went in front crying 'Remember Justice Godfrey' while a pantomime Jesuit ran among the crowd 'giving pardons very freely to those who would murder Protestants'. An effigy of the dead magistrate was then drawn through the streets 'in the habit he usually wore, the cravat wherewith he was murdered about his neck, with spots of blood on his wrists, shirt and white gloves'. Jesuits with 'bloody daggers' followed behind, to be succeeded by 'Popish bishops', while bringing up the rear came a hugely expensive wax image of the Pope himself with the devil whispering in his ear.[40] All London turned out to watch over 600 apprentices carry this effigy through the streets, and according to one contemporary account the many thousands gathered 'expressed their loyalty and good will to the Protestant religion by calling always No Pope, No Papist, God bless the King and the Duke of Monmouth'.[41]

The high tide of Whig triumph came when Parliament reassembled in October 1680. Whig propaganda had now reached a climax with stories about a black box which was supposed to contain evidence of Charles's secret marriage to Monmouth's mother, Lucy Walter. The Whigs gained a ringing victory in the elections to the City of London's institutions and, encouraged by such success, Shaftesbury resolved to have the Middlesex Grand Jury try James as a papist and Louise de Kéroualle as a prostitute. He failed in this, but so strong was the current running in favour of the Whigs that it was clear that they would re-introduce a Bill to exclude James and that they might even impeach him. The belief now spread among some of Charles's ministers that he would buckle under the pressure and agree to Exclusion. Some even made overtures to William of Orange, assuming that he would be the benefi-ciary of Charles's surrender. Indeed, so great were the divisions among his advisers that Charles himself was left isolated and obliged to rely on his determination alone. It was evident that he was sorely tried. His halting opening speech to Parliament was unconvincing, while his request for money to reinforce the English garrison at Tangier (which had been ambushed by the Moors) was ignored. The Tory leaders could do little save force an amendment to the Exclusion Bill which, while acknowledging that James's right had been abolished, nonethe-less left the question of the succession open. The Bill then passed its third reading in the Commons and went up before the Lords.

And it was at this point that the tide began to turn in Charles's favour. The Tory propagandists had been extremely active in their attempts to 'reduce the deluded multitude to their just allegiance'.[42] Like the Whigs, they too relied on the politics of fear, but where Shaftesbury and his associates could draw on the deep wells of anti-Catholic feeling in the country, the Tories knew that they could stir frightened memories of the worst excesses of the civil war and the Protectorate. After all, what were the Whigs but the children of that brood of sectaries, Nonconformists and raging fundamentalists who two decades earlier had spread the worst excesses of anarchy across the land? They were subversives who threatened the security of the church and state. Old fears of the tyranny of popular government were revived, and a night-mare image of rabble rule was enthusiastically promoted. Only an unencumbered monarchy could save the people from this threat, and in the last resort Charles could be seen as a quasi-mystical figure sublimely poised above faction: 'God's Servant, not the People's Slave'.[43]

A growing number of frightened people was prepared to accept such an argument, and it was naturally agreeable to many of the peers. Charles himself, somewhat less confident of his divine status, knew that he must work if he were to ensure his survival. He attended the debate in the Lords, scowled when his opponents spoke and showed evident pleasure at his supporters' speeches. None of these last was more determined or more nimble than that given by Halifax. For ten long, gruelling hours he parried every argument that Shaftesbury could produce. He dwelt on the dangers of revolution that the passing of the Exclusion Bill might bring in its wake. He dwelt on the prestige of the Duke of York. He pointed out the benefits that would come from wise limitations on James's power rather than outright exclusion. As the night drew on, Shaftesbury became 'much disconcerted'. He knew that both in the House and outside his support was beginning to falter. He had raised fears that were for many insupportable, and his autocratic methods had alienated a number of his followers. The Whigs in the Commons were being made to seem increasingly intransigent and impractical, while in the Lords Halifax's oratory eventually persuaded the peers by a substantial majority to refuse a first reading of the Exclusion Bill. Now, with the tide beginning to run for him and with the Whigs bickering ever more acrimoniously among themselves, Charles dissolved Parliament and began to prepare the greatest political coup of his career.

Although the second attempt to pass the Exclusion Bill had failed, Charles knew that his struggle with the Whigs was not yet over. He had not completely defeated them. That the party still had plenty of fight was suggested the day after the failure of the Bill when Shaftesbury, 'sick in health yet in action nimble busy as a body louse', moved a motion designed to separate Charles from his Queen.[44] He hoped that a new Protestant wife might provide a new Protestant heir which he now regarded as 'the sole remaining chance of liberty, security and religion'.[45] The Lords were unimpressed, but as Charles made his feelings for his wife clear by dining in public with her, so the Whigs determined to add the names of the five imprisoned Catholic peers to the list of those already tried and executed for supposed collusion in the Popish Plot. Hysteria had to be maintained. Old Lord Stafford was their most obviously vulnerable victim, and perjured evidence sent him to his death sure that he was 'totally innocent of what he is accused of, and confident of God's mercy'.[46] Charles himself signed his warrant with 'tears in my eyes', but in the savage atmosphere about him he felt that he could extend no more mercy to the old man than ensuring that the more terrible punishments usually inflicted on traitors were remitted in his case.

Those close to Charles noted a new 'severity in his disposition'; and in his resolve to outstare the crisis that threatened his survival he himself felt that he was growing harder, more inured to the terrible realities of power. 'Men ordinarily become more timid as they grow old,' he would declare; 'as for me, I shall be, on the contrary, bolder and firmer.'[47] His tactics for the endgame of the Exclusion Crisis were to prove this to be the case. There would be no compromise, no going halfway to meet his opponents on their own ground. Instead, he would give them enough rope to hang themselves. He would subtly encourage them to work their own destruction and reveal the apparently crippling limitations of what his Poet Laureate, John Dryden, called 'the dregs of a democracy'.[48] Charles himself would then emerge triumphant in the full and legitimate power of his royal prerogative. He would become the king he had always sought to be.

To this end, Charles asked for the judges' opinion on whether he could ban unlicensed publications on the grounds that they threatened public order and received a favourable reply. He also busied himself with examining the royal warrants by which municipal corporations were granted their charters and voting rights. In this way he hoped to check the large number of Whig MPs returned by the boroughs, but beyond this he did not directly concern himself with the Tory election campaign. He knew not only that his efforts would bring him little reward but that by appearing remote and aloof he would preserve the mystique of his authority. Charles was not seeking power through votes but rather the means to make those votes eventually appear redundant. Avoiding too active a public role, he resorted instead to secret negotiation. While the Whig propaganda campaign reached its apogee and seemed to show that the party would be able to force Exclusion on the country, guarantee the Protestant religion and limit the power of the King, Charles listened to the overtures being made to him by Louis XIV. These were comforting indeed. The new direction of the French King's territorial ambitions made it desirable that Charles be kept from interfering in European politics, but Louis was also motivated by more pressing ideological considerations, and it was in these that the true Popish Plot lay. The fantasies of Oates and his kind, powerful though these seemed, were flimsy indeed compared to the deepest concerns of the King of France.

In September 1679, Louis had written that the basic purpose of all his policies towards England was what he himself called 'la confirmation de la royauté et de la religion Catholique en Angleterre', the maintenance of royal supremacy and the Catholic faith in the country.[49] He genuinely believed that Catholic beliefs could be re-established in England if he were to help support a strong monarchy there. Long experience had led him to think that Charles himself was feckless and would be of little help in furthering these aims, and he told Barrillon as much, writing to say that he could not put any trust 'in the treaties which the King of England might make with me'.[50] Nonetheless, if Louis had largely lost his faith in Charles, he would not abandon his Catholic brother. He had confidence in James, and as he concluded an agreement whereby he would pay the English King an initial 2,000,000 crowns and then subsidies of 500,000 crowns in each of the two succeeding years, so he hoped his generosity might be a first step in establishing Catholic absolutism. It was Louis' devout wish that the money he gave him would allow Charles to relax the penal laws and so 'no longer call down upon himself the wrath of God for the unjust persecution of the Catholics'.[51] For all the comprehensive brilliance of his diplomacy, the King of France had proved himself to be, at bottom, an idealist.

Assured by Louis' generosity, Charles prepared to display the political guile he had acquired through a lifetime. To underline his confidence, he decreed that Parliament should meet in Royalist Oxford. It was his right to do so, and as a seething, resentful London was placed under the military control of the Earl of Craven, Charles prepared the situation with the greatest care. While the Whigs rode into Oxford with a posse of armed guards and blue satin ribbons in their hats woven with the motto 'No Popery! No Slavery!', Charles himself once again looked over the 'subtle and crafty' speech he had written for the opening session of Parliament. His tone would be that of firm but sweet reasonableness. He would uphold traditional constitutional decencies in the face of what appeared to many to be the Whig desire for absolute power.

While 'no irregularities in Parliaments shall make me out of love with them', Charles declared, he made it clear he was determined not to be bullied, not to be pushed into a corner by mere elected representatives.[52] 'I, who will never use arbitrary government myself,' he explained, 'am resolved not to suffer it in others.'[53] He was the true embodiment of a just constitution, and the Whigs should take their cue from him and 'make the laws of the land your rule, because I am resolved they shall be mine'.[54] Charles then dismissed the idea of Exclusion, but dangled before the assembled MPs the new idea of a regency which would take effective control of the country and leave James with little more than the empty title of a king.

The idea was an attractive one and had many merits (not the least of which was its appeal to William of Orange, the man most likely to be appointed regent) and Charles had carefully prepared speakers to argue his case at length. The Whigs, as he had hoped, dismissed the idea out of hand. Exclusion had become their obsession and they would let nothing stand in its way. Such intransigence suited Charles's purposes perfectly. The Whigs would reveal themselves as a dangerous, obsessive and fundamentally unconstitutional body of men whom the country would be well advised to shun. Not only this. By ensuring that they concentrated on a single issue, Charles could rely on the fact that the Whigs would find neither the time nor the energy to renew the legal prohibition on imports from France which had expired in the early part of the year. Luxury goods were now flowing into the country with a consequently healthy effect on customs duties and so, in addition to his French subsidy, Charles could rely on a swelling income from international trade. Parliamentary supply was becoming ever less necessary to him.

There was only one fly in the ointment. Louise de Kéroualle had employed an obscure and dubious Irish spy named Edward Fitzharris to discover if the Whigs were still plotting to besmirch her reputation. Fitzharris set about his task with a surge of imaginative energy and had soon assembled a quantity of spurious information which suggested that Whig extremists were indeed at work. Louise abandoned the man when his absurd machinations were exposed, and Fitzharris decided that his strongest suit lay in defecting to the Whigs and spreading allegations about Louise herself, about the Duke of York, the Queen and various leading Tories. The Whigs believed they now had in their hands a valuable means of prolonging the Parliamentary session and stirring the fires of national hysteria. Charles, realising how dangerous this could be, at once had the wretched Fitzharris removed from Oxford and imprisoned in the Tower of London. The man knew too much. He had to be silenced if the King were to make a success of the show-trials he had planned for the Whig leaders in the aftermath of his triumph.

There remained now the altogether more important task of destroying the Whigs themselves. They had acted exactly as Charles had hoped. They had been acrimonious, intransigent, unreasonable. They had declared that their instructions from their constants demanded they insist on Exclusion. They had refused utterly to consider Charles's proposals for a regency. They had been loud in their objections to the treatment meted out to Fitzharris. They remained determined to move a new Exclusion Bill and resolved to publish their proceedings as their appeal to a nation which they believed was hungrily anticipating their success. They even complained that the buildings in which they were housed were too cramped, and Charles – ever compliant and courteous – promised to make the beauties of the Sheldonian Theatre available to them, and himself went to examine the alterations he had commanded should be made there in order that the opposition might be comfortably housed.

Then, on Monday 28 March, while the Whigs were debating the first reading of their third attempt to pass an Exclusion Bill, Charles took his customary place among the Lords in the Hall of Christ Church. From there he sent Black Rod to summon the Commons before him. The excited Members obeyed his command, sure that some new and great concession was about to be made. They squeezed their way down the narrow flight of steps at the entrance to the Hall, gabbling so loudly that the Sergeant of Arms had to call three times for silence before the company became fully aware of a robed Charles seated on his throne, the crown of England upon his head.

A wave of awe fell across the room. Charles was no longer the shifty, manipulative and fallible man the Whigs believed they had in their grasp. He was arrayed in the sumptuous pageantry of a quasi-divine power. He was the Lord's anointed, vested with a holy authority and incorruptible. Where the dismayed Whigs drew their arguments from reason he drew his power from God, and it was with this assurance (helpfully backed up by French money) that Charles now spoke, dismissing democracy with a single sentence because it clearly did not work. 'All the world may see to what a point we are come,' he said with feigned dismay, adding: 'we are not like to have a good end when the divisions at the beginning are such'.[55] With that he left the Hall and then, having eaten a hurried meal, rode in his coach to Windsor along the heavily guarded roads. He would never call a parliament again.

The Years of Personal Rule

L oyal addresses poured in from a grateful people. Their King had outstared the nation's madness, and the spectre of anarchy had disappeared. Charles had survived the greatest crisis of his reign but, for all this, he knew that his work was not yet done. He had emerged from the recent contest with his prerogative powers intact, with the greater part of his people faithful to him, and with his finances in a healthier state than they had ever been. But it was not enough that he should win. Others must lose and be seen to have lost. Charles resolved on vigorous action against the Whigs.

Great and small alike would suffer as justice was polluted for political ends. Charges were brought against the wretched Edward Fitzharris – the turncoat Charles had sent from Oxford to the Tower – and when his case came to court it was revealed with more enthusiasm than truth that Fitzharris was a Roman Catholic Irishman who had libelled the crown and plotted to disturb the nation's peace by bringing in the French. He was summarily despatched to Tyburn. An indictment was also brought against one Stephen College, a boisterous London joiner who was said to have appeared in Oxford 'armed cap-a-pee' with every intention of seizing the King.[1] It was in vain that College himself protested that nothing had been proved against him save the possession of a horse, a sword and a pair of pistols. Examples were to be made, and when an exhausted jury finally delivered a verdict of guilty, a shout of triumph echoed round the courtroom. Equally shameful was the trial of an altogether greater man, Oliver Plunkett, the Roman Catholic Archbishop of Armagh. Plunkett was convicted on Oates's trumped-up evidence of conspiring to bring a French army into Ireland. He was entirely innocent of this, but he could produce few witnesses for his defence and was sent to Tyburn 'generally pitied and believed to die very innocent of what he was condemned'.[2]

But the greatest prize was to be Shaftesbury. The day after Fitzharris and Plunkett were executed, the Whig leader was sent to the Tower on a charge of high treason. It was alleged against him that he had planned to make war on the King by using force to compel him to Exclusion. It was further alleged that he had determined to repeal the laws against Dissenters, and the familiar gang of disreputables was prepared to testify that he had spoken treasonable words. Shaftesbury was himself by this time seriously ill, and he sent a message to Charles promising that he would withdraw into private life if the prosecution against him were dropped. He would take refuge in Dorset or even in Carolina, where he had business interests. Charles was not prepared to be merciful for he believed that 'Little Sincerity', as he called him, would never abandon his political ambitions. He resolved instead to leave Shaftesbury to the law, but the trial of a man who had been so popular would not necessarily prove straightforward. Although a new Lord Chief Justice did everything in his power to secure a conviction, an impressive London jury of strongly Whig principles meant that Charles failed to get his way. The allegations against Shaftesbury could not be made to stick, and in defiance of the clear will of the King the jury returned an *ignoramus* verdict – there was no case for Shaftesbury to answer. Exultant Whigs issued a medal showing a radiant sun emerging from the clouds over the Tower of London and illuminating the Latin motto 'Rejoice!'

A furious Charles refused to be thwarted. If the Whigs in his capital had the temerity to go against his wishes, then the Whig authorities would have to be removed. Pressure was brought to bear. While the greatest of a long line of Restoration political satires, Dryden's

Absalom and Achitophel, lampooned Shaftesbury, exposed the supposed fallacies of his political thinking, and exalted the 'Godlike' qualities of Charles himself, more dubious means of influence were also applied. Overtures were made to the London Tories, and while plays and pamphlets set out to denigrate the Whigs, those prosperous tradesmen who supplied the court and the navy were left in no doubt as to the true direction of Charles's wishes. The Justices of the Peace were encouraged to move against London Dissenters, who had for the most part enthusiastically supported the Whigs. To make the royal will still clearer, the City militia was much in evidence. Considerable chicanery was then employed to ensure that Tory sheriffs were returned at the next elections and, having been returned, they provided Charles with the opportunity to investigate the legal grounds on which the City held its charter. The Court of King's Bench was instructed to investigate the matter. Charges of disrespectful petitioning and the raising of illegal taxes were soon produced and were declared to be sufficiently heinous offences for the charter to be withdrawn. As the usefully pliant Judge Jeffreys expressed the matter: 'the King of England is likewise King of London'. This indeed proved to be the case and Shaftesbury, aware that the last bastion of his power had crumbled before the law, fled to Amsterdam, where he died at the start of 1683, the defeated and disillusioned advocate of English Parliamentary democracy.

Even then the Whig threat was not finally quashed. In the early summer of that year a muddle-headed attempt to assassinate Charles and his brother was revealed. The so-called Rye House Plot actually consisted of two conspiracies. The first, which gave the plan its name, was an intrigue by City radicals who decided to use a house conveniently situated on a narrow part of the Newmarket road as the place from which to launch the assassination attempt. The parallel conspiracy was hatched by a group of aristocratic Whigs who planned to overcome Charles's Lifeguards, seize the King himself and force him to accede to their demands. The first plot failed when an accidental fire obliged Charles and James to leave Newmarket earlier than they had expected, but the exposure of the Whig notables in the attempt kindled all the desire for vengeance smouldering in a Charles still smarting from his failure to convict Shaftesbury.

He ordered the Whigs' immediate arrest, and while the once loyal Essex evaded the King's anger by committing suicide, Lord William Russell and Algernon Sidney – the latter a great 'Commonwealthsman' who had only just escaped with his life in 1660 – were brought to trial. Charles personally took charge of their examination before the Council. There, wise from his experience of the entanglements woven by Oates, he refused to allow witnesses to construct a 'growing evidence' and concentrated instead on the barest facts. He was resolved to show no mercy even towards so great an aristocrat as Russell. 'All that is true,' he said when pleas of mitigation were entered in Russell's defence, 'but it is as true that if I do not take his life he will soon have mine.'[3] Russell was duly executed and then, towards the end of the year, in a trial shamefully manipulated by Judge Jeffreys, Algernon Sidney too was found guilty and went to his death 'very stoutly and like a true republican'.[4]

For Charles himself, the execution of the Rye House conspirators was a vindication of his just contempt for the Whig cause, but if the deaths of Russell and Sidney were public statements of his political position there was private grief here too. Many of the Whigs still regarded his illegitimate son, the Duke of Monmouth, as the desirable and even rightful heir to the throne, and Monmouth himself had done everything he could to promote his spurious cause. The acclamations lavished on him during the Exclusion Crisis still echoed loudly enough to confuse his shallow and febrile mind. Besides, he was quite unable to accept the fact that, though his father loved him, Charles's affection was not as limitless as he supposed. Monmouth was undaunted by the fact that when he stood bail for the arrested Shaftesbury his father gave his erstwhile offices to his half-brothers. When the Duke was removed from the Chancellorship of Cambridge University and his portrait was burned, he still refused to take the hint.

At last Monmouth's presence could no longer be endured at court and he revived the habit Shaftesbury had taught him of making triumphal progresses around the country. He had already proved himself to be a natural showman. In the high summer of 1682 he made an ostentatious visit to the Whig magnates in Staffordshire, and so great a crowd turned out at the Wallasey horse races that 'it wanted only a *vive le roy* to complete the rebellion'.[5] Luck and charm were both on his side. Monmouth won a plate at the races and presented it to the local mayor's newly christened daughter. He won a couple of footraces, 'first stripped and then in his boots'. The applause was so loud that he had to ask the admiring audience to cease their cheers. At Liverpool, he had the temerity to touch for the King's Evil, and so great was his following that it was considered necessary to arrest him. But by early 1683 the climate of opinion had radically changed. Stunts no longer won over an admiring crowd. When Monmouth rode into Chichester, the High Sheriff appeared with a troop of horse, and when the 'Protestant Duke' attended a service in the cathedral the chaplain preached so pointed a sermon that Monmouth felt obliged to hurry ignominiously away. In the aftermath of the Rye House Plot a grand jury found against him and a reward was put on his head, but even now the King was lenient. As Russell and Sidney went to their deaths, Charles consented to an angry and sorrowful meeting with his son, who, for all his air of repentance, refused to betray his Whig friends and stormed out of his father's presence to exile. Charles eventually granted him an allowance of £6000 a year, but even his indulgence did not stretch to permitting his son to return home, and it was while he was abroad that Monmouth matured the plans for the last act of his tragedy.

Meanwhile, the Duke of York was the chief beneficiary of his absence. Having successfully resisted the attempts to exclude his brother from power, Charles now began quietly to return James to a position of influence. He was careful not to overplay his hand, for if he was determined to act ruthlessly against those who opposed him he was also resolved that none of his immediate circle of advisers should have precedence as they jockeyed for position. James was ordered to attend all the Council's investigations into the Rye House Plot, and by May 1684 Charles had so managed matters that James was able to take over effective control of the navy once again, despite the proscriptions of the Test Act. Charles nonetheless refused to allow himself to be dominated by his brother's hard-line opinions, just as he refused to allow himself to be dominated by anybody else.

He had emerged from the Exclusion Crisis as an unfettered sovereign, and as such he would remain. He distanced himself from his Tory supporters, refusing them the privileges they might legitimately have expected. Indeed, Charles was determined to lower the levels of political consciousness and excitement in the country as a whole, and to reduce the influence of party activity especially. What he sought was a nation united in passive loyalty to the crown, a nation at peace with itself and prosperously pursuing the manifold forms of private enterprise rather than the dangerous stimulation of public and political commitment. Charles had vowed not to recall Parliament, and it was made clear that he would not accept petitions on matters of national concern from the public at large. He took steps to impose censorship and to control the 'intolerable liberties of the press'. Certain now that the greater number of boroughs were in the hands of men sympathetic to his aims, he also delegated much of the day-to-day business of government to the carefully balanced rivals around him and enjoyed the hours of leisure afforded by Newmarket, Windsor and the new palace he was building for himself at Winchester.

The last project absorbed much of the King's time and a great deal of his spare money. Sir Christopher Wren had completed designs for the palace by September 1682 when Evelyn described Charles as being 'mightily pleased' with the plans for a building of 160 rooms crowned by a graceful cupola.[6] This miniature version of Versailles was never completed, but the concept was lavish indeed. Marble columns presented by the Duke of Tuscany were to ornament the grand staircase, great fountains were planned for the surrounding parkland, where the King could also hunt, and there was to be a street connecting the palace to Winchester Cathedral, while the nearby ports provided convenient anchorage for Charles's yachts.

The building of the palace was a sign of the King's new-found sense of security, but the content that largely characterised his private life in these years was made the richer for the affectionate relationships he had with the greater number of his illegitimate children. Seven mistresses had provided him with twelve bastards. Lady Castlemaine was the mother of five of them, Nell Gwynn of two, while Elizabeth Killigrew, Catherine Pegge, Moll Davis and Louise de Kéroualle had added one each to that number. Only the troublesome Monmouth remained to remind Charles of his fraught affair with the long-dead Lucy Walter. The King was generous to all his offspring, boys and girls alike. Six sons received nine dukedoms, and if none of the boys came close to rivalling their father in intelligence and political acumen, several of them made decent careers for themselves. One of Barbara's sons, the handsome Duke of Grafton, became a sailor. The Earl of Plymouth was a soldier who died young at Tangier, while Nell Gwynn's boy, the Duke of St Albans, was a 'very pretty' youth who was given an education in France before going off to fight the Turks in Hungary.[7]

It was the King's relationship with Louise de Kéroualle that nonetheless brought him the greatest happiness. An apparently deep and genuine affection grew up between them and somehow managed to survive criticism from the outside world, political pressure, temptation and moments of personal difficulty. Louise had suffered cruelly during the tribulations of the Popish Plot, her discomfort being made the worse by her own vapidity and foolishness. Her fears were not without foundation, for she was an unpopular French Catholic mistress in a period when Catholics had come to personify all that was most alien to the English way of life. At times she was terrified, and Barrillon wrote to Louis XIV informing him that she would prefer to flee the country while she still retained the King's affection than 'by staying longer . . . expose herself to the rage of a whole nation'.[8]

Precisely how venomous that rage could be was suggested by the articles of high treason drawn up against her and offered to the House of Commons for their perusal. The paper presented Louise as a foreign whore wracked by 'foul, nauseous, and contagious distempers'.[9] It seemed there was nothing to which she could not have been imagined to stoop, and rumours circulated that she had even employed a French Catholic confectioner in her attempt to lure the King into eating poisoned sweets. There were those who thought she had played a decisive part in persuading Charles to prorogue Parliament, and the French still wrongly considered that she had considerable political influence. In fact, she was politically naive in the extreme, which was part of the attraction she had for Charles and also the reason why he chose to ignore her desperate tacking and veering during the height of the Exclusion Crisis. Indeed, rather than dismissing her from his affections as an exasperating woman, his tenderness for her only seemed to grow and, as his feelings warmed, so did the generosity with which he responded to her every wish and need.

When Louise fell ill and her doctors advised that a stay in France might be beneficial to her health, Charles insisted that Barrillon write to his master asking him to receive her with every courtesy. Both Louis and his ambassador believed they were now getting full value from Louise. 'She has', Barrillon wrote, 'shown great, constant, and intelligent zeal for Your Majesty's interests, and given me numberless useful hints and pieces of information.'[10] As a consequence, when Louise arrived at the French court, the sometime impoverished lady-in-waiting was treated as if she were a queen and behaved accordingly. For all that she was supposed to have come from a dependent and poverty-stricken English court, she was weighed down with jewels. She lost a fortune at the gambling tables, and she was surrounded everywhere she went with a vast and sumptuously liveried equipage. The homage Louis himself paid her was 'like sunshine gilding and glorifying an insignificant object', and when she returned to London she did so as an international celebrity for whom Charles was determined to do all that he could. He lavished honours on the son she had borne him, and persuaded Louis to make her a duchesse in her own right. It seemed that she could do no wrong, and when she momentarily faltered Charles willingly forgave her weakness.

That weakness arrived in England in the repulsive form of Philippe de Vendôme, the Grand Prior of France. He was a young man of exceptional looks and predatory sexual habits who had never, he said, gone to bed sober in his life. Louise found him utterly intriguing and, falling for him, realised she had exposed herself to the greatest danger. The normally tolerant Charles was for once insanely jealous and vented his fury on the arrogant young man. Vendôme was given to understand that he was not to visit Louise's apartments, but he contemptuously refused the hint. Barrillon was employed to tell him that he was no longer welcome in England, but he merely said that he would stay until he heard the order from Charles's own mouth. Barrillon begged Charles to give the man an interview. For a while the King refused to stoop so low, but when he eventually agreed Vendôme merely told him that he had no intention of leaving the country. It was only when that arch-diplomat Louis XIV became involved in the affair and sent word via Vendôme's brother that the young man should come home that Louise was freed from the embarrassment in which she had become entangled. Charles returned to the penitent embraces of his beloved Fubbs and, to celebrate the occasion, Louise issued a medal which displayed Cupid and the motto *omnia vincit*.

The involvement of Louis XIV in the most personal details of Charles's life suggests the continuing influence he also had over him in the wider sphere of politics. Passive financial dependence on the French suited Charles well, provided that he could avoid being drawn into Louis' interminable wars. This was not always easily achieved, and a crisis occurred late in 1681 when the French blockaded Luxembourg, thereby threatening the security of William of Orange. It clearly behoved a Protestant king to become involved in the conflict but this would inevitably mean a recall of Parliament to raise the necessary subsidies, and Charles told Barrillon that he was extremely reluctant to do this since 'they are devils who want my ruin'.[11] It was essential that an 'expedient' be found, and Charles begged Barrillon to 'tell the king my brother to relieve me of my embarrassment'. Realising the delicacy of the situation, Louis adroitly arranged a diplomatic scheme by which Charles was appointed as an international mediator who, by prearrangement with Louis, determined that the Spanish retain control of Luxembourg on the condition that its defences were destroyed. The handling of this neat compromise earned Charles an increase in his subsidy along with the deepening mistrust of William of Orange.

William indeed proved the most difficult of all the foreign problems that Charles had to face. It was one of William's principal aims to secure English resources to continue his struggle with Louis XIV, and it was one of Charles's prime objectives to prevent this. He knew that William had extensive contacts in England and, though he probably overestimated the importance of these, Charles devoted much of his time and energy to minimising their usefulness. William's attempts to interfere in domestic policies riled him and, in an angry interview with the Dutch ambassador, he showed how much he knew about William's involvement. When the Prince himself paid a state visit to England, Charles told him bluntly that he was not prepared to call another Parliament or to offer William soldiers to defend Flanders. Anglo–Dutch relations seriously deteriorated, and when in 1683 William proposed another state visit, Charles promptly vetoed it, fearing that its only purpose was to drag him into the expensive morass of continental warfare.

In the meantime the self-indulgent life of the English court continued to beguile the ageing roués who populated it. Evelyn described in characteristically censorious terms a little soirée that took place on 1 February 1685. It was a Sunday, and Evelyn was shocked by 'the inexpressible luxury and profaneness, gaming and all dissoluteness' which he was obliged to watch. He described 'the King sitting and toying with his concubines, Portsmouth, Cleveland and Mazarin' – once rival mistresses but now, it seems, companions of a sort. The party was entertained by a French boy singing love songs, 'whilst about twenty of the great courtiers and other dissolute persons were at basset round a large table, a bank of at least two thousand in gold before them'.[12]

But this was the last occasion on which Charles was to enjoy himself in so characteristic a fashion. He rose the following morning pale and irritable. His usual fast walk had become a preoccupied pacing up and down. He tottered and nearly fell. He spent an unusually long time in his privy closet, and when Chiffinch eventually led him out of it his speech was slurred and disjointed. He managed to sip a little sherry and China Orange and then sat down to the ministrations of his barber, as was his wont. Suddenly, as the barber was wrapping the linen cloth around his master's neck, Charles let out a piercing shriek and sank back unconscious. The pretence that nothing was wrong could no longer be maintained, and doctors were hurriedly sent for. They bled Charles's comatose body, while an anxious message was despatched to the Duke of York and the Privy Council requiring their immediate attention.

With the great men of the nation assembled, the doctors continued their terrible ministrations. Twenty-four ounces of blood were drained from the King's nerveless arm, and eventually his speech returned. He asked to see his Queen. As he returned to his bed, the usual bands of guards about Whitehall were reinforced, a ban was placed on ships entering or leaving the country, and Barrillon alone was allowed to get a message out to Louis XIV. In this moment of crisis it was essential that at one and the same time the French should be informed of what was happening and that Monmouth and William of Orange kept in ignorance. Inevitably, the news leaked out to the London streets, and while the dignitaries of the City sent a loyal address to the Duke of York, the ordinary people 'cried as they walked' and there was 'great sadness in all faces, and great crowds at all the gates'.[13]

By the time Charles had his second fit on the following day, twelve doctors had gathered in that bedroom where the King's dogs had customarily whelped and the King's clocks ticked and struck the hours in a random cacophony of mechanical noise. A horrifying series of remedies was proposed and applied to Charles's sinking body. His head, nose and feet were all tortured in the effort to save his life. He was liberally dosed with enemas and emetics. A witch's brew of hellebore, rock salt, vitriol, syrup of buckthorn and a stone removed from the stomach of a goat swirled in agonising and useless chaos through his wracked intestines. Red-hot irons were placed on his shaved skull, and the doctors shook their heads as they examined his scalding urine, his inflamed tongue and his teeth, which had become twisted during his convulsions. Even so, he rallied, but was forbidden to speak.

Louise de Kéroualle wept and swooned, and Nell Gwynn 'lay roaring behind the door'.[14] Queen Catherine, prostrate with grief, was carried to her rooms. The chamber was crowded all the same. Seventy-five of the great and the good had gathered in the expectation of the King's death. Five of these men were bishops, and it was Ken of Bath and Wells who spoke for them all, begging the King to take communion and declare himself a member of the Church of England. Charles muttered that he was too feeble . . . that there was no hurry. But his condition was slowly worsening. His body was tormented with fever as what were almost certainly his diseased kidneys caused him ever more dreadful pain. In the meantime, Bishop Ken read the Prayers for the Sick out of the Book of Common Prayer. Charles listened, the Duke of York listened, but their minds were not on what they heard. They were preoccupied with a matter altogether too dangerous to broach until the King's final moments should come.

While they hesitated, Barrillon paid a visit to the tearful Louise. She lamented that she was rarely able to see her dying friend since the Queen was often at his side. She lamented, too, the presence of the Anglican bishops, for she knew with a lover's knowledge that 'at the bottom of his heart the King is a Catholic'.[15] Could not a priest be smuggled into the dying man's room? Barrillon had a word in the Duke of York's ear. James quietly replied that he knew there was little time to lose and declared that he 'would rather risk everything than not do my duty'.[16] It was a characteristic reply, but what needed to be done was difficult to achieve. The bishops and the bigwigs still crowded the room and could not easily be commanded to leave. James bent over his brother's death-bed. There was an anxious, barely audible muttering, and the King was heard to say: 'Yes, with all my heart.' He was a dying man and would not go lying into eternity. He was a dying king, but politics were no longer his prime concern. He had throughout his life maintained the outward appearance of holding the beliefs that the greater number of his subjects held. In these last moments it was no longer necessary for him to do so. He wanted a priest.

Neither those priests who attended the Queen nor those who attended the Duke of York could be considered remotely suitable for the task of receiving the dying Charles into the Catholic church. The Queen's priests spoke Portuguese, the Duke's were generally despised. Messengers were sent to the house of the Venetian ambassador in the hope that he might help. But Providence had, perhaps, decreed a different end. As the messengers sent to the Venetian ambassador passed through the Queen's rooms, so they encountered a simple, modest, holy man. Nearly three decades before he had shown Charles a little manuscript called *A Short and Plain Way to the Faith and Church.*

The fugitive King had read it through and declared that he had 'not seen anything more clear or plain upon this subject!' He had then put the manuscript down and had said: 'The arguments here are drawn from succession and are so conclusive, I do not see how they can be denied.' Now, they no longer could be.

The good Father Huddleston, disguised in a cassock and a wig, was about to perform his last and greatest service for his King. Huddleston waited in a little closet off Charles's room while others were sent to find a Host. He heard the Duke of York peremptorily declare: 'Gentlemen, the King wishes everybody to retire except the Earls of Bath and Feversham.' These two Protestants were to be the witnesses to Charles's voluntary conversion. When the rest had gone, Chiffinch ushered Huddleston into the King's presence. A look of joy suffused his dying face as he cried out with what strength remained: 'You that saved my body are now come to save my soul!'

The priest set about his task. Did the King of England wish to die in the faith and communion of the holy Roman Catholic Church? The quiet but distinct answer was yes. Did the King wish to make a full confession of his sins? The answer again was yes. Charles was 'most heartily sorry' that he had delayed this supreme moment for so long, and when the confession was over he commended his soul to God. 'Mercy, Sweet Jesus, Mercy.' He was given absolution and asked if he would receive the Blessed Sacrament.

'If I were worthy of it, Amen.'

But the Host had not yet been delivered, and it was only when Huddleston had anointed the King with holy oil in the Sacrament of Extreme Unction that a Portuguese priest came to the threshold carrying the sacred wafer. Charles wanted to receive it kneeling but he was too weak. Huddleston told him that God would understand. Prone on his death-bed, Charles took his first and final Catholic communion. Then he grasped the proffered crucifix in his hands to meditate on Christ's Passion.

'Beseech Him with all humility', Huddleston urged, 'that His most precious Blood may not be shed in vain for you . . . And when it shall please him to take you out of this transitory world, to grant you a joyful resurrection, and an eternal crown of glory in the next.'

But still Charles lingered in that world whose deceits and glories he had manipulated with so cynical a hand. He was, in a phrase he almost certainly did not use, 'a most unconscionable time dying'.[17] He apologised to those about him for keeping them so long. Still he remained conscious. The dreadful doctors returned to torture him again, and the clocks ticked and chimed to remind him that 'my business will shortly be done'. The Queen came to bid him farewell, but she was overcome with tears and had to be hurried from the room. She sent a message begging Charles's pardon for any offence she had caused him.

'Alas! Poor Woman,' he said, 'she beg my pardon! I beg hers with all my heart.'

He begged his weeping brother for pardon too. He commended all his children save Monmouth into the Duke's care. Then, recalling his mistresses, he asked his brother earnestly to look after Louise de Kéroualle and 'not let poor Nelly starve'.

The long hours of the night wore on, and at six Charles asked for the heavy curtains round his bed to be drawn back so that he could see the dawn for the last time. Day broke across his dying face, but still his spirit lingered. The hours passed, his voice failed, and by ten o'clock he had slipped into a coma. Two hours later, the great survivor was dead.

Afterword

The autopsy showed that Charles's body was so over-charged with blood that it was surprising he had survived so long. The cause of his death was nonetheless of little importance compared to the fact of his demise. The King was dead, long live the King! While the fatty tissues of the dissected corpse were left to soak down a drain before a modest funeral was held in Westminster Abbey, James ascended peacefully to his throne. It was not the least of Charles's achievements that his brother could succeed without a hint of disorder, but the next four years were to show that Charles's abilities had been directed only to continuous short-term measures. He had survived by guile and had effected no major institutional changes that were permanently satisfactory to the country at large. He had exalted the monarchy, but the prerogative powers he had handled with such dexterity were used so clumsily by James that profound constitutional change became inevitable.

It was James's devout and principal wish to promote the interests of his co-religionists. He did not wish to impose Catholicism on the country, but he was determined to remove the impediments under which the papists laboured by repealing the penal laws and the Test Act. At first he tried to do this by Parliamentary means. Blinded by the glare of his good intentions, he was unable to see that Whigs and Tories,

Anglicans and Dissenters, were united in one thing only: their vehement opposition to allowing Roman Catholics freedom of worship. Popery meant absolutism, and as James pursued his disastrous plans, so suspicions that he wished to become an absolute king gathered ever more ominously about him.

There were those among the Whigs who were resolved to oppose him by force of arms. Many of the Whig exiles believed that the succession of a Catholic monarch would be so unpopular that the country would rally to their cause. Chronic mismanagement and a naive inability to read the true temper of the people ensured disaster. After six months of discussion the rebels decided that a two-pronged approach would serve their interests best. The Earl of Argyll was to land in Scotland and raise an army among his fearful Highlanders. Acrimony and division in the council of war made certain that this did not come about, but while Argyll's efforts ended in fiasco those of the Duke of Monmouth led to tragedy. Realising that an assault on London would be foolhardy in the extreme, Charles's illegitimate son sailed for the Puritan West Country, landing at Lyme on 11 June 1685. He declared himself king and promised annual parliaments, religious toleration and the abolition of a standing army. Four thousand men rallied to his standard but were more than matched by the local militia, who roundly defeated him at Sedgemoor on 6 July. Monmouth himself was taken to London where, having cringingly and vainly begged for his life, he was duly executed. His followers were then consigned to the horrors of the so-called Bloody Assizes. The terrible Judge Jeffreys conducted these with sadistic self-righteousness and, convinced that God was on his side, sent so many of Monmouth's supporters to their deaths that the blood from their hanged and quartered bodies was said to have run ankle-deep through Somerset.

Judicial carnage appeared to have wrought the final destruction of the Whigs, but it did nothing to endear James to the Tories. He had used the rebellion as a pretext for greatly increasing the size of his standing army, and the new battalions were liberally sprinkled with Catholic officers. His natural supporters began muttering loudly against him and James, with the political clumsiness that was so thoroughly characteristic of him, prorogued the ardently monarchist Parliament that a few months earlier had welcomed him to his throne. He resolved to change his tactics rather than his tune. If Tories would not help him then surely the Dissenters would. It gradually became clear to James that these good people had been driven to sedition and Whiggery purely by that heretic Anglican church which had so conspicuously snubbed him. A Parliament of Dissenters would surely grant toleration to themselves and, in gratitude, to the Catholics as well. The greater number of James's new allies were nonetheless men of modest economic and social status and were in no position to compete with the magnates who dominated the Tory heartlands. It was clearly necessary to offer them extraordinary support, and this James now resolved to do.

Grey areas of the royal prerogative were examined in the light of his prejudices. It was generally recognised that under the most exceptional circumstances the King could exempt certain individuals from the rigour of the law. The judges' decision in the test case of *Godden* v *Hales* appeared to uphold this, and James persuaded himself that the ruling gave him carte blanche to exempt the whole nation from complying with the penal laws and the Test Act. Both were suspended by royal order, and the sight of their king emasculating major legislation in this way made men ever more certain that James was aiming for absolutism. Their worries seemed confirmed when, having made public office available to those very minorities the bulk of the nation most greatly feared, James embarked on a campaign of arm-twisting and gerrymandering to make sure that his new Parliament was packed with those he believed would back his plans. He was to be sadly disappointed by their ingratitude. The Dissenters believed as fervidly as the Anglicans that all papists were committed to destroying Protestantism root and branch, and it soon became clear that James had lost the support of the Anglican and Tory gentry without gaining that of the modest and marginal Dissenters. His clumsiness had brought him to this impasse when, late in 1687, his Queen at last became pregnant.

The nation waited on the birth with deepening pessimism. What if James produced a male heir? Would the Catholic menace never go away? As the Queen's time approached and she gave birth to a son, these anxious questions turned to ever darkening suspicion. So terrible were the facts that people felt obliged to think themselves the victims of a fraud. The boy was not James's child at all, they said. It was a changeling and, as everybody knew, it had been smuggled into Whitehall hidden in a warming pan. Uneasiness grew daily, but if the acquittal of the seven bishops who had been imprisoned for refusing to allow their clergy to read James's Declaration of Indulgence caused widespread rejoicing, men felt there was little they could do to break the national deadlock. Help, if it were to come at all, would have to come from outside.

It was at this point that the ever observant William of Orange offered to invade England 'if he was invited by some men of the best interest to . . . come and rescue the nation and the religion'.[1] William's propaganda machine had already made it clear that if he were to be offered power in the right of his wife then, while he and Mary were prepared to consider toleration for Catholics and other religious minorities, they would refuse to countenance a repeal of the Test Act. All men who were not communicating Anglicans would still be banned from public office. It was a decision that had a wide appeal, and the eyes of the establishment looked with increasing confidence to Holland.

A wide range of considerations had led William to make his historic decision to involve himself personally in the affairs of England. Desire for the crown itself was, of course, one element in his thinking, but he was also motivated by far more than personal ambition. William wanted to secure his wife's right to succeed to the English throne on James's death, and he wanted to secure a freely elected parliament. This last, he hoped, would make war on Louis XIV, who he now believed wished to conquer the whole of the Low Countries as part of his campaign to dominate the rest of Western Europe. If Louis were to succeed, he would surely eradicate Protestantism across his territories and secure their trade for France. Supplies voted by an English parliament would help put an end to this peril, while succession to the throne itself would place the nation's entire resources at William's disposal.

The balance of European power was at this critical point when seven of the great and the good wrote to William assuring him that the exasperated people of England would welcome a change of government and that James's standing army would not fight. With the courage and competence that were second nature to him, William planned a winter landing in England. He was gambling for the highest possible stakes. Louis XIV may have been currently preoccupied with his struggle against the Habsburgs, but he might at any time redirect his army to a Holland temporarily deprived of its great military leader. William's plans also relied heavily on English assurances that James's army would not resist him. And, in addition, there were the hazards of the winter weather to contend with. So severe were the storms that now blew up that William was at first driven back to port. Then, with a suddenness many were to attribute to Providence, the winds veered and carried his fleet safely down the Channel, allowing him to land at Torbay on that most atavistic of all Protestant anniversaries, 5 November.

James's fleet remained bottled up in the Thames and the gentry showed no eagerness to hurry to his side. They had been promised a free parliament and confidently expected to be returned to those privileges which they considered to be rightly theirs. James, with the courage of his obstinacy, refused to bow under pressure. He had a large army, but as he tried to march it westwards along the frozen, slippery roads his disaffected men started to desert, and news reached him that the gentry of the north were arming against him. James retreated to London and tried to buy time by pretending to negotiate even while he was planning to flee. He believed that his life was in peril and sensed that his ambitions had come to an end. But even now he would not abandon his cause. He had a male heir, and that boy's life and future were precious to him above all other things. He would save him and rear him for some future happy time. The boy would not fall a victim to the Anglican gentry. ''Tis my son they aim at,' he declared, 'and 'tis my son I must endeavour to preserve, whatever becomes of me.'[2] The boy was hurried into France along with his mother, and James determined to join them.

Even now misfortune dogged him. As he tried to slip away, James was caught by a group of fishermen who thought he was a Jesuit and he was brought back to London. The City was convulsed with two days of anti-Catholic rioting, and while William set about the task of reimposing order and receiving the submission of the populace and the army he also arranged for James to flee. He quietly gave orders that the English guards around Whitehall be replaced at midnight by Dutchmen. One back door was deliberately left unattended. Messengers from William then crept up to the sleeping James and woke him with the advice that he should flee for his own safety. He agreed and suggested that he leave by way of Rochester. William, greatly relieved, provided him with a Dutch guard to escort him down the river, and on Christmas morning 1688 James arrived in France. His ignominious reign had come to its end four years after it had begun, just as his brother had predicted that it would. Charles's prophecy had shown him to be as worldly-wise as ever, but he could not have foreseen – and certainly would not have welcomed – the profound changes that were to affect the English monarchy in the wake of William's bloodless victory – that victory which generations were to refer to as the Glorious Revolution.

References

Preface

1. Halifax, 'A Character of King Charles the Second', in *Works*, p. 251.

Chapter One: The Black Boy

1. Edward Hyde, Earl of Clarendon, *History of the Rebellion and Civil Wars in England*, I, p. 33; hereafter cited as Clarendon, *History*.
2. *Calendar of State Papers Domestic*, 21 Dec. 1628; hereafter cited as *CSPD*.
3. Ibid., 13 May 1629; Henrietta Maria's letter quoted in Carola Oman, *Henrietta Maria*, p. 67.
4. Quoted in Oman, op. cit., p. 68.
5. Ibid.
6. *Calendar of State Papers Venetian*, XXII, p. 350; hereafter cited as *CSPV*.
7. *CSPD*, 27 June 1630.
8. Oman, op. cit., p. 69.
9. Quoted in Hester Chapman, *The Tragedy of Charles II*, p. 22.
10. Quoted in Agnes Strickland, *Lives of the Queens of England*, V, p. 52.
11. Quoted in Antonia Fraser, *King Charles II*, p. 9.
12. *Letters of Henrietta Maria*, pp. 17–18.
13. *CSPD*, 10 Jan. 1631.
14. Quoted in Chapman, op. cit., p. 28.
15. Ibid. p. 29.
16. *CSPV*, 28 Feb. 1629.
17. Quoted in Charles Carlton, *Charles I: The Personal Monarch*, p. 120.

18. Quoted in Chapman, op. cit., p. 18.

19. Lucy Hutchinson, *Memoirs of the Life of Colonel Hutchinson*, p. 67.

20. Quoted in Oman, op. cit., p. 95.

21. Stage direction to *Salmacida Spolia*, quoted in Roy Strong, *Splendour at Court*, pp. 241–2.

22. Sir Simonds D'Ewes, *Autobiography*, quoted in Carlton, op. cit., p. 138.

23. J. Mayor, *Two Lives of Nicholas Ferrar*, pp. 115–294.

24. Quoted in Christopher Hill, *God's Englishman*, p. 44.

25. Quoted in Chapman, op. cit., pp. 41–2.

26. Quoted in Strickland, op. cit., p. 266.

27. *The Letters, Speeches and Declarations of King Charles II*, p. 3; hereafter cited as *Letters*.

28. For an account of monarchical theory see Mark Kishlansky, *A Monarchy Transformed*, pp. 34–40, to which this paragraph is indebted.

29. James I, *Works*, p. 529.

30. Quoted in Carlton, op. cit., p. 206.

Chapter Two: The End of Peace

1. Quoted in Chapman, op. cit., p. 45.

2. Quoted in Alison Plowden, *The Stuart Princesses*, p. 64.

3. Quoted in Chapman, op. cit., p. 51.

4. Ibid., p. 49.

5. Ibid.

6. Quoted in Richard Ollard, *Clarendon and his Friends*, p. 68.

7. Quoted in Chapman, op. cit., p. 57.

8. Ibid., and Carlton, op. cit., p. 243.

9. J. R. Phillips, *Memoirs of the Civil War in Wales and the Marches*, I, p. 18.

10. See Carlton, op. cit., pp. 246–7.

11. Quoted in Fraser, op. cit., p. 28.

12. James II's account of the battle quoted in Young, *Edgehill*, p. 115.

13. Quoted in Chapman, op. cit., p. 63–4.

14. Quoted in Samuel Gardiner, *Civil War*, I, p. 151.

15. Quoted in Charles Carlton, *Going to the Wars*, p. 93.

16. Clarendon, *History*, IV, p. 13.

17. Ibid., pp. 7–8.

18. Ibid., quoted in Fraser, op. cit., p. 37.

19. For the Clubman movement see Carlton, op. cit., pp. 294–5.

20. Clarendon, *History*, p. 547.
21. Quoted in Kenyon, *The Civil Wars of England*, p. 154.
22. Quoted in S. Elliott Hoskins, *Charles the Second in the Channel Islands*, I, p. 346.
23. Ibid., p. 361.
24. Ibid., p. 364.
25. Ibid., p. 366.
26. Ibid., p. 381.
27. Ibid., p. 383.
28. Ibid., p. 386.
29. Ibid.
30. Quoted in Chapman, op. cit., p. 89.
31. Quoted in Hoskins, op. cit., p. 443.
32. Ibid., p. 444.

Chapter Three: The Prince in France and Holland

1. Quoted in Eva Scott, *The King in Exile*, p. 18.
2. Madame de Montpensier, *Mémoires*, I, p. 99.
3. *Nicholas Papers*, I, pp. 71–3.
4. Clarendon, *History*, IV, p. 312.
5. Madame de Motteville, *Mémoires*, III, p. 102.
6. de Montpensier, op. cit., I, p. 126.
7. de Motteville, op. cit., II, p. 188.
8. de Montpensier, op. cit., I, p. 102.
9. Ibid., p. 127.
10. Ibid., p. 138.
11. Quoted in Chapman, op. cit., p. 100.
12. de Montpensier, op. cit., I, p. 140.
13. Ibid.
14. Quoted in Chapman, op. cit., p. 100.
15. de Montpensier, op. cit., I, p. 141.
16. Quoted in Vita Sackville-West, *Daughter of France*, p. 57.
17. Bussy-Rabuton to Madame de Sévigné, quoted in ibid., p. 56.
18. Quoted in Scott, op. cit., p. 37.
19. For the Levellers, see Christopher Hill, *The World Turned Upside Down*, pp. 107–50.
20. Quoted in Fraser, op. cit., p. 57.
21. Quoted in Pieter Geyl, *Orange and Stuart*, p. 42.
22. Ibid., p. 44.
23. Quoted in Scott, op. cit., p. 47.
24. Quoted in Brian Masters, *The Mistresses of Charles II*, pp.15–16.
25. Quoted in Scott, op. cit., p. 57.
26. *Clarendon State Papers*, II, p. 416.
27. Quoted in Scott, op. cit., p. 59.
28. *Nicholas Papers*, quoted in ibid., p. 64.
29. Quoted in Scott, op. cit., p. 63.
30. Ibid., p. 48.
31. See Carlton, *Charles I: The Personal Monarch*, p. 334.
32. Quoted in Scott, op. cit., p. 71.

33. Charles II, *Letters*, p. 7.
34. Quoted in Fraser, op. cit., p. 77.

Chapter Four: The Treaty of Breda

1. Quoted in Fraser, op. cit., p. 82.
2. Quoted in Scott, op. cit., p. 80.
3. Carte, *Letters*, I, p. 250, quoted in ibid., p. 83.
4. *Clarendon State Papers*, II, p. 470.
5. Quoted in Chapman, op. cit., p. 126.
6. Quoted in Scott, op. cit., p. 92.
7. Quoted in Chapman, op. cit., p. 123.
8. Ibid., p. 130.
9. Quoted in Scott, op. cit., p. 98.
10. Ibid., p. 99.
11. Ibid., pp. 99–100.
12. *Nicholas Papers*, I, p. 116.
13. Quoted in Scott, op. cit., p. 106.
14. Ibid., p. 107.
15. Ibid.
16. Ibid., p. 108.
17. Quoted in Chapman, op. cit., p. 136.
18. Evelyn, *Diary*, p. 132.
19. Clarendon, *History*, XII, p. 60.
20. Ibid., pp. 62–3.
21. Ibid., p. 64.
22. Carte, *Letters* I, p. 306, quoted in Scott, op. cit., p. 117.
23. Scott, op. cit., p. 121.
24. Quoted in ibid., p. 123.
25. Ibid., p. 124.
26. Ibid., pp. 121–2.
27. Ibid., pp. 129–30.
28. Ibid., p. 135.
29. Ibid.
30. *Clarendon State Papers*, III, pp. 13–15.
31. Quoted in Scott, op. cit., p. 138.
32. Ibid.
33. Ibid., p. 138.
34. Ibid., p. 145.
35. Ibid., p. 155.
36. *Clarendon State Papers*, II, pp. 528–9.
37. Ibid., app. lxiv.
38. Quoted in Scott, op. cit., p. 158

Chapter Five: A Fading Crown

1. Quoted in Scott, op. cit., p. 164.
2. Quoted in Chapman, op. cit., p. 164.
3. Clarendon, *History*, XIII, p. 5.
4. Sir Edmund Walker, quoted in Scott, op. cit., p. 167.
5. Ibid.
6. Ibid., p. 168.
7. Quoted in Chapman, op. cit., p. 164.
8. Quoted in Scott, op. cit., p. 172.
9. Ibid., p. 176.

10. Ibid., p. 177.
11. 'The Dean of Tuam's Conference with the King', in Carte, *Letters*, I, p. 391, quoted in Scott, op. cit., pp. 179–80.
12. Scott, op. cit., pp. 179–80.
13. Ibid., p. 182.
14. Quoted in Tony Barnard, *The English Republic*, p. 79.
15. Quoted in John Kenyon, *The Civil Wars of England*, p. 215.
16. Quoted in Fraser, op. cit., p. 95.
17. See Scott, op. cit., pp. 186–7.
18. Quoted in ibid., p. 189.
19. Ibid., p. 190.
20. Ibid., p. 191.
21. Ibid., p. 192.
22. Ibid., p. 194.
23. Somers, *Tracts*, VI, pp. 118–41.
24. Quoted in Fraser, op. cit., p. 98.
25. Quoted in Scott, op. cit., p. 195.
26. Ibid.
27. Ibid., p. 198.
28. Carte, *Letters*, II, p. 15.
29. Quoted in Scott, op. cit., p. 200.
30. Ibid., p. 206.
31. Ibid., p. 207.
32. Clarendon, *History*, XIII, p. 72.
33. Ibid., p. 62.
34. Quoted in Kenyon, op. cit., p. 218.
35. Quoted in Scott, op. cit., p. 213.
36. *CSPD*, 1651, p. 437.
37. Quoted in Scott, op. cit., p. 214.
38. Richard Baxter, *Autobiography*, p. 68.

Chapter Six: The Fugitive

1. Quoted in Richard Ollard, *The Escape of Charles II after the Battle of Worcester*, p. 23.
2. Quoted in Scott, op. cit., p. 224.
3. Ibid., pp. 224–5.
4. Ibid.
5. Ibid., p. 226.
6. Ibid., p. 228.
7. Ibid., p. 229.
8. Ibid., p. 230.
9. Ibid.
10. Ollard, *Escape of Charles II*, p. 38.
11. Quoted in Scott, op. cit., p. 231.
12. Ibid., p. 232.
13. Ibid., p. 233.
14. Ibid.
15. Quoted in Ollard, *Escape of Charles II*, p. 46.
16. Ibid., p. 49.
17. Quoted in Scott, op. cit., p. 240.
18. Quoted in Ollard, *Escape of Charles II*, p. 61.
19. Ibid., p. 62.
20. Ibid., p. 65.
21. Ibid., p. 83.
22. Ibid.
23. Ibid., p. 112.
24. Ibid., p. 122.
25. Ibid., p. 127.

26. Ibid., p. 123.
27. Ibid., p. 127.
28. Ibid., p. 129.
29. Ibid.
30. Ibid., p. 131.
31. Ibid., p. 132.

Chapter Seven: Exile in France

1. Quoted in Scott, op. cit., p. 280.
2. Ibid., p. 281.
3. Ibid., p. 334.
4. Clarendon, *History*, XIII, p. 145.
5. Quoted in Scott, op. cit., p. 316.
6. Ibid., p. 317.
7. Ibid., p. 453.
8. Ibid., p. 337.
9. *Mercurius Politicus*, 5–15 Nov. 1651.
10. Quoted in Scott, op. cit., pp. 340–1.
11. de Montpensier, op. cit., pp. 319–35.
12. Quoted in Scott, op. cit., p. 352.
13. Ibid., p. 353.
14. Evelyn, quoted in ibid., p. 358.
15. *Nicholas Papers*, II, p. 11.
16. Quoted in Scott, op. cit., p. 374.
17. Ibid., p. 377.
18. Ibid., p. 380.
19. Ibid., p. 386.
20. Ibid.
21. *Clarendon State Papers*, III, p. 314.
22. Quoted in Scott, op. cit., p. 409.
23. Ibid., p. 414.
24. Ibid., p. 416.
25. Quoted in Kishlansky, op. cit., p. 187.
26. Ibid.
27. Quoted in Scott, op. cit., p. 421.
28. Ibid.
29. Ibid., p. 420.
30. Ibid., pp. 447–8.
31. *Clarendon State Papers*, III, p. 170.
32. Ibid., p. 171.
33. Ibid., p. 117.
34. Ibid.
35. Quoted in Scott, op. cit., p. 447.
36. Ibid., p. 449.
37. Ibid., p. 469.
38. Clarendon, *History*, XIV, p. 65.
39. Quoted in Scott, op. cit., p. 473.
40. Ibid., p. 474.
41. Ibid.
42. Ibid., p. 476.
43. Ibid., p. 478.
44. Ibid., p. 479.
45. Quoted in Sackville-West, op. cit., p. 56.
46. Quoted in Scott, op. cit., pp. 482–3.
47. Ibid., p. 490.
48. Ibid., p. 491.
49. Ibid.
50. Ibid., p. 495.

Chapter Eight: The Wanderer

1. Quoted in Scott, op. cit., p. 493.
2. Clarendon, *History*, XIV, p. 98.
3. Ibid., p. 101.
4. Quoted in Chapman, op. cit., p. 262.
5. Quoted in Eva Scott, *Travels of the King*, p. 8.
6. Ibid., p. 6.
7. *Clarendon State Papers*, II, p. 382.
8. Scott, *Travels of the King*, p. 13.
9. Ibid.
10. Ibid.
11. Ibid.
12. Ibid.
13. *Nicholas Papers*, II, p. 91.
14. Quoted in Chapman, op. cit., p. 275.
15. *Clarendon State Papers*, II, pp. 403–21.
16. Quoted in Chapman, op. cit., p. 276.
17. Ibid., p. 278.
18. *CSPV*, XXIX, pp. 282–3.
19. For Naylor's case see Barnard, op. cit., pp. 58–9, and R. J. Acheson, *Radical Puritans in England*, pp. 69 ff.
20. See Chapman, op. cit., pp. 303–5.
21. Quoted in Fraser, op. cit., p. 145.
22. Quoted in Scott, *The King in Exile*, p. 2.
23. Quoted in Fraser, op. cit., p. 146.
24. Ibid.
25. Ibid., p. 153.
26. Ibid., p. 156.
27. See Masters, op. cit., pp. 36 ff.
28. Ibid., p. 38.
29. See ibid., pp. 38 ff.
30. Ibid., p. 40.
31. Ibid., p. 42.
32. Quoted in Fraser, op. cit., p. 156.
33. Ibid., p. 145.
34. *Clarendon State Papers*, III, p. 307.

Chapter Nine: A King! A King!

1. *Clarendon State Papers*, III, p. 412.
2. Quoted in Chapman, op. cit., p. 341.
3. Ibid., p. 342.
4. Ibid.
5. Quoted in Scott, *Travels of the King*, p. 376.
6. Ibid.
7. Ibid.
8. For Mordaunt, see ibid., pp. 378 ff.
9. For Booth, see ibid., pp. 393 ff.
10. *Clarendon State Papers*, IV, p. 400.
11. Carte, *Letters*, II, p. 186.
12. Charles II, *Letters*, p. 80.
13. Quoted in Fraser, op. cit., p. 170.

14. Ibid.
15. Ibid., p. 168.
16. Charles II, *Letters*, p. 83.
17. Ibid., pp. 86 ff.
18. Ibid.
19. Pepys, quoted in Chapman, op. cit., p. 373.
20. Ibid., p. 377.
21. Ibid., pp. 372–3.
22. Ibid., p. 374.
23. Quoted in Fraser, op. cit., p. 174.
24. Quoted in Chapman, op. cit., p. 375.
25. Ibid., pp. 376–7.
26. For touching the King's Evil, see Liza Picard, *Restoration London*, pp. 79–82.
27. Quoted in Masters, op. cit., p. 52.
28. Quoted in Chapman, op. cit., p. 379.
29. Ibid.
30. Ibid., p. 382.
31. Ibid., p. 383.
32. *CSPV*, XXI, p. 155.
33. Quoted in Chapman, op. cit., p. 385.
34. Ibid.
35. Quoted in J. R. Jones, ed., *The Restored Monarch*, p. 34.
36. Quoted in Fraser, op. cit., p. 183.
37. Quoted in Jones, op. cit., p. 34.
38. Quoted in John Miller, *Charles II*, p. 33.

Chapter Ten: The Promised Land

1. Quoted in Miller, op. cit., p. 46.
2. Ibid., p. 47.
3. Ibid., p. 42.
4. Jones, op. cit., p. 5.
5. Ibid., p. 37.
6. Ibid., p. 158.
7. Quoted in Fraser, op. cit., p. 199.
8. Ibid., p. 200.
9. For the Anglican church at the Restoration see R. A. Beddard, 'The Restoration Church', in Jones, op. cit., pp. 155 ff.
10. Quoted in Chapman, op. cit., p. 362.
11. Quoted in Miller, op. cit., p. 95.
12. Ibid.
13. Ibid., p. 96.
14. Quoted in Masters, op. cit., p. 97.
15. Ibid., pp. 56–7.
16. Quoted in Miller, op. cit., p. 97.
17. Ibid.
18. Quoted in Fraser, op. cit., p. 206.
19. Quoted in Masters, op. cit., p. 60.
20. Charles II, *Letters*, p. 126.
21. Quoted in Masters, op. cit., p. 60.
22. Ibid., p. 70.
23. Ibid., p. 69.
24. Ibid.
25. Ibid., p. 71.
26. Ibid., p. 72.
27. Quoted in Fraser, op. cit., p. 213.

Chapter Eleven: The Horsemen of the Apocalypse

1. Quoted in David Ogg, *England in the Reign of Charles II*, p. 222.
2. Ibid., pp. 235–6.
3. Pepys, *Diary*, 30 April 1664.
4. Quoted in J. R. Jones, *The Anglo-Dutch Wars of the Seventeenth Century*, p. 92.
5. See Ogg, op. cit., pp. 287 ff.
6. Dryden, *Essay of Dramatic Poesy*, quoted in Ogg, op. cit., p. 288.
7. See Ogg, op. cit., pp. 291 ff.
8. Ibid.
9. Evelyn, *Diary*, pp. 209–16.
10. Dryden, *Annus Mirabilis*, quoted in Fraser, op. cit., p. 246.
11. For the rebuilding of London, see W. G. Bell, *The Great Fire of London*, pp. 230 ff.
12. Quoted in Fraser, op. cit., p. 246.
13. Quoted in Ogg, op. cit., p. 312.
14. Quoted in Fraser, op. cit., p. 250.
15. Quoted in Miller, op. cit., p. 131.
16. Pepys, *Diary*, 13 June 1667.
17. Quoted in *The Poems and Letters of Andrew Marvell*, I, p. 347.
18. Marvell, 'The Last Instructions to a Painter', ibid., p. 147, 1.12.
19. Quoted in Fraser, op. cit., p. 241.
20 Quoted in Ollard, *Clarendon and his Friends*, p. 288.

Chapter Twelve: The Grand Design

1. Pepys, *Diary*, 10 Sept. 1667.
2. Quoted in Fraser, op. cit., p. 256.
3. Charles II, *Letters*, p. 219.
4. Ibid., p. 236.
5. Pepys, *Diary*, 13 November 1668.
6. Quoted in J. R. Jones, *Charles II: Royal Politician*, p. 85.
7. Ibid., p. 84.
8. Quoted in Miller, op. cit., p. 140.
9. Quoted in Fraser, op. cit., p. 266.
10. Quoted in Maurice Ashley, *Charles II: The Man and the Statesman*, p. 156.
11. Quoted in Vincent Cronin, *Louis XIV*, p. 189.
12. Quoted in C. H. Hartmann, *The King my Brother*, p. 209.
13. Charles II, *Letters*, p. 214.
14. Quoted in Hartmann, op. cit., p. 214.
15. See Jones, *Charles II: Royal Politician*, p. 88. I am grateful to this work and to Ashley, op. cit., for their analyses of these complex and devious negotiations.
16. Charles II, *Letters*, p. 230.
17. Quoted in Fraser, op. cit., p. 271.
18. Quoted in Cronin, op. cit., p. 191.
19. See Fraser, op. cit., p. 258.
20. Quoted in Ashley, op. cit., p. 167.
21. Ibid.
22. Ibid.

23. Ibid., p. 170.
24. Quoted in Hartmann, op. cit., p. 321.
25. Ibid.
26. Evelyn, *Diary*, p. 244.
27. Quoted in Fraser, op. cit., p. 305.
28. Ibid., p. 306.
29. Quoted in Ashley, op. cit., p. 173.
30. Quoted in Jones, *Charles II: Royal Politician*, p. 98.
31. Quoted in Fraser, op. cit., p. 306.
32. See ibid., p. 271.

Chapter Thirteen: The King at Play

1. Quoted in Fraser, op. cit., p. 292. I am grateful to this work for details of Charles's sporting interests.
2. Ibid., p. 290.
3. Ibid., p. 292.
4. Evelyn, *Diary*, p. 242.
5. Quoted in Fraser, op. cit., p. 295.
6. Ibid., p. 297.
7. Quoted in Masters, op. cit., p. 78.
8. Ibid., p. 77.
9. Ibid., pp. 80–1.
10. Ibid.
11. Quoted in Fraser, op. cit., p. 285.
12. Ibid.
13. Evelyn, *Diary*, p. 252.
14. Pepys, *Diary*, 11 Jan. 1668.
15. Quoted in Masters, op. cit., p. 81.
16. Ibid., p. 86.
17. See ibid., pp. 82–3.
18. Ibid., p. 83.
19. Quoted in Fraser, op. cit., p. 224.
20. *Burnet's History*, I, p. 167.
21. Evelyn, *Diary*, pp. 318–19.
22. Ibid., p. 200.
23. Ibid.
24. Ibid., p. 232.
25. Ibid., p. 233.
26. Ibid.
27. Ibid.
28. See Fraser, op. cit., p. 331.
29. Evelyn, *Diary*, p. 403.
30. Ibid., p. 193.
31. Quoted in Ashley, op. cit., illustrative supplement, p. 2.
32. Evelyn, *Diary*, pp. 318–19.
33. Ibid., p. 216.
34. Ibid., pp. 283–4.
35. Ibid.
36. Quoted in Graham Parry, *The Seventeenth Century: The Intellectual and Cultural Context of English Literature*, p. 148.
37. Ibid., p. 147.
38. See ibid.
39. Quoted in Stephen Coote, *The Penguin Short History of English Literature*, p. 224.
40. Dryden, *Essays*, I, p. 176.
41. Quoted in Parry, op. cit., p. 114.
42. *A Satyr Against Reason and Mankind*, II. 25–30.
43. See Masters, op. cit., pp. 97–8.

44. Quoted in Fraser, op. cit., p. 299.
45. Pepys, *Diary*, 2 March 1667.
46. Ibid., 7 May 1668.
47. Ibid., 1 May, 1667.
48. Quoted in Masters, op. cit., p. 107.
49. Ibid., p. 96.
50. Evelyn, *Diary*, p. 231.
51. Quoted in Masters, op. cit., p. 134.
52. Ibid., p. 135.
53. Ibid., p. 136.
54. Ibid., p. 137.
55. Ibid.
56. Ibid., p. 148.
57. Quoted in Bryan Bevan, *King William III*, p. 23.
58. Ibid., p. 24.
59. Ibid., p. 26.

Wars of the Seventeenth Century, p. 199.
9. Ibid.
10. Quoted in idem, *Charles II: Royal Politician*, p. 104.
11. Quoted in Ogg, op. cit., p. 368.
12. Quoted in Jones, *The Anglo-Dutch Wars of the Seventeenth Century*, p. 203.
13. Ibid., p. 204.
14. Ibid., p. 206.
15. Ibid., p. 211.
16. Ibid., p. 214.
17. Ibid.
18. Ibid., pp. 214–15.
19. Ibid.
20. Ibid.
21. Quoted in idem, *Charles II: Royal Politician*, p. 107.

Chapter Fourteen: The Tightening Net

1. See Jones, *The Anglo-Dutch Wars of the Seventeenth Century*, p. 180.
2. Quoted in Fraser, op. cit., p. 307.
3. Quoted in Cronin, op. cit., pp. 193–4.
4. Quoted in Bevan, op. cit., p. 32.
5. Ibid., p. 35.
6. Ibid., p. 38.
7. Quoted in Jones, *Charles II: Royal Politician*, p. 103.
8. Quoted in idem, *The Anglo-Dutch*

Chapter Fifteen: Politics and Parties

1. Quoted in Jones, *Charles II: Royal Politician*, p. 110.
2. Ibid., p. 117.
3. Quoted in Ogg, op. cit., p. 532.
4. Quoted in J. P. Kenyon, *The Popish Plot*, p. 24.
5. Quoted in Ogg, op. cit., p. 537.
6. Quoted in Masters, op. cit., p. 156.
7. Ibid.
8. Ibid., p. 157.

9. Ibid., p. 159.
10. Quoted in Jones, *Charles II: Royal Politician*, p. 122.
11. Ibid., p. 121.
12. Quoted in Bevan, op. cit., p. 49.
13. Ibid., p. 50.
14. Ibid.
15. Ibid., p. 52.
16. Quoted in Kenyon, *The Popish Plot*, p. 60.

Chapter Sixteen: The Popish Conspirators

1. Quoted in Ogg, op. cit., p. 599.
2. Quoted in Kenyon, *The Popish Plot*, p. 1.
3. Ibid., pp. 2–3.
4. Ibid., p. 4.
5. Ibid., p. 56.
6. Ibid., p. 59.
7. Ibid., p. 61.
8. Ibid., p. 79.
9. Ibid., p. 80.
10. Ibid.
11. Ibid., p. 81.
12. Ibid., p. 84.
13. Ibid., p. 85.
14. Ibid., p. 84.
15. Quoted in Ogg, op. cit., p. 572.
16. Ibid.
17. Quoted in Kenyon, *The Popish Plot*, p. 91.
18. Ibid., p. 96.
19. Quoted in Ogg, p. 573.
20. Quoted in Kenyon, *The Popish Plot*, p. 97.
21. Ibid., p. 103.
22. Ibid., p. 116.
23. Ibid., pp. 127–8.
24. Ibid., p. 126.
25. Ibid., p. 130.
26. Ibid., p. 50.
27. Ibid., p. 146.
28. Ibid.
29. Quoted in Ogg, op. cit., pp. 577–8.
30. Quoted in Fraser, op. cit., p. 391.
31. Quoted in Jones, *Charles II: Royal Politician*, p. 143.
32. Ibid., p. 145.
33. Quoted in Fraser, op. cit., p. 368.
34. Ibid., p. 369.
35. Ibid., pp. 369–70.
36. Ibid., p. 370.
37. Quoted in Jones, *Charles II: Royal Politician*, p. 146.
38. Quoted in Fraser, op. cit., p. 382.
39. Quoted in Tim Harris, *London Crowds in the Reign of Charles II*, p. 99.
40. Quoted in Ogg, op. cit., pp. 595–6.
41. Quoted in Harris, op. cit., p. 178.
42. Ibid., p. 131.
43. Ibid., p. 150.
44. Quoted in Fraser, op. cit., p. 398.
45. Ibid.
46. Ibid., p. 400.

47. Ibid., p. 397.

48. *Absalom and Achitophel*, 1. 227.

49. Quoted in Ogg, op. cit., p. 601.

50. Ibid.

51. Ibid.

52. Quoted in Fraser, op. cit., p. 403.

53. Ibid.

54. Quoted in Jones, *Charles II: Royal Politician*, p. 168.

55. Quoted in Fraser, op. cit., p. 405.

Chapter Seventeen: The Years of Personal Rule

1. Quoted in Ogg, op. cit., p. 627.

2. Quoted in Fraser, op. cit., p. 409.

3. Ibid., p. 429.

4. Ibid.

5. Quoted in Ogg, op. cit., p. 646.

6. Quoted in Fraser, op. cit., p. 431.

7. Ibid., p. 415.

8. Quoted in Masters, op. cit., p. 163.

9. Ibid., p. 164.

10. Ibid., p. 167.

11. Quoted in Fraser, op. cit., p. 430.

12. Quoted in Masters, op. cit., p. 173.

13. Quoted in Fraser, op. cit., p. 446.

14. Ibid., p. 447.

15. Ibid., p. 452.

16. Ibid.

17. The phrase appears to be an invention of Macaulay's in his *History of England*.

Afterword

1. Bishop Burnet, quoted in John Miller, *The Glorious Revolution*, p. 12.

2. Ibid., p. 15.

Bibliography

Acheson, R. J., *Radical Puritans in England, 1550–1660*, Longman, 1990.

Ashley, Maurice, *Charles II: The Man and the Statesman*, Weidenfeld & Nicolson, 1971.

————, *Life in Stuart England*, Batsford, 1964.

————, *The Golden Century: Europe, 1598–1715*, Weidenfeld & Nicolson, 1969.

Barbour, Violet, *Henry Bennet, Earl of Arlington*, American Historical Association, 1914.

Barnard, Toby, *The English Republic, 1649–1660*, Longman, 1982.

Baxter, Richard, *The Autobiography of Richard Baxter*, abridged J. M. Lloyd Thomas, ed. with Introduction N. H. Keeble, Dent, rev. edn, 1985.

Bell, Walter George, *The Great Fire of London*, 1923; repr., Bracken Books, 1994.

Bennett, Martyn, *The English Civil War*, Longman, 1995.

Bevan, Bryan, *Charles the Second's French Mistress*, Hale, 1972.

————, *King William III: Prince of Orange, the first European*, Rubicon Press, 1997.

————, *Nell Gwynn*, Hale 1969.

Bragg, Melvyn, with Ruth Gardiner, *On Giants' Shoulders: Great Scientists and their Discoveries from Archimedes to DNA*, Hodder & Stoughton, 1998.

Bryant, Arthur, ed., *The Letters, Speeches and Declarations of King Charles II*, Cassell, 1935.

Burnet's History of my own Time, ed.

Osmund Airy, 2 vols, Oxford University Press, 1897, 1900.

Calendar of State Papers Domestic.

Calendar of State Papers Venetian.

Carlton, Charles, *Charles I: The Personal Monarch*, 1983; 2nd edn, Routledge, 1995.

————, *Going to the Wars: The Experience of the English Civil Wars, 1638–1651*, Routledge, 1992.

Carte, Thomas, *A Collection of Original Papers and Letters . . . Found Among the Duke of Ormode's Papers*, 2 vols, 1739.

Chandaman, C. D., *The English Public Revenue, 1660–1688*, Oxford Clarendon Press, 1975.

Chapman, Hester W., *The Tragedy of Charles II in the Years 1630–1660*, Jonathan Cape, 1964.

Clarendon State Papers.

Clark, Sir George, *The Later Stuarts, 1660–1714*, 2nd edn, Oxford Clarendon Press, 1955.

Coote, Stephen, *The Penguin Short History of English Literature*, Penguin Books, 1993.

Coward, Barry, *Social Change and Continuity in Early Modern England, 1550–1750*, Longman, 1988.

Cronin, Vincent, *Louis XIV*, 1964; repr., Harvill Press, 1996.

Davies, Godfrey, *The Restoration of*

Charles II, 1658–1660, Huntingdon Library, San Marino, 1955.

Delpech, Jeanine, *Life and Times of the Duchess of Portsmouth*, Elek, 1953.

Dryden, John, *Essays*, ed. W. P. Ker, 2 vols, Dent, 1926.

Earle, Peter, *James II*, Weidenfeld & Nicolson, 1972.

Evelyn, John, *The Diary of John Evelyn*, selected and ed. John Bowle, Oxford University Press, 1985.

Fellows, Nicholas, *Charles II and James II*, Hodder & Stoughton, 1995.

Forneron, H., *Louise de Keroualle, Duchesse of Portsmouth*, 1887.

Fraser, Antonia, *King Charles II*, Weidenfeld & Nicolson, 1979.

Geyl, Pieter, *Orange and Stuart, 1641–72*, trans. Arnold Pomerans, Weidenfeld & Nicolson, 1969.

Halifax, George Saville, Marquis of, *Complete Works*, ed. J. P. Kenyon, Penguin Books, 1969.

Harris, Tim, *London Crowds in the Reign of Charles II: Propaganda and Politics from the Restoration until the Exclusion Crisis*, Cambridge University Press, 1987.

Hartmann, C. H., *The King my Brother*, Heinemann, 1954.

Hill, Christopher, *God's Englishman: Oliver Cromwell and the English*

Revolution, 1970; repr., Pelican Books, 1972.

———, *The World Turned Upside Down*, 1972; repr., Pelican Books, 1975.

Holmes, Geoffrey, *The Making of a Great Power: Late Stuart and Early Georgian Britain, 1660–1722*, Longman, 1993.

Hoskins, S. Elliott, *Charles the Second in the Channel Islands: A Contribution to Biography and to the History of his Age*, 2 vols, 1854.

Hutchinson, Lucy, *Memoirs of the Life of Colonel Hutchinson*, ed. J. Sutherland, Oxford University Press, 1973.

Hutton, Ronald, *Charles the Second, King of England, Scotland, and Ireland*, Clarendon Press, 1989.

———, *The Restoration: A Political and Religious History of England and Wales, 1658–1667*, Oxford University Press, 1985.

Hyde, Edward; Earl of Clarendon, *The History of the Rebellion and Civil Wars in England*, 6 vols, Oxford, 1888.

Jones, J. R., *The Anglo-Dutch Wars of the Seventeenth Century*, Longman, 1996.

———, *Charles II: Royal Politician*, Allen & Unwin, 1987.

———, *Country and Court: England, 1658–1714*, Arnold, 1978.

———, *The First Whigs: The Politics of the Exclusion Crisis, 1678–1683*, Oxford University Press, 1961.

———, ed., *The Restored Monarchy, 1660–1688*, Macmillan, 1979.

Kenyon, J. P., *The Civil Wars of England*, 1988; repr., Orion Books, 1996.

———, *The Popish Plot*, 1972; repr., Penguin Books, 1974.

Kishlansky, Mark, *A Monarchy Transformed: Britain, 1603–1714*, Allen Lane, The Penguin Press, 1996.

Legouis, Pierre, *Andrew Marvell: Poet, Puritan, Patriot*, Clarendon Press, 1968.

Lynch, Michael, *The Interregnum, 1649–1660*, Hodder & Stoughton, 1994.

Lyon, C. J., *Personal History of King Charles the Second . . .*, 1851.

Marvell, Andrew, *The Poems and Letters of Andrew Marvell*, 2 vols, ed. H. M. Margoliouth; 3rd edn, rev. Pierre Legouis with the collaboration of E. E. Duncan-Jones, Clarendon Press, 1971.

Masters, Brian, *The Mistresses of Charles II*, 1979; repr., Constable, 1997.

Mercurius Politicus.

Miller, John, *Charles II*, Weidenfeld & Nicolson, 1991.

———, *The Glorious Revolution*, Longman, 1983.

———, *Popery and Politics in England, 1660–1688*, Cambridge University Press, 1973.

———, *The Restoration and the England of Charles II*, 2nd edn, Cambridge University Press, 1997.

de Montpensier, Madame, *Mémoires*, 1891.

de Motteville, Madam, *Mémoires*, 1824.

Mullett, Michael, *James II and English Politics, 1678–1688*, Routledge, 1994.

Nicholas Papers.

Norrington, Ruth, ed., *My Dearest Minette: Letters between Charles II and his Sister, the Duchesse d'Orléans*, Peter Owen, 1996.

Ogg, David, *England in the Reign of Charles II*, Oxford University Press, 2nd edn, 1956; repr., 1972.

Ollard, Richard, *Clarendon and his Friends*, Hamish Hamilton, 1987.

———, *The Escape of Charles II after the Battle of Worcester*, Hodder & Stoughton, 1966.

Oman, Carola, *Henrietta Maria*, Hodder & Stoughton, 1936.

Parry, Graham, *The Golden Age Restor'd: The Culture of the Stuart Court, 1603–42*, Manchester University Press, 1981.

———, *The Seventeenth Century: The Intellectual and Cultural Context of English Literature, 1603–1700*, Longman, 1989.

Pennington, D. H., *Europe in the Seventeenth Century*, 1970; 2nd edn, Longman, 1989.

Pepys, Samuel, *The Shorter Pepys*, selected and ed. Robert Latham, 1985; repr., Penguin Books, 1987.

Phillips, J. R., *Memoirs of the Civil War and the Marches, 1642–1649*, 1874.

Picard, Lisa, *Restoration London*, Weidenfeld & Nicolson, 1997.

Plowden, Alison, *The Stuart Princesses*, 1996; repr., Alan Sutton, 1997.

Plumb, J. H., *The Growth of Political Stability in England, 1675–1725*, Macmillan, 1967.

Quintrell, Brian, *Charles I, 1625–1640*, Longman, 1993.

Roseveare, Henry, *The Financial Revolution, 1660–1760*, Longman, 1991.

Russell, Conrad, *The Crisis of Parliaments: English History, 1509–1660*, Oxford University Press, 1971; rev. edn, 1974.

Sackville-West, Vita, *Daughter of France: The Life of Anne Marie Louise d'Orléans, Duchesse de Montpensier, 1627–1693 – La Grande Mademoiselle*, Michael Joseph, 1959.

Scott, Eva, *The King in Exile: The Wanderings of Charles II from June 1646 to July 1654*, Constable, 1904.

——, *Travels of the King: Charles II in Germany and Flanders, 1654–1660*, Constable, 1907.

Scott, George, *Lucy Walter: Wife or Mistress?*, Harrap, 1947.

Seaward, Paul, *The Restoration, 1660–1688*, Macmillan, 1991.

Somer's, *Tracts*.

Stevenson, David, *Revolution and Counter-Revolution in Scotland, 1664–1651*, Royal Historical Society, 1977.

Strickland, Agnes, *Lives of the Queens of England*, 1851.

Strong, Roy, *Splendour at Court: Renaissance Spectacle and the Theatre of Power*, Houghton Mifflin, 1973.

Trease, Geoffrey, *Portrait of a Cavalier: William Cavendish, First Duke of Newcastle*, Macmillan, 1979.

Whitcombe, D. T., *Charles II and the Cavalier House of Commons*, Manchester University Press, 1966.

Wilkinson, Richard, *Louis XIV, France and Europe, 1661–1715*, Longman, 1993.

Willcock, John, *The Great Marquis: Life and Times of Archibald, 8th Earl, and 1st (and only) Marquess of Argyll*, 1903.

Wrightson, Keith, *English Society, 1580–1680*, Hutchinson, 1982.

Wyndham, Violet, *The Protestant Duke: A Life of Monmouth*, Weidenfeld & Nicolson, 1976.

Young, Peter, *Edgehill, 1642*, Roundwood, 1967.

Index

JOHN CHARMLEY

SPLENDID ISOLATION

In *Splendid Isolation?* John Charmley uses his celebrated shrewd, analytical style to upset traditionally held views, and offers a radically new interpretation of Britain's role in the world in the period leading up to the First World War.

A dramatic account of Disraeli's political methods in foreign policy is revealed using new evidence drawn from private papers. A heady mixture of high politics and low intrigue gives an insight into the political rise of Lord Salisbury, and of the underhand methods by which the reputation of Lord Derby and his wife were destroyed.

'This is an original and meticulous book about British foreign policy at the zenith of empire'   *Country Life*

'Deeply researched and passionately argued book'
                                                    Morning Star

'This book has punch and purpose'   *The Sunday Times*

'Charmley proceeds to cut a broad revisionist swathe through the various foreign secretaries and prime ministers'
                                                    The Spectator

HODDER AND STOUGHTON PAPERBACKS

STEPHEN COOTE

W. B. YEATS A LIFE

'Yeats was . . . one of those few whose history is the history of our own time, who are part of the consciousness of their age, which cannot be understood without them'.

T. S. Eliot

In his masterful new biography of W. B. Yeats (1865–1939), acclaimed biographer Stephen Coote shows how through lifetime of tumultuous creativity Yeats strove to give new meaning to poetry, vision and politics. The profoundly original poet rose through the despair of unrequited love to become one of the leading figures of the decadent 1890s; the friend of Wilde, Morris and the doomed poets of the Rymers' Club. He was also the prime mover behind the foundation of the Abbey Theatre in Dublin.

Stephen Coote skilfully weaves Yeats's own life into the developing consciousness of his nation and reveals him as the ardent nationalist creating in his work an Irish soul that would soar above materialism to the timeless world of myth and magic. The bitterly disillusioned observer of the Irish Civil War emerges from his famous Tower to become the Senator powerfully advocating greater freedom for Ireland even while interesting himself in the rise of Fascism and the cause of the Irish Blueshirts. From the great conflicts of his old age arise some of the supreme poems of the twentieth century 'Sailing to Byzantium' and 'A prayer for my Daughter'.

HODDER AND STOUGHTON PAPERBACKS

GILES MILTON

NATHANIEL'S NUTMEG

Nathaniel's Nutmeg is the extraordinary story of nutmeg, the spice of trade, the island of Run and a heroic English adventurer.

'Beautifully touching . . . To write a book that makes the reader, after finishing it, sit in a trance, lost in his passionate desire to pack a suitcase and go, somehow, to the fabulous place – that, in the end, is something one would give a sack of nutmeg for'.   Philip Hensher, *The Spectator*

'Giles Milton tells his adventurous and sometimes grisly tale with relish . . . The thoroughness and intelligence of his research underpins the lively confidence with which he deploys it.'   John Spurling, *The Times Literary Supplement*

'Milton has created a truly gripping tale of jingoistic pride, atrocious cruelty, avarice and double-dealing . . . His research is impeccable and his narrative reads in part like a modern-day Robert Louis Stevenson novel. Once embarked upon the journey of the book, one is loath, sometimes unable, as were the characters within it, to turn back and abandon it.'
          Martin Booth, *The Sunday Times*

HODDER AND STOUGHTON PAPERBACKS

GEORDIE GREIG

LOUIS AND THE PRINCE

Louis and the Prince is the unlikely yet fascinating story of the powerful friendship between Scottish naval surgeon, Louis Greig, and the future George VI.

Greig, a war hero and rugby international, became mentor, physician and friend to the young and hesitant Prince Albert. His influence helped to guide the prince from a stammering, shy schoolboy to become one of the most respected constitutional monarchs, seeing the nation through the Second World War and bringing the royal family closer to the people.

'Remarkably rich in insights into twentieth-century history . . . he writes well and handles his excellent material with aplomb. A fine biography and a fascinating read . . . Emphatically not just a "royal book"'   *Literary Review*

'A treasure trove that throws new and entertaining light on the workings of the court and the domestic life of the royal family . . . It could be the title of a fairy tale but the central figure comes as enthrallingly off the pages as the hero in a yarn by John Buchan'   *The Times*

'Geordie Greig, a stylish journalist, now emerges as an accomplished biographer in this lively work'   *The Spectator*

'A revealing insight into the world of the royals . . . fascinating'   *Observer*

'Charming, intriguing, well-written'   *The Sunday Times*

'Essential reading'   *Mail on Sunday*

HODDER AND STOUGHTON PAPERBACKS

JOHN MACLEOD

DYNASTY
THE STUARTS 1560–1807

Dynasty is the tale of the most glamorous, foolish and unlikely families ever to sit on our thrones.

From the serial husbands of Mary, Queen of Scots, to the eccentric cardinal with a taste for pretty young men, award winning writer John Macleod unfolds the complex, calamitous and entertaining history of the Stuarts.

Stuart kings were stabbed or hacked to death, deposed, killed by their own cannon or, like bold 'King Billy', felled by a common molehill.

Scots, and especially the Highlanders, suffered much at the hands of Stuart ineptitude. Yet, thorough the farce and tumult of their years in power, a new and vigorous religion emerged; a United Kingdom; radical new thoughts and institutions and the foundations of a modern democracy.

In this extraordinary story of intrigue and battle, from the glories of Robert the Bruce to an overindulgent queen, John Macleod unfolds their darkly funny history with detail, anecdote and wit.

HODDER AND STOUGHTON PAPERBACKS

STEPHEN COOTE

JOHN KEATS A LIFE

'Follows Keats lovingly to the end, using a wide range of sources but never losing touch with the poems themselves . . . I cannot recall a biography of Keats which made more sense of his cockney origins nor one which made so clear a case regarding his complete love for Fanny Brawne . . . Here is a life of Keats which brings Keats back to life outside his poems'
Robert Nyr in the *Scotsman*

'An uncluttered biography, a tragic story racily told, that importantly sends us back to poems themselves . . . Enjoy this biography, weep a little, and be instructed'
Danny Abse in the *Independent on Sunday*

'Coote is first-rate in his large evocation of Keats as a great friend . . . In language which is plain, modest, and highly serviceable, Coote renders the personal tragedy and the personal achievement which rises to impersonality'
Christopher Ricks in *The Sunday Times*

John Keats was the last of the great romantics to be born and the first to die. In this vivid and moving new life, Stephen Coote uses a wide range of contemporary sources to throw new light on the poems and rediscovers a poet who set his face against authoritarian state. Above all, he gives us back a Keats of real vitality – a man profoundly original, challenging and deeply human.

HODDER AND STOUGHTON PAPERBACKS